THE OXFOR[D]
O[F]
FRIEND[SHIP]

D. J. Enright is a distinguished poet and critic and the editor of several anthologies, including *The Oxford Book of Contemporary Verse 1945–1980*, *The Oxford Book of Death* (1983), and *The Faber Book of Fevers and Frets* (1989). A new volume of his *Selected Poems* was published in 1990.

David Rawlinson is Senior Lecturer in English at La Trobe University, Melbourne, and the author of *The Practice of Criticism* (1968).

THE OXFORD BOOK
OF
FRIENDSHIP

CHOSEN AND EDITED BY

D. J. ENRIGHT

AND

DAVID RAWLINSON

Oxford   New York

OXFORD UNIVERSITY PRESS

1992

Oxford University Press, Walton Street, Oxford OX2 6DP

Oxford New York Toronto
Delhi Bombay Calcutta Madras Karachi
Petaling Jaya Singapore Hong Kong Tokyo
Nairobi Dar es Salaam Cape Town
Melbourne Auckland

and associated companies in
Berlin Ibadan

Oxford is a trade mark of Oxford University Press

Introduction and compilation © D. J. Enright and David Rawlinson 1991

First published 1991
First issued as an Oxford University Press paperback 1992

British Library Cataloguing in Publication Data
Data available
ISBN 0-19-282967-X

Library of Congress Cataloging in Publication Data
The Oxford book of friendship / chosen and edited by
D. J. Enright and David Rawlinson
p.   cm.
Includes index.
1. Friendship—Literary collections.   I. Enright, D. J. (Dennis
Joseph), 1920-   . II. Rawlinson, David H.
PN6071.F7094 1991   302.3'4—dc20   90-7540
ISBN 0-19-282967-X

Printed in Great Britain by
Biddles Ltd.
Guildford and King's Lynn

CONTENTS

EDITORS' NOTE

DATES are of first publication, or occasionally of composition, when known; otherwise, as also in the case of posthumous publication, the author's dates are given. When no translator is credited, the editors are responsible for the English version.

The editors are obliged to the following for help of various kinds: Toby Buchan, Gerry Keenan, Shirley Chew, Ernst de Chickera, Madeleine Enright, Judith Luna, Derick Marsh, Brian Mooney, George Parfitt, Rod Settle, John Silverlight, Jacqueline Simms, Piotr Sommer, Christopher Watson, Anthony Weale, and John Wiltshire.

D.J.E.
D.H.R.

I wonder whether you ever think of the place of friendship
in life; what determines it; what it is; what it has of
destiny; what it is of design; what of momentary nearness,
and passing mood; what of eternity?

JOHN MASEFIELD, letter to Audrey Napier-Smith

From quiet homes and first beginning,
  Out to the undiscovered ends,
There's nothing worth the wear of winning,
  But laughter and the love of friends.

HILAIRE BELLOC, 'Dedicatory Ode'

This poem goes on too long because our friendship has
  been long, long for this life and these times, long
  as art is long and uninterruptable,
and I would make it as long as I hope our friendship
  lasts if I could make poems that long.

FRANK O'HARA, 'Poem Read at Joan Mitchell's'

The Nature of Friendship

FRIENDSHIP is an ancient and honourable institution, Thoreau said, 'older than Hindostan and the Chinese Empire'. The present compilation opens with 'our general ancestor' pleading for fellowship and the 'rational delight' it affords. That in the event Adam was given a wife is beside the point (or, rather, has its own point). A touching expression in New Guinea pidgin is *wantok*, possibly dating back to the blackbirding era when labourers, speaking diverse languages, were brought in from all over the South Pacific. A lonely worker would hope to meet someone from his home territory with whom he could converse directly, requiring no intermediary: a 'one-talk'. It was not good, the Lord God declared in Genesis, that the man should be alone. He felt no need to elaborate on the statement.

Others have felt that need, philosophers in particular. Plato's Socrates must have enjoyed himself in demonstrating that, though he has a passion for friends, he is unable to define 'a friend'. (The *Concise Oxford Dictionary* might have helped: 'One joined to another in intimacy and mutual benevolence independently of sexual or family love.') The discussion is broken up, somewhat ironically, by the irruption of the 'tutors' or attendants who appear to have been drinking together. More positively, Aristotle claims that to have a friend is to enjoy a supplementary life, awareness of the other's existence and nature making us more fully aware of our own; the point is developed by later writers, rather grandly in Dryden's lines: 'The Souls of Friends like Kings in Progress are; / Still in their own, though from the Palace far.'

The question of benefits accruing is a ticklish one. We know that, as Proverbs 19 has it, 'Many will intreat the favour of the prince: and every man is a friend to him that giveth gifts.' Friendship, traditionally associated with virtue, ought to be its own reward; but a reward is a reward, however disinterested and uncalculating the recipient. Ecclesiastes sums up the gains: a solitary person is cold, two people keep each other warm. Bacon is frank on the subject: a friend is a second *you*, and will look after your affairs when you have gone. And La Rochefoucauld is more brutal: the phenomenon is no more than 'a reciprocal management of interests'. Cicero, however, maintains that, though material advantage may well ensue, we do not value friendship as a source of it. Benefits unsought and incidental surely carry no taint; benevolence implies the possibility of benefaction.

Death—to revert to Bacon's utilitarian considerations—may be reckoned a critical emergency (a friend in need is indeed a friend), but many observers have insisted that what we appreciate most in our friends is ordinary little attentions rather than succour at times of crisis. And, at the back of our minds, confidence that help would be forthcoming should unhappy circumstance demand it.

Schopenhauer touches on the narrowness, the constriction of sympathy, involved in friendship: having friends suggests that other people are not friends, so you care nothing for them. It has been held that friendship is actually immoral in that it entails giving preferential treatment to people who may neither need nor deserve it more than others. In the *Proceedings of the Aristotelian Society* 1970–1, Elizabeth Telfer offered as the only possible answer that in this sphere the utility of the practice is 'high enough to compensate for the fact that some measure of injustice is involved in it'. (Which might have been Burke's answer to Goldsmith's complaint that he gave up to party what was meant for mankind.) Once any substantially damaging nepotism is left aside, the fuss over the theoretical injustice arising out of friendship must seem absurd when we think of the injustices deriving from so many other causes. It could equally well be reasoned that marriage is immoral because it denies one's estimable self to all the other potential spouses, equally deserving or needful.

C. S. Lewis believed that in modern times we have fallen away from the Ancients, for whom friendship was 'the crown of life', the happiest and most human of all forms of love. The subject was indeed pre-eminent then, as notably in our sixteenth and seventeenth centuries. Under the unpredictable sway of corrupt emperors and despotic rulers, friendship with someone of known integrity was much to be desired, and could prefigure the possibility of a better, more generous, and humane society. But, like unrequited love, friendship might lend itself to set literary exercises; it could indulge the resentment provoked by the tyranny of sexuality (itself a theme not readily to be written about), or by the banality and burdensomeness of family life. Friendship, among men at least, had an impeccably noble ring to it. Leigh Hunt was thinking along similar lines when he described it as the 'most spiritual of the affections' in that one's *kindred*, on the other hand, partook of one's flesh and blood.

The contents of this book, we hope, will show that Lewis was mistaken in supposing that for the modern world friendship is 'quite marginal . . . something that fills up the chinks of one's time'. We are more reticent these days, on some subjects, or afraid of sounding highflown or mawkish or naïve. 'What an odious thing it is to be thought to love a wife in good company,' remarks a character in a Restoration comedy. In good company you don't need to talk about having friends; in bad company you wouldn't dream of doing so.

But Lewis is right in judging that friendship is 'the least *natural* of loves', being the least instinctive, biological, or necessary. This he intends in no derogatory sense—reason not the need!—but distinctly the reverse. Friendship, Emerson said, resembles the immortality of the soul in that it is too good to be believed. Obviously he did believe in it. 'I awoke this morning with devout thanksgiving for my friends, the old and the new. Shall I not call God the Beautiful, who daily showeth himself so to me in his gifts?'

Is it better to have many friends or few? Should they be like us or unlike? Are old friends best, or should we take care to make new ones? Is *make* the right word? Isn't our natural egoism so strong that the existence of friendship must be as questionable as that of the sea serpent? While in this anthology we aim to display diverse and often mutually contra-dictory views of the subject, its nature and duties, pleasures and pains, we shall spend little time on abstract generalities and far more on particular instances, in life and in literature, in some of their innumerable varieties, phases, manifestations, and effects. As George Eliot said of 'love', 'friendship' is 'a word of all work'.

———

As thus he spake, each bird and beast behold
Approaching two and two, these cow'ring low
With blandishment, each bird stooped on his wing.
I named them as they passed, and understood
Their nature; with such knowledge God endued
My sudden apprehension. But in these
I found not what methought I wanted still,
And to the heav'nly Vision thus presumed:
    'O by what name, for thou above all these,
Above mankind, or aught than mankind higher,

Surpassest far my naming, how may I
Adore thee, Author of this universe,
And all this good to man, for whose well-being
So amply, and with hands so liberal
Thou hast provided all things? But with me
I see not who partakes. In solitude
What happiness? Who can enjoy alone,
Or all enjoying, what contentment find?'
Thus I presumptuous; and the Vision bright,
As with a smile more brightened, thus replied:

'What call'st thou solitude? Is not the earth
With various living creatures, and the air
Replenished, and all these at thy command
To come and play before thee? Know'st thou not
Their language and their ways? They also know,
And reason not contemptibly; with these
Find pastime, and bear rule; thy realm is large.'
So spake the universal Lord, and seemed
So ordering. I with leave of speech implored,
And humble deprecation, thus replied:

'Let not my words offend thee, heav'nly Power;
My Maker, be propitious while I speak.
Hast thou not made me here thy substitute,
And these inferior far beneath me set?
Among unequals what society
Can sort, what harmony or true delight?
Which must be mutual, in proportion due
Giv'n and received; but in disparity,
The one intense, the other still remiss
Cannot well suit with either, but soon prove
Tedious alike. Of fellowship I speak
Such as I seek, fit to participate
All rational delight, wherein the brute
Cannot be human consort; they rejoice
Each with their kind, lion with lioness;
So fitly them in pairs thou hast combined;
Much less can bird with beast, or fish with fowl
So well converse, nor with the ox the ape;
Worse then can man with beast, and least of all.'
Whereto th'Almighty answered, not displeased:

'A nice and subtle happiness, I see,
Thou to thyself proposest, in the choice
Of thy associates, Adam, and wilt taste
No pleasure, though in pleasure, solitary.'

JOHN MILTON, *Paradise Lost*, 1667

First I must tell you that I am one who from my childhood upward have set my heart upon a certain thing. All people have their fancies; some desire horses, and others dogs; and some are fond of gold, and others of honour. Now, I have no violent desire of any of these things; but I have a passion for friends; and I would rather have a good friend than the best cock or quail in the world: I would even go further, and say the best horse or dog . . . And when I see you and Lysis, at your early age, so easily possessed of this treasure, and so soon, he of you, and you of him, I am amazed and delighted, seeing that I myself, although I am now advanced in years, am so far from having made a similar acquisition, that I do not even know in what way a friend is acquired. But I want to ask you a question about this, for you have experience: tell me then, when one loves another, is the lover or the beloved the friend; or may either be the friend?

Either may, I should think, be the friend of either.

Do you mean, I said, that if only one of them loves the other, they are mutual friends?

Yes, Menexenus said; that is my meaning.

But what if the lover is not loved in return? which is a very possible case.

Yes.

Or is, perhaps, even hated? which is a fancy which sometimes is entertained by lovers respecting their beloved. Nothing can exceed their love; and yet they imagine either that they are not loved in return, or that they are hated. Is not that true?

Yes, he said, quite true.

In that case, the one loves, and the other is loved?

Yes.

Then which is the friend of which? Is the lover the friend of the beloved, whether he be loved in return, or hated; or is the beloved the friend; or is there no friendship at all on either side, unless they both love one another?

There would seem to be none at all . . .

Then they are not lovers of horses, whom the horses do not love in return; nor lovers of quails, nor of dogs, nor of wine, nor of gymnastic exercises, who have no return of love; no, nor of wisdom, unless wisdom loves them in return.

Then what is to be done? Or rather is there anything to be done? I can only, like the wise men who argue in courts, sum up the arguments:—If neither the beloved, nor the lover, nor the like, nor the unlike, nor the good, nor the congenial, nor any other of whom we spoke—for there were such a number of them that I cannot remember all—if none of these are friends, I know not what remains to be said.

Here I was going to invite the opinion of some older person, when suddenly we were interrupted by the tutors of Lysis and Menexenus, who came upon us like an evil apparition with their brothers, and bade them go home, as it was getting late. At first, we and the bystanders drove them off; but afterwards, as they would not mind, and only went on shouting in their barbarous dialect, and got angry, and kept calling the boys—they appeared to us to have been drinking rather too much at the Hermaea, which made them difficult to manage—we fairly gave way and broke up the company.

I said, however, a few words to the boys at parting: O Menexenus and Lysis, how ridiculous that you two boys, and I, an old boy, who would fain be one of you, should imagine ourselves to be friends—this is what the bystanders will go away and say—and as yet we have not been able to discover what is a friend!

PLATO (?429–347 BC), *Lysis*; tr. Benjamin Jowett

Nature assigns the Sun—
That—is Astronomy—
Nature cannot enact a Friend—
That—is Astrology.

EMILY DICKINSON (1830–86), 'Nature assigns the Sun'

The truest kind of friendship is that which exists between good men, as we have said more than once. For it is agreed that what is good or pleasant absolutely is lovable and desirable absolutely, and what is good or pleasant for a particular person is lovable and desirable for that person. But friendship between good men rests on both grounds—the good are good and pleasant absolutely, and good and pleasant to each other. And when men wish well to those they love for their own sakes, this goodwill is not an emotion but a fixed disposition. Liking seems to be an emotion, but friendship a disposition; liking may just as much be felt for inanimate objects, but mutual affection is a matter of deliberate choice, and this springs from a fixed disposition. In loving a friend men are loving their own good, as a good man benefits a person whose affection he wins. Each party to a friendship therefore both promotes his own good and makes an equal return in goodwill and in the pleasure that he gives. There is a saying, 'Amity is equality', and this is most fully realized in the friendships between good men.

Friendship is essentially a partnership. Also a friend is a second self, so that our consciousness of a friend's existence, when given reality by intercourse with him, makes us more fully conscious of our own existence.

ARISTOTLE (384–322 BC), *Nicomachean Ethics*; tr. H. Rackham

> Then wonder not to see this Soul extend
> The bounds, and seek some other self, a Friend:
> As swelling Seas to gentle Rivers glide,
> To seek repose, and empty out the Tide;
> So this full Soul, in narrow limits pent,
> Unable to contain her, sought a vent,
> To issue out, and in some friendly breast
> Discharge her Treasures, and securely rest:
> T'unbosom all the secrets of her Heart,
> Take good advice, but better to impart.
> For 'tis the bliss of Friendship's holy state
> To mix their Minds, and to communicate;
> Though Bodies cannot, Souls can penetrate.
> Fixt to her choice; inviolably true;
> And wisely choosing, for she chose but few.
> Some she must have; but in no one could find
> A Tally fitted for so large a Mind.

>   The Souls of Friends like Kings in Progress are;
>   Still in their own, though from the Palace far:
>   Thus her Friend's Heart her Country Dwelling was,
>   A sweet Retirement to a coarser place:
>   Where Pomp and Ceremonies enter'd not;
>   Where Greatness was shut out, and Bus'ness well forgot.

>   JOHN DRYDEN, from 'Eleonora: A Panegyrical Poem, Dedicated
>   to the Memory of the late Countess of Abingdon', 1692

Well, then, it has very often occurred to me when thinking about friendship, that the chief point to be considered was this: is it weakness and want of means that make friendship desired? I mean, is its object an interchange of good offices, so that each may give that in which he is strong, and receive that in which he is weak? Or is it not rather true that, although this is an advantage naturally belonging to friendship, yet its original cause is quite other, prior in time, more noble in character, and springing more directly from our nature itself? The Latin word for friendship—*amicitia*—is derived from that for love—*amor*; and love is certainly the prime mover in contracting mutual affection.

For as we are not beneficent and liberal with any view of extorting gratitude, and do not regard an act of kindness as an investment, but follow a natural inclination to liberality; so we look on friendship as worth trying for, not because we are attracted to it by the expectation of ulterior gain, but in the conviction that what it has to give us is from first to last included in the feeling itself.

Indeed I am inclined to think that friends ought at times to be in want of something. For instance, what scope would my affections have had if Scipio had never wanted my advice or co-operation at home or abroad? It is not friendship, then, that follows material advantage, but material advantage friendship.

>   MARCUS TULLIUS CICERO (106–43 BC), *On Friendship*; tr. E. S.
>   Shuckburgh

Two are better than one; because they have a good reward for their labour.

For if they fall, the one will lift up his fellow: but woe to him that is alone when he falleth; for he hath not another to help him up.

Again, if two lie together, then they have heat: but how can one be warm alone?

And if one prevail against him, two shall withstand him; and a threefold cord is not quickly broken.

Ecclesiastes 4

A Principall Fruit of *Frendship*, is the Ease and Discharge of the Fulnesse and Swellings of the Heart, which Passions of all kinds doe cause and induce. We know that Diseases of Stoppings, and Suffocations, are the most dangerous in the body; and it is not much otherwise in the Minde: You may take *Sarʒa* to open the Liver; *Steele* to open the Spleene; *Flower of Sulphur* for the Lungs; *Castoreum* for the Braine. But no Receipt openeth the Heart, but a true *Frend*, to whom you may impart Griefes, Joyes, Feares, Hopes, Suspicions, Counsels, and whatsoever lieth upon the Heart, to oppresse it, in a kind of Civill Shrift or Confession. . . .

Certainly, if a Man would give it a hard Phrase, Those that want *Frends* to open themselves unto, are Canniballs of their owne *Hearts*. . . .

There is as much difference, betweene the *Counsell* that a *Frend* giveth, and that a Man giveth himselfe, as there is betweene the *Counsell* of a *Frend*, and of a *Flatterer*. For there is no such *Flatterer* as is a Man's Selfe; and there is no such Remedy, against *Flattery* of a Man's Selfe, as the Liberty of a *Frend*. . . .

Cast and see, how many Things there are, which a Man cannot doe Himselfe, and then it will appeare, that it was a Sparing Speech of the Ancients, to say, *That a Frend is another Himselfe*: For that a *Frend* is farre more than *Himselfe*. Men have their Time, and die many times in desire of some Things, which they principally take to Heart: the bestowing of a Child, the Finishing of a Worke, or the like. If a Man have a true *Frend*, he may rest almost secure, that the Care of those Things will continue after Him. So that a Man hath as it were two Lives in his desires.

SIR FRANCIS BACON, 'Of Frendship', 1597

What helps us in friendship is not so much the help our friends actually give as the assurance we feel concerning that help.

EPICURUS (341–270 BC), *Gnomologium Vaticanum*

In estimating the value of an acquaintance or even a friend, we give a preference to intellectual or convivial over moral qualities. The truth is, that in our habitual intercourse with others, we much oftener require to be amused than assisted. We consider less, therefore, what a person with whom we are intimate is ready to do for us in critical emergencies, than what he has to say on ordinary occasions.

WILLIAM HAZLITT, *Characteristics*, 1823

That friendship may be at once fond and lasting, there must not only be equal virtue on each part, but virtue of the same kind; not only the same end must be proposed, but the same means must be approved by both. We are often, by superficial accomplishments and accidental endearments, induced to love those whom we cannot esteem; we are sometimes, by great abilities and incontestable evidences of virtue, compelled to esteem those whom we cannot love. But friendship, compounded of esteem and love, derives from one its tenderness, and its permanence from the other; and therefore requires not only that its candidates should gain the judgement, but that they should attract the affections; that they should not only be firm in the day of distress, but gay in the hour of jollity; not only useful in exigences, but pleasing in familiar life; their presence should give chearfulness as well as courage, and dispel alike the gloom of fear and of melancholy.

SAMUEL JOHNSON, *The Rambler*, 27 October 1750

... I really thought you would know yourself to be so certainly entitld to my Friendship, that twas a possession, you cou'd not imagine needed any further Deeds or Writings to assure you of it. It is an honest Truth, there's no one living or dead of whom I think oft'ner, or better than yourself. I look upon You to be, (as to me) in a State between both: you have from me all the passions, & good wishes, that can attend the Living; & all that Respect & tender Sense of Loss, that we feel for the Dead. Whatever you seem to think of your withdrawn & separate State, at this distance, & in this absence, Dr Swift lives still in England, in ev'ry place & company where he woud chuse to live; & I find him in all the conversations I keep, & in all the Hearts in which I wou'd have any Share. We have never met these many Years without mention of you. . . . My Friendships are increas'd by new ones, yet no part of the warmth I felt for the old is diminish'd. Aversions I have none but to Knaves, (for Fools I have learn'd to bear with) & those I cannot be commonly Civil to: For I think those are next of knaves who converse with them.

ALEXANDER POPE, letter to Swift, August 1723

Your Notions of Friendship are new to me; I believe every man is born with his quantum, and he can not give to one without Robbing another. I very well know to whom I would give the first place in my Friendship, but they are not in the way, I am condemned to another Scene, and therefore I distribute it in pennyworths to those about me, and who displease me least and should do the same to my fellow Prisoners if I were Condemned to a Jayl. I can likewise tolerate knaves much better than Fools because their knavery does me no hurt in the Commerce I have with them which however I own is more dangerous, tho' not so troublesome as that of Fools, I have often endeavoured to establish a Friendship among all Men of Genius, and would fain have it done. They are seldom above three or four Cotemporaries and if they could be united would drive the world before them; I think it was so among the Poets in the time of Augustus, but Envy and party and pride have hindred it among us. I do not include the subalterns of which you are Seldom without a large Tribe under the Name of Poets and Scriblers; I suppose you mean the Fools you are content to see sometimes when they happen to be modest, which was not frequent among them while I was in the world.

JONATHAN SWIFT, letter to Pope, 20 September 1723

Lamb says somewhere that if, of three friends (A, B, and C), A should die, then B loses not only A but 'A's part in C', while C loses not only A but

'A's part in B'. In each of my friends there is something that only some other friend can fully bring out.

C. S. LEWIS, The Four Loves, 1960

We have as many sides to our character as we have friends to show them to. Quite unconsciously I find myself witty with one friend, large and magnanimous with another, petulant and stingy with another, wise and grave with another, and utterly frivolous with another. I watch with surprise the sudden and startling changes in myself as I pass from the influence of one friend to the influence of some one else. But my character with each particular friend is constant. I find myself, whenever I meet him, with much the same emotional and mental tone. If we talk, there is with each one some definite subject upon which we always speak and which remains perennially fresh and new. If I am so unfortunate as to stray accidentally from one of these well-worn fields into another, I am instantly reminded of the fact by the strangeness and chill of the atmosphere. We are happy only on our familiar levels, but on these we feel that we could go on exhaustless forever, without a pang of ennui. And this inexhaustibility of talk is the truest evidence of good friendship.

Friends do not, on the other hand, always talk of what is nearest to them. Friendship requires that there be an open channel between friends, but it does not demand that that channel be the deepest in our nature. It may be of the shallowest kind and yet the friendship be of the truest. For all the different traits of our nature must get their airing through friends, the trivial as well as the significant. We let ourselves out piecemeal it seems, so that only with a host of varied friends can we express ourselves to the fullest. Each friend calls out some particular trait in us, and it requires the whole chorus fitly to teach us what we are. This is the imperative need of friendship. A man with few friends is only half-developed; there are whole sides of his nature which are locked up and have never been expressed. He cannot unlock them himself, he cannot even discover them; friends alone can stimulate him and open them. Such a man is in prison; his soul is in penal solitude. A man must get friends as he would get food and drink for nourishment and sustenance. And he must keep them, as he would keep health and wealth, as the infallible safeguards against misery and poverty of spirit.

RANDOLPH BOURNE, 'The Excitement of Friendship', 1912

On the third evening, one of his friends, to whom I had not had an opportunity before of speaking, conversed with me at great length; and I overheard him telling Saint-Loup how much he had been enjoying himself. And indeed we sat talking together almost all evening, leaving our glasses of sauterne untouched on the table before us, isolated, sheltered from the others by the sumptuous curtains of one of those intuitive sympathies between man and man which, when they are not based upon any physical attraction, are the only kind that is altogether mysterious. Of such an enigmatic nature had seemed to me, at Balbec, that feeling which Saint-Loup had for me, which was not to be confused with the interest of our conversations, a feeling free from any material association, invisible, intangible, and yet a thing of the presence of which in himself, like a sort of inflammatory gas, he had been so far conscious as to refer to it with a smile. And yet there was perhaps something more surprising still in this sympathy born here in a single evening, like a flower that had budded and opened in a few minutes in the warmth of this little room.

MARCEL PROUST, *Remembrance of Things Past: The Guermantes Way I*, 1920; tr. C. K. Scott Moncrieff

You know about a person who deeply interests you more than you can be told. A look, a gesture, an act, which to everybody else is insignificant tells you more about that one than words can . . . If he wished to conceal something from you it would be apparent. It is as if a bird told you. Something of moment occurs. Your friend designs that it shall be a secret to you. Vain wish! You will know it, and his design. He says consciously nothing about it, yet as he is necessarily affected by it, its effect is visible to you. From this effect you infer the cause. Have you not already anticipated a thousand possible accidents? Can you be surprised? You unconsciously through sympathy make the right supposition. No other will account for precisely this behavior. You are disingenuous, and yet your knowledge exceeds the woodcraft of the cunningest hunter. It is as if you had a sort of trap, knowing the haunts of your game, what lures attract it, and its track, etc. You have foreseen how it will behave when it is caught, and now you only behold what you anticipated.

HENRY DAVID THOREAU, *Journal*, 20 February 1859

My friends have come to me unsought. The great God gave them to me. By oldest right, by the divine affinity of virtue with itself, I find them, or rather not I, but the Deity in me and in them derides and cancels the thick walls of individual character, relation, age, sex, circumstance, at which he usually connives, and now makes many one.

There are two elements that go to the composition of friendship, each so sovereign that I can detect no superiority in either, no reason why either should be first named. One is Truth. A friend is a person with whom I may be sincere. Before him I may think aloud. I am arrived at last in the presence of a man so real and equal, that I may drop even those undermost garments of dissimulation, courtesy, and second thought, which men never put off, and may deal with him with the simplicity and wholeness with which one chemical atom meets another. Sincerity is the luxury allowed, like diadems and authority, only to the highest rank, *that* being permitted to speak truth, as having none above it to court or conform unto ... Almost every man we meet requires some civility —requires to be humoured; he has some fame, some talent, some whim of religion or philanthropy in his head that is not to be questioned, and which spoils all conversation with him. But a friend is a sane man who exercises not my ingenuity, but me. My friend gives me entertainment without requiring any stipulation on my part. A friend, therefore, is a sort of paradox in nature. I who alone am, I who see nothing in nature whose existence I can affirm with equal evidence to my own, behold now the semblance of my being, in all its height, variety, and curiosity, reiterated in a foreign form; so that a friend may well be reckoned the masterpiece of nature.

The other element of friendship is tenderness. We are holden to men by every sort of tie, by blood, by pride, by fear, by hope, by lucre, by lust, by hate, by admiration, by every circumstance and badge and trifle, but we can scarce believe that so much character can subsist in another as to draw us by love. Can another be so blessed, and we so pure, that we can offer him tenderness? When a man becomes dear to me, I have touched the goal of fortune ... The end of friendship is a commerce the most strict and homely that can be joined; more strict than any of which we have experience. It is for aid and comfort through all the relations and passages of life and death. It is fit for serene days, and graceful gifts, and country rambles, but also for rough roads and hard fare, shipwreck, poverty, and persecution. It keeps company with the sallies of the wit and the trances of religion. We are to dignify to each other the daily needs and offices of man's life, and embellish it by courage, wisdom, and unity. It should never fall into something usual and settled, but should be alert and inventive, and add rhyme and reason to what was drudgery.

RALPH WALDO EMERSON, 'Friendship', *Essays: First Series*, 1841

Friendship is almost always the union of a part of one mind with a part of another; people are friends in spots. Friendship sometimes rests on sharing early memories, as do brothers and schoolfellows, who often, but for that now affectionate familiarity with the same old days, would dislike and irritate one another extremely. Sometimes it hangs on passing pleasures and amusements, or on special pursuits; sometimes on mere convenience and comparative lack of friction in living together. One's friends are that part of the human race with which one can be human. But there are youthful friendships of quite another quality, which I seem to have discovered flourishing more often and more frankly in England than in other countries; brief echoes, as it were, of that love of comrades so much celebrated in antiquity. I do not refer to the 'friendship of virtue' mentioned by Aristotle, which means, I suppose, community in allegiance or in ideals. It may come to that in the end, considered externally; but community in allegiance or in ideals, if genuine, expresses a common disposition, and its roots are deeper and more physical than itself. The friendship I have in mind is a sense of this initial harmony between two natures, a union of one whole man with another whole man, a sympathy between the centres of their being, radiating from those centres on occasion in unanimous thoughts, but not essentially needing to radiate. Trust here is inwardly grounded; likes and dislikes run together without harness, like the steeds of Aurora; you may take agreement for granted without words; affection is generously independent of all tests or external bonds; it can even bear not to be mutual, not to be recognized; and in any case it shrinks from the blatancy of open vows. In such friendships there is a touch of passion and of shyness; an understanding which does not need to become explicit or complete.

GEORGE SANTAYANA, *Soliloquies in England*, 1922

The men whose familiarity and society I hunt after, are those which are called honest, virtuous, and sufficient: the image of whom doth distaste and divert me from others. It is (being rightly taken) the rarest of our forms; and a form or fashion chiefly due unto nature.

The end or scope of this commerce is principally and simply familiarity, conference and frequentation: the exercise of minds, without other fruit. In our discourses all subjects are alike to me: I care not though they want either weight or depth; grace and pertinency are never wanting; all therein is tainted with a ripe and constant judgement, and commixed with goodness, liberty, cheerfulness, and kindness. It is not only in the subject of Laws and affairs of Princes, that our spirit sheweth its beauty, grace and vigour: It sheweth them as much in private conferences. I know my people by their very silence and smiling, and peradventure discover them better at a Table than sitting in serious counsel.

Hippomacus said, he discerned good Wrestlers but by seeing them march through a Street. If learning vouchsafe to step into our talk, she shall not be refused; yet must not she be stern, mastering, imperious and importunate, as commonly she is; but assistant and docile of herself. Therein we seek for nothing but recreation and pastime: when we shall look to be instructed, taught and resolved, we will go seek and sue to her in her throne.

MICHEL DE MONTAIGNE, 'Of Three Commerces or Societies', *Essays*, 1580; tr. John Florio, 1603

What is commonly honored with the name of Friendship is no very profound or powerful instinct. Men do not, after all, *love* their Friends greatly. I do not often see the farmers made seers and wise to the verge of insanity by their Friendship for one another. They are not often transfigured and translated by love in each other's presence. I do not observe them purified, refined, and elevated by the love of a man. If one abates a little the price of his wood, or gives a neighbor his vote at town-meeting, or a barrel of apples, or lends him his wagon frequently, it is esteemed a rare instance of Friendship. Nor do the farmers' wives lead lives consecrated to Friendship. I do not see the pair of farmer Friends of either sex prepared to stand against the world. There are only two or three couples in history. To say that a man is your Friend, means commonly no more than this, that he is not your enemy. Most contemplate only what would be the accidental and trifling advantages of Friendship, as that the Friend can assist in time of need, by his substance, or his influence, or his counsel; but he who foresees such advantages in this relation proves himself blind to its real advantage, or indeed wholly inexperienced in the relation itself. Such services are particular and menial, compared with the perpetual and all-embracing service which it is. Even the utmost good-will and harmony and practical kindness are not sufficient for Friendship, for Friends do not live in harmony merely, as some say, but in melody.

THOREAU, *A Week on the Concord and Merrimack Rivers*, 1849

What restored and refreshed me chiefly, was the solaces of other friends, with whom I did love, what instead of Thee I loved: and this was a great fable, and protracted lie, by whose adulterous stimulus, our soul, which lay itching in our ears, was being defiled. But that fable would not die to me, so oft as any of my friends died. There were other things which in them did more take my mind; to talk and jest together, to do kind offices by turns; to read together honied books; to play the fool or be earnest together; to dissent at times without discontent, as a man might with his own self; and even with the seldomness of these dissentings, to season our more frequent consentings; sometimes to teach, and sometimes learn; long for the absent with impatience; and welcome the coming with joy. These and the like expressions, proceeding out of the hearts of those that loved and were loved again, by the countenance, the tongue, the eyes, and a thousand pleasing gestures, were so much fuel to melt our souls together, and out of many make but one.

This is it that is loved in friends; and so loved, that a man's conscience condemns itself, if he love not him that loves him again, or love not again him that loves him, looking for nothing from his person, but indications of his love. Hence that mourning, if one die, and darkenings of sorrows, that steeping of the heart in tears, all sweetness turned to bitterness; and upon the loss of life of the dying, the death of the living. Blessed whoso loveth Thee, and his friend in Thee, and his enemy for Thee. For he alone loses none dear to him, to whom all are dear in Him Who cannot be lost. And who is this but our God, the *God that made heaven and earth*, and *filleth them*, because by filling them He created them?

ST AUGUSTINE, *Confessions, c.* 397–400; tr. E. B. Pusey

'As the sun is in the firmament, so is friendship in the world', a most divine and heavenly band. As nuptial love makes, this perfects mankind, and is to be preferred (if you will stand to the judgment of Cornelius Nepos) before affinity or consanguinity; *plus in amicitia valet similitudo morum, quam affinitas*, etc., the cords of love bind faster than any other wreath whatsoever. Take this away, and take all pleasure, joy, comfort, happiness, and true content out of the world; 'tis the greatest tie, the surest indenture, strongest band, and . . . is much to be preferred before the rest.

A faithful friend is better than gold, a medicine of misery, an only possession; yet this love of friends, nuptial, heroical, profitable, pleasant, honest, all three loves put together, are little worth, if they proceed not from a true Christian illuminated soul, if it be not done *in ordine ad Deum*, for God's sake.

Robert Burton, *The Anatomy of Melancholy*, 1621

Now with my friend I desire not to share or participate, but to engross, his sorrows; that, by making them mine own, I may more easily discuss them; for in mine own reason, and within my self, I can command that which I cannot intreat without my self, and within the circle of another. I have often thought those noble pairs and examples of friendship not so truly Histories of what had been, as fictions of what should be; but I now perceive nothing in them but possibilities, nor any thing in the Heroick examples of Damon and Pythias, Achilles and Patroclus, which methinks upon some grounds I could not perform within the narrow compass of my self. That a man should lay down his life for his Friend, seems strange to vulgar affections, and such as confine themselves within that Worldly principle, *Charity begins at home.* For mine own part I could never remember the relations that I held unto my self, nor the respect that I owe unto my own nature, in the cause of God, my Country, and my Friends. Next to these three, I do embrace my self. I confess I do not observe that order that the Schools ordain our affections, to love our Parents, Wives, Children, and then our Friends; for, excepting the injunctions of Religion, I do not find in my self such a necessary and indissoluble Sympathy to all those of my blood. I hope I do not break the fifth Commandment, if I conceive I may love my friend before the nearest of my blood, even those to whom I owe the principles of life. I never yet cast a true affection on a woman; but I have loved my friend as I do virtue, my soul, my God.

Sir Thomas Browne, *Religio Medici*, 1642

'If I had to choose between betraying my country and betraying my friend, I hope I should have the guts to betray my country.' This statement by Mr E. M. Forster reminds us how far we have wandered from the ancient conception of friendship, of treating a kindred soul as an end not a means. 'The Chinese poet recommends himself as a friend, the Western poet as a lover,' writes Arthur Waley; but the Western prose-writer also used to recommend himself as a friend; the seventeenth and eighteenth centuries elaborated friendship and all but made it their religion. In the circle of Johnson, of Walpole and Madame du Deffand or of the Encyclopedists nobody could live without his friend. They loved them and even a misanthropic philosopher like La Bruyère could grow sentimental over the theme. Only the invalid Pascal demolished friendship on the ground that if we could read each other's thoughts it would disappear.

Now the industrialization of the world, the totalitarian State, and the egotism of materialism have made an end to friendship; the first through speeding up the tempo of human communication to the point where no one is indispensable, the second by making such demands on the individual that comradeship can be practised between workers and colleagues only for the period of their co-operation, and the last by emphasizing whatever is fundamentally selfish and nasty in people, so that we are unkind about our friends and resentful of their intimacy because of something which is rotting in ourselves. We have developed sympathy at the expense of loyalty.

CYRIL CONNOLLY, *The Unquiet Grave*, 1944

I remember a certain meeting in Moscow in the Red Square in which thousands of young people from all over the world participated. I have never experienced more strongly the deep meaning of camaraderie than when all together, each in his own language, we sang the *International*. If the word 'mystique' did not then have a pejorative sense for us, I would have spoken of a mystic communion among these young people. Between comrades the distinction between 'mine' and 'yours' no longer existed; it went without saying that each shared all. A fervent militant went so far as to offer his wife's companionship to a professional propagandist of the party whom he supposed to be long deprived of women because of his work.

From many points of view camaraderie can be mistaken for friendship. Yet it is not friendship. What is important in camaraderie is infinitely less the person of the comrade than his participation in a common struggle. It is true that bonds of particular affinity, of interpersonal predilection can be established, in which case we can say that comrades are also friends. But this friendship always remains subordinate to the exigencies of combat and necessarily obeys the directives of the party.

IGNACE LEPP, *The Ways of Friendship*, 1964; tr. Bernard Murchland

I much better understand the Duties of Friendship & the Merits of Virtue in Private life, than those of Public: and should never love my Country if I did not love the Best men in it.

POPE, letter to Hugh Bethel, 14 April 1741

To be attached to the subdivisions, to love the little platoon we belong to in society, is the first principle (the germ as it were) of public affections.

EDMUND BURKE, *Reflections on the Revolution in France*, 1790

That outlook which values the collective above the individual necessarily disparages Friendship; it is a relation between men at their highest level of individuality . . . To say 'These are my friends' implies 'Those are not'.

C. S. LEWIS, *The Four Loves*

We can love nothing except in relation to ourselves, and we only follow our taste and our pleasure when we prefer our friends to ourselves; nevertheless it is thanks to that preference alone that friendship can be true and perfect.

What people have called friendship is nothing but an association, a reciprocal management of interests, and an exchange of good offices; in short it is nothing but a transaction from which the self always means to gain something.

We are easily consoled for the afflictions suffered by our friends when these help us to show our affection.

When we exaggerate the affection our friends have for us, it is often less out of gratitude than to create an impression of our merit.

The greater effort of friendship lies not in revealing our faults to a friend but in getting him to see his own.

It is not in proportion to their merits that we regret the loss of our friends, but according to our needs, and the opinion we believe we have given them of our worth.

It is more shameful to distrust one's friends than to be deceived by them.

However rare true love may be, it is less so than true friendship.

FRANÇOIS, DUC DE LA ROCHEFOUCAULD, *Maximes*, 1665

The temple of friendship has long been a household word, but it is well known that the place has been very little frequented . . . Orestes, Pylades, Pirithous, Achates, and the tender Nisus, they were all genuine friends and great heroes; but alas they existed only in fable.

VOLTAIRE, *Dictionnaire Philosophique*, 1764

The real friendships among men are so rare that when they occur they are famous.

CLARENCE DAY, *This Simian World*, 1920

True and genuine friendship presupposes a strong sympathy with the weal and woe of another—purely objective in its character and quite disinterested; and this in its turn means an absolute identification of self with the object of friendship. The egoism of human nature is so strongly antagonistic to any such sympathy, that true friendship belongs to that class of things—the sea serpent, for instance—with regard to which no one knows whether they are fabulous or really exist somewhere or other.

Still, in many cases, there is a grain of true and genuine friendship in the relations of man to man, though generally, of course, some secret personal interest is at the bottom of them—some one among the many forms that selfishness can take. But in a world where all is imperfect, this grain of true feeling is such an ennobling influence that it gives some warrant for calling those relations by the name of friendship, for they stand far above the ordinary friendships that prevail amongst mankind. The latter are so constituted that, were you to hear how your dear friends speak of you behind your back, you would never say another word to them.

With the ancients *friendship* was one of the chief elements in morality. But friendship is only limitation and partiality; it is the restriction to one individual of what is the due of all mankind, namely, the recognition that a man's own nature and that of mankind are identical. At most it is a compromise between this recognition and selfishness.

I observed once to Goethe, in complaining of the illusion and vanity of life, that when a friend is with us we do not think the same of him as when he is away. He replied: 'Yes! because the absent friend is yourself, and he exists only in your head; whereas the friend who is present has an individuality of his own, and moves according to laws of his own; which cannot always be in accordance with those which you form for yourself.'

ARTHUR SCHOPENHAUER, *Parerga and Paralipomena*, 1851; tr. T. Bailey Saunders

We are all liars, because
the truth of yesterday becomes a lie tomorrow,
whereas letters are fixed,
and we live by the letter of truth.

The love I feel for my friend, this year,
is different from the love I felt last year.
If it were not so, it would be a lie.
Yet we reiterate love! love!

as if it were coin with a fixed value
instead of a flower that dies, and opens a different bud.

D. H. LAWRENCE (1885–1930), 'Lies about Love'

Friendship's an empty name, made to deceive
Those whose good nature tempts them to believe:
There's no such thing on earth, the best that we
Can hope for here is faint neutrality.

SIR SAMUEL TUKE, *The Adventures of Five Hours*, 1663

But perhaps there are some that . . . rest satisfi'd in the enjoyment of their
Friends, calling friendship the most desirable of all things; more necessary than either air, fire, or water; so delectable, that he that shall take it
out of the World had as good put out the Sun; and lastly so commendable,
if yet that make any thing to the matter, that neither the Philosophers
themselves doubted to reckon it among their chiefest good. But what if I
shew you that I am both the beginning and end of this so great good also?
Nor shall I go about to prove it by Fallacies, Sorites, Dilemmas, or other
the like subtilties of Logicians, but after my blunt way, point out the thing
as clearly as 'twere with my finger.

And now tell me, if to wink, slip over, be blind at, or deceiv'd in, the
vices of our friends, nay, to admire and esteem them for Virtues, be not at
least the next degree to folly? What is it when one kisses his Mistresses
freckle Neck, another the Wart on her Nose? When a Father shall swear
his squint-ey'd Child is more lovely than Venus? What is this, I say, but
meer folly? And so, perhaps you'l cry, it is; and yet 'tis this onely that
joyns friends together, and continues them so joyn'd. I speak of ordinary
men, of whom none are born without their imperfections, and happy is he
that is prest with the least: for among wise Princes there is either no
friendship at all, or if there be, 'tis unpleasant and reserv'd, and that too
but amongst a very few, 'twere a crime to say none. For that the greatest
part of mankind are fools, nay there is not any one that dotes not in many
things; and friendship, you know, is seldome made but amongst equalls.
And yet if it should so happen that there were a mutual good-will
between them, it is in no wise firm nor very long liv'd; that is to say,

among such as are morose and more circumspect than needs, as being Eagle-sighted into his friends' faults, but so blear-ey'd to their own that they take not the least notice of the Wallet that hangs behind their own Shoulders. Since then the nature of Man is such that there is scarce any one to be found that is not subject to many errors, add to this the great diversity of minds and studies, so many slips, oversights and chances of humane life, and how is it possible there should be any true friendship between those Argus's, so much as one hour, were it not for that which the Greeks excellently call εὐήθειαν? and you may render by Folly or good Nature, chuse you whether. But what? Is not the Author and Parent of all our Love, Cupid, as blind as a beetle? and as with him all colours agree, so from him is it that every one likes his own Sweeter-kin best, though never so ugly, and 'that an old man dotes on his old wife, and a boy on his girle'. These things are not onely done every where but laught at too, yet as ridiculous as they are, they make society pleasant, and, as it were, glew it together. . . .

In fine, I am so necessary to the making of all society and manner of life both delightful and lasting, that neither would the people long endure their Governors, nor the Servant his Master, nor the Master his Footman, nor the Scholar his Tutor, nor one friend another, nor the Wife her Husband, nor the Userer the Borrower, nor a Souldier his Commander, nor one Companion another, unlesse all of them had their interchangeable failings, one while flattering, other while prudently conniving, and generally sweetning one another with some small relish of Folly.

DESIDERIUS ERASMUS, The Praise of Folly, 'An Oration, of feigned matter, spoken by Folly in her own Person', 1511; tr. John Wilson, 1668

Only reflect to yourself how various are the feelings, how divided the opinions, even among your closest acquaintances, how even the same opinions are of a quite different rank or intensity in the heads of your friends than they are in yours; how manifold are the occasions for misunderstanding, for hostility and rupture. After reflecting on all this you must tell yourself: how uncertain is the ground upon which all our alliances and friendships rest, how close at hand are icy downpours or stormy weather, how isolated each man is! When one realizes this, and realizes in addition that all the opinions of one's fellow men, of whatever kind they are and with whatever intensity they are held, are just as

necessary and unaccountable as their actions; if one comes to understand
this inner necessity of opinions originating in the inextricable interweav-
ing of character, occupation, talent, environment—perhaps one will then
get free of that bitterness of feeling with which the sage cried: 'Friends,
there are no friends!' One will, rather, avow to oneself: yes, there are
friends, but it is error and deception regarding yourself that led them to
you; and they must have learned how to keep silent in order to remain
your friend; for such human relationships almost always depend upon
the fact that two or three things are never said or even so much as touched
upon: if these little boulders do start to roll, however, friendship follows
after them and shatters. Are there not people who would be mortally
wounded if they discovered what their dearest friends actually know
about them?—Through knowing ourselves and regarding our own
nature as a moving sphere of moods and opinions, and thus learning to
despise ourself a little, we restore our proper equilibrium with others. It is
true we have good reason to think little of each of our acquaintances,
even the greatest of them; but equally good reason to direct this feeling
back on to ourself.—And so, since we can endure ourself, let us also
endure other people; and perhaps to each of us there will come the more
joyful hour when we exclaim:

> 'Friends, there are no friends!' thus said the dying sage;
> 'Foes, there are no foes!' say I, the living fool.

FRIEDRICH NIETZSCHE, *Human, All Too Human*, 1878; tr. R. J.
Hollingdale

What are friends?
Why, they are people for love of whom one goes
    out and eagerly borrows what one to them eagerly
    lends,
Who in return assure one that if one were about to be eaten
    by an octopus they would dive fathoms deep to the
    rescue at the risk of contracting the bends,
But who, if one faces any more prosaic emergency such as
    asking if they would mind one's bringing along an
    extra girl, one is making a mistake if one on them
    depends.
They are people on whose entertainment one's entire
    income one hospitably and hebdomadally spends,

And who at one's house eat birthright and at their house
      one eats pottage and other odds and ends,
And for whose behaviour one is to one's foes constantly
      making amends,
Yes, that's what are friends.
What then are foes?
Why they are the least of anybody sensible's woes,
Because if there is one thing that you might of anybody
      sensible suppose,
It is that he wouldn't have anything to do with people who
      prove to be foes,
Because obviously if one tarries blithely among one's
      proven foemen,
Why whom has one to blame but oneself if one receives
      a poisoned barb in the small of the back or a poisoned
      comment on the large of the abdomen?
Yes, friends are unavoidable and epidemic and therefore
      friend trouble is forgivable but I have no sympathy
      for him who circles Robin Hood's barn and exposes
Himself to foeses.
I maintain that foes are very nice people as long as a
      reasonable distance separates oneself and them, whereas
      a friend in need or in his cups can reach you across
      mountains of glass and lakes of fire, with which
      remark I shall now close,
Simply pausing to add that compared to a friend at the
      front door I find foes at a reasonable distance rather
      restful, and from now on I shall ever think of them
      as *Comme Il Fauts*.

> OGDEN NASH, 'A Friend In Need Will Be Around In Five
> Minutes', 1942

If you're ever in a jam,
    Here I am.
If you're ever in a mess,
    S.O.S.
If you ever feel so happy you land in jail,
    I'm your bail.

It's friendship, friendship,
Just a perfect blendship.
When other friendships have been forgot,
Ours will still be hot.

If you're ever up a tree,
 Phone to me.
If you're ever down a well,
 Ring my bell.
If you ever lost your teeth and you're out to dine,
 Borrow mine.

It's friendship, friendship,
Just a perfect blendship.
When other friendships have been forgate,
Ours will still be great.

If they ever black your eyes,
 Put me wise.
If they ever cook your goose,
 Turn me loose.
If they ever put a bullet through your brain,
 I'll complain.

It's friendship, friendship,
Just a perfect blendship.
When other friendships have been forgit,
Ours will still be it.

COLE PORTER, 'Friendship', *Du Barry Was A Lady*, 1939

Dos and Don'ts

To lay down rules would make friendship seem a mechanical operation —the passage of Schopenhauer's, cited later, while it corrects sentimentality, smacks of cold-blooded policy in recommending the admixture of 'a grain of disdain', as does the Jewish saying, 'Descend a step in taking a wife; ascend a step in choosing a friend'—but some proposals can fairly be submitted.

'Neither a borrower nor a lender be ...' The passing of money between friends has occupied many minds, with opinions as to its propriety ranging from the unreserved generosity envisaged by George Herbert to the word of warning dropped by Mark Twain. Mr Wemmick, Dickens's clerk, holds the balance: the head advises against investing cash in a friend, the heart thinks otherwise. Hazlitt echoes Johnson's rejection of the idea that you should test a friend by asking him needlessly for a loan, when he says, in a passage not included here, that we stand in need of many other comforts aside from meat and drink and clothing, and it may well be that a man will open his mind to us who wouldn't pull out his purse. Johnson, in whose nature there was a persistent element of quite simple gentleness, would surely have rejected the Italian adage too: 'Test your friend with a falsehood, and if he keeps it a secret, tell him the truth.' A quick way of losing a friend before you have made one.

Disagreement also occurs over whether the exchange of harsh words will strengthen the bonds of friendship or sever them. As so often, Johnson, though himself devoted to argument, is the most convincing voice, in the anecdote reported by Mrs Thrale. Elsewhere he observed that if he had once said something to hurt a man—perhaps in a thrust of wit, that 'unruly engine'—then he would never recover lost ground no matter how many pleasing things he might tell him later. This seems truer, or more often the case, than Proverbs 28: 'He that rebuketh a man afterwards shall find more favour than he that flattereth with the tongue.' Like other coiners of proverbs, Solomon could contradict himself: 'A soft answer turneth away wrath: but grievous words stir up anger', 15.

Should we seek friends among those who are like or unlike us? They should be both: without some likeness a relationship will hardly begin, without some unlikeness it will soon die of inanition. Success, as Emerson sees it, lies in the *not-mine* coming to be *mine*: the recipe applies equally well to love. John Pomfret's poetical anatomy of the perfect specimen appears thoroughly acceptable—predictable, no doubt, and perhaps unrealistically sanguine—until we hear that his friends are to be faithful to Caesar as well as true to their Maker. In accommodating secular with religious obligations, Christ was evading the snares of the Pharisees, whereas in Pomfret's mouth the sentiment sounds merely unctuous.

Apropos of the Revd Colton's allusion to the lack of any text bidding us to forgive our friends, it is worth noting that in his essay 'Of Revenge' Bacon reported in rather shocked tones that Cosimo I, Duke of Florence, uttered 'a desperate saying against perfidious or neglecting friends': 'You shall read (saith he) that we are commanded to forgive our enemies; but you never read that we are commanded to forgive our friends.' Mighty contests rise from trivial things, and ruptures commonly have small causes. Such as failure to keep an appointment (Hazlitt). We need to remember that, like us, our friends are only human; Goethe's advice is that we shouldn't use too fine a scales in which to weigh their failings. This may be the drift of the (putative) Chinese injunction: 'Do not remove a fly from your friend's forehead with a hatchet.'

———

Instead of a friend become not an enemy; for thereby thou shalt inherit an ill name, shame, and reproach: even so shall a sinner that hath a double tongue . . .

Sweet language will multiply friends: and a fairspeaking tongue will increase kind greetings.

Be in peace with many: nevertheless have but one counsellor of a thousand.

If thou wouldst get a friend, prove him first, and be not hasty to credit him.

For some man is a friend for his own occasion, and will not abide in the day of thy trouble.

And there is a friend, who being turned to enmity and strife will discover thy reproach.

Again, some friend is a companion at the table, and will not continue in the day of thy affliction.

But in thy prosperity he will be as thyself, and will be bold over thy servants.

If thou be brought low, he will be against thee, and will hide himself from thy face.

Separate thyself from thine enemies, and take heed of thy friends.

A faithful friend is a strong defence: and he that hath found such an one hath found a treasure.

Nothing doth countervail a faithful friend, and his excellency is invaluable.

A faithful friend is the medicine of life; and they that fear the Lord shall find him.

Whoso feareth the Lord shall direct his friendship aright: for as he is, so shall his neighbour be also.

Ecclesiasticus 6

That life may be more comfortable yet,
And all my joys refined, sincere, and great,
I'd choose two friends, whose company would be
A great advance to my felicity:
Well-born, of humours suited to my own,
Discreet, and men as well as books have known;
Brave, gen'rous, witty, and exactly free
From loose behaviour, or formality;
Airy and prudent, merry, but not light,
Quick in discerning, and in judging right.
Secret they should be, faithful to their trust;
In reas'ning cool, strong, temperate, and just;
Obliging, open, without huffing brave,
Brisk in gay talking, and in sober, grave;
Close in dispute, but not tenacious; tried
By solid reason, and let that decide;
Not prone to lust, revenge, or envious hate,
Nor busy meddlers with intrigues of state;
Strangers to slander, and sworn foes to spite,
Not quarrelsome, but stout enough to fight;
Loyal, and pious, friends to Caesar; true,
As dying martyrs, to their Maker too.

In their society I could not miss
A permanent, sincere, substantial bliss.

JOHN POMFRET, from 'The Choice', 1700

I do not wish to treat friendships daintily, but with roughest courage. When they are real, they are not glass threads or frostwork, but the solidest thing we know.

Friendship requires that rare mean betwixt likeness and unlikeness, that piques each with the presence of power and of consent in the other party. Let me be alone to the end of the world, rather than that my friend should overstep, by a word or a look, his real sympathy. I am equally balked by antagonism and by compliance. Let him not cease an instant to be himself. The only joy I have in his being mine, is that the *not mine* is *mine*. I hate, where I looked for a manly furtherance, or at least a manly resistance, to find a mush of concession. Better be a nettle in the side of your friend than his echo. The condition which high friendship demands is ability to do without it. That high office requires great and sublime parts. There must be very two, before there can be very one. Let it be an alliance of two large, formidable natures, mutually beheld, mutually feared, before yet they recognize the deep identity which beneath these disparities unites them.

We talk of choosing our friends, but friends are self-elected. Reverence is a great part of it. Treat your friend as a spectacle. Of course he has merits that are not yours, and that you cannot honour, if you must needs hold him close to your person. Stand aside; give those merits room; let them mount and expand. Are you the friend of your friend's buttons, or of his thought? To a great heart he will still be a stranger in a thousand particulars, that he may come near in the holiest ground. Leave it to girls and boys to regard a friend as property, and to suck a short and all-confounding pleasure, instead of the noblest benefit.

EMERSON, 'Friendship'

The extent to which uniformity of mood is productive of good fellowship may be measured by its effects upon a large company. When, for instance, a great many people are gathered together and presented with some objective interest which works upon all alike and influences them in a similar way, no matter what it be—a common danger or hope, some great news, a spectacle, a play, a piece of music, or anything of that kind—you will find them roused to a mutual expression of thought, and a display of sincere interest. There will be a general feeling of pleasure amongst them; for that which attracts their attention produces a unity of mood by overpowering all private and personal interests.

And in default of some objective interest of the kind I have mentioned, recourse is usually had to something subjective. A bottle of wine is not an uncommon means of introducing a mutual feeling of fellowship; and even tea and coffee are used for a like end.

The only way to attain superiority in dealing with men, is to let it be seen that you are independent of them.

And in this view it is advisable to let everyone of your acquaintance —whether man or woman—feel now and then that you could very well dispense with their company. This will consolidate friendship. Nay, with most people there will be no harm in occasionally mixing a grain of disdain with your treatment of them; that will make them value your friendship all the more. *Chi non istima vien stimato*, as a subtle Italian proverb has it—to disregard is to win regard. But if we really think very highly of a person, we should conceal it from him like a crime. This is not a very gratifying thing to do, but it is right. Why, a dog will not bear being treated too kindly, let alone a man!

Schopenhauer, Parerga and Paralipomena; tr. T. Bailey Saunders

He that toucheth pitch shall be defiled therewith; and he that hath fellowship with a proud man shall be like unto him.

Burden not thyself above thy power while thou livest; and have no fellowship with one that is mightier and richer than thyself: for how agree the kettle and the earthen pot together? For if the one be smitten against the other, it shall be broken . . .

All flesh consorteth according to kind, and a man will cleave to his like.

What fellowship hath the wolf with the lamb? So the sinner with the godly.

What agreement is there between the hyena and a dog? And what peace between the rich and the poor?

Ecclesiasticus 13

Disproportioned friendships ever terminate in disgust . . . Let us keep to companions of our own rank.

> OLIVER GOLDSMITH, *The Vicar of Wakefield*, 1766

In all societies it is advisable to associate if possible with the highest; not that the highest are always the best, but, because if disgusted there, we can at any time descend;—but if we begin with the lowest, to ascend is impossible. In the grand theatre of human life, a *box ticket* takes us through the house.

It is always safe to learn, even from our enemies—seldom safe to venture to instruct, even our friends.

We generally most covet that particular trust which we are least likely to keep. He that thoroughly knows his friends might, perhaps, with safety, confide his wife to the care of one, his purse to another, and his secrets to a third, when to permit them to make their own choice would be his ruin.

It is true that we are enjoined to forgive our enemies, but I remember no text that enforces a similar conduct with regard to our *friends*.

> REVD CHARLES CALEB COLTON, *Lacon: or, Many Things in Few Words*, Vol. I, 1820

Be a friend to thyself, and others will befriend thee.

> Proverb

Turn him, and see his threads; look if he be
    Friend to himself, that would be friend to thee.
For that is first required, a man be his own.
    But he that's too much that is friend of none.

> BEN JONSON, from 'An Epistle to Master Arthur Squib', published posthumously in 1640

Yet here, Laertes? Aboard, aboard, for shame!
The wind sits in the shoulder of your sail,
And you are stayed for. There—my blessing with thee.
And these few precepts in thy memory
Look thou character. Give thy thoughts no tongue,
Nor any unproportioned thought his act.
Be thou familiar, but by no means vulgar.
Those friends thou hast, and their adoption tried,
Grapple them unto thy soul with hoops of steel.
But do not dull thy palm with entertainment
Of each new-hatched, unfledged courage. Beware
Of entrance to a quarrel. But, being in,
Bear't that th'opposèd may beware of thee.
Give every man thine ear, but few thy voice.
Take each man's censure, but reserve thy judgement.
Costly thy habit as thy purse can buy,
But not expressed in fancy; rich, not gaudy;
For the apparel oft proclaims the man,
And they in France of the best rank and station
Are of a most select and generous chief in that.
Neither a borrower nor a lender be,
For loan oft loses both itself and friend,
And borrowing dulleth edge of husbandry.
This above all: to thine own self be true,
And it must follow, as the night the day,
Thou canst not then be false to any man.
Farewell. My blessing season this in thee!

WILLIAM SHAKESPEARE, *Hamlet*, 1600–1; Polonius to his son

I must in a particular manner recommend to you a strict care in the choice of your friendships. Perhaps the best are not without their objections, but however, be sure that yours may not stray from the rules which the wiser part of the world hath set to them. The leagues offensive and defensive seldom hold in politics, and much less in friendships. The violent intimacies, when once broken, of which they scarce ever fail, make such a noise; the bag of secrets untied, they fly about like birds let loose from a cage, and become the entertainment of the town. Besides, these great dearnesses by degrees grow injurious to the rest of your acquaintance, and throw them off from you. There is such an offensive distinction when the Dear Friend cometh into the room that it is flinging stones at the company, who are not apt to forgive it.

Do not lay out your friendship too lavishly at first, since it will, like other things, be so much the sooner spent. Neither let it be of too sudden a growth, for as the plants which shoot up too fast are not of that continuance as those which take more time for it, so too swift a progress in pouring out your kindness is a certain sign that by the course of nature it will not be long lived.

GEORGE SAVILE, MARQUESS OF HALIFAX, *A Lady's New Year's Gift, or Advice to a Daughter*, 1688

Be upon your guard against those who, upon very slight acquaintance, obtrude their unasked and unmerited friendship and confidence upon you; for they probably cram you with them only for their own eating; but, at the same time, do not roughly reject them upon that general supposition. Examine further, and see whether those unexpected offers flow from a warm heart and a silly head, or from a designing head and a cold heart; for knavery and folly have often the same symptoms. In the first case, there is no danger in accepting them, *valeant quantum valere possunt*. In the latter case, it may be useful to seem to accept them, and artfully to turn the battery upon him who raised it.

LORD CHESTERFIELD, letter to his son, 19 December 1749

It was on the 10th Day of August 1770 that I saw Mr [William] Fitzherbert for the first Time . . . Johnson says that it is by having *no* Wit, & pretending to none, that he has gained such a considerable Ground upon the World, that 'tis now half a Disgrace not to be acquainted with Fitzherbert: he added a peculiarity of Character which doubtless contributes to forward his *Reputation—Reception* I mean; & that is, that no Man is less welcome to Fitzherbert either for his Virtues or for his Vices; he is as willing, says Johnson, to shew Friendship to Sam: Johnson as to Dick Swift [a famous robber]—to *Rousseau* as to *Saint Austin*.

On the 3rd of January this famous Fitzherbert hanged himself, leaving
Mankind much astonished at his conduct: And now, says Johnson, see
what it is to have a diffus'd Acquaintance and not one Friend.

> HESTER LYNCH THRALE, *Thraliana: The Diary of Mrs Hester Lynch
> Thrale, 1776–1809*

It is now long since we saw one another; and whatever has been the
reason neither you have written to me, nor I to you. To let friendship die
away by negligence and silence, is certainly not wise. It is voluntarily to
throw away one of the greatest comforts of this weary pilgrimage, of
which when it is, as it must be, taken finally away, he that travels on alone
will wonder how his esteem could be so little. Do not forget me; you see
that I do not forget you. It is pleasing in the silence of solitude to think,
that there is one at least, however distant, of whose benevolence there is
little doubt, and whom there is yet hope of seeing again.

> JOHNSON, letter to Bennet Langton, 20 March 1782

> Though you are in your shining days,
> Voices among the crowd
> And new friends busy with your praise,
> Be not unkind or proud,
> But think about old friends the most:
> Time's bitter flood will rise,
> Your beauty perish and be lost
> For all eyes but these eyes.

> W. B. YEATS, 'The Lover Pleads with his Friend for Old Friends',
> 1899

He said to Sir Joshua Reynolds, 'If a man does not make new acquaintance as he advances through life, he will soon find himself alone. A man,
Sir, should keep his friendship *in constant repair*.'

> JAMES BOSWELL, *Life of Johnson*, 1755: 'at a subsequent period of
> his life, the opinion of Johnson'

The holy passion of Friendship is of so sweet and steady and loyal and enduring a nature that it will last through a whole lifetime, if not asked to lend money.

MARK TWAIN, *Pudd'nhead Wilson*, 1894

BOSWELL: 'I have known a man resolve to put friendship to the test, by asking a friend to lend him money merely with that view, when he did not want it.' JOHNSON: 'That is very wrong, Sir. Your friend may be a narrow man, and yet have many good qualities: narrowness may be his only fault. Now you are trying his general character as a friend, by one particular singly, in which he happens to be defective, when, in truth, his character is composed of many particulars.'

BOSWELL, *Life of Johnson*, 3 April 1778

The fact was, that when the five hundred pounds had come into my pocket, a thought had come into my head which had been often there before; and it appeared to me that Wemmick was a good person to advise with, concerning such thought.

He had already locked up his safe, and made preparations for going home. He had left his desk, brought out his two greasy office candlesticks and stood them in line with the snuffers on a slab near the door, ready to be extinguished; he had raked his fire low, put his hat and great-coat ready, and was beating himself all over the chest with his safe-key as an athletic exercise after business.

'Mr Wemmick,' said I, 'I want to ask your opinion. I am very desirous to serve a friend.'

Wemmick tightened his post-office and shook his head, as if his opinion were dead against any fatal weakness of that sort.

'This friend,' I pursued, 'is trying to get on in commercial life, but has no money, and finds it difficult and disheartening to make a beginning. Now, I want somehow to help him to a beginning.'

'With money down?' said Wemmick, in a tone drier than any sawdust.

'With *some* money down,' I replied, for an uneasy remembrance shot across me of that symmetrical bundle of papers at home; 'with *some* money down, and perhaps some anticipation of my expectations.'

'Mr Pip,' said Wemmick, 'I should like just to run over with you on my fingers, if you please, the names of the various bridges up as high as Chelsea Reach. Let's see; there's London, one; Southwark, two; Blackfriars, three; Waterloo, four; Westminster, five; Vauxhall, six.' He had checked off each bridge in its turn, with the handle of his safe-key on the palm of his hand. 'There's as many as six, you see, to choose from.'

'I don't understand you,' said I.

'Choose your bridge, Mr Pip,' returned Wemmick, 'and take a walk upon your bridge, and pitch your money into the Thames over the centre arch of your bridge, and you know the end of it. Serve a friend with it, and you may know the end of it too—but it's a less pleasant and profitable end.'

I could have posted a newspaper in his mouth, he made it so wide after saying this.

'This is very discouraging,' said I.

'Meant to be so,' said Wemmick.

'Then is it your opinion,' I inquired, with some little indignation, 'that a man should never——'

'——Invest portable property in a friend?' said Wemmick. 'Certainly he should not. Unless he wants to get rid of the friend—and then it becomes a question how much portable property it may be worth to get rid of him.'

'And that,' said I, 'is your deliberate opinion, Mr Wemmick?'

'That,' he returned, 'is my deliberate opinion in this office.'

'Ah!' said I, pressing him, for I thought I saw him near a loophole here; 'but would that be your opinion at Walworth?'

'Mr Pip,' he replied with gravity, 'Walworth is one place, and this office is another ... They must not be confounded together. My Walworth sentiments must be taken at Walworth; none but my official sentiments can be taken in this office.'

'Very well,' said I, much relieved, 'then I shall look you up at Walworth, you may depend upon it.'

'Mr Pip,' he returned, 'you will be welcome there, in a private and personal capacity.'

CHARLES DICKENS, *Great Expectations*, 1860–1

Few things tend more to alienate friendship than a want of punctuality in our engagements. I have known the breach of a promise to dine or sup to break up more than one intimacy ... I myself once declined an invitation to meet Talma, who was an admirer of Shakespeare, and who idolized Buonaparte, to keep an appointment with a person who had *forgot* it!

HAZLITT, 'On the Spirit of Obligations', 1824

Candid and generous and just,
Boys care but little whom they trust,
   An error soon corrected—
For who but learns in riper years,
That man, when smoothest he appears,
   Is most to be suspected?

Who seeks a friend, should come dispos'd
T'exhibit in full bloom disclos'd
   The graces and the beauties
That form the character he seeks,
For 'tis an union that bespeaks
   Reciprocated duties.

A man renown'd for repartee
Will seldom scruple to make free
   With friendship's finest feeling,
Will thrust a dagger at your breast,
And say he wounded you in jest,
   By way of balm for healing.

Religion should extinguish strife,
And make a calm of human life;
   But friends that chance to differ
On points, which God has left at large,
How fiercely will they meet and charge,
   No combatants are stiffer!

The man that hails you Tom or Jack,
And proves by thumps upon your back
   How he esteems your merit,
Is such a friend, that one had need
Be very much his friend indeed
   To pardon or to bear it.

Oh Friendship! if my soul forgo
Thy dear delights while here below,
   To mortify and grieve me,
May I myself at last appear
Unworthy, base, and insincere,
   Or may my friend deceive me!

WILLIAM COWPER, from 'Friendship', 1800

Whoso casteth a stone at the birds frayeth them away: and he that upbraideth his friend breaketh friendship.

Though thou drewest a sword at thy friend, yet despair not: for there may be a returning to favour.

If thou hast opened thy mouth against thy friend, fear not; for there may be a reconciliation: except for upbraiding, or pride, or disclosing of secrets, or a treacherous wound: for for these things every friend will depart.

Whoso discovereth secrets loseth his credit; and shall never find friend to his mind.

Love thy friend, and be faithful unto him: but if thou bewrayest his secrets, follow no more after him.

For as a man hath destroyed his enemy, so hast thou lost the love of thy neighbour.

Ecclesiasticus 22, 27

The company of professed wits and poets is extremely inviting to most young men; who, if they have wit themselves, are pleased with it, and if they have none, are sillily proud of being one of it: but it should be frequented with moderation and judgement, and you should by no means give yourself up to it. A wit is a very unpopular denomination, as it carries terror along with it; and people in general are as much afraid of a live wit, in company, as a woman is of a gun, which she thinks may go off of itself and do her a mischief.

LORD CHESTERFIELD, letter to his son, 12 October 1748

Wit's an unruly engine, wildly striking
Sometimes a friend, sometimes the engineer.
Hast thou the knack? pamper it not with liking:
But if thou want it, buy it not too deare . . .

Thy friend put in thy bosome: wear his eyes
Still in thy heart, that he may see what's there.
If cause require, thou art his sacrifice;
Thy drops of bloud must pay down all his fear:
    But love is lost, the way of friendship's gone,
    Though *David* had his *Jonathan*, *Christ* his *John*.

GEORGE HERBERT, The Church-Porch, 1633

I was angry with my friend;
I told my wrath, my wrath did end.
I was angry with my foe;
I told it not, my wrath did grow.

WILLIAM BLAKE, from 'A Poison Tree', 1784

Words beget Anger: Anger brings forth blows:
Blows make of dearest friends immortal Foes.
For which prevention (Sociate) let there be
Betwixt us two no more *Logomachie*.
Far better 'twere for either to be mute,
Than for to murder friendship, by dispute.

ROBERT HERRICK, 'To his friend to avoid contention of words',
1648

I wrastle not with rage
    While furies flame doth burne:
It is in vaine to stop the streme,
    Untill the tide doth turne.

But when the flame is out
   And ebbing wrath doth end:
I turne a late enraged foe
   Into a quiet frend.

Robert Southwell, from 'Content and Rich', 1595

We were likewise talking today at Breakfast of Mr Shenstone's Rule for keeping up kindness between Lovers, Friends or Relations: some little Quarrel, says he, should now & then be kindled, that the Soul may feel her own elastick Force; & return to the beloved Object with renewed Delight: Why now what a pernicious Maxim this is, cries Johnson, surely all Quarrels ought to be avoided as nobody can possibly tell where they will end; besides that lasting Detestation is often the Consequence of occasional Disgust; and that the Cup of Life is already sufficiently displeasing, without making it more bitter by a Dash of Resentment.

Hester Lynch Thrale, *Thraliana*

Dear George,

To give pain ought always to be painful, and I am sorry that I have been the occasion of any uneasiness to you, to whom I hope never to do anything but for your benefit or your pleasure. Your uneasiness was without any reason on your part, as you had written with sufficient frequency to me, and I had only neglected to answer then, because as nothing new had been proposed to your study no new direction or incitement could be offered you . . .

I write thus largely on this suspicion which you have suffered to enter your mind, because in youth we are apt to be too rigorous in our expectations, and to suppose that the duties of life are to be performed with unfailing exactness and regularity, but in our progress through life we are forced to abate much of our demands, and to take friends such as we can find them, not as we would make them.

These concessions every wise man is more ready to make to others as he knows that he shall often want them for himself; and when he remembers how often he fails in the observance or cultivation of his best friends, is willing to suppose that his friends may in their turn neglect him without any intention to offend him.

When therefore it shall happen, as happen it will, that you or I have disappointed the expectation of the other, you are not to suppose that you have lost me or that I intended to lose you; nothing will remain but to repair the fault, and to go on as if it never had been committed.

> JOHNSON, letter to George Strahan, 14 July 1763. The recipient, then aged 19 and at Abingdon School, was the son of Johnson's old friend, the printer William Strahan; he became a clergyman and was to edit Johnson's prayers and meditations

I had delayed because in truth I had nothing to say but what I thought; and when my friends and I do not think alike, I prefer silence to contradictions or disputes, for I cannot say what I do not think, especially to my friends; to other people one can talk a good deal of nonsense which serves instead of thinking.

> HORACE WALPOLE, letter to the Revd William Mason, 27 November 1775

Nothing will reconcile friends but love. They make a fatal mistake when they go about like foes to explain and treat with one another. It is a mutual mistake. None are so unmanageable.

One of the best men I know often offends me by uttering made words—the very best words, of course, or dinner speeches, most smooth and gracious and fluent repartees, a sort of talking to Buncombe, a dash of polite conversation, a graceful bending, as if I were Master Slingsby of promising parts, from the University. O would you but be simple and downright! Would you but cease your palaver! It is the misfortune of being a gentleman and famous. The conversation of gentlemen after dinner! One of the best of men and wisest, to whom this diabolical formality will adhere. Repeating himself, shampooing himself! Passing the time of day, as if he were just introduced! No words are so tedious. Never a natural or simple word or yawn. It produces an appearance of phlegm and stupidity in me the auditor. I am suddenly the closest and most phlegmatic of mortals, and the conversation comes to naught. Such speeches as an ex-Member of Congress might make to an ex-Member of Parliament.

To explain to a friend is to suppose that you are not intelligent of one another. If you are not, to what purpose will you explain?

SPAN   THOREAU, *Journal*, 19 February 1841, 17 December 1851

There can be no Friendship where there is no *Freedom*. Friendship loves a *free* Air, and will not be penned up in streight and narrow Enclosures. It will speak *freely*, and *act* so too; and take nothing ill where no ill is meant; nay, where it is, 'twill *easily* forgive, and forget too, upon small Acknowledgments.

SPAN   WILLIAM PENN, *Some Fruits of Solitude*, 1693

Mutual respect implies discretion and reserve even in love itself; it means preserving as much liberty as possible to those whose life we share. We must distrust our instinct of intervention, for the desire to make one's own will prevail is often disguised under the mask of solicitude.

SPAN   HENRI-FRÉDÉRIC AMIEL, *Journal*, 7 November 1862; tr. Mrs Humphry Ward

I want relations which are not purely personal, based on purely personal qualities; but relations based upon some unanimous accord in truth or belief, and a harmony of *purpose*, rather than of personality. I am weary of personality . . . Let us be easy and impersonal, not forever fingering over our own souls, and the souls of our acquaintances, but trying to create a new life, a new common life, a new complete tree of life from the roots that are within us.

SPAN   D. H. LAWRENCE, Letter to Katherine Mansfield, 12 December 1915

With men I get on rather better: for I feel that one must weigh them by avoirdupois weight, and not by the jeweller's scales; as, unfortunately,

friends too often weigh one another in their hypochondriacal humours
and in an over-exacting spirit.

> JOHANN WOLFGANG VON GOETHE, 'Naples, 17 March 1787',
> *Travels in Italy*; tr. John Oxenford

A benevolent man should allow a few faults in himself, to keep his friends
in countenance.

> BENJAMIN FRANKLIN (1706–90), *Autobiography*

It should be a part of our private ritual to devote a quarter of an hour
every day to the enumeration of the good qualities of our friends. When
we are not *active*, we fall back idly upon defects, even of those whom we
most love.

> MARK RUTHERFORD (1831–1913), *Last Pages from a Journal*

When I condole with you for the loss of your only son, in order to enter
into your grief I do not consider what I, a person of such a character and
profession, should suffer, if I had a son, and if that son were unfortunately
to die: but I consider what I should suffer, if I was really you, and I do
not only change circumstances with you, but I change persons and
characters.

> ADAM SMITH, *The Theory of Moral Sentiments*, 1759

> Lord, make me coy and tender to offend:
> In friendship, first I think, if that agree,
>   Which I intend,
>   Unto my friend's intent and end.
> I would not use a friend, as I use Thee.

If any touch my friend, or his good name,
It is my honour and my love to free
                His blasted fame
         From the least spot or thought of blame.
I could not use a friend, as I use Thee.

My friend may spit upon my curious floor:
Would he have gold? I lend it instantly;
                But let the poor,
         And thou within them, starve at door.
I cannot use a friend, as I use Thee.

When that my friend pretendeth to a place,
I quit my interest, and leave it free:
                But when thy grace
         Sues for my heart, I thee displace.
Nor would I use a friend, as I use Thee.

Yet can a friend what thou hast done fulfil?
O write in brass, *My God upon a tree*
                His blood did spill
         Only to purchase my good-will.
Yet use I not my foes, as I use Thee.

                    GEORGE HERBERT, 'Unkindness', 1633

Alike he thwarts the hospitable end,
Who drives the free, or stays the hasty friend;
True friendship's laws are by this rule exprest,
Welcome the coming, speed the parting guest.

                    HOMER (?8th century BC), *Odyssey*; tr. Pope, 1725–6

Among Men

TROUBLED times can be a great incentive to friendship, and an enhancement of its value. In the otherwise light-hearted poem of invitation included here, Ben Jonson assures his guests that no spies will be present and they need have no fears the next day as to what they may have uttered during the merry-making. And the poem by the prototype Cavalier poet Lovelace, ostensibly another invitation to conviviality, doesn't refer solely to the season of winter when it speaks of 'this cold Time and frozen Fate'; the poet was in prison in 1648, when he put together his collection, *Lucasta*.

Besides demonstrating loyalty to a dead friend and the risks attending it, the correspondence between Cicero and Gaius Matius, also set in a perilous age, shows how affection linked with respect can come to terms with political differences. This would seem one of the larger of those 'allowances' we are urged to make. And Henry King's poem indicates that friendship could, if with difficulty, transcend class barriers even in the hierarchic world of the seventeenth century.

We have naturally given accounts of some of the most famous friendships: between David and Jonathan (together with a cynical codicil by Voltaire), Orestes and Pylades, Theseus and Pirithous, Damon and Pythias. Also the less celebrated friendship of Montaigne and Etienne de la Boétie, which G. H. Lewes took as an exemplar of the union of kindred natures. Professional friendship between writers is represented by Goethe and Schiller, Robert Frost and Edward Thomas, Pound and Eliot, Yeats and Gogarty, and (more ambiguous) Rimbaud and Verlaine. Such associations—love me, love my book—incline to be ticklish, as Jonson hints in his epistle to Selden. Perhaps it is appropriate in this connection to cite Gorky's remark that he was not an orphan on the earth so long as Tolstoy was living on it.

Fellowship does not always exist on such heights of intellect or sensibility. The most popular of current television soap operas both feature a public house, a casual social centre, albeit quarrels are more frequent there than amicable interludes, and 'Lyrick Feasts' are rare. 'What men, unless they had their wives with them, can find to talk about,

I can't think': Mrs Caudle's remonstrations provide a humble gloss on the
starry-eyed project for an all-male retreat mentioned by St Augustine.
We end this section with some curious reflections on friendship, or a
surrogate for it, as observed in clubs of the more exclusive kind.

———

Live to that point I will, for which I am man,
　　And dwell as in my centre as I can,
Still looking to, and ever loving, heaven;
　　With reverence using all the gifts thence given.
'Mongst which, if I have any friendships sent,
　　Such as are square, well-tagged, and permanent,
Not built with canvas, paper, and false lights,
　　As are the glorious scenes at the great sights,
And that there be no fevery heats, nor colds,
　　Oily expansions, or shrunk dirty folds,
But all so clear and led by reason's flame,
　　As but to stumble in her sight were shame;
These I will honour, love, embrace, and serve,
　　And free it from all question to preserve.
So short you read my character, and theirs
　　I would call mine, to which not many stairs
Are asked to climb. First give me faith, who know
　　Myself a little. I will take you so,
As you have writ yourself. Now stand, and then,
　　Sir, you are sealèd of the tribe of Ben.

　　　　BEN JONSON, from 'An Epistle Answering to One that Asked to be
　　　　Sealed of the Tribe of Ben', written 1623

I ne'er was dress'd in forms; nor can I bend
My pen to flatter any, nor commend,
Unless desert or honour do present
Unto my verse a worthy argument.

You are my friend, and in that word to me
Stand blazon'd in your noblest heraldry;
That style presents you full, and does relate
The bounty of your love, and my own fate,
Both which conspir'd to make me yours. A choice,
Which needs must, in the giddy people's voice,
That only judge the outside, and, like apes,
Play with our names, and comment on our shapes,
Appear too light: but it lies you upon,
To justify the disproportion.

Truth be my record, I durst not presume
To seek to you, 'twas you that did assume
Me to your bosom. Wherein you subdu'd
One that can serve you, though ne'er could intrude
Upon great titles; nor knows how t'invade
Acquaintance: Like such as are only paid
With great men's smiles; if that the passant Lord
Let fall a forc'd salute, or but afford
The nod regardant. It was test enough
For me, you ne'er did find such servile stuff
Couch'd in my temper; I can freely say,
I do not love you in that common way
For which Great Ones are lov'd in this false time:
I have no wish to gain, nor will to climb;
I cannot pawn my freedom, nor outlive
My liberty, for all that you can give . . .

Know, best of friends, however wild report
May justly say, I am unapt to sort
With your opinion or society
(Which truth would shame me, did I it deny),
There's something in me says, I dare make good,
When honour calls me, all I want in blood.

Put off your giant titles, then I can
Stand in your judgement's blank an equal man.
Though hills advancèd are above the plain,
They are but higher earth, nor must disdain
Alliance with the vale: we see a spade

Can level them, and make a mount a glade.
Howe'er we differ in the Heralds' book,
He that mankind's extraction shall look
In Nature's rolls, must grant we all agree
In our best part's immortal pedigree.

HENRY KING, from 'A Letter', 1657

Lawrence, of virtuous father virtuous son,
   Now that the fields are dank and ways are mire,
   Where shall we sometimes meet, and by the fire
   Help waste a sullen day, what may be won
From the hard season gaining? Time will run
   On smoother, till Favonius reinspire
   The frozen earth, and clothe in fresh attire
   The lily and rose, that neither sowed nor spun.
What neat repast shall feast us, light and choice,
   Of Attic taste, with wine, whence we may rise
   To hear the lute well touched, or artful voice
Warble immortal notes and Tuscan air?
   He who of those delights can judge, and spare
   To interpose them oft, is not unwise.

MILTON, sonnet to Edward Lawrence, 1655

Thou best of men and friends! we will create
   A genuine Summer in each other's breast;
And spite of this cold Time and frozen Fate,
   Thaw us a warm seat to our rest.

Our sacred hearths shall burn eternally
   As vestal flames; the North-wind, he
Shall strike his frost-stretch'd wings, dissolve, and fly
   This Etna in epitome.

Dropping December shall come weeping in,
　　Bewail th' usurping of his reign;
But when in show'rs of old Greek we begin,
　　Shall cry he hath his crown again.

Night as clear Hesper shall our tapers whip
　　From the light casements where we play,
And the dark hag from her black mantle strip,
　　And stick there everlasting day.

Thus richer than untempted kings are we,
　　That asking nothing, nothing need:
Though lord of all what seas embrace, yet he
　　That wants himself is poor indeed.

> RICHARD LOVELACE, from 'The Grasshopper, To My Noble
> Friend Mr Charles Cotton', 1649

Come, when no graver cares employ,
Godfather, come and see your boy:
　　Your presence will be sun in winter,
Making the little one leap for joy.

For, being of that honest few,
Who give the Fiend himself his due,
　　Should eighty-thousand college-councils
Thunder 'Anathema', friend, at you;

Should all our churchmen foam in spite
At you, so careful of the right,
　　Yet one lay-hearth would give you welcome
(Take it and come) to the Isle of Wight;

Where, far from noise and smoke of town,
I watch the twilight falling brown
　　All round a careless-order'd garden
Close to the ridge of a noble down.

You'll have no scandal while you dine,
But honest talk and wholesome wine,
   And only hear the magpie gossip
Garrulous under a roof of pine:

For groves of pine on either hand,
To break the blast of winter, stand;
   And further on, the hoary Channel
Tumbles a billow on chalk and sand;

Where, if below the milky steep
Some ship of battle slowly creep,
   And on thro' zones of light and shadow
Glimmer away to the lonely deep,

We might discuss the Northern sin
Which made a selfish war begin;
   Dispute the claims, arrange the chances;
Emperor, Ottoman, which shall win:

Or whether war's avenging rod
Shall lash all Europe into blood;
   Till you should turn to dearer matters,
Dear to the man that is dear to God;

How best to help the slender store,
How mend the dwellings, of the poor;
   How gain in life, as life advances,
Valour and charity more and more.

Come, Maurice, come: the lawn as yet
Is hoar with rime, or spongy-wet;
   But when the wreath of March has blossom'd,
Crocus, anemone, violet,

Or later, pay one visit here,
For those are few we hold as dear;
   Nor pay but one, but come for many,
Many and many a happy year.

   ALFRED LORD TENNYSON, 'To the Rev. F. D. Maurice, January,
  1854'

A quiet valley with no man's footprints,
An empty garden lit by the moon.
Suddenly my dog barks and I know
A friend with a bottle is knocking at the gate.

ŎM ŬI-GIL, 'Sitting at Night', 17th century; Korean poet writing
in Chinese, tr. Kim Jong-gil

Tonight, grave sir, both my poor house and I
    Do equally desire your company;
Not that we think us worthy such a guest,
    But that your worth will dignify our feast
With those that come; whose grace may make that seem
    Something, which else could hope for no esteem.
It is the fair acceptance, sir, creates
    The entertainment perfect, not the cates.
Yet shall you have, to rectify your palate,
    An olive, capers, or some better salad
Ushering the mutton; with a short-legged hen,
    If we can get her, full of eggs, and then
Lemons, and wine for sauce; to these, a coney
    Is not to be despaired of, for our money;
And though fowl now be scarce, yet there are clerks,
    The sky not falling, think we may have larks.
I'll tell you of more, and lie, so you will come:
    Of partridge, pheasant, woodcock, of which some
May yet be there; and godwit, if we can;
    Knat, rail and ruff, too. Howsoe'er, my man
Shall read a piece of Virgil, Tacitus,
    Livy, or of some better book to us,
Of which we'll speak our minds, amidst our meat;
    And I'll profess no verses to repeat;
To this, if aught appear which I not know of,
    That will the pastry, not my paper, show of.
Digestive cheese and fruit there sure will be;
    But that which most doth take my muse and me
Is a pure cup of rich Canary wine,
    Which is the Mermaid's now, but shall be mine;
Of which had Horace or Anacreon tasted,

Their lives, as do their lines, till now had lasted.
Tobacco, nectar, or the Thespian spring
   Are all but Luther's beer to this I sing.
Of this we will sup free, but moderately;
   And we will have no Poley or Parrot by;
Nor shall our cups make any guilty men,
   But at our parting we will be as when
We innocently met. No simple word
   That shall be uttered at our mirthful board
Shall make us sad next morning, or affright
   The liberty that we'll enjoy tonight.

> JONSON, 'Inviting a Friend to Supper', 1616; Poley and Parrot
> were government spies

Ah *Ben*!
  Say how, or when
  Shall we thy Guests
Meet at those *Lyrick* Feasts,
  Made at the *Sun*,
The *Dog*, the triple *Tunne*?
Where we such clusters had,
As made us nobly wild, not mad;
  And yet each Verse of thine
Out-did the meate, out-did the frolick wine.

My *Ben*
  Or come agen,
  Or send to us
Thy wit's great over-plus;
  But teach us yet
Wisely to husband it;
  Lest we that Talent spend:
And having once brought to an end
  That precious stock, the store
Of such a wit the world should have no more.

> HERRICK, 'Ode to Ben Jonson', 1648

30 December [*1813*]. After dinner a rubber at Lamb's; then went with Lamb and Burney to Rickman's. Hazlitt there. Cards, as usual, were our amusement. Lamb was in a pleasant mood. Rickman produced one of Chatterton's forgeries. In one manuscript there were seventeen different kinds of *e*'s. 'Oh,' said Lamb, 'that must have been written by one of the "Mob of gentlemen who write with ease".'

HENRY CRABB ROBINSON, Diary

The person whose doors I enter with most pleasure, and quit with most regret, never did me the smallest favour. I once did him an uncalled-for service, and we nearly quarrelled about it. If I were in the utmost distress, I should just as soon think of asking his assistance, as of stopping a person on the highway. Practical benevolence is not his *forte*. He leaves the profession of that to others. His habits, his theory are against it as idle and vulgar. His hand is closed, but what of that? His eye is ever open, and reflects the universe: his silver accents, beautiful, venerable as his silver hairs, but not scanted, flow as a river. I never ate or drank in his house; nor do I know or care how the flies or spiders fare in it, or whether a mouse can get a living. But I know that I can get there what I get nowhere else—a welcome, as if one was expected to drop in just at that moment, a total absence of all respect of persons and of airs of self-consequence, endless topics of discourse, refined thoughts, made more striking by ease and simplicity of manner—the husk, the shell of humanity is left at the door, and the spirit, mellowed by time, resides within!

HAZLITT, 'On the Spirit of Obligations'

I

If you were riding in a coach
And I were wearing a *li*,   *peasant's straw hat*
And one day we met in the road,
You would get down and bow.
If you were carrying a *tĕng*   *hawker's umbrella*
And I were riding on a horse,
And one day we met in the road
I would get down for you.

2

Shang Ya!
I want to be your friend
For ever and ever without break or decay.
When the hills are all flat
And the rivers are all dry,
When it lightens and thunders in winter,
When it rains and snows in summer,
When Heaven and Earth mingle—
Not till then will I part from you.

    'Oaths of Friendship', Chinese, 1st century AD; tr. Arthur Waley

The ancients argued that friendship could never last.
A few old friends, we walk on the mountain's milder slopes,
Discussing their reasons. The wind lifts our coats.
An hour passes, and we find we are shaking our staffs,
We are out of breath. We must have been quarrelling!
Some prophecies, if you listen to them, come true.
Quickly we drop the topic, open the picnic baskets,
And pour the wine. How sad it would be to drink alone!
Someone recites a poem on the sorrow of separation.
It seems the famous sages were not unfailingly right.

    TAO TSCHUNG YU, 'Quarrelling', ?18th century

Sentiments are nice, 'The Lonely Crowd',
a rift in the clouds appears above the purple,
you find a birthday greeting card with violets
which says 'a perfect friend' and means
'I love you' but the customer is forced to be
shy. It says less, as all things must.
                            But
grease sticks to the red ribs shaped like a
sea shell, grease, light and rosy that smells of
sandalwood: it's memory! I remember JA
staggering over to me in the San Remo and murmuring
'I've met SOMEONE MARVELLOUS!' That's friendship
for you, and the sentiment of introduction.

And now that I have finished dinner I can continue.

What is it that attracts one to one? Mystery?
I think of you in Paris with a red beard, a
theological student; in London talking to a friend
who lunched with Dowager Queen Mary and offered
her his last cigarette; in Los Angeles shopping
at the Supermarket; on Mount Shasta, looking . . .
above all on Mount Shasta in your unknown youth
and photograph.
                    And then the way you straighten
people out. How ambitious you are! And that you're
a painter is a great satisfaction, too. You know how
I feel about painters. I sometimes think poetry
only describes.
                    Now I have taken down the underwear
I washed last night from the various light fixtures
and can proceed.
                    And the lift of our experiences
together, which seem to me legendary. The long subways
to our old neighborhood the near East 49th and 53rd,
and before them the laughing in bars till we cried,
and the crying in movies till we laughed, the tenting
tonight on the old camp grounds! How beautiful it is
to visit someone for instant coffee! and you visiting
Cambridge, Massachusetts, talking for two weeks worth
in hours, and watching Maria Tallchief in the Public
Gardens while the swan-boats slumbered. And now,
not that I'm interrupting again, I mean your now,
you are 82 and I am 03. And in 1984 I trust we'll still
be high together. I'll say 'Let's go to a bar'
and you'll say 'Let's go to a movie' and we'll go to both;
like two old Chinese drunkards arguing about their
favorite mountain and the million reasons for them both.

                    FRANK O'HARA (1926–66), 'John Button Birthday'

And Saul said unto his servants, Provide me now a man that can play
well, and bring him to me.

Then answered one of the servants, and said, Behold, I have seen a son of Jesse the Bethlehemite, that is cunning in playing, and a mighty valiant man, and a man of war, and prudent in matters, and a comely person, and the LORD is with him.

Whereupon Saul sent messengers unto Jesse, and said, Send me David thy son, which is with the sheep.

And Jesse took an ass laden with bread, and a bottle of wine, and a kid, and sent them by David his son unto Saul.

And David came to Saul, and stood before him: and he loved him greatly; and he became his armourbearer.

And Saul sent to Jesse, saying, Let David, I pray thee, stand before me; for he hath found favour in my sight.

And it came to pass, when the evil spirit from God was upon Saul, that David took an harp, and played with his hand: so Saul was refreshed, and was well, and the evil spirit departed from him.

And it came to pass, when he had made an end of speaking unto Saul, that the soul of Jonathan was knit with the soul of David, and Jonathan loved him as his own soul.

And Saul took him that day, and would let him go no more home to his father's house.

Then Jonathan and David made a covenant, because he loved him as his own soul.

And Jonathan stripped himself of the robe that was upon him, and gave it to David, and his garments, even to his sword, and to his bow, and to his girdle.

And David fled from Naioth in Ramah, and came and said before Jonathan, What have I done? what is mine iniquity? and what is my sin before thy father, that he seeketh my life?

And he said unto him, God forbid; thou shalt not die: behold, my father will do nothing either great or small, but that he will shew it me: and why should my father hide this thing from me? it is not so.

And David sware moreover, and said, Thy father certainly knoweth that I have found grace in thine eyes; and he saith, Let not Jonathan know this, lest he be grieved: but truly as the LORD liveth, and as thy soul liveth, there is but a step between me and death.

Then said Jonathan unto David, Whatsoever thy soul desireth, I will even do it for thee.

Now the Philistines fought against Israel: and the men of Israel fled from before the Philistines, and fell down slain in mount Gilboa.

And the Philistines followed hard upon Saul and upon his sons; and the Philistines slew Jonathan, and Abinadab, and Melchishua, Saul's sons.

And the battle went sore against Saul, and the archers hit him; and he was sore wounded of the archers.

And David lamented with this lamentation over Saul and over Jonathan his son: . . .

The beauty of Israel is slain upon thy high places: how are the mighty fallen!

Tell it not in Gath, publish it not in the streets of Askelon; lest the daughters of the Philistines rejoice, lest the daughters of the uncircumcised triumph.

Ye mountains of Gilboa, let there be no dew, neither let there be rain, upon you, nor fields of offerings: for there the shield of the mighty is vilely cast away, the shield of Saul, as though he had not been anointed with oil.

From the blood of the slain, from the fat of the mighty, the bow of Jonathan turned not back, and the sword of Saul returned not empty.

Saul and Jonathan were lovely and pleasant in their lives, and in their death they were not divided: they were swifter than eagles, they were stronger than lions.

Ye daughters of Israel, weep over Saul, who clothed you in scarlet, with other delights, who put on ornaments of gold upon your apparel.

How are the mighty fallen in the midst of the battle! O Jonathan, thou wast slain in thine high places.

I am distressed for thee, my brother Jonathan: very pleasant hast thou been unto me: thy love to me was wonderful, passing the love of women.

How are the mighty fallen, and the weapons of war perished!

I Samuel 16, 18, 20, 31; II Samuel 1

The only friendship spoken of among the Jews was that which existed between David and Jonathan. It is said that David loved Jonathan with a love surpassing that of women; but it is also reported that, after the death of his friend, David dispossessed Mephibosheth, Jonathan's son, and caused him to be put to death.

VOLTAIRE, *Dictionnaire Philosophique*

Iphigenia. Stranger, if I can save thee, wilt thou bear
    To Argos and the friends who loved my youth
    Some word? . . .
    Help me! Be saved! Thou also hast thy part,
    Thy life for one light letter. . . . For thy friend,
    The Law compelleth. He must bear the end
    By Artemis ordained, apart from thee.
Orestes. Strange woman, as thou biddest let it be,
    Save one thing. 'Twere for me a heavy weight
    Should this man die. 'Tis I and mine own fate
    That steer our goings. He but sails with me
    Because I suffer much. It must not be
    That by his ruin I should 'scape mine own,
    And win thy grace withal. 'Tis simply done.
    Give him the tablet. He with faithful will
    Shall all thy hest in Argolis fulfil.
    And I . . . who cares may kill me. Vile is he
    Who leaves a friend in peril and goes free
    Himself. And, as it chances, this is one
    Right dear to me; his life is as my own.
Pylades. I cannot live for shame if thou art dead.
    I sailed together with thee; let us die
    Together. What a coward slave were I,
    Creeping through Argos and from glen to glen
    Of wind-torn Phocian hills! And most of men—
    For most are bad—will whisper how one day
    I left my friend to die and made my way
    Home. They will say I watched the sinking breath
    Of thy great house and plotted for thy death
    To wed thy sister, climb into thy throne. . . .
    I dread, I loathe it.—Nay, all ways but one
    Are shut. My last breath shall go forth with thine,
    Thy bloody sword, thy gulf of fire be mine
    Also. I love thee and I dread men's scorn.
Orestes. Peace from such thoughts! My burden can be borne;
    But where one pain sufficeth, double pain
    I will not bear . . .
        And fare thee well. I have no friend like thee
    For truth and love, O boy that played with me,
    And hunted on Greek hills, O thou on whom

Hath lain the hardest burden of my doom!
Farewell. The Prophet and the Lord of Lies
Hath done his worst. Far out from Grecian skies
With craft forethought he driveth me, to die
Where none may mark how ends his prophecy!
I trusted in his word. I gave him all
My heart. I slew my mother at his call;
For which things now he casts me here to die.
Pylades. Thy tomb shall fail thee not. Thy sister I
Will guard for ever. I, O stricken sore,
Who loved thee living and shall love thee more
Dead. But for all thou standest on the brink,
God's promise hath not yet destroyed thee. Think!
How oft, how oft the darkest hour of ill
Breaks brightest into dawn, if Fate but will!
Orestes. Enough. Nor god nor man can any more
Aid me.

EURIPIDES, *Iphigenia in Tauris*, c.411 BC; tr. Gilbert Murray

Touching the friendshippe betwixt Pirithous and Theseus, it is sayed it beganne thus. The renowne of his valliancy was marvelously blowen abroade through all Grece, and Pirithous desirous to knowe it by experience, went even of purpose to invade his countrye, and brought awaye a certaine bootie of oxen of his taken out of the countrye of Marathon. Theseus being advertised thereof, armed straight, and went to the rescue. Pirithous hearing of his comming, fled not at all, but returned backe sodainly to mete him. And so sone as they came to see one another, they both wondred at eche others beawtie and corage, and so had they no desire to fight. But Pirithous reaching out his hande first to Theseus, sayed unto him, I make your selfe judge of the damage you have susteined by my invasion, and with all my harte I will make suche satisfaction, as it shall please you to assesse it at. Theseus then dyd not only release him, of all the damages he had done, but also requested him he would become his friend, and brother in armes. Hereupon they were presently sworne brethren in the field.

PLUTARCH (c.50–c.125), *Lives of the Noble Grecians and Romans*; tr. Sir Thomas North, 1579, from the French of Jacques Amyot

Alexander the Great appears not more glorious from his victories, than amiable for his friendship. Hephaestion was the constant companion of his pleasures, and dear to him through the sweetness of his nature; they were nearly of the same age, but Hephaestion was the more handsome. When Sysigambis, the captive mother of Darius, entered Alexander's tent, she threw herself at Hephaestion's feet; he modestly retired, and the empress felt abashed at her mistake. The generous conqueror said, 'You have not erred, madam, for he too is Alexander.'

SHOLTO and REUBEN PERCY, *The Percy Anecdotes*, Vol. XII, 1823

From Cicero to Matius greetings . . .

As far back into the past as my memory extends, no friend of mine is older than yourself. But length of acquaintance is something which many share in some degree, affection is not. I cared for you from the first day we met and believed that you cared for me. Your subsequent departure for a long period, together with my pursuit of a political career and the difference between our modes of life, debarred us from cementing our friendly feelings by constant intercourse. But I had fresh evidence of your disposition towards me many years before the Civil War, when Caesar was in Gaul. Through your efforts Caesar came to look upon me as one of his circle, the object of his regard and friendly attentions; a result which you considered highly advantageous to me and not disadvantageous to Caesar himself . . .

There followed the time when, whether impelled by my sensitivity to criticism or by obligation or by fortune, I went to join Pompey. Your devoted service was never wanting either to me in my absence or to my family on the spot. In the judgement of them all, neither they nor I had a better friend.

I arrived in Brundisium. Do you think I have forgotten how swiftly, the moment you heard the news, you rushed over to me from Tarentum, how you sat beside me, talking and encouraging me in the dejection to which fear of the common calamities had reduced me?

At long last we took up residence in Rome. Our familiar friendship was now complete. In the most important matters, in determining how to conduct myself towards Caesar, I availed myself of your advice; in others, of your good offices. Was there any man but me, Caesar excepted, whose house you chose to frequent, and often spend many hours in the most delightful conversation? . . .

You may wonder where all this discourse (longer than I had envisaged) is tending. The truth is, I am astonished that you, who ought to know all this, should have believed me guilty of any action against the spirit of our friendship. For besides the well-attested and manifest facts which I have mentioned above, I have many others of a less conspicuous nature in mind, such as I cannot easily express in words. All about you delights me, but your most notable characteristics attract me most: loyalty to friendship, judgement, responsibility, steadfastness on the one hand, charm, humanity, literary culture on the other . . .

But a scholar like yourself will not be unaware that if Caesar was a despot, which seems to me to be the case, your ethical position can be argued in two ways. On the one side it can be maintained (and this is the line I take) that in caring for your friend even after he is dead you show commendable loyalty and good feeling. According to the other view, which is adopted in some quarters, the freedom of one's country should come before a friend's life. I only wish that my argumentations arising from such talk had been conveyed to you. At any rate no one recalls more readily and more often than I the two facts which above all others redound to your honour, namely, that yours was the weightiest influence both against embarking on a civil war and in favour of a moderate use of victory. In this I have found nobody who did not agree with me.

So I am grateful to our good friend Trebatius for giving me occasion to write this letter. If you do not believe in its sincerity, you will be setting me down as a stranger to all sense of obligation and good feeling. Nothing can be more grievous to me than such a verdict, or more uncharacteristic of yourself.

Tusculum, mid October(?) 44 BC

Matius to Cicero greetings.

Your letter gave me great pleasure, because it told me that you think of me as I had expected and desired . . .

I am well aware of the criticisms which people have levelled at me since Caesar's death. They make it a point against me that I bear the death of a friend hard and am indignant that the man I loved has been destroyed. They say that country should come before friendship—as though they have already proved that his death was to the public advantage. But I shall not make debating points. I acknowledge that I have not yet arrived at that philosophical level. It was not Caesar I followed in the civil conflict, but a friend whom I did not desert, even though I did not like what he was doing. I never approved of civil war or indeed of the origin of the conflict, which I did my very utmost to get nipped in the bud. And so, when my friend emerged triumphant, I was not caught by the lure of office or money, prizes of which others, whose influence with Caesar was less than my own, took immoderate advantage . . .

Why are they angry with me for praying that they may be sorry for what they have done? I want every man's heart to be sore for Caesar's death. But I shall be told that as a citizen I ought to wish the good of the commonwealth. Unless my past life and hopes for the future prove that I so desire without words of mine, then I do not ask anyone to accept it because I say so . . .

However, I don't doubt that the moderation of my career will be a strong enough defence against false reports in time to come; and I am equally confident that even those who do not love me because of my loyalty to Caesar would rather have friends like me than like themselves . . .

I am most grateful to our friend Trebatius for revealing the straight-forward and amicable nature of your sentiments towards me, thus adding to the reasons why I ought to pay respect and attention to one whom I have always been glad to regard as a friend.

Rome, in reply to the foregoing; both letters tr. D. R. Shackleton Bailey

Damon being condemned to death by Dionysius, Tyrant of Syracuse, obtained liberty to visit his wife and children, leaving his friend Pythias [correctly, Phintias] as a pledge for his return, on condition that, if he failed, Pythias should suffer in his stead. At the appointed time, Damon failed in appearing, and the tyrant had the curiosity to visit Pythias in prison. 'What a fool you were,' said he, 'to rely on Damon's promise! How could you imagine that he would sacrifice his life for you or for any man?' 'My lord,' said Pythias, with a firm voice and noble aspect, 'I would suffer a thousand deaths, rather than my friend should fail in any article of honour. He cannot fail. I am confident of his virtue, as I am of my own existence. But I beseech the gods to preserve his life. Oppose him, ye winds! Disappoint his eagerness, and suffer him not to arrive until my death has saved a life of much greater consequence than mine, necessary to his lovely wife, to his little innocents, to his friends, to his country. Oh! let me not die the cruellest of deaths in that of my Damon.'

Dionysius was confounded, and awed with the magnanimity of these sentiments. He wished to speak; he hesitated; he looked down, and retired in silence. The fatal day arrived. Pythias was brought forth, and with an air of satisfaction walked to the place of execution. He ascended the scaffold, and addressed the people. 'My prayers are heard; the gods are propitious; the winds have been contrary. Damon could not conquer impossibilities; he will be here tomorrow, and my blood shall ransom that of my friend.' As he pronounced these words, a buzz arose; a distant voice was heard; the crowd caught the words, and 'Stop, stop, executioner!' was repeated by every person. A man came at full speed. In the same instant he was off his horse, on the scaffold, and in the arms of Pythias. 'You are safe,' he cried, 'you are safe, my friend. The gods be praised, you are safe.' Pale and half speechless in the arms of his Damon, Pythias replied in broken accents: 'Fatal haste; cruel impatience! What envious powers have wrought impossibilities against your friend! but I will not be wholly disappointed. Since I cannot die to save you, I will die to accompany you.'

Dionysius heard and beheld with astonishment. His eyes were opened; his heart was touched; and he could no longer resist the power of virtue. He descended from his throne, and ascended the scaffold. 'Live, live, ye incomparable pair. Ye have demonstrated the existence of virtue, and consequently of a God who rewards it. Live happy, live revered; and as you have invited me by your example, form me by your precepts to participate worthily of a friendship so divine.'

The Percy Anecdotes

And many of us friends conferring about, and detesting the turbulent turmoils of human life, had debated and now almost resolved on living apart from business and the bustle of men; and this was to be thus obtained; we were to bring whatever we might severally procure, and make one household of all; so that through the truth of our friendship nothing should belong especially to any; but the whole thus derived from all, should as a whole belong to each, and all to all. We thought there might be some ten persons in this society; some of whom were very rich, especially Romanianus our townsman, from childhood a very familiar friend of mine, whom the grievous perplexities of his affairs had brought up to court; who was the most earnest for this project; and therein was his voice of great weight, because his ample estate far exceeded any of the rest. We had settled also, that two annual officers, as it were, should provide all things necessary, the rest being undisturbed. But when we began to consider whether the wives, which some of us already had, others hoped to have, would allow this, all that plan, which was being so well moulded, fell to pieces in our hands, was utterly dashed and cast aside. Thence we betook us to sighs, and groans, and our steps to follow the *broad and beaten ways* of the world; for many thoughts were in our heart, *but Thy counsel standeth for ever.* Out of which counsel Thou didst deride ours, and preparedst Thine own; purposing to *give us meat in due season, and to open Thy hand, and to fill our souls with blessing.*

ST AUGUSTINE, *Confessions*

And sometimes they'd get talking, low and mysterious like, about 'Th' Eureka Stockade'; and if we didn't understand and asked questions, 'What was the Eureka Stockade?' or 'What did they do it for?' father'd say: 'Now, run away, sonny, and don't bother; me and Mr So-and-so want to talk.' Father had the mark of a hole on his leg, which he said he got through a gun accident when a boy, and a scar on his side, that we saw when he was in swimming with us; he said he got that in an accident in a quartz-crushing machine. Mr So-and-so had a big scar on the side of his forehead that was caused by a pick accidentally slipping out of a loop in the rope, and falling down a shaft where he was working. But how was it they talked low, and their eyes brightened up, and they didn't look at each other, but away over sunset, and had to get up and walk about, and take a stroll in the cool of the evening when they talked about Eureka?

And, again they'd talk lower and more mysterious like, and perhaps mother would be passing the wood-heap and catch a word, and ask:

'Who was she, Tom?'

And Tom—father—would say:

'Oh, you didn't know her, Mary; she belonged to a family Bill knew at home.'

And Bill would look solemn till mother had gone, and then they would smile a quiet smile, and stretch and say, 'Ah, well!' and start something else.

They had yarns for the fireside, too, some of those old mates of our father's, and one of them would often tell how a girl—a queen of the diggings—was married, and had her wedding-ring made out of the gold of that field; and how the diggers weighed their gold with the new wedding-ring—for luck—by hanging the ring on the hook of the scales and attaching their chamois-leather gold bags to it (whereupon she boasted that four hundred ounces of the precious metal passed through her wedding-ring); and how they lowered the young bride, blindfolded, down a golden hole in a big bucket, and got her to point out the drive from which the gold came that her ring was made out of. The point of this story seems to have been lost—or else we forgot it—but it was characteristic. Had the girl been lowered down a duffer, and asked to point out the way to the gold, and had she done so successfully, there would have been some sense in it . . .

Those old mates had each three pasts behind them. The two they told each other when they became mates, and the one they had shared.

And when the visitor had gone by the coach we noticed that the old man would smoke a lot, and think as much, and take great interest in the fire, and be a trifle irritable perhaps.

Those old mates of our father's are getting few and far between, and only happen along once in a way to keep the old man's memory fresh, as it were. We met one today, and had a yarn with him, and afterwards we got thinking, and somehow began to wonder whether those ancient friends of ours were, or were not, better and kinder to their mates than we of the rising generation are to our fathers; and the doubt is painfully on the wrong side.

HENRY LAWSON, from 'An Old Mate of Your Father's', 1893

He became impatient to see Captain Hardy, and, as that officer, though often sent for, could not leave the deck, Nelson feared that some fatal cause prevented him, and repeatedly cried, 'Will no one bring Hardy to me? He must be killed! He is surely dead!' An hour and ten minutes elapsed from the time when Nelson received his wound before Hardy could come to him. They shook hands in silence; Hardy in vain struggling to suppress the feelings of that most painful and yet sublimest moment. 'Well, Hardy,' said Nelson, 'how goes the day with us?' 'Very well,' replied Hardy; 'ten ships have struck, but five of their van have tacked, and show an intention of bearing down upon the *Victory*. I have called two or three of our fresh ships round, and have no doubt of giving them a drubbing.' 'I hope,' said Nelson, 'none of our ships have struck?' Hardy answered, 'There was no fear of that.' Then, and not till then, Nelson spoke of himself. 'I am a dead man, Hardy,' said he; 'I am going

fast; it will be all over with me soon. Come nearer to me. Let my dear
Lady Hamilton have my hair, and all other things belonging to me.'
Hardy observed that he hoped Mr Beatty could yet hold out some
prospect of life. 'Oh, no!' he replied, 'it is impossible. My back is shot
through. Beatty will tell you so.' Captain Hardy then once more shook
hands with him, and with a heart almost bursting hastened upon deck . . .

   Captain Hardy, some fifty minutes after he had left the cockpit,
returned; and again taking the hand of his dying friend and commander,
congratulated him on having gained a complete victory. How many of
the enemy were taken he did not know, as it was impossible to perceive
them distinctly; but fourteen or fifteen at least. 'That's well,' cried Nelson,
'but I bargained for twenty.' And then in a stronger voice he said,
'Anchor, Hardy, anchor.' Hardy upon this hinted that Admiral Collingwood would take upon himself the direction of affairs. 'Not while I live,
Hardy!' said the dying Nelson, ineffectually endeavouring to raise
himself from the bed; 'do you anchor.' . . . Presently, calling Hardy back,
he said to him in a low voice, 'Don't throw me overboard'; and he desired
that he might be buried by his parents, unless it should please the King to
order otherwise. Then reverting to private feelings, 'Take care of my dear
Lady Hamilton, Hardy; take care of poor Lady Hamilton. Kiss me,
Hardy,' said he. Hardy knelt down and kissed his cheek, and Nelson said,
'Now I am satisfied. Thank God I have done my duty.' Hardy stood over
him in silence for a moment or two, then knelt again and kissed his
forehead. 'Who is that?' said Nelson; and being informed, he replied,
'God bless you, Hardy.' And Hardy then left him—for ever.

                        ROBERT SOUTHEY, *The Life of Nelson*, 1813

His Chaplaine, Dr Lushington, was a very learned and ingeniose man,
and they loved one another. The Bishop sometimes would take the key of
the wine-cellar, and he and his Chaplaine would goe and lock themselves
in and be merry. Then first he layes downe his Episcopall hat—*There lyes
the Doctor.* Then he putts off his gowne—*There lyes the Bishop.* Then twas,
Here's to thee, Corbet, and *Here's to thee, Lushington* . . .

   The last words he sayd were, *Good night, Lushington.*

          JOHN AUBREY, (1626–97), 'Richard Corbet', *Brief Lives*

Those we ordinarily call friends and amities, are but acquaintances and familiarities, tied together by some occasion or commodities, by means whereof our minds are entertained ... If a man urge me to tell wherefore I loved him [Etienne de la Boétie], I feel it cannot be expressed, but by answering: Because it was he, because it was myself. There is beyond all my discourse, and besides what I can particularly report of it, I know not what inexplicable and fatal power, a mean and mediatrix of this indissoluble union. We sought one another before we had seen one another, and by the reports we heard one of another; which wrought a greater violence in us, than the reason of reports may well bear; I think by some secret ordinance of the heavens, we embraced one another by our names. And at our first meeting, which was by chance at a great feast, and solemn meeting of a whole township, we found our selves so surprised, so known, so acquainted, and so combinedly bound together, that from thence forward, nothing was so near unto us as one unto another's.

Montaigne, 'Of Friendship'

There are few nobler spectacles than the friendship of two great men; and the History of Literature presents nothing comparable to the friendship of Goethe and Schiller. The friendship of Montaigne and Etienne de la Boétie was, perhaps, more passionate and entire; but it was the union of two kindred natures, which from the first moment discovered their affinity, not the union of two rivals incessantly contrasted by partisans, and originally disposed to hold aloof from each other. Rivals Goethe and Schiller were, and are; natures in many respects directly antagonistic; chiefs of opposing camps, and brought into brotherly union only by what was highest in their natures and their aims.

To look on these great rivals was to see at once their profound dissimilarity. Goethe's beautiful head had the calm victorious grandeur of the Greek ideal; Schiller's the earnest beauty of a Christian looking towards the Future. The massive brow, and large-pupilled eyes—like those given by Raphael to the infant Christ, in the matchless Madonna di San Sisto—the strong and well-proportioned features, lined indeed by thought and suffering, yet showing that thought and suffering have troubled, but not vanquished, the strong man—a certain healthy vigour in the brown skin, and an indescribable something which shines out from the face, make Goethe a striking contrast to Schiller, with his eager eyes, narrow brow—tense and intense—his irregular features lined by thought and suffering, and weakened by sickness. The one *looks*, the other *looks out*. Both are majestic; but one has the majesty of repose, the other of conflict . . .

'An air that was beneficial to Schiller acted on me like poison,' Goethe said to Eckermann. 'I called on him one day, and as I did not find him at home, I seated myself at his writing-table to note down various matters. I had not been seated long, before I felt a strange indisposition steal over me, which gradually increased, until at last I nearly fainted. At first I did not know to what cause I should ascribe this wretched and to me unusual state, until I discovered that a dreadful odour issued from a drawer near me. When I opened it, I found to my astonishment that it was full of rotten apples. I immediately went to the window and inhaled the fresh air, by which I was instantly restored. Meanwhile his wife came in, and told me that the drawer was always filled with rotten apples, because the scent was beneficial to Schiller, and he could not live or work without it.' . . .

In comparing one to a Greek ideal, the other to a Christian ideal, it has already been implied that one was the representative of Realism, the other of Idealism. Goethe has himself indicated the capital distinction between them: Schiller was animated with the idea of Freedom; Goethe, on the contrary, was animated with the idea of Nature. This distinction runs through their works: Schiller always pining for something greater than Nature, wishing to make men Demigods; Goethe always striving to let Nature have free development, and produce the highest forms of Humanity. The Fall of Man was to Schiller the happiest of all events, because thereby men fell away from pure *instinct* into conscious *freedom*; with this sense of freedom came the possibility of Morality. To Goethe this seemed paying a price for Morality which was higher than Morality was worth; he preferred the ideal of a condition wherein Morality was unnecessary. Much as he might prize a good police, he prized still more a society in which a police would never be needed . . .

Having touched upon the points of contrast, it will now be needful to say a word on those points of resemblance which served as the basis of their union . . . They were both profoundly convinced that Art was no luxury of leisure, no mere amusement to charm the idle, or relax the careworn; but a mighty influence, serious in its aims although pleasurable in its means; a sister of Religion, by whose aid the great world-scheme was wrought into reality . . . They believed that Culture would raise Humanity to its full powers; and they, as artists, knew no Culture equal to that of Art . . .

At this time, then, that these two men seemed most opposed to each other, and *were* opposed in feeling, they were gradually drawing closer and closer in the very lines of their development, and a firm basis was prepared for solid and enduring union. Goethe was five-and-forty, Schiller five-and-thirty. Goethe had much to give, which Schiller gratefully accepted; and if he could not in return influence the developed mind of his great friend, or add to the vast stores of its knowledge and experience, he could give him that which was even more valuable, *sympathy* and *impulse*. He excited Goethe to work. He withdrew him from the engrossing pursuit of science, and restored him once more to poetry. He urged him to finish what was already commenced, and not to leave his works all fragments. They worked together with the same purpose and with the same earnestness, and their union is the most glorious episode in the lives of both, and remains as an eternal exemplar of a noble friendship.

G. H. Lewes, *Life of Goethe*, 1855

Now, Thackeray, I lay you ten thousand pounds that you will be thoroughly disappointed when we come together—our letters have been so warm, that we shall expect each minute to contain a sentence like those in our letters. But in letters we are not always together: there are no blue devilish moments: one of us isn't kept waiting for the other: and above all in letters there is Expectation! I am thus foreboding because I have felt it—and put you on your guard very seriously about it, for the disappoint-ment of such hopes has caused a flatness, then a disgust, and then a coldness betwixt many friends, I'll be bound. So think of meeting me not as I am in my letters (for they being written when in a good humour, and read when you have nothing better to do, make all seem alert and agreeable) but as you used to see me in London, Cambridge, etc. If you come to think, you will see there is a great difference. Do not think I speak this in a light-hearted way about the tenacity of our friendship, but with a very serious heart anxious lest we should disappoint each other, and so lessen our love a little—I hate this subject and to the devil with it.

Edward FitzGerald, letter to Thackeray, 10 October 1831

Here is the third letter I have begun, dear Edward, in reply to that noble
one w^h I have just received from you—the two first were full of thanks,
but I think I had better leave you to fancy these, finding it myself so
difficult to describe them—What I like to think of better than your
generosity or the cause of it, is the noble & brotherly love, w^h I believe
unites us together; my dear friend & brother, may God grant that no time
or circumstance ever should diminish this love between us; it seems to me
a thing w^h one should cultivate & preserve as a virtue, as a kind of
religion, of w^h it seems to have usurped the place & I hope to exercise this
power,—I might fill sheets with this kind of talk as I have done before;
but I find when I look at what has been written that I have not expressed
what I wanted—I wonder how sentimental writers manage to clothe fine
thoughts in fine sentences—I suppose because they only act them
—when they come to feel them they must be tongue-tied as I am.—. . .

> WILLIAM MAKEPEACE THACKERAY, letter to FitzGerald, 8
> October 1834

Old Fitz, who from your suburb grange,
    Where once I tarried for a while,
Glance at the wheeling Orb of change,
    And greet it with a kindly smile;
Whom yet I see as there you sit
    Beneath your sheltering garden-tree,
And while your doves about you flit,
    And plant on shoulder, hand and knee,
Or on your head their rosy feet . . .
              but none can say
That Lenten fare makes Lenten thought,
    Who reads your golden Eastern lay,
Than which I know no version done
    In English more divinely well;
A planet equal to the sun
    Which cast it, that large infidel
Your Omar; and your Omar drew
    Full-handed plaudits from our best
In modern letters, and from two,
    Old friends outvaluing all the rest,
Two voices heard on earth no more;
    But we old friends are still alive,

And I am nearing seventy-four,
    While you have touched at seventy-five,
And so I send a birthday line
    Of greeting; and my son, who dipt
In some forgotten book of mine
    With sallow scraps of manuscript,
And dating many a year ago,
    Has hit on this, which you will take
My Fitz, and welcome, as I know
    Less for its own than for the sake
Of one recalling gracious times,
    When, in our younger London days,
You found some merit in my rhymes,
    And I more pleasure in your praise.

TENNYSON, from 'To E. FitzGerald', written in June 1883; Tennyson intended to send it together with his poem 'Tiresias', but FitzGerald died a few days later

They crossed the Channel on Tuesday 27 May [1873], and Verlaine was immediately delighted with Camden Town. 'A very gay district,' he wrote on 30 May ... 'You'd think you were in Brussels,' he added. And on 21 June he even went so far as to say: 'London is charming.' On that day an advertisement appeared in the *Daily Telegraph*:

> Leçons de français en français.
> Perfection, finesse, par deux
> gentlemen parisiens.—Verlaine,
> 8 Great College St, Camden Town.

On the surface everything seemed to be going well for the two Parisian gentlemen—Verlaine (29) and Rimbaud (18)—but the latter, busy writing his *Season in Hell*, was in a suitably devilish mood. Verlaine was taunted and tormented until he could stand no more. It ended with the incident of the herring (or was it a mackerel?) hurled through the air at 8 Great College Street on Thursday morning, 3 July.

Verlaine had been doing the shopping (it was Rimbaud's turn to tidy the room) and was returning down Plender Street with the herring in one hand, a bottle of oil in the other. Rimbaud, watching at the open window, saw Verlaine a long way off as he walked down the middle of the wide street with his fish and his oil. As he drew near, the younger man, elegantly propped against the window, called out: 'If you could only see what a clot you look!' Verlaine burst up the stairs, threw the fish at his friend (but not, fortunately, the bottle) and immediately began to pack.

Soon he was striding towards St Katharine's Dock to catch the next boat for Belgium, while Rimbaud hurried after pleading with him not to go. Even when Verlaine was safely aboard with the gangplank up, Rimbaud still cried out from the quayside, begging him not to leave a poor compatriot stranded in the big city. But Verlaine for once was adamant and the ship bore him away down the Thames.

Rimbaud returned to 8 Great College Street in tears and sought consolation from the landlady, Mrs Alexander Smith. A hectic exchange of letters then followed, ending with a telegram from Verlaine on Tuesday 8 July to say he was joining the Spanish Army. This was too much for Rimbaud—he said goodbye to Mrs Smith and caught a boat to Antwerp after pawning two pairs of Verlaine's trousers to pay for the ticket. Unfortunately, in the rush to save his friend from a glorious death in Spain, he forgot to take Verlaine's laundry and some other possessions left at Great College Street. Verlaine was peeved and wrote to Mrs Smith in English . . .

We do not know if Mrs Smith sent the box, or even understood the request. In any case Verlaine did not go to Paris. He was detained in Belgian prisons for the next eighteen months for shooting and wounding the aforesaid M. Rimbaud.

DAVID ARKELL, *Ententes Cordiales*, 1989

When Longfellow read verse, it was with a hollow, with a mellow resonant murmur, like the note of some deep-throated horn. His voice was very lulling in quality, and at the Dante Club it used to have early effect with an old scholar who sat in a cavernous armchair at the corner of the fire, and who drowsed audibly in the soft tone and the gentle heat. The poet had a fat terrier who wished always to be present at the meetings of the Club, and he commonly fell asleep at the same moment with that dear old scholar, so that when they began to make themselves heard in concert, one could not tell which it was that most took our thoughts from the text of the *Paradiso*. When the duet opened, Longfellow would look up with an arch recognition of the fact, and then go gravely on to the end of the canto. At the close he would speak to his friend and lead him out to supper as if he had not seen or heard anything amiss.

The supper was very plain: a cold turkey, which the host carved, or a haunch of venison, or some braces of grouse, or a platter of quails, with a deep bowl of salad, and the sympathetic companionship of those elect vintages which Longfellow loved, and which he chose with the inspiration of affection. We usually began with oysters, and when some one who was expected did not come promptly, Longfellow invited us to raid his plate, as a just punishment of his delay. One evening Lowell remarked, with the cayenne poised above his blue-points, 'It's astonishing how fond these fellows are of pepper.'

The old friend of the cavernous armchair was perhaps not wide enough awake to repress an 'Ah?' of deep interest in this fact of natural history, and Lowell was provoked to go on. 'Yes, I've dropped a red pepper pod into a barrel of them, before now, and then taken them out in a solid mass, clinging to it like a swarm of bees to their queen.'

'Is it possible?' cried the old friend; and then Longfellow intervened to save him from worse, and turned the talk.

No doubt he had his resentments, but he hushed them in his heart, which he did not suffer them to embitter. While Poe was writing of 'Longfellow and other Plagiarists', Longfellow was helping to keep Poe alive by the loans which always made themselves gifts in Poe's case ...

He was patient of all things, and gentle beyond all mere gentlemanliness. But it would have been a great mistake to mistake his mildness for softness ... If he did not find it well to assert himself, he was prompt in behalf of his friends, and one of the fine things told of him was his resenting some censures of Sumner at a dinner in Boston during the old pro-slavery times: he said to the gentlemen present that Sumner was his friend, and he must leave their company if they continued to assail him.

At the services held in the house before the obsequies at the cemetery, I saw the poet for the last time, where 'Dead he lay among his books', in the library behind his study ... All who were left of his old Cambridge were present, and among those who had come farther was Emerson. He went up to the bier, and with his arms crossed on his breast, and his elbows held in either hand, stood with his head pathetically fallen forward, looking down at the dead face. Those who knew how his memory was a mere blank, with faint gleams of recognition capriciously coming and going in it, must have felt that he was struggling to remember who it was lay there before him; and for me the electly simple words confessing his failure will always be pathetic with his remembered aspect: 'The gentleman we have just been burying,' he said to the friend who had come with him, 'was a sweet and beautiful soul; but I forget his name.'

WILLIAM DEAN HOWELLS, *Literary Friends and Acquaintance*, 1900

Dear Edward

I am within a hair of being precisely as sorry and as glad as you are.

You are doing it for the self-same reason I shall hope to do it for if my time ever comes and I am brave enough, namely, because there seems nothing else for a man to do.

You have let me follow your thought in almost every twist and turn toward this conclusion. I know pretty well how far down you have gone and how far off sideways. And I think the better of you for it all. Only the very bravest could come to the sacrifice in this way . . .

I have never seen anything more exquisite than the pain you have made of it. You are a terror and I admire you. For what has a man locomotion if it isn't to take him into things he is between barely and not quite standing.

I should have liked you anyway—no friend ever has to strive for my approval—but you may be sure I am not going to like you less for this.

All belief is one. And this proves you are a believer.

I can't think what you would ask my forgiveness for unless it were saying my poetry is better than it is. You are forgiven as I hope to be forgiven for the same fault. Some day I hope I can afford to lean back and deprecate as excessive the somewhat general praise I may have won for what I may have done.

Your last poem Aspens seems the loveliest of all. You must have a volume of poetry ready for when you come marching home.

I wonder if they are going to let you write to me as often as ever.

Affectionately R. F.

ROBERT FROST, letter to Edward Thomas, 31 July 1915

The sun used to shine while we two walked
Slowly together, paused and started
Again, and sometimes mused, sometimes talked
As either pleased, and cheerfully parted

Each night. We never disagreed
Which gate to rest on. The to be
And the late past we gave small heed.
We turned from men or poetry

To rumours of the war remote
Only till both stood disinclined
For aught but the yellow flavorous coat
Of an apple wasps had undermined;

Or a sentry of dark betonies,
The stateliest of small flowers on earth,
At the forest verge; or crocuses
Pale purple as if they had their birth

In sunless Hades fields. The war
Came back to mind with the moonrise
Which soldiers in the east afar
Beheld then. Nevertheless, our eyes

Could as well imagine the Crusades
Or Caesar's battles. Everything
To faintness like those rumours fades—
Like the brook's water glittering

Under the moonlight—like those walks
Now—like us two that took them, and
The fallen apples, all the talks
And silences—like memory's sand

When the tide covers it late or soon,
And other men through other flowers
In those fields under the same moon
Go talking and have easy hours.

EDWARD THOMAS, 'The sun used to shine', written 22 May 1916;
recalling a holiday spent with Frost in Herefordshire in August
1914

Dear Helen

People have been praised for self-possession in danger. I have heard Edward doubt if he was as brave as the bravest. But who was ever so completely himself right up to the verge of destruction, so sure of his thought, so sure of his word? He was the bravest and best and dearest man you and I have ever known. I knew from the moment when I first met him at his unhappiest that he would some day clear his mind and save his life. I have had four wonderful years with him. I know he has done this all for you: he is all yours. But you must let me cry my cry for him as if he were *almost* all mine too.

Of the three ways out of here, by death where there is no choice, by death where there is a noble choice, and by death where there is a choice not so noble, he found the greatest way. There is no regret—nothing that I will call regret. Only I can't help wishing he could have saved his life without so wholly losing it and come back from France not too much hurt to enjoy our pride in him. I want to see him to tell him something. I want to tell him, what I think he liked to hear from me, that he was a poet. I want to tell him that I love those he loved and hate those he hated. (But the hating will wait: there will be a time for hate.) I had meant to talk endlessly with him still, either here in our mountains as we had said or, as I found my longing was more and more, there at Ledington where we first talked of war.

It was beautiful as he did it. And I don't suppose there is anything for us to do to show our admiration but to love him forever.

                                                                    Robert

ROBERT FROST, letter to Helen Thomas, 27 April 1917

Gogarty admired Yeats as the greatest living poet and thought him the finest talker he had ever heard. He admired also his public courage. This did not prevent him from parading tales and witty remarks about the poet's eccentricities, in the taverns and eating-houses of the city. 'Yeats is becoming so aristocratic, he's evicting imaginary tenants,' he quipped to J. B. Priestley. On another occasion, he told a medical acquaintance of Yeats's reaction to the Steinach operation, which he had undergone to improve his sexual powers. The acquaintance was shocked that Gogarty should speak of a friend in this way ... Yeats knew quite well that Gogarty made him the centre of many a tale, behind his back, but he knew the nature of such tales—carefully embroidered fantasies, thought out as Oscar Wilde might have invented them, only with an individual touch of Gogartian derision. It made no difference to his friendship with Gogarty. In their daily meetings, he knew that Gogarty could stoke the fire-born moods of his mind, which was all that mattered when art and imagination were primary concerns. Most days, Gogarty snatched time to run out in his car to Riverdale in Rathfarnham, for a chat with Yeats. One day he had to bring with him what amounted to a death sentence. A Spanish doctor had written a report on Yeats couched in quaint medical jargon: 'We have here an antique cardiosclerotic of advanced years.' Gogarty tried to withhold the news from him at first, but Yeats insisted on hearing the truth. 'It is my letter, Gogarty. I must see it.' As he read it he rolled the word 'cardiosclerotic' lovingly on his tongue. He looked up, his great shock of white hair tumbling over his bronzed features: 'You know, Gogarty, I'd rather be called cardiosclerotic, than Lord of Lower Egypt.'

ULICK O'CONNOR, *Oliver St John Gogarty*, 1964

Caro mio: MUCH improved. I think your instinct had led you to put the remaining superfluities at the end. I think you had better leave 'em, abolish 'em altogether or for the present.

IF you MUST keep 'em, put 'em at the beginning before the 'April cruelest month'. The POEM ends with the 'Shantih, shantih, shantih'.

One test is whether anything would be lacking if the last three were omitted. I don't think it would.

The song has only two lines which you can use in the body of the poem. The other two, at least the first, does not advance on earlier stuff. And even the sovegna doesn't hold with the rest; which does hold.

(It also, to your horror probably, reads aloud very well. Mouthing out his OOOOOOze.)

I doubt if Conrad is weighty enough to stand the citation.

The thing now runs from 'April . . .' to 'shantih' without a break. That is 19 pages, and let us say the longest poem in the English langwidge. Don't try to bust all records by prolonging it three pages further.

The bad nerves is O.K. as now led up to.

My squibs are now a bloody impertinence. I send 'em as requested; but don't use 'em with *Waste Land*.

You can tack 'em onto a collected edtn, or use 'em somewhere where they would be decently hidden and swamped by the bulk of accompanying matter. They'd merely be an extra and wrong note with the 19 page version.

Complimenti, you bitch. I am wracked by the seven jealousies, and cogitating an excuse for always exuding my deformative secretions in my own stuff, and never getting an outline. I go into nacre and objets d'art. Some day I shall lose my temper, blaspheme Flaubert, lie like a ———— and say 'Art should embellish the umbelicus.'

SAGE HOMME

These are the poems of Eliot
By the Uranian Muse begot;
A Man their Mother was,
A Muse their Sire.

How did the printed Infancies result
From Nuptials thus doubly difficult?

If you must needs enquire
Know diligent Reader
That on each Occasion
Ezra performed the Caesarean Operation.

Cauls and grave clothes he brings,
Fortune's outrageous stings,
About which odour clings,
            Of putrefaction,
Bleichstein's dank rotting clothes
Affect the dainty nose,
He speaks of common woes
            Deploring action.

He writes of A.B.C.s
And flaxseed poultices,
Observing fate's hard decrees
            Sans satisfaction;
Breeding of animals,

> *Humans and cannibals,*
> *But above all else of smells*
> *Without attraction*

Vates cum fistula

It is after all a grrrreat litttttterary period.
Thanks for the Aggymemnon.

> EZRA POUND, letter to T. S. Eliot, Paris, 24 December 1921; on
> *The Waste Land*

Cher maître: Criticisms accepted so far as understood, with thanks.
  Glowed on the marble where the glass
  Sustained by standards wrought with fruited vines
  Wherefrom . . . ??
Footsteps shuffled on the stair . . .
  A closed car. I can't use taxi more than once.
  Departed, *have* left no addresses . . . ???
What does THENCE mean (To luncheon at the Cannon St. Hotel)???
Would D's [Pound's wife, Dorothy] difficulty be solved by inverting to
  Drifting logs
  The barges wash . . . ???
1. Do you advise printing 'Gerontion' as a prelude in book or pamphlet
     form?
2. Perhaps better omit Phlebas also???
3. Wish to use Caesarean Operation in italics in front.
4. Certainly omit miscellaneous pieces.
5. Do you mean not use the Conrad quote or simply not put Conrad's
     name to it? It is much the most appropriate I can find, and somewhat
     elucidative.
  Complimenti appreciated, as have been excessively depressed. ----
  I would have sent Aeschule before but have been in bed with flu, now
out, but miserable.
Would you advise working sweats with tears etc. into nerves mono-
logue; only place where it can go?
  Have writ to Thayer [editor at *The Dial*] asking what he can offer for
this.

> T. S. ELIOT, letter to Ezra Pound, London, ?24 January 1922

Filio dilecto mihi: I merely queeried the dialect of 'thence'; dare say it is O.K.

D was fussing about some natural phenomenon, but I thought I had crossed out her query. The wake of the barges washes etc., and the barges may perfectly well be said to wash. I should leave it as it is, and NOT invert.

I do *not* advise printing 'Gerontion' as preface. One don't miss it *at* all as the thing now stands. To be more lucid still, let me say that I advise you NOT to print 'Gerontion' as prelude.

I DO advise keeping Phlebas. In fact I more'n advise. Phlebas is an integral part of the poem; the card pack introduces him, the drowned phoen. sailor. And he is needed ABsolootly where he is. Must stay in.

Do as you like about my obstetric effort.

Ditto re Conrad; who am I to grudge him his laurel crown?

Aeschylus not so good as I had hoped, but haven't had time to improve him, yet.

I dare say the sweats with tears will wait. ————

POUND, letter to Eliot, Paris, ?27 January 1922

I know to whom I write. Here, I am sure,
Though I am short, I cannot be obscure;
Less shall I for the art or dressing care,
Truth and the Graces best when naked are.
Your book, my Selden, I have read, and much
Was trusted, that you thought my judgement such
To ask it; though in most of works it be
A penance, where a man may not be free,
Rather than office, when it doth or may
Chance that the friend's affection proves allay
Unto the censure. Yours all need doth fly
Of this so vicious humanity,
Than which there is not unto study a more
Pernicious enemy.

JONSON, from 'An Epistle to Master John Selden', prefixed to Selden's *Titles of Honour*, 1614

There are, who to my person pay their court:
I cough like Horace, and, though lean, am short,
Ammon's great son one shoulder had too high,
Such Ovid's nose, and 'Sir! you have an eye'—
Go on, obliging creatures, make me see
All that disgraced my betters, met in me.
Say for my comfort, languishing in bed,
'Just so immortal Maro held his head':
And when I die, be sure you let me know
Great Homer died three thousand years ago.

Why did I write? what sin to me unknown
Dipped me in ink, my parents' or my own?
As yet a child, nor yet a fool to fame,
I lisped in numbers, for the numbers came.
I left no calling for this idle trade,
No duty broke, no father disobeyed.
The Muse but served to ease some friend, not wife,
To help me through this long disease, my life,
To second, ARBUTHNOT! thy art and care,
And teach the being you preserved, to bear.

But why then publish? Granville the polite,
And knowing Walsh, would tell me I could write;
Well-natured Garth inflamed with early praise;
And Congreve loved, and Swift endured my lays;
The courtly Talbot, Somers, Sheffield read,
Even mitred Rochester would nod the head,
And St John's self (great Dryden's friends before)
With open arms received one poet more.
Happy my studies, when by these approved!
Happier their author, when by these beloved!

POPE, from *An Epistle to Dr Arbuthnot*, 1735

My dear G. B. S.,

Since I wrote you, I have learnt that I shall have to undergo an operation one of these days—I go into a nursing home tomorrow. I don't know that the operation is a very serious one, and as a matter of fact I feel as fit as a fiddle, so I suppose my chances are pretty good. Still, accidents will happen, and this episode gives me an excuse for saying, what I hope you don't doubt—namely, that though I may sometimes have played the part of the all-too candid mentor, I have never wavered in my admiration and affection for you, or ceased to feel that the Fates had treated me kindly in making me your contemporary and friend. I thank you from my heart for forty years of good comradeship . . .

Ever yours,

W. A.

> WILLIAM ARCHER, letter to George Bernard Shaw, 17 December 1924. Archer died ten days later, and the news, Shaw said, 'threw me into a transport of fury . . . I still feel that when he went he took a piece of me with him.'

Much later, in the time after Zelda had what was then called her first nervous breakdown and we happened to be in Paris at the same time, Scott [Fitzgerald] asked me to have lunch with him at Michaud's restaurant on the corner of the rue Jacob and the rue des Saints-Pères. He said he had something very important to ask me that meant more than anything in the world to him and that I must answer absolutely truly. I said that I would do the best that I could. When he would ask me to tell him something absolutely truly, which is very difficult to do, and I would try it, what I said would make him angry, often not when I said it but afterwards, and sometimes long afterwards when he had brooded on it. My words would become something that would have to be destroyed and sometimes, if possible, me with them.

He drank wine at the lunch but it did not affect him and he had not prepared for the lunch by drinking before it. We talked about our work and about people and he asked me about people that we had not seen lately. I knew that he was writing something good and that he was having great trouble with it for many reasons, but that was not what he wanted to talk about. I kept waiting for it to come, the thing that I had to tell the absolute truth about; but he would not bring it up until the end of the meal, as though we were having a business lunch.

Finally when we were eating the cherry tart and had a last carafe of wine he said, 'You know I never slept with anyone except Zelda.'

'No, I didn't.'

'I thought I had told you.'

'No. You told me a lot of things but not that.'

'That is what I have to ask you about.'

'Good. Go on.'

'Zelda said that the way I was built I could never make any woman happy and that was what upset her originally. She said it was a matter of measurements. I have never felt the same since she said that and I have to know truly.'

'Come out to the office,' I said.

'Where is the office?'

'*Le water,*' I said.

We came back into the room and sat down at the table.

'You're perfectly fine,' I said. 'You are O.K. There's nothing wrong with you. You look at yourself from above and you look foreshortened. Go over to the Louvre and look at the people in the statues and then go home and look at yourself in the mirror in profile.'

'Those statues may not be accurate.'

'They are pretty good. Most people would settle for them.'

'But why would she say it?'

'To put you out of business. That's the oldest way in the world of putting people out of business. Scott, you asked me to tell you the truth and I can tell you a lot more but this is the absolute truth and all you need. You could have gone to see a doctor.'

'I didn't want to. I want you to tell me truly.'

'Now do you believe me?'

'I don't know,' he said.

'Come on over to the Louvre,' I said. 'It's just down the street and across the river.'

We went over to the Louvre and he looked at the statues but still he was doubtful about himself.

'It is not basically a question of the size in repose,' I said. 'It is the size that it becomes. It is also a question of angle.' I explained to him about using a pillow and a few other things that might be useful for him to know . . .

But he was still doubtful.

'Should we go and see some pictures?' I asked. 'Have you ever seen anything in here except the Mona Lisa?'

'I'm not in the mood for looking at pictures,' he said. 'I promised to meet some people at the Ritz bar.'

ERNEST HEMINGWAY (1898–1961), *A Moveable Feast*

Olmutz, Moravia: Wittgenstein
   is walking side by side
with Engelmann, who lived to write
   after his friend had died,

'I sought, between the world that is
   and the world that ought to be,
in my own troubled self the source
   of the discrepancy,

'and in his lonely mind this touched
   a sympathetic chord.
I offered friendship, and was given
   his friendship, a reward

'no gift of mine could match.' They walk
   as friends do, late at night,
two men of cultivated taste
   talking, in reason's light,

of music (Wittgenstein had learned
   to play the clarinet;
could whistle, too, in perfect pitch,
   one part from a quartet)

and of the pure veracity
   Wittgenstein prized in art.
'Count Eberhard's Hawthorn', Uhland's poem,
   profoundly touched his heart:

Felicitous, simple: Eberhard
   rode by a hawthorn spray,
and in his iron helmet placed
   a tender sprig of may,

which, preserved through the wars, he brought
   home from his pilgrimage.
It grew into a branching tree
   to shelter his old age.

Above his dreams a flowering arch
   by whispering breezes fanned
recalled the far time when he was
   young, in the Holy Land.

One day when Wittgenstein was ill
   and could not leave his bed,
Engelmann's mother sent her son
   with gruel to see him fed.

Engelmann climbing up the stairs
   slipped with the saucepan full,
and steaming oatmeal porridge splashed
   his coat of threadbare wool.

'You are showering me with kindnesses,'
   said grateful Wittgenstein,
and Engelmann, 'I am showering,
   it seems, this coat of mine.'

—*He was mightily amused.* The stiff
   unfunny joke survives
through solemn reminiscences
   to illuminate two lives.

Philosopher and architect
   walk through the flaking town,
Wittgenstein in his uniform
   of red and chocolate brown,

formal and courteous they talk
   of the Count's hawthorn flower;
how nature and our thought conform
   through words' mysterious power;

how propositions cannot state
   what they make manifest;
of the ethical and mystical
   that cannot be expressed;

how the world is on one side of us,
   and on the other hand
language, the mirror of the world;
   and God is, *how things stand.*

Europe lies sick in its foul war.
   Armies choke in clay.
But these friends keep their discourse clear
   as the white hawthorn spray,

one a great genius, and both
   humble enough to seek
the simple sources of that truth
   whereof one cannot speak.

GWEN HARWOOD, 'Wittgenstein and Engelmann', 1981

The thoughtful reader must have noted with some displeasure that I have scarcely, whether at college or at home, used the word 'friendship' with respect to any of my companions. The fact is, I am a little puzzled by the specialty and singularity of poetical and classic friendship. I get, distinctively, attached to places, to pictures, to dogs, cats, and girls: but I have had, Heaven be thanked, many and true friends, young and old, who have been of boundless help and good to me,—nor I quite helpless to them; yet for none of whom have I ever obeyed George Herbert's mandate, 'Thy friend put in thy bosom; wear his eyes, still in thy heart, that he may see what's there; if cause require, thou art his sacrifice', etc. Without thinking myself particularly wicked, I found nothing in my heart that seemed to me worth anybody's seeing; nor had I any curiosity for insight into those of others; nor had I any notion of being a sacrifice for them, or the least wish that they should exercise for my good any but their most pleasurable accomplishments,—Dawtrey Drewitt, for instance, being farther endeared because he could stand on his head, and catch vipers by the tail; Gershom Collingwood because he could sing French songs about the Earthly Paradise; and Alic Wedderburn, because he could swim into tarns and fetch out water-lilies for me, like a water-spaniel. And I never expected that they should care much for *me*, but only that they should read my books; and looking back, I believe they liked and like me, nearly as well as if I hadn't written any.

JOHN RUSKIN, *Praeterita*, 1885–9

My father was in a café, so he told me, with Sidney Pawling, Heinemann's partner, and Peter Chalmers Mitchell who directed the London Zoo and was subsequently knighted. Wilde came in, looked round him, then went out. Mitchell said, 'That's Wilde. I'll go and speak to him.' He was away ten minutes. On his return, he said, 'I don't see why you should cut a man because he's had a scandal. I've no use for fair-weather friends who drink a man's wine when he's in favour and look the other way when he's in trouble.' He was so persistent and generally self-righteous that finally Pawling said, 'What are you making all this fuss about? Waugh doesn't know him. I've scarcely met him. Don't be such an ass, Mitchell, finish up your beer.'

ALEC WAUGH, *My Brother Evelyn and Other Profiles*, 1967

And so you've gone and joined a club? The Skylarks, indeed! A pretty skylark you'll make of yourself! But I won't stay and be ruined by you. No: I'm determined on that. I'll go and take the dear children, and you may get who you like to keep your house. That is, as long as you have a house to keep—and that won't be long, I know.

How any decent man can go and spend his nights in a tavern!—oh, yes, Mr Caudle; I dare say you *do* go for rational conversation. I should like to know how many of you would care for what you call rational conversation, if you had it without your filthy brandy-and-water; yes, and your more filthy tobacco-smoke. I'm sure the last time you came home, I had the headache for a week . . .

How any man can leave his own happy fireside to go and sit, and smoke, and drink, and talk with people who wouldn't one of 'em lift a finger to save him from hanging—how any man can leave his wife—and a good wife, too, though I say it—for a parcel of pot-companions—oh, it's disgraceful, Mr Caudle; it's unfeeling. No man who had the least love for his wife could do it.

And I suppose this is to be the case every Saturday? . . . There was a time, when you were as regular at your fireside as the kettle. That was when you were a decent man, and didn't go amongst Heaven knows who, drinking and smoking, and making what you think your jokes. I never heard any good come to a man who cared about jokes. No respectable tradesman does . . .

And all the Club married men and fathers of families. The more shame for 'em! Skylarks, indeed! They should call themselves Vultures; for they can only do as they do by eating up their innocent wives and children. Eighteen-pence a week! And if it was only that,—do you know what fifty-two eighteen-pences come to in a year? . . .

Going and sitting for four hours at a tavern! What men, unless they had their wives with them, can find to talk about, I can't think. No good, of course.

DOUGLAS JERROLD, *Mrs Caudle's Curtain Lectures*, 1846

Our eager parties, when the lunar light
Throws its full radiance on the festive night,
Of either sex, with punctual hurry come,
And fill, with one accord, an ample room;
Pleased, the fresh packs on cloth of green they see,
And seizing, handle with preluding glee;
They draw, they sit, they shuffle, cut and deal;
Like friends assembled, but like foes to feel;
But yet not all,—a happier few have joys
Of mere amusement, and their cards are toys;
No skill nor art, nor fretful hopes have they,
But while their friends are gaming, laugh and play.

Next is the club, where to their friends in town,
Our country neighbours once a month come down;
We term it *Free-and-Easy*, and yet we
Find it no easy matter to be free:
Ev'n in our small assembly, friends among,
Are minds perverse, there's something will be wrong.
Men are not equal; some will claim a right
To be the kings and heroes of the night;
Will their own favourite themes and notions start,
And you must hear, offend them, or depart.
There comes Sir Thomas from his village seat,
Happy, he tells us, all his friends to meet;
He brings the ruin'd brother of his wife,
Whom he supports, and makes him sick of life;
A ready witness whom he can produce
Of all his deeds—a butt for his abuse;
Soon as he enters, has the guests espied,

Drawn to the fire, and to the glass applied—
'Well, what's the subject—what are you about?
The news, I take it—come, I'll help you out';
And then, without one answer he bestows
Freely upon us all he hears and knows;
Gives us opinions, tells us how he votes,
Recites the speeches, adds them to his notes,
And gives old ill-told tales for new-born anecdotes;
Yet cares he nothing what we judge or think,
Our only duty's to attend and drink;
At length, admonish'd by his gout he ends
The various speech, and leaves at peace his friends;
But now alas! we've lost the pleasant hour,
And wisdom flies from wine's superior power.

The Poor Man has his Club; he comes and spends
His hoarded pittance with his chosen friends;
Nor this alone,—a monthly dole he pays,
To be assisted when his health decays;
Some part his prudence from the day's supply,
For cares and troubles in his age, lays by;
The printed rules he guards with painted frame,
And shows his children where to read his name;
Those simple words his honest nature move,
That bond of union tied by laws of love.

Early in life, when we can laugh aloud,
There's something pleasant in a social crowd,
Who laugh with us—but will such joy remain,
When we lie struggling on the bed of pain?
When our physician tells us with a sigh,
No more on hope and science to rely,
Life's staff is useless then; with labouring breath
We pray for Hope divine—the staff of Death;—
This is a scene which few companions grace,
And where the heart's first favourites yield their place.
Here all the aid of man to man must end,
Here mounts the soul to her eternal Friend;
The tenderest love must here its ties resign,
And give th'aspiring heart to love divine.

> Men feel their weakness, and to numbers run,
> Themselves to strengthen, or themselves to shun;
> But though to this our weakness may be prone,
> Let's learn to live, for we must die, alone.
>
> GEORGE CRABBE, from 'Clubs and Social Meetings', *The Borough*,
> 1810

I visited several clubs in St James's, Pall Mall and Carlton Terrace, than which nothing can be more richly decorated or more comfortable. The entrance to these palaces is truly royal; vast vestibules, superb double staircases, furnished with beautiful carpets and lit by a hundred gas brackets, the whole heated by hot-water pipes ... There is no passably well-appointed club which does not have a French cook. The chef (the culinary artist preserves the grandiose title from the other side of the Channel) is the soul of the establishment ... Such are the great material advantages derived from shared interests; let us now examine the intellectual returns.

What do they do, these two or three hundred members of a club? Do they genuinely seek to be enlightened on important social questions? Do they talk about business and politics? Literature, theatre, the arts? No. They go there to eat well, drink good wines, play cards, and escape from the boredom of home life; they come to find a shelter from the day's tribulations, not to give themselves over to the fatigue of a sustained discussion on whatever subject. Besides, whom could they converse with? They do not know one another; the terms of membership do not include the obligation to speak to fellow members or even to greet them. Each of them enters the rooms with his hat on his head, neither glancing at nor nodding to anyone. There is nothing more comic than to see a hundred men *gathered* in these huge rooms, like items of *furniture*. One, sitting in an armchair, reads a new pamphlet; another writes at a table, next to somebody he has never exchanged a word with; a third is asleep, stretched out on a sofa; some walk to and fro; others speak in whispers, so as not to disturb the sepulchral silence, as though they were in church. What pleasure can these men find—I asked myself as I watched—in coming together like this? They all looked extremely bored. Amazed by this mode of associating, I imagined at times that I was observing a collection of automatons. I asked the Englishman who accompanied me why there was not more intercourse between the members of these clubs.

'What!' he replied, 'Would you have people address a man they don't know, about whom they know nothing? Ignorant of whether he is rich or poor, Tory or Whig or Radical, they would risk wounding him in his pride or his opinions, without concern for the consequences! Only the French could behave so imprudently.'

'Then why,' I resumed, 'do you admit people you do not know?'

'Because a certain number of subscriptions is needed to cover the club's expenses, and as regards the respectability of candidates, it is enough that they have been proposed by two members of the club and accepted by the committee.'

This reply illustrates the English mentality perfectly; in any association they always have some material advantage in view. Do not ask them to bring in their ideas, their sentiments, their moral being, for they will not understand you.

FLORA TRISTAN, *Promenades dans Londres*, 1840; the author, socialist and feminist, was Gauguin's maternal grandmother

At twelve o'clock George walked across the park to one of his clubs. He belonged to three. The park was empty. He blew across it like a solitary late leaf. The light snow was turning Whitehall black, and spat on his gold glasses, but he arrived, a little breathless, but ready to deal with that bugbear of old men: protective sympathy.

'George! You ought not to be out on a day like this!' several said. One put his arm round his shoulder. They were a sneezing and coughing lot with slack affectionate faces and friendly overburdened bellies, talking of snowed-up roads, late trains and scrambles for taxis.

'You *walked* through this! Why didn't you make your chauffeur bring you?'

'No car.'

'Or a cab?'

'Fares have gone up. I'm too mean.'

'Or a bus?'

'Oh, no, no, you see,' said George, glittering at them. 'I don't know if I told you'—he had told them innumerable times—'when you're brought up by a rich brute of a father, as I was—oh, yes, he was very rich—you get stingy. I'm very stingy. I must have told you about my father. Oh, well, now, there's a story,' he began eagerly. But the bar was crowded;

slow to move, George Clark found his listener had been pushed away
and had vanished. He stood suddenly isolated in his autobiography.

'Oh, God,' he groaned loudly, but in a manner so sepulchral and
private that people moved respectfully away. It was a groan that seemed
to come up from the earth, up from his feet, a groan of loneliness that was
raging and frightening to the men round him . . .

For him the dining-room was one more aspect of the general battle-
field. Where should he place his guns? Next to Doyle? No, he was 'a
Roman'. George hated 'Romans'. He hated 'Protestants' too. He was an
atheist who never found anyone sufficiently atheistical. George was tired
of telling Doyle how he had happened to be in Rome in 'o5 staying with
one of the great families ('she was a cousin of the Queen's') and had, for a
year, an unparalleled inside view of what was going on in the Vatican.
'Oh, yes, you see, a Jesuit, one of their relations, became a great friend
and exposed the whole hocus-pocus to me. You see, I have often been in a
position to know more of what is going on than most people. I was close
to Haig in the war.' There was Gregg, the painter—but it was intolerable
to listen to Academicians; there was Foster who had been opposed to
Munich and George could not stand that. There was Macdonald—but
Scots climb. Look at Lang! There was Jeffries, such a bore about divorce
reform: the bishops want it but daren't say so. 'I told the Archbishop in
this club that the moment you drag in God you lose your reason. My
mother ought to have got a divorce. You should have seen his face. Oh,
no, oh, no, he didn't like it. Not a bit.'

George looked at the tops of heads and the tableloads of discarded
enemies, casualties of his battles, with a grin. At last, glancing round him,
he chose a seat beside a successful, smirking pink man of fifty whose
name he had forgotten. 'Pretty harmless,' muttered George. 'He thinks
Goya a great painter when we all know he is just a good painter of the
second rank. Ah, he's eating oysters.' This stirred a memory. The man
was talking to a deaf editor but on the other side there were empty chairs.
It was against George's military sense to leave an exposed flank, but the
chance of attacking the club oysters was too good to miss.

'I see you've risked the oysters. I never eat oysters in this club,' said
George, sitting down. 'Poisonous. Oh, yes, yes—didn't I tell you? Oh,
you see, it was an awful thing, last year—'

'Now, George,' said the man, 'you told me that story before.'

'Did I? Nothing in that,' sniffed George. 'I always repeat myself, you
see I make a point of telling my stories several times. I woke up in the
night—'

'Please, George,' said the man more sternly, 'I want to enjoy my lunch.'

'Oh, ah, ah, ah,' said George, sniffing away. 'I'll watch your plate. I'll warn you if I see a bad one.'

'Oh, really, George!' said the young man.

'You're interrupting our conversation, George,' the editor called across. 'I was telling Trevor something very interesting about my trip to Russia.'

'I doubt if it is interesting,' said George in a loudish whisper to the other man. 'Interesting! I never found a Whig interesting.'

'Dear George is old. He talks too much,' said the deaf editor, speaking louder than he knew.

'Not a lot of rot,' said George in a loud mutter.

'What's he say?' said the deaf editor.

'You see,' George continued to interrupt, 'I talk a lot because I live alone. I probably talk more than anyone in this club and I am more interesting than most people. You see, I've often been in a position to know more than most people here. I was in Rome in '05 . . .'

But George looked restlessly at the vacant chair beside him. 'I hope,' he said, suddenly nervous, 'some awful bore is not going to sit here. You never know who, who—oh, no, oh, no, no . . .'

V. S. PRITCHETT, from 'The Skeleton', 1969

Among Women

THE most famous friendship between women is that of Ruth and Naomi; and Vera Brittain comments that it has had precious few rivals. That this section is half the size of the preceding is not due to bias on the editors' part; we could pick and choose among friendships between men, examples of friendship between women (in literature, be it understood) we had to seek out.

There has been a feeling, not confined to male witnesses, that female friendships are of little substance, watery imitations of male camaraderie, either shallow or morbid ('copious outpourings of grief,' says Randolph Bourne, the comparing of notes on illness and the misfortunes of others) or else (especially when the talk is of men) over-intimate and embarrassing to imagine. And also, compared with male friendships, short-lived, soon terminated by vanity or selfishness or, of course, jealousy. No doubt it is understandable that men should like to see friendship between young women as a substitute for erotic love (a pathetic substitute for *them*) or a preparation for it. Once women have tasted love, La Rochefoucauld declares, most of them will find friendship boring. It seems only fair that women have responded by detecting or claiming to detect an element of homosexuality in male friendships; they have some reason to distrust associations that involve late hours, heavy drinking and its aftermath, and the squandering of money rightly owing to the household.

In the past women have written less about friendship because they have written less about anything; or less of it has survived. In *Persuasion*, during an argument over the relative constancy of the sexes, Anne Elliot bursts out: 'If you please, no reference to examples in books. Men have had every advantage of us in telling their own story . . . the pen has been in their hands.' Close acquaintance often forms at work, in shared endeavours; set against the great outside world, the scene of momentous events where men have reckoned to spend their best energies, the bosom of the family is not a rich breeding ground for friendships. Until recent times, women have had few opportunities to lay down their life for a friend, although Kilvert records a comparable sacrifice that one sister made for the other.

Even so, male writers have depicted female friendship with admiration and force. *As You Like It* wouldn't be very much without Rosalind and Celia, and Maria and Caroline are the liveliest and most intelligent characters in Robert Bage's *Hermsprong*. It was with his daughter in mind that Yeats wished for 'the heart-revealing intimacy that chooses right' in finding friends. On the other hand, women writers have been sharp-tongued concerning their own sex; notably, in what follows, Jane Austen (sharp about many things) and Dorothy Sayers. More gently, though firmly, George Eliot strives to persuade the ardent Edith Simcox to divert her affections towards a man, intending what we assume the Lord God meant when he said it was not good to be alone. Perhaps it ought to be mentioned that Christina Stead's Nellie is a trouble-maker, an 'imp of Satan'.

Richardson's Colonel Morden is conventionally wise in taking for granted that marriage, 'the highest state of friendship', generally soaks up friendship between women—so it can, and it can dissolve or dilute friendship between man and man—yet his account of the 'remarkable exception', even if it reads rather like a formal testimonial, is eminently cogent, both warm and weighty.

———

From the days of Homer the friendships of men have enjoyed glory and acclamation, but the friendships of women, in spite of Ruth and Naomi, have usually been not merely unsung, but mocked, belittled and falsely interpreted. I hope that Winifred's story [Winifred Holtby's] may do something to destroy these tarnished interpretations, and show its readers that loyalty between women is a noble relationship which, far from impoverishing, actually enhances the love of a girl for her lover, of a wife for her husband, of a mother for her children.

Some feminine individualists believe that they flatter men by fostering the fiction of women's jealous inability to love and respect one another. Other sceptics are roused by any record of affection between women to suspicions habitual among the over-sophisticated.

VERA BRITTAIN, *Testament of Friendship*, 1940

Now it came to pass in the days when the judges ruled, that there was a famine in the land. And a certain man of Bethlehem-judah went to sojourn in the country of Moab, he, and his wife, and his two sons.

And the name of the man was Elimelech, and the name of his wife Naomi, and the name of his two sons Mahlon and Chilion . . .

And Elimelech Naomi's husband died; and she was left, and her two sons.

And they took them wives of the women of Moab; the name of the one was Orpah, and the name of the other Ruth: and they dwelled there about ten years.

And Mahlon and Chilion died also both of them; and the woman was left of her two sons and her husband.

Then she arose with her daughters in law, that she might return from the country of Moab: for she had heard in the country of Moab how that the Lord had visited his people in giving them bread.

Wherefore she went forth out of the place where she was, and her two daughters in law with her; and they went on the way to return unto the land of Judah.

And Naomi said unto her two daughters in law, Go, return each to her mother's house: the Lord deal kindly with you, as ye have dealt with the dead, and with me.

The Lord grant you that ye may find rest, each of you in the house of her husband. Then she kissed them; and they lifted up their voice, and wept.

And they said unto her, Surely we will return with thee unto thy people.

And Naomi said, Turn again, my daughters: why will ye go with me? are there yet any more sons in my womb, that they may be your husbands? . . .

And they lifted up their voice, and wept again: and Orpah kissed her mother in law; but Ruth clave unto her.

And she said, Behold, thy sister in law is gone back unto her people, and unto her gods: return thou after thy sister in law.

And Ruth said, Intreat me not to leave thee, or to return from following after thee: for whither thou goest, I will go; and where thou lodgest, I will lodge: thy people shall be my people, and thy God my God:

Where thou diest, will I die, and there will I be buried: the Lord do so to me, and more also, if ought but death part thee and me.

When she saw that she was steadfastly minded to go with her, then she left speaking unto her.

So they two went until they came to Bethlehem.

Ruth 1

Celia. O my poor Rosalind, whither wilt thou go?
　　Wilt thou change fathers? I will give thee mine.
　　I charge thee, be not thou more grieved than I am.
Rosalind. I have more cause.
Cel. 　　　　　　　　Thou hast not, cousin.
　　Prithee, be cheerful; knowest thou not the Duke
　　Hath banished me, his daughter?
Ros. 　　　　　　　　That he hath not.
Cel. No, hath not? Rosalind lacks then the love
　　Which teacheth thee that thou and I am one.
　　Shall we be sundered? Shall we part, sweet girl?
　　No, let my father seek another heir.
　　Therefore devise with me how we may fly,
　　Whither to go, and what to bear with us,
　　And do not seek to take your change upon you,
　　To bear your griefs yourself and leave me out;
　　For, by this heaven, now at our sorrows pale,
　　Say what thou canst, I'll go along with thee.
Ros. Why, whither shall we go?
Cel. To seek my uncle in the Forest of Arden.
Ros. Alas, what danger will it be to us,
　　Maids as we are, to travel forth so far?
　　Beauty provoketh thieves sooner than gold.
Cel. I'll put myself in poor and mean attire
　　And with a kind of umber smirch my face.
　　The like do you; so shall we pass along
　　And never stir assailants.
Ros. 　　　　　　　　Were it not better,
　　Because that I am more than common tall,
　　That I did suit me all points like a man?
　　A gallant curtle-axe upon my thigh,
　　A boar-spear in my hand, and in my heart
　　Lie there what hidden woman's fear there will,
　　We'll have a swashing and a martial outside,
　　As many other mannish cowards have
　　That do outface it with their semblances.
Cel. What shall I call thee when thou art a man?
Ros. I'll have no worse a name than Jove's own page,
　　And therefore look you call me 'Ganymede'.
　　But what will you be called?

Cel. Something that hath a reference to my state:
  No longer 'Celia', but 'Aliena'.

SHAKESPEARE, *As You Like It*, ?1599

'Pray, my dear, have you ever made an estimate of the quantity of your
father's affection?'

'An estimate! Sure, Maria, it is inestimable.'

'Yes, my dear, when in full growth. But Lord Grondale's doesn't seem
to be in that state of dimension.'

'This is a subject, Maria, that lies very near my heart.'

'I understand the reproof, my dear. But that heart I want to take a
naked peep into; to see if it is composed of true feminine matter; if it
prefer girandoles [candelabra] and the heartache, to a simple candle
and content.'

'I see the extent of your question, my dear Maria. But suppose I could
determine to buy peace with the loss of fortune, would not that peace be
as much wounded by my own breach of filial obligation, as by my father's
unkindness? If then,' continued Miss Campinet with a faint smile, 'the
heartache must be borne, one may as well have the girandoles along with
it.'

'Why, this now, Caroline, is ingenious, and I dare say ingenuous; it is
so like the rest of the daughters of Eve: and yet it leaves me still in doubt,
whether this meek and humble duty has its foundation in love, money, or
one or other of the ten commandments.'

'You are very whimsical, Maria.'

'And you, Caroline, instructive. I had got into the foolish way of
thinking that women did not love tyrants, whether husbands or fathers.'

'It is a sight of every day, Maria, that women, wives at least, continue
to love the tyrants, when the tyranny has become almost insupportable.'

'Depend upon it, it is nothing but a habit of fondness the silly things
have acquired, and not had time to get rid of.'

'But, Maria, a tyrant is a very harsh term; too harsh, I hope, to be
properly applied to Lord Grondale.'

'Oh, quite! for what has he done, but governed with absolute sway, as
great men ought; and turned his daughter out of doors, to make room for
persons of merit?'

'And Mrs Stone has merit, Maria; let us do her justice; and if my father chooses to treat her more as a friend than a servant, what right have I to complain?'

'Oh, no!—he might have married her, and begot you a few loving brothers.'

'Certainly he might; and had he given me a respectable mother, so far from considering it an injury, I should have rejoiced at the event.'

'Well, Caroline, since you are so fond of respectable stepmothers, I will try to accommodate you. I have some thoughts of taking that dignity upon myself, and am glad to find you in such dutiful inclinations.'

'And have you consulted Lord Grondale, mamma?'

'Yes, his eyes; and eyes will sometimes betray the secrets of elderly gentlemen as well as of young maidens. So God bless you, my dear child! be a good girl, and go quietly to sleep.'

'My dear,' said Miss Fluart, . . . 'whilst I have life and limb I will never be your stepmother; and yet you do want some such body to take care of you.'

'Indeed I am little able to take care of myself.'

'Now, Caroline, keep the fifth commandment, and honour your father,—if you can. No doubt it is a very pretty duty when it is possible to be performed. Where it is not, children must do as well as they can. Dissimulation, I hope, is not one of the seven deadly sins; for it is monstrous convenient on certain occasions.'

'If it ever is a necessity, Maria, sure it is the most disagreeable one that can be imposed upon an ingenuous mind; and yet you, my dear, have taken it voluntarily upon you.'

'No, indeed. It is a necessity imposed by friendship.'

'My heart thanks you, Maria; but my judgement is against you.'

'I am content with your heart, my dear.'

'When Lord Grondale discovers the deceit, as soon he must, shall I be the better treated for it?'

'I think, my dear, I can make his lordship dance the dance of expectation a couple of years at least; and whilst I am mother-expectant, I hope I may be able to dispose of my daughter in an honourable manner.'

So saying, this mother-expectant withdrew in a most matronly manner to her own dressing-room.

ROBERT BAGE, *Hermsprong*, 1796

On retiring from service at Court, I should like to live in a large and pleasing house. Naturally my family would be staying there too. One of the wings would be kept for a friend, an elegant lady-in-waiting to the Empress, with whom I could converse. Whenever we so wished, we would meet and discuss new poems and other interesting topics. When a letter came for my friend, we would read it together, and frame an answer. Should someone come to visit my friend when she was away, I would receive him in one of the charmingly decorated rooms, and if a storm or something of that nature prevented him from leaving, then I would invite him cordially to stay. Whenever my friend was called to the Palace, I would help her prepare and make sure she had everything necessary for the occasion. Anything to do with those of noble birth enchants me.

But I dare say these fancies of mine sound rather odd.

SEI SHŌNAGON, *Pillow Book, c.* 1000

I have examin'd and do find,
    Of all that favour me,
There's none I grieve to leave behind
    But only, only thee.
To part with thee I needs must die,
Could parting sep'rate thee and I.

But neither Chance nor Compliment
    Did element our Love;
'Twas sacred Sympathy was lent
    Us from the quire above.
That Friendship Fortune did create,
Still fears a wound from Time or Fate.

Our chang'd and mingled souls are grown
    To such acquaintance now,
That if each would resume their own,
    Alas! we know not how.
We have each other so engrost,
That each is in the union lost.

And thus we can no Absence know,
   Nor shall we be confin'd;
Our active souls will daily go
   To learn each other's mind.
Nay, should we never meet to Sense,
Our souls would hold Intelligence.

Inspired with a flame divine,
   I scorn to court a stay;
For from that noble soul of thine
   I ne'er can be away.
But I shall weep when thou dost grieve;
Nor can I die whilst thou dost live.

By my own temper I shall guess
   At thy felicity,
And only like my happiness
   Because it pleaseth thee.
Our hearts at any time will tell,
If thou, or I, be sick, or well.

All Honour sure I must pretend,
   All that is good or Great;
She that would be Rosania's Friend,
   Must be at least complete.
If I have any bravery,
'Tis cause I have so much of thee.

Thy lieger soul in me shall lie,
   And all thy thoughts reveal;
Then back again with mine shall fly,
   And thence to me shall steal.
Thus still to one another tend;
Such is the sacred Name of Friend.

Thus our twin-souls in one shall grow,
   And teach the World new love,
Redeem the age and sex, and show
   A flame Fate dares not move:
And courting Death to be our friend,
Our lives together too shall end.

A dew shall dwell upon our Tomb
   Of such a quality,
That fighting armies, thither come,
   Shall reconcilèd be.
We'll ask no Epitaph, but say
   ORINDA and ROSANIA.

   KATHERINE PHILIPS (1631–64), 'To Mrs M. A. at parting'

My dear and tender friend, we are both sensible how much time, habit, and your kindness have rendered our attachment more strong and indissoluble. As to myself, your absence daily becomes more insupportable, and I can now no longer live for a moment without you. The progress of our friendship is more natural than it appears to be; it is founded not only on a similarity of character, but of condition. As we advance in years, our affections begin to centre on one point. We every day lose something that was dear to us, which we can never replace. Thus we perish by degrees, till at length, being wholly devoted to self-love, we lose life and sensibility, even before our existence ceases. But a susceptible mind arms itself with all its force against this anticipated death: when a chillness begins to seize the extremities, it collects all the genial warmth of nature round its own centre; the more connections it loses, the closer it cleaves to those which remain, and all its former ties are combined to attach it to the last object.

   JEAN-JACQUES ROUSSEAU, *Julie, or the New Eloisa*, 1761: letter from Julie to Claire; tr. anon.

For there is no friend like a sister
In calm or stormy weather;
To cheer one on the tedious way,
To fetch one if one goes astray,
To lift one if one totters down,
To strengthen whilst one stands.

   CHRISTINA ROSSETTI, *Goblin Market*, 1862

9 June 1872. I went to see Mrs Prosser at the Swan, a young pretty woman dying I fear of consumption which she caught of her sister, Mrs Hope of the Rose and Crown in Hay. It was a sad beautiful story. She was warned not to sleep with her sister who was dying of decline and told that if she did she herself would probably be infected with the disease. But her sister begged her so hard not to leave her and to go on sleeping with her that she gave way. 'What could I do?' she said. 'She was my only sister and we loved each other so. I have been married seven years,' she said, 'and now my first child has just come, a little girl, and it does seem so hard to go away and leave her. But if it is the Lord's will to take me I must be content to go. My left lung is quite gone,' she said looking at me with her lip trembling and her beautiful eyes full of tears.

REVD FRANCIS KILVERT, *Diary*

Catherine was delighted with this extension of her Bath acquaintance, and almost forgot Mr Tilney while she talked to Miss Thorpe. Friendship is certainly the finest balm for the pangs of disappointed love.

Their conversation turned upon those subjects, of which the free discussion has generally much to do in perfecting a sudden intimacy between two young ladies; such as dress, balls, flirtations, and quizzes. Miss Thorpe, however, being four years older than Miss Morland, and at least four years better informed, had a very decided advantage in discussing such points; she could compare the balls of Bath with those of Tunbridge; its fashions with the fashions of London; could rectify the opinions of her new friend in many articles of tasteful attire; could discover a flirtation between any gentleman and lady who only smiled on each other; and point out a quiz through the thickness of a crowd. These powers received due admiration from Catherine, to whom they were entirely new.

The progress of the friendship between Catherine and Isabella was quick as its beginning had been warm, and they passed so rapidly through every gradation of increasing tenderness, that there was shortly no fresh proof of it to be given to their friends or themselves. They called each other by their Christian name, were always arm in arm when they walked, pinned up each other's train for the dance, and were not to be divided in the set; and if a rainy morning deprived them of other enjoyments, they were still resolute in meeting in defiance of wet and dirt, and shut themselves up, to read novels together.

The following conversation, which took place between the two friends in the Pump-room one morning, after an acquaintance of eight or nine days, is given as a specimen of their very warm attachment, and of the delicacy, discretion, originality of thought, and literary taste which marked the reasonableness of that attachment.

They met by appointment; and as Isabella had arrived nearly five minutes before her friend, her first address naturally was—'My dearest creature, what can have made you so late? I have been waiting for you at least this age!'

'Have you, indeed!—I am very sorry for it; but really I thought I was in very good time. It is but just one. I hope you have not been here long?'

'Oh! these ten ages at least. I am sure I have been here this half hour. But now, let us go and sit down at the other end of the room, and enjoy ourselves. I have an hundred things to say to you. In the first place, I was so afraid it would rain this morning, just as I wanted to set off; it looked very showery, and that would have thrown me into agonies! Do you know, I saw the prettiest hat you can imagine, in a shop window in Milsom-street just now—very like yours, only with coquelicot ribbons instead of green; I quite longed for it. But, my dearest Catherine, what have you been doing with yourself all this morning?—Have you gone on with Udolpho?'

'Yes, I have been reading it ever since I woke; and I am got to the black veil.'

'Are you, indeed? How delightful! Oh! I would not tell you what is behind the black veil for the world! Are you not wild to know?'

'Oh! yes, quite; what can it be?—But do not tell me—I would not be told upon any account. I know it must be a skeleton, I am sure it is Laurentina's skeleton. Oh! I am delighted with the book! I should like to spend my whole life in reading it. I assure you, if it had not been to meet you, I would not have come away from it for all the world.'

'Dear creature! how much I am obliged to you; and when you have finished Udolpho, we will read the Italian together; and I have made out a list of ten or twelve more of the same kind for you.'

'Have you, indeed! How glad I am!—What are they all?'

'I will read you their names directly; here they are, in my pocket-book. Castle of Wolfenbach, Clermont, Mysterious Warnings, Necromancer of the Black Forest, Midnight Bell, Orphan of the Rhine, and Horrid Mysteries. Those will last us some time.'

'Yes, pretty well; but are they all horrid, are you sure they are all horrid?'

'Yes, quite sure; for a particular friend of mine, a Miss Andrews, a sweet girl, one of the sweetest creatures in the world, has read every one of them. I wish you knew Miss Andrews, you would be delighted with her. She is netting herself the sweetest cloak you can conceive. I think her as beautiful as an angel, and I am so vexed with the men for not admiring her!—I scold them all amazingly about it.'

'Scold them! Do you scold them for not admiring her?'

'Yes, that I do. There is nothing I would not do for those who are really my friends. I have no notion of loving people by halves, it is not my nature. My attachments are always excessively strong. I told Capt. Hunt at one of our assemblies this winter, that if he was to tease me all night, I would not dance with him, unless he would allow Miss Andrews to be as beautiful as an angel. The men think us incapable of real friendship you know, and I am determined to shew them the difference. Now, if I were to hear anybody speak slightingly of you, I should fire up in a moment: —but that is not at all likely, for *you* are just the kind of girl to be a great favourite with the men.'

'Oh! dear,' cried Catherine, colouring, 'how can you say so?'

'I know you very well; you have so much animation, which is exactly what Miss Andrews wants, for I must confess there is something amazingly insipid about her.'

JANE AUSTEN (1775–1817), *Northanger Abbey*

'What a brown patch I am by the side of you, Rosy! You are the most unbecoming companion.'

'Oh no! No one thinks of your appearance, you are so sensible and useful, Mary. Beauty is of very little consequence in reality,' said Rosamond, turning her head towards Mary, but with eyes swerving towards the new view of her neck in the glass.

'You mean *my* beauty,' said Mary, rather sardonically.

Rosamond thought, 'Poor Mary, she takes the kindest things ill.' . . .

'. . . I mean, there is a gentleman who may fall in love with you, seeing you almost every day.'

A certain change in Mary's face was chiefly determined by the resolve not to show any change.

'Does that always make people fall in love?' she answered, carelessly; 'it seems to me quite as often a reason for detesting each other.'

'Not when they are interesting and agreeable. I hear that Mr Lydgate is both.'

'Oh, Mr Lydgate!' said Mary, with an unmistakable lapse into indifference. 'You want to know something about him,' she added, not choosing to indulge Rosamond's indirectness.

'Merely, how you like him.'

'There is no question of liking at present. My liking always wants some little kindness to kindle it. I am not magnanimous enough to like people who speak to me without seeming to see me.'

'Is he so haughty?' said Rosamond, with heightened satisfaction. 'You know that he is of good family?'

'No; he did not give that as a reason.'

'Mary! you are the oddest girl. But what sort of looking man is he? Describe him to me.'

'How can one describe a man? I can give you an inventory: heavy eyebrows, dark eyes, a straight nose, thick dark hair, large solid white hands—and—let me see—oh, an exquisite cambric pocket handkerchief. But you will see him. You know this is about the time of his visits.'

Rosamond blushed a little, but said, meditatively, 'I rather like a haughty manner. I cannot endure a rattling young man.'

'I did not tell you that Mr Lydgate was haughty; but *il y en a pour tous les goûts*, as little Mamselle used to say, and if any girl can choose the particular sort of conceit she would like, I should think it is you, Rosy.'

'Haughtiness is not conceit; I call Fred conceited.'

'I wish no one said any worse of him.'. . .

'It is of no use saying anything to you, Mary. You always take Fred's part.'

'Why should I not take his part?' said Mary, lighting up. 'He would take mine. He is the only person who takes the least trouble to oblige me.'

'You make me feel very uncomfortable, Mary,' said Rosamond, with her gravest mildness; 'I would not tell mamma for the world.'

'What would you not tell her?' said Mary, angrily.

'Pray do not go into a rage, Mary,' said Rosamond, mildly as ever.

'If your mamma is afraid that Fred will make me an offer, tell her that I would not marry him if he asked me. But he is not going to do so, that I am aware. He certainly never has asked me.'

'Mary, you are always so violent.'

'And you are always so exasperating.'

'I? What can you blame me for?'

'Oh, blameless people are always the most exasperating. There is the bell—I think we must go down.'

'I did not mean to quarrel,' said Rosamond, putting on her hat.

'Quarrel? Nonsense; we have not quarrelled. If one is not to get into a rage sometimes, what is the good of being friends?'

GEORGE ELIOT, *Middlemarch*, 1871–2

Harriet Smith's intimacy at Hartfield was soon a settled thing. Quick and decided in her ways, Emma lost no time in inviting, encouraging, and telling her to come very often; and as their acquaintance increased, so did their satisfaction in each other . . .

Harriet certainly was not clever, but she had a sweet, docile, grateful disposition; was totally free from conceit; and only desiring to be guided by any one she looked up to. Her early attachment to herself was very amiable; and her inclination for good company, and power of appreciating what was elegant and clever, shewed that there was no want of taste, though strength of understanding must not be expected. Altogether she was quite convinced of Harriet Smith's being exactly the young friend she wanted—exactly the something which her home required. Such a friend as Mrs Weston was out of the question. Two such could never be granted. Two such she did not want. It was quite a different sort of thing—a sentiment distinct and independent. Mrs Weston was the object of a regard, which had its basis in gratitude and esteem. Harriet would be loved as one to whom she could be useful. For Mrs Weston there was nothing to be done; for Harriet every thing.

'But Harriet Smith—I have not half done about Harriet Smith. I think her the very worst sort of companion that Emma could possibly have. She knows nothing herself, and looks upon Emma as knowing every thing. She is a flatterer in all her ways; and so much the worse, because undesigned. Her ignorance is hourly flattery. How can Emma imagine she has any thing to learn herself, while Harriet is presenting such a delightful inferiority? And as for Harriet, I will venture to say that *she* cannot gain by the acquaintance. Hartfield will only put her out of conceit with all the other places she belongs to. She will grow just refined enough to be uncomfortable with those among whom birth and circumstances have placed her home. I am much mistaken if Emma's doctrines give any

strength of mind, or tend at all to make a girl adapt herself rationally to
the varieties of her situation in life.—They only give a little polish.'

> JANE AUSTEN, *Emma*, 1816; the speaker in the second extract is
> Mr Knightley

GEORGE ELIOT AND FRIENDSHIP

My brightest spot, next to my love of *old* friends, is the deliciously calm
new friendship that Herbert Spencer gives me. We see each other every
day, and have a delightful *camaraderie* in everything. But for him my life
would be desolate enough. What a wretched lot of old shrivelled
creatures we shall be by-and-by. Never mind—the uglier we get in the
eyes of others, the lovelier we shall be to each other; that has always been
my firm faith about friendship, and now it is in a slight degree my
experience.

> GEORGE ELIOT, letter to Miss Sara Hennell, 27 May 1852

What divergence there has been in our different careers! As 'George
Eliot' I have traced you as far as possible and with an interest which few
could feel; not many knew you as intimately as I once did, tho' we have
been necessarily separated for so long. My heart has ever yearned after
you, and pleasant is it truly in the evening of life to find the old love still
existing.

> MARIA LEWIS, letter, 22 September 1874, to George Eliot,
> who had sent a cheque for £10 on learning of her straitened
> circumstances

Dear Miss Evans,
    If I were a german girl I would add: 'much adored', but we Dutch are
not überschwänglich in affectionate expressions, as we are too much
fulfilled with respect for those who awake our best soul ... since I
finished with reading Middlemarch I could not resist something within
me that draws me nearer to you ... You must have experienced

much—you must much have felt. There are cries of the heart that awake an echo in every maiden's soul.

Jeanne Buskes, letter to George Eliot, 26 December 1874

I kissed her again and again and murmured broken words of love. She bade me not exaggerate. I said I didn't—nor could, and then scolded her for not being satisfied with letting me love her as I did—as in present reality—and proposing instead that I should save my love for some imaginary he. She said—expressly what she has often before implied to my distress—that the love of men and women for each other must always be more and better than any other and bade me not wish to be wiser than 'God who made me'—in pious phrase. I hung over her caressingly and she bade me not think too much of her—she knew all her own frailty and if I went on, she would have to confess some of it to me. Then she said—perhaps it would shock me—she had never all her life cared very much for women—it must seem monstrous to me—I said I had always known it. She went on to say, what I also knew, that she cared for the womanly ideal, sympathized with women and liked for them to come to her in their troubles, but while feeling near to them in one way, she felt far off in another—the friendship and intimacy of men was more to her. Then she tried to add what I had already imagined in explanation that when she was young, girls and women seemed to look on her as somehow 'uncanny' while men were always kind.

Edith Simcox, 'Autobiography of a Shirt Maker' (MS); of a visit to George Eliot, 9 March 1880

In friendship George Eliot had the unconscious exactingness of a full nature. She was intolerant of a vacuum in the mind or character, and she was indifferent to admiration that did not seem to have its root in fundamental agreement with those first principles she held to be most 'necessary to salvation'. Where this sympathy existed, her generous affection was given to a fellow-believer, a fellow-labourer, with singularly little reference to the fact that such full sympathy was never unattended with profound love and reverence for herself as a living witness to the truth and power of the principles thus shared. To love her was a strenuous pleasure, for in spite of the tenderness for all human weakness that was natural to her, and the scrupulous charity of her overt judgements, the fact remained that her natural standard was ruthlessly out of reach, and it was a painful discipline for her friends to feel that she was compelled to lower it to suit their infirmities. The intense humility of her self-appreciation, and the unfeigned readiness with which she would even herself with any sinner who sought her counsel, had the same effect upon those who could compare what she condemned in herself with what she tolerated in them. And at the same time, no doubt, this total absence of self-sufficiency had something to do with the passionate tenderness with which commonplace people dared to cherish their immortal friend . . . her character seemed to include every possibility of action and emotion: no human passion was wanting in her nature, there were no blanks or negations; and the marvellous thing was to see how, in this wealth of impulses and desires, there was no crash of internal discord, no painful collisions with other human interests outside; how, in all her life, passions of volcanic strength were harnessed in the service of those nearest her, and so inspired by the permanent instinct of devotion to her kind, that it seemed as if it were by their own choice they spent themselves there only where their force was welcome.

> EDITH SIMCOX, 'George Eliot, a valedictory article', *The Nineteenth Century*, May 1881

I am glad to know as much as possible of all Her friends. I am not sorry that I do not find amongst them all any to whom She Herself was more than She was and is to me.

> EDITH SIMCOX, 'Autobiography'; after reading George Eliot's letters to Mme Bodichon

'I want to know you,' Olive said, on this occasion; 'I felt that I must last night, as soon as I heard you speak. You seem to me very wonderful. I don't know what to make of you. I think we ought to be friends; so I just asked you to come to me straight off, without preliminaries, and I believed you would come. It is so *right* that you have come, and it proves how right I was.' These remarks fell from Miss Chancellor's lips one by one, as she caught her breath, with the tremor that was always in her voice, even when she was the least excited, while she made Verena sit down near her on the sofa, and looked at her all over in a manner that caused the girl to rejoice at having put on the jacket with the gilt buttons. It was this glance that was the beginning; it was with this quick survey, omitting nothing, that Olive took possession of her . . . It was just as she was that she liked her; she was so strange, so different from the girls one usually met, seemed to belong to some queer gipsy-land or transcendental Bohemia. With her bright, vulgar clothes, her salient appearance, she might have been a rope-dancer or a fortune-teller; and this had the immense merit, for Olive, that it appeared to make her belong to the 'people', threw her into the social dusk of that mysterious democracy which Miss Chancellor held that the fortunate classes know so little about, and with which (in a future possibly very near) they will have to count. Moreover, the girl had moved her as she had never been moved, and the power to do that, from whatever source it came, was a force that one must admire. Her emotion was still acute, however much she might speak to her visitor as if everything that had happened seemed to her natural; and what kept it, above all, from subsiding was her sense that she found here what she had been looking for so long—a friend of her own sex with whom she might have a union of soul. It took a double consent to make a friendship, but it was not possible that this intensely sympathetic girl would refuse . . .

'Will you be my friend, my friend of friends, beyond every one, everything, forever and forever?' Her face was full of eagerness and tenderness.

Verena gave a laugh of clear amusement, without a shade of embarrassment or confusion. 'Perhaps you like me too much.'

'Of course I like you too much! When I like, I like too much. But of course it's another thing, your liking me,' Olive Chancellor added. 'We must wait—we must wait. When I care for anything, I can be patient.' She put out her hand to Verena, and the movement was at once so appealing and so confident that the girl instinctively placed her own in it. So, hand in hand, for some moments, these two young women sat looking at each other . . .

Verena wondered afterward why she had not been more afraid of her—why, indeed, she had not turned and saved herself by darting out of the room. But it was not in this young woman's nature to be either timid or cautious; she had as yet to make acquaintance with the sentiment of fear. She knew too little of the world to have learned to mistrust sudden enthusiasms, and if she had had a suspicion it would have been (in accordance with common worldly knowledge) the wrong one—the suspicion that such a whimsical liking would burn itself out. She could not have that one, for there was a light in Miss Chancellor's magnified face which seemed to say that a sentiment, with her, might consume its object, might consume Miss Chancellor, but would never consume itself. Verena, as yet, had no sense of being scorched; she was only agreeably warmed. She also had dreamed of a friendship, though it was not what she had dreamed of most, and it came over her that this was the one which fortune might have been keeping.

An immense pity for Olive sat in her heart, and she asked herself how far it was necessary to go in the path of self-sacrifice. Nothing was wanting to make the wrong she should do her complete; she had deceived her up to the very last; only three months earlier she had reasserted her vows, given her word, with every show of fidelity and enthusiasm. There were hours when it seemed to Verena that she must really push her inquiry no further, but content herself with the conclusion that she loved as deeply as a woman could love and that it didn't make any difference. She felt Olive's grasp too clinching, too terrible. She said to herself that she should never dare, that she might as well give up early as late; that the scene, at the end, would be something she couldn't face; that she had no right to blast the poor creature's whole future. She had a vision of those dreadful years; she knew that Olive would never get over the disappointment. It would touch her in the point where she felt everything most keenly; she would be incurably lonely and eternally humiliated. It was a very peculiar thing, their friendship; it had elements which made it probably as complete as any (between women) that had ever existed. Of course it had been more on Olive's side than on hers, she had always known that; but that, again, didn't make any difference. It was of no use for her to tell herself that Olive had begun it entirely and she had only responded out of a kind of charmed politeness, at first, to a tremendous appeal. She had lent herself, given herself, utterly, and she ought to have known better if she didn't mean to abide by it. At the end of the three weeks she felt that her inquiry was complete, but that after all nothing was gained except an immense interest in Basil Ransom's views and the prospect of an eternal heartache. He had told her he wanted her to know him, and now she knew him pretty thoroughly. She knew him and she adored him, but it didn't make any difference. To give him up or to give Olive up—this effort would be the greater of the two.

HENRY JAMES, *The Bostonians*, 1886

Nellie stretched her legs out and said a perfect friendship was a fine thing. Had Caroline ever had a friend?

'I had plenty of friends, at school and in the church, everywhere. Dozens I suppose if you count them all.'

Nellie said earnestly that was not what she meant, 'You can't have dozens of friends. You can only have one, one true friend. Have you never had a true friend?'

'Oh, yes, when I was about eighteen I had one. We used to take long walks together. We were both interested in serious questions. She was lovely: so true.'

'And she was your true friend, pet?'

'We got on because we weren't too close and weren't alike. That's best. Our lives ran parallel and never met: no friction. And she's loyal and so am I.'

'Ah, no, your lives didn't run parallel; they met.'

'No, my life never met anyone's till I met Barry, my husband. He was more like a best friend. I was very happy. I knew the risk I was taking coming home.'

She paused and Nellie waited. Caroline continued, 'We live through everything. Sometimes I think life is a strange disease that attacks different people in different ways; and at different ages it attacks you differently.'

'Aye, but with a true friend you can fight off that disease; you can hold on to the true solution, the cure.'

'What's the cure?' Caroline laughed sadly.

'There are two, sweetheart: love, and death.'

'Oh, both those are diseases, too.'

'Ah, you're depressed, love. You see, you never understood what friendship is. The friendship at school and at church, that's good; but it's the loaf of bread; it's not the wine.' . . .

Nellie went on in a sweet thin craven tone, asking if Caroline thought they could be friends.

'You're missing something if you haven't a friend.'

'But we are friends, aren't we? I know it's early.'

'It's early for an ordinary companionship, aye; but where there's a genuine basis, it ought to begin at once. It only needs the act of willing and knowing. Would you say we couldn't be friends now?'

Caroline looked at her, still puzzled.

Nellie went on in a dreamy coaxing tone, 'It's no good playing the ascetic, no; the thick armour of self-sufficiency which you have, pet, covers a wound, a scar is there. Self-knowledge must be struggled for. Confess what you know, confess what you don't know. You need a friend for that, to tell your inmost secrets to.'

'I'll tell you the truth,' said Caroline and paused.

'Ah, now, that's better: let's be frank.'

'I've written to Barry, but had no reply. He never caused me any pain. I feel quite sensible now. It was harmony with him, as you say. If he is free, I would go there now.'

She looked at Nellie as if she had told her whole story.

Nellie said, 'Then there's no hope for us as friends?'

'Why not?'

Caroline looked at her eccentric face and topknot and the glasses standing before her sympathetically. She added, with warmth, 'You know, I think it is you who don't know about friendship. For a woman the best friend is a man. There's no deeper feeling.'

Nellie cried in a rage, 'That's a damn hypocritical superior attitude. I won't take it from you or anyone else. So women are second-class citizens. Like families in slums who need housing. Subjects for pity!'

Caroline sat up in angry astonishment.

Nellie cried, 'So that's it. Women are inferior, incapable of friendship. Of all the goddamn backward bourgeois attitudes. A woman's not the equal of a man. I resent it. You can't put that over on me. So we're second-class citizens to you.'

Caroline said indignantly, 'Well, if it seems that way to you.'

'You see what a bourgeois you are? The superiority feeling in everything! You're incapable of a decent human relation with another woman.'

Caroline did not reply.

Nellie began to lament, 'You see how contorted your attitudes are? You're formed by the middle-class marriage hunt; man first, last and always. Aren't you ashamed, a little ashamed? Ashamed to put your sisters on such a level?'

'I can't see what you mean. If Barry answers, he will be all to me.'

'That's a terrible confession.'

Caroline said, 'A confession?'

'A confession; a terrible confession.'

'Of what?'

'Of weakness, inferiority, of needing the superior conquering sex.'

Caroline began to laugh weakly, 'You make everything so unusual. I want to get married again; that's all. I'm glad to have some women friends.'

She felt she had hurt Nellie and added, 'We were brought up so differently.'

'Yes, we were. I was not brought up with pretty pictures painted on me eyelids.'

'If you're my friend, shouldn't you try to understand me?'

Nellie said bitterly, 'I understand you very well . . .'

CHRISTINA STEAD, *Cotters' England*, 1966

She sat on the floor—that was her first impression of Sally—she sat on the floor with her arms round her knees, smoking a cigarette. Where could it have been? The Mannings'? The Kinloch-Jones's? At some party (where she could not be certain), for she had a distinct recollection of saying to the man she was with, 'Who is *that*?' . . . But all that evening she could not take her eyes off Sally. It was an extraordinary beauty of the kind she most admired, dark, large-eyed, with that quality which, since she hadn't got it herself, she always envied—a sort of abandonment, as if she could say anything, do anything; a quality much commoner in foreigners than in Englishwomen. Sally always said she had French blood in her veins, an ancestor had been with Marie Antoinette, had his head cut off, left a ruby ring . . . They sat up till all hours of the night talking. Sally it was who made her feel, for the first time, how sheltered the life at Bourton was. She knew nothing about sex—nothing about social problems. She had once seen an old man who had dropped dead in a field—she had seen cows just after their calves were born. But Aunt Helena never liked discussion of anything (when Sally gave her William Morris, it had to be wrapped in brown paper). There they sat, hour after hour, talking in her bedroom at the top of the house, talking about life, how they were to reform the world. They meant to found a society to abolish private property, and actually had a letter written, though not sent out. The ideas were Sally's, of course—but very soon she was just as excited—read Plato in bed before breakfast; read Morris; read Shelley by the hour.

Sally's power was amazing, her gift, her personality. There was her way with flowers, for instance. At Bourton they always had stiff little vases all the way down the table. Sally went out, picked hollyhocks, dahlias—all sorts of flowers that had never been seen together—cut their heads off, and made them swim on the top of water in bowls. The effect was extraordinary—coming in to dinner in the sunset. (Of course Aunt Helena thought it wicked to treat flowers like that.) Then she forgot her sponge, and ran along the passage naked. That grim old housemaid, Ellen Atkins, went about grumbling—'Suppose any of the gentlemen had seen?' Indeed she did shock people. She was untidy, Papa said.

The strange thing, on looking back, was the purity, the integrity, of her feeling for Sally. It was not like one's feeling for a man. It was completely disinterested, and besides, it had a quality which could only exist between women, between women just grown up. It was protective, on her side; sprang from a sense of being in league together, a presentiment of something that was bound to part them (they spoke of marriage always as a catastrophe), which led to this chivalry, this protective feeling which was much more on her side than Sally's. For in those days she was completely reckless; did the most idiotic things out of bravado; bicycled round the parapet on the terrace; smoked cigars. Absurd, she was—very absurd. But the charm was overpowering, to her at least, so that she could remember standing in her bedroom at the top of the house holding the hot-water can in her hands and saying aloud, 'She is beneath this roof. . . . She is beneath this roof!'

Virginia Woolf, Mrs Dalloway, 1925

I first met Marianne Moore in the spring of 1934 when I was a senior at Vassar College, through Miss Fanny Borden, the college librarian . . .

I was very frightened, but I put on my new spring suit and took the train to New York. I had never seen a picture of Miss Moore; all I knew was that she had red hair and usually wore a wide-brimmed hat. I expected the hair to be bright red and for her to be tall and intimidating. I was right on time, even a bit early, but she was there before me (no matter how early one arrived, Marianne was always there first) and, I saw at once, not very tall and not in the least intimidating. She was forty-seven, an age that seemed old to me then, and her hair was mixed with white to a faint rust pink, and her rust-pink eyebrows were frosted with white. The large flat black hat was as I'd expected it to be. She wore a blue tweed suit that day and, as she usually did then, a man's 'polo shirt', as they were called, with a black bow at the neck. The effect was quaint, vaguely Bryn Mawr 1909, but stylish at the same time. I sat down and she began to talk.

It seems to me that Marianne talked to me steadily for the next

thirty-five years, but of course that is nonsensical. I was living far from
New York many of those years and saw her at long intervals. She must
have been one of the world's greatest talkers: entertaining, enlightening,
fascinating, and memorable; her talk, like her poetry, was quite different
from anyone else's in the world. I don't know what she talked about at
that first meeting; I wish I had kept a diary. Happily ignorant of the poor
Vassar girls before me who hadn't passed muster, I began to feel less
nervous and even spoke some myself. I had what may have been an
inspiration, I don't know—at any rate, I attribute my great good fortune
in having known Marianne as a friend in part to it. Ringling Bros. and
Barnum & Bailey Circus was making its spring visit to New York and I
asked Miss Moore (we called each other 'Miss' for over two years) if she
would care to go to the circus with me the Saturday after next. I didn't
know that she *always* went to the circus, wouldn't have missed it for
anything, and when she accepted, I went back to Poughkeepsie in the
grimy day coach extremely happy.

Sometimes we went to movies together, to *Kon-Tiki* twice, I recall. I
never attempted to lure her to any dramatic or 'artistic' films. Since Dr
and Mrs Sibley Watson were her dearest friends, she must have seen his
early experimental films, such as *Lot in Sodom*. I heard the sad story of two
young men, however, who when they discovered that she had never seen
Eisenstein's *Potemkin* insisted on taking her. There was a short before
Potemkin, a Walt Disney film; this was when the Disney films still had
charm and humour. After the movies they went to tea and Marianne
talked at length and in detail about the ingenuity of the Disney film, and
nothing more. Finally they asked her what she had thought of *Potemkin*.
Her opinion was brief but conclusive: 'Life,' she said, 'is not like that.'

ELIZABETH BISHOP, from 'Efforts of Affection: A Memoir of
Marianne Moore', *c.*1969

Esther, Liz and Alix, who in Jane Austen's day would never have met at
all, met in Cambridge in 1952. Just before Christmas, when they were up
for interview from their respective schools. Alix was applying to read
English Literature, Liz to read Natural Sciences (with a view to medicine)
and Esther to read Modern Languages. This should have safely prevented any rapport between them, but did not. There were, it is true,
many awkwardnesses in their first communications, for none of them

was much used to speaking to strangers, but this lack of practice was balanced by a strong desire on the part of all three of them to enter upon a new life in which speaking to strangers was possible. Otherwise, each had separately recognized, the future was circumscribed. Somehow, haltingly, over dinner in Hall (chicken, leeks and tinned spaghetti, a mixture delicious to each after years of post-war whale meat and school meals) they lurched into conversation, having found themselves for no good reason sitting together: Liz and Alix discovered that both came from Yorkshire, and that neither played lacrosse, nor had ever seen it being played, and Esther joined the discussion by volunteering that she had herself managed to avoid playing netball for the past three years on the grounds that she was too small. 'I said I was unfairly handicapped, and they let me do extra Latin instead,' she said. The fact that both Liz and Alix seemed to accept that extra Latin might be preferable to netball indicated that further interchange might be possible, and they continued to talk, through the fruit tart and custard, of the nature of intellectual and physical education, of matter and spirit, of Descartes (brought up by Esther), of T. S. Eliot (brought up by Alix) and of schizophrenia (brought up by Liz). The matter was abstract, for none of them knew anything other than abstractions, and the tone lofty. It was what they had expected of University, but had not hoped so soon to find.

It would be wrong to give the impression that Liz, Alix and Esther fell into one another's arms with cries of delight when they met again that October, or to suggest that they proved thereafter inseparable. But they were, nevertheless, pleased to rediscover one another, and sat up late on their first evening in Esther's room, which had already begun to put out hints of its later decorative eccentricities. They talked of their summer adventures, of their hopes for the future, but mostly of their own provenance. Liz attempted her first sketch of her mother, her first outline for the outside world of the domestic ghost with which she had lived so long: Alix spoke of her relief at escaping from the small boarding school world in which her parents and her contemporaries all knew one another far too well: Esther conjured up visions of both deprivation and splendour in her own past. They did not know then, were not to know for many years, were never fully to understand what it was that held them together—a sense of being on the margins of English life, perhaps, a sense of being outsiders, looking in from a cold street through a lighted window into a warm lit room that later might prove to be their own? Removed from the mainstream by a mad mother, by a deviant ideology, by refugee status and the war-sickness of Middle Europe? None of this would have meant anything to them, then, as they drank their Nescafé, which in those days came not in granules in jars but in powder in tins with brown, cream and white labels: tins which cost 2s.6d. each. They thought they found one another interesting. And so they became friends.

Liz, Alix, Esther. No, it was not an unbroken friendship, they did not become inseparable; they had distant patches, patches of estrangement that lasted for years at times, when they met rarely, or distantly. Alix and Esther did not care to see much of Charles, nor he of them, as we have seen, and there were periods when the Liz–Charles alliance was dominant in Liz's life and excluded other interests. Alix sometimes removed herself into her work, sometimes simply went silent, and answered the telephone forbiddingly. Esther went abroad for months at a time, or took up a new acolyte who absorbed her attention for a while. But by the end of 1979, when this account opens, they had settled down into what looked like being a semi-permanent pattern. They would meet for an evening meal, once a week, once a fortnight, once a month—if a monthly gap occurred, each would feel the need for apology, explanation. They met alone, without their men, as over the years they more often than not had done: a pattern of relationship that was considered mildly eccentric by some, mildly avant-garde by others, but to themselves was natural.

They would eat, drink and talk. They exchanged ideas. Sometimes they exchanged them so successfully that a year later Alix would be putting forward a proposition that she had energetically refuted when Liz had proposed it a year earlier: only to find that Liz, influenced by Alix, had subsequently shifted her ground and herself rejected it. It can only have been through Esther that Liz and Alix began to look at paintings at all, that the Albers' squares hung on the Harley Street stairs. Some of their notions swam, unallocated, in the space between them. The origins of some of their running jokes had been forgotten.

Their professional worlds overlapped and, between them, their frame of reference was quite wide, although they had been educated at the same college of the same university.

As their professional worlds overlap, so do their diversions—or one, at least, of their diversions. They share, perhaps surprisingly, a love of walking, of the English countryside. . . .

Men are not usually invited. Charles is a sporting man, or was once a sporting man, but he is not a walker. Esther's friends have rarely been seen out of doors, even by Esther. Brian has accompanied them once or twice, for Brian loves to walk, but the women tease him about his walking boots. 'How can you lift your feet up, in those great things?' they mockingly wonder. They refuse to let him carry the picnic in his rucksack. So Brian does not often go, although they sometimes invite him. Alix has a photograph, taken by Brian on one of these expeditions; it shows the three of them crouching under a hedge, in the roots of hawthorns, in driving rain, eating a wet sandwich. None of them is looking at the camera: they are looking in different directions, wetly, miserably. Liz has her back to Alix; Esther is sitting some way away staring at the ground. They are very fond of this dismal photograph: the essence of the English landscape, Esther declares. The essence of togetherness.

Margaret Drabble, The Radiant Way, 1987

At M—— we arrived in a few hours; and on sending in our names were immediately admitted to Sophia, the Wife of Edward's freind. After having been deprived during the course of 3 weeks of a real freind (for such I term your Mother) imagine my transports at beholding one, most truly worthy of the Name. Sophia was rather above the middle size; most elegantly formed. A soft languor spread over her lovely features, but increased their Beauty—. It was the Charectarestic of her Mind—. She was all sensibility and Feeling. We flew into each others arms and after having exchanged vows of mutual Freindship for the rest of our Lives, instantly unfolded to each other the most inward secrets of our Hearts—. We were interrupted in the delightfull Employment by the entrance of Augustus, (Edward's freind) who was just returned from a solitary ramble.

Never did I see such an affecting Scene as was the meeting of Edward and Augustus.

'My Life! my Soul!' (exclaimed the former) 'My adorable angel!' (replied the latter) as they flew into each others arms. It was too pathetic for the feelings of Sophia and myself—We fainted alternately on a sofa.

Jane Austen, aged about fifteen, Love and Freindship

'A little *change of companionship* is good for *everybody*. I've known so many *happy friendships* spoilt by people seeing *too much* of one another.'

'They couldn't have been *real* friendships, then,' asserted the girl, dogmatically. 'Mary and I are *absolutely* happy together.'

'Still,' said Miss Climpson, 'if you don't mind an *old woman* giving you a word of warning, I should be inclined not to keep the bow *always* bent. Suppose Miss Whittaker, for instance, wanted to go off and have a day in Town on her own, say—or go to stay with friends—you would have to learn not to mind that.'

'Of course I shouldn't mind. Why—' she checked herself. 'I mean, I'm quite sure that Mary would be every bit as loyal to me as I am to her.'

'That's right,' said Miss Climpson. 'The longer I live, my dear, the more *certain* I become that *jealousy* is the most *fatal* of feelings. The Bible calls it "cruel as the grave", and I'm sure that is so. *Absolute* loyalty, without jealousy, is the essential thing.'

'Yes. Though naturally one would hate to think that the person one was really friends with was putting another person in one's place . . . Miss Climpson, you do believe, don't you, that a friendship ought to be "fifty-fifty"?'

'That is the ideal friendship, I suppose,' said Miss Climpson, thoughtfully, 'but I think it is a *very rare thing*. Among women, that is. I doubt very much if I've ever seen an example of it. *Men*, I believe, find it easier to give and take in that way—probably because they have so many outside interests.'

'Men's friendships—oh yes! I know one hears a lot about them. But half the time, I don't believe they're *real* friendships at all. Men can go off for years and forget all about their friends. And they don't really confide in one another. Mary and I tell each other all our thoughts and feelings. Men seem just content to think each other good sorts without ever bothering about their inmost selves.'

'Probably that's why their friendships last so well,' replied Miss Climpson. 'They don't make such demands on one another.'

DOROTHY L. SAYERS, *Unnatural Death*, 1927

A good friendship, strange to say, has little place for mutual consolations and ministrations. Friendship breathes a more rugged air. In sorrow the silent pressure of the hand speaks the emotions, and lesser griefs and misfortunes are ignored or glossed over. The fatal facility of women's friendships, their copious outpourings of grief to each other, their sharing of wounds and sufferings, their half-pleased interest in misfortune—all this seems of a lesser order than the robust friendship of men, who console each other in a much more subtle, even intuitive way—by a constant pervading sympathy which is felt rather than expressed. For the true atmosphere of friendship is a sunny one. Griefs and disappointments do not thrive in its clear, healthy light. When they do appear, they take on a new color. The silver lining appears, and we see even our own personal mistakes and chagrins as whimsical adventures. It is almost impossible seriously to believe in one's bad luck or failures or incapacity while one is talking with a friend. One achieves a sort of transfiguration of personality in those moments.

RANDOLPH BOURNE, 'The Excitement of Friendship'

Lovelace to Belford

But thinkest thou (and yet I think thou dost) that there is any-thing in these high flights among the Sex? Verily, Jack, these vehement friendships are nothing but chaff and stubble, liable to be blown away by the very wind that raises them. Apes! mere apes of *us!* they think the word *friendship* has a pretty sound with it; and it is much talked of; a fashionable word: And so, truly, a single woman, who thinks she has a Soul, and knows that she wants something, would be thought to have found a fellow-soul for it in her own Sex. But I repeat, that the word is a *mere* word, the thing a *mere* name with them; a cork-bottomed shuttle-cock, which they are fond of striking to and fro, to make one another glow in the frosty weather of a Single State; but which, when a *man* comes in between the pretended *inseparables*, is given up, like their Music, and other maidenly amusements; which, nevertheless, may be necessary to keep the pretty rogues out of active mischief. They then, in short, having caught the *fish*, lay aside the *net*.

. . . this I pronounce, as a truth, which all experience confirms; that friendship between women never holds to the sacrifice of capital gratifications, or to the endangering of life, limb, or estate, as it often does in our nobler Sex.

Clarissa to Anna

What pain, my dearest friend, does your kind solicitude for my welfare give me! How much more binding and tender are the Ties of pure Friendship, and the Union of Like minds, than the Ties of Nature! Well might the Sweet Singer of Israel, when he was carrying to the utmost extent the praises of the friendship between him and his beloved friend, say, that the Love of Jonathan to him was wonderful; that it surpassed the *Love of women!* What an exalted idea does it give of the Soul of Jonathan, sweetly attempered for the sacred band, if we may suppose it but equal to that of my Anna Howe for her fallen Clarissa!—But, altho' I can glory in your kind Love for me, think, my dear, what concern must fill a mind, not ungenerous, when the obligation lies all *on one side*.

Colonel Morden to Belford
There never was a firmer and nobler friendship in women, than that between my dear Cousin and Miss Howe, to which this wretched man has given a period.

Friendship, generally speaking, Mr Belford, is too fervent a flame for female minds to manage: A light, that but in few of their hands burns steady, and often hurries the Sex into flight and absurdity. Like other extremes, it is hardly ever durable. Marriage, which is the highest state of friendship, generally absorbs the most vehement friendships of female to female; and that whether the wedlock be happy, or not.

What female mind is capable of two fervent friendships at the same time?

This I mention as a *general observation:* But the friendship that subsisted between these two Ladies affords a remarkable exception to it: Which I account for from those qualities and attainments in *both*, which, were they more common, would furnish more exceptions still in favour of the Sex.

Both had an *enlarged*, and even a *liberal* education: Both had minds thirsting after virtuous knowlege: Great readers both: Great writers —(And *early familiar writing* I take to be one of the greatest openers and improvers of the mind, that man or woman can be employed in.) Both generous. High in fortune; therefore above that dependence each on the other, that frequently destroys the familiarity which is the cement of friendship. Both excelling in *different ways*, in which neither sought to envy the other. Both blessed with clear and distinguishing faculties; with solid sense; and from their first intimacy . . . each seeing something in the other to *fear*, as well as to *love*; yet making it an indispensable condition of their friendship, each to tell the other of her failings; and to be thankful for the freedom taken. One by nature *gentle*; the other *made so*, by her *love* and *admiration* of her exalted friend—Impossible that there could be a friendship better calculated for duration.

SAMUEL RICHARDSON, *Clarissa*, 1747–8

If one could be friendly with women, what a pleasure—the relationship so secret & private compared with relations with men. Why not write about it? truthfully?

VIRGINIA WOOLF, *Diary*, 1 November 1924

Between Men and Women

THOUGH experts have done their assiduous best to separate friendship from love, our efforts to exclude the latter have not met with total success. Where is the dividing line? Not inevitably at the bedroom door.

La Bruyère maintains that amicable relations between the sexes, being neither 'genuine' friendship nor (that greater or lesser thing) love, constitute a class of their own. Montaigne has doubts, expressed somewhat obscurely, concerning the stability of such relations in view of the seductive power of the 'corporal senses', and Sydney Smith, though apparently himself an exception to the rule he hints at, thinks that, given the manners of the age, friendship between men and women is (perhaps like the immortality of the soul) too good to be believed. Early this century, the Spanish-born American philosopher George Santayana pointed to a subtler obstacle: friends are generally of the same sex, 'for when men and women agree, it is only in their conclusions; their reasons are always different'. Conclusions matter in both love and friendship, but love inclines to spend less time on reasons.

Cornelius Whur had no reservations, but has rarely been taken seriously; it seems that no one has ever queried, not even in our meanly suspicious times, the nature of his female friend's accomplishments and charms. Most likely they coincided with the 'endearing elegance of female friendship' which the old astronomer in *Rasselas* sadly confessed to having missed.

The relationship between Tchaikovsky and Nadezhda von Meck never slid into passion; for one thing, they never met in the flesh. The case of Frederica in A. S. Byatt's novel is virtually the opposite: she wanted to be a friend, not a girl-friend, and hoped to slide into friendship by way of sex. William Penn's reflection, that difference of sex was of no account 'since in Souls there is none: And they are the Subjects of Friendship', would have been of little help; the souls she desired to cultivate were reluctant to yield themselves up, or scared to.

A recurrent complaint has it that whereas male friends are content to take you as you are, women usually want to change and improve you. In *Orthodoxy* (1909) Chesterton extended the charge: 'A man's friend likes him but leaves him as he is: his wife loves him and is always trying to turn him into somebody else.'

Yet there are stirring examples on record: Pope (very much, one might have thought, a man's man) and the Blounts, and Walpole and the Berrys, a pair of sisters whose charms were of remarkable durability. Most touching is the friendship between John Masefield and Audrey Napier-Smith; it was also a friendship between old and young: 'Do not ever think that if the head becomes stupider the heart is deader.' The 'rather grim piece of work' that prevented Masefield from writing at greater length in his last letter was the job of dying.

> Friendship's an abstract of Love's noble flame.
>   'Tis love refined, and purged from all its dross,
>   'Tis next to angel's love, if not the same,
>   As strong as passion is, though not so gross . . .

Thus Katherine Philips. For the greater part, the judges gathered here place friendship above love: it is more serious-minded ('founded on principle'), a partnership of equals, tolerant, neither violent nor invasive, it lasts longer and age is less apt to wither it. According to British authorities, 'L'amitié est l'amour sans ailes' is a French proverb, whereas the French attribute the saying to Byron. At face value it seems to mean that friendship is earthbound, while love, supernal, soars aloft. For Byron, however, what love's wings do is carry it off, so that 'no trace of thee remains behind', except for pain. In an enigmatic variation, the brothers Hare, Julius Charles and Augustus William, state in their *Guesses at Truth* (1827): 'Friendship is Love, without either flowers or veil.'

Friendship needs its champions, for when love appears at the door it often flies out of the window. 'In love, who respects friend?' asks Proteus in *The Two Gentlemen of Verona*. And 'Friendship is constant in all things,' says Claudio in *Much Ado About Nothing*, 'save in the office and affairs of love.' The fate of Tristan and Isolde shows the danger in wooing by proxy, and while Claudio happens to be mistaken on the occasion in question, the story of Palamon and Arcite indicates some truth in the generalization, 'Love is a greater law.' Friendship, as C. S. Lewis perceived, is not conspicuously biological.

A female character in Gay's *Dione* (1720) asks, 'Who shall compare love's mean and gross desire / To the chaste zeal of friendship's sacred fire?', but a jealous male alleges, 'A woman's friendship ever ends in love.' The consensus of opinion is that while friendship may easily turn to love, the reverse will never happen, the assumption being that when love dies, it is succeeded only by hatred, contempt, or apathy. At best, as a line of Peter Porter's has it, 'Proud lovers end as pallid friends.' Mme de Sévigné appears as a phenomenon, a veritable nonpareil, since her would-be lovers were able to reconcile themselves to remaining merely good friends. The lovers could take no credit for this; the virtue lay elsewhere.

———

Like a French poem is life; being only perfect in structure
When with the masculine rhymes mingled the feminine are.

HENRY WADSWORTH LONGFELLOW, 'Elegiac Verse', VII, 1882

A man needs something which is more than friendship and yet is not love as it is generally understood. This something nevertheless a woman only can give.

MARK RUTHERFORD, *Last Pages from a Journal*

The company of fair and society of honest women is likewise a sweet commerce for me: *Nam nos quoque oculus eruditos habemus*, 'For we also have learned eyes.' If the mind have not so much to solace herself as in the former, the corporal senses, whose part is more in the second, bring it to a proportion near unto the other: although in mine opinion not equal. But it is a society wherein it behoveth a man somewhat to stand upon his guard: and especially those that are of a strong constitution, and whose body can do much, as in me. In my youth I heated myself therein and was very violent: and endured all the rages and furious assaults which Poets say happen to those who, without order or discretion, abandon themselves over-loosely and riotously unto it.

MONTAIGNE, 'Of Three Commerces or Societies'

Friendships should be formed with persons of all ages and conditions, and with both sexes . . . It is a great happiness to form a sincere friendship with a woman; but a friendship among persons of different sexes rarely or ever takes place in this country. The austerity of our manners hardly admits of such a connection;—compatible with the most perfect innocence, and a source of the highest possible delight to those who are fortunate enough to form it.

SYDNEY SMITH; in *A Memoir*, by his daughter, Lady Holland, 1855

. . . to say the truth, I do not perceive that inferiority of understanding which the levity of rakes, the dullness of men of business, or the austerity of the learned, would persuade us of in women. As for my woman, I declare I have found none of my own sex capable of making juster observations on life, or of delivering them more agreeably; nor do I believe any one possessed of a faithfuller or braver friend. And sure as this friendship is sweetened with more delicacy and tenderness, so is it confirmed by dearer pledges than can attend the closest male alliance; for what union can be so fast as our common interest in the fruits of our embraces?

HENRY FIELDING, *Joseph Andrews*, 1742

Friendship can last between people of different sexes, even exempt from all grossness. However, a woman always regards a man as a man, and reciprocally a man regards a woman as a woman. Such a relationship is neither passion nor pure friendship: it forms a class apart.

JEAN DE LA BRUYÈRE, 'Du Coeur', *Les Caractères*, 1688

Women are perfectly able to make friends with a man; but to maintain the friendship perhaps requires the assistance of a slight physical antipathy.

NIETZSCHE, *Human, All Too Human*

ST FRANCIS AND ST CLARE

This wonderful woman, clear alike in name and in deed, belonged to a family of no small lustre of the city of Assisi. Having been first a fellow citizen of the Blessed Francis on earth, she afterwards came to reign with him on high . . .

Hearing of the now famous name of Francis, who, like a new man, had restored by new virtues the path of perfection forgotten in the world, Clare at once was desirous to hear and see him, being moved thereto by the Father of Spirits, whose first promptings both had followed, albeit in a different manner. And Francis, struck by the fair fame of so favoured a maiden, was not less wishful to see her and hold converse with her, for, being wholly eager for spoils and having come to depopulate the kingdom of this world, he would fain in some way snatch this noble prey from the wicked world and restore her to her God. Francis visited Clare and she more often visited him, so ordering the times of their visits that their holy meetings might neither become known by man nor disparaged by public rumour. For, accompanied by a single confidential companion, the girl, going forth from her paternal home in secret, frequently visited the man of God: to her his words seemed a flame and his deeds more than human.

THOMAS OF CELANO, *The Life of St Clare*, c.1255–61; tr. Paschal Robinson, OFM

According to one legend, Francis and Clare were journeying together from Spello to Assisi and went into a house to ask for a little bread and water on their way. They noticed the people looking askance at them and heard them making covert allusions to their mutual relationship. They continued their way through the snow-covered countryside, for it was winter. Twilight fell. St Francis suddenly said: 'Sister, did you understand what these people were saying?' St Clare did not answer, for her distress was such that she dared not speak. 'It is time we should part,' continued the father. 'You will reach the convent before nightfall and I will go on alone, following where God leads me.' St Clare knelt down in the middle of the road, prayed a while and then walked on with bowed head without looking round. But after some time she found herself in a wood and had not the heart to continue on her way without a word of consolation or leave-taking, so she waited for St Francis and when he came up to her she said: 'Father, when shall we meet again?' The blessed father replied: 'When summer returns and the roses blossom again.' Then a miracle took place, and all the juniper bushes around and the frosty hedges were covered with roses. When St Clare had recovered from her amazement, she went and picked a bunch of roses and gave them to St Francis. And, so says the legend, the Saints parted no more.

Otto Karrer, *St Francis of Assisi: The Legends and Lauds*, 1947; tr. N. Wydenbruck

S^r
In my opinion you doe not understande the Law's of freindship right; tis generaly beleeved it owes it's birth to an agreement & conformity of humors, and that it lives no longer then tis preserved by the Mutuall care of those that bred it, tis wholy Governde by Equality, and can there bee such a thing in it, as a distinction of Power? noe sure, if wee are friends wee must both comande & both obay alike . . . I meant to chide you for the shortnesse of your last letter and to tell you that if you doe not take the same liberty of telling mee of all my faults, I shall not think you are my freind. In Earnest tis true you must use to tell mee freely of any thing you see amisse in mee, whither I am too stately or not enough, what humor pleases you and what do's not, what you would have mee doe & what avoyde, with the same freedom that you would use to a person over whome you had an absolute Power and were concerned in; these are the Laws of ffriendship as I understande them, and I beleeve I understande them right, for I am Certaine noe body can bee more perfectly a friend then I am Yours

My B. [brother] would perswade mee there is noe such thing in the worlde as a constante friendship, People (hee say's) that marry with great passion for one another, as they think, come afterwards to loose it they know not how, besydes the multitude of such as are false and meane it. I cannot bee of his opinion, (though I confesse there are too many Examples on't), I have alway's beleeved there might bee a friendship perfect like that you discribe and mee thinks I finde somthing like it in my selfe, but sure tis not to bee taught, it must come Naturaly to those that have it, and those that have it not can ne're bee made to understand it . . . Last night, I was in the Garden till Eleven a clock, it was the sweetest night that ere I saw, the Garden looked soe well, and the Jessomin smelt beyond all perfumes, and yet I was not pleased. The place had all the Charmes it used to have when I was most sattisfied with it and had you bin there I should have liked it much more than Ever I did, but that not being it was noe more to mee then the next feilde, and only served mee for a place to resve [dream] in without disturbance.

> DOROTHY OSBORNE, letters to William Temple, 2 July and 16 July 1653

Dear Ladies,—I think myself obligd to desire, you would not put off any Diversion you may find, in the prospect of seeing me on Saturday, which is very uncertain. I Take this occasion to tell you once for all, that I design no longer to be a constant Companion when I have ceas'd to be an agreable one. You only have had, as my friends, the priviledge of knowing my Unhappiness; and are therefore the only people whom my Company must necessarily make melancholy. I will not bring myself to you at all hours, like a Skeleton, to come across your diversions, and dash your pleasures: Nothing can be more shocking than to be perpetually meeting the Ghost of an old acquaintance, which is all you can ever see of me.

You must not imagine this to proceed from any Coldness, or the least decrease of Friendship to you. If You had any Love for me, I should be always glad to gratify you with an Object that you thought agreable. But as your regard is Friendship & Esteem; those are things that are as well, perhaps better, preservd Absent than Present. A Man that you love is a joy to your eyes at all times; a Man that you Esteem is a solemn kind of thing, like a Priest, only wanted at a certain hour to do his Office: Tis like Oyl in a Sallet, necessary, but of no manner of Taste. And you may depend upon it, I will wait upon you on every real occasion, at the first summons, as long as I live.

Let me open my whole heart to you: I have some times found myself inclined to be in love with you: and as I have reason to know from your Temper & Conduct how miserably I should be used in that circumstance, it is worth my while to avoid it: It is enough to be Disagreable, without adding Fool to it, by constant Slavery. I have heard indeed of Women that have had a kindness for Men of my Make; but it has been after Enjoyment, never before; and I know to my Cost you have had no Taste of that Talent in me, which most Ladies would not only Like better, but Understand better, than any other I have.

I love you so well that I tell you the truth, & that has made me write this Letter. I will see you less frequently this winter, as you'll less want company: When the Gay Part of the world is gone, I'll be ready to stop the Gap of a vacant hour whenever you please. Till then I'll converse with those who are more Indifferent to me, as You will with those who are more Entertaining. I wish you every pleasure God and Man can pour upon ye; and I faithfully promise you all the good I can do you, which is, the Service of a Friend, who will ever be Ladies, Entirely Yours.

> POPE, letter to Teresa and Martha Blount, ?late 1717; the unhappiness referred to was probably caused by the loss of 'one of the best of Fathers'

I am not a little disappointed and mortified at the post bringing me no letter from you today; you promised to write on the road . . .

I passed so many evenings of the last fortnight with you, that I almost preferred it to our two honeymoons, and consequently am the more sensible to the deprivation—and how dismal was *Sunday* evening compared to those of last autumn! If you both felt as I do, we might surpass any events in the annals of Dunmow: Oh! what a prodigy it would be if a husband and *two wives* should present themselves and demand the flitch of bacon on swearing that not one of the three in a year and a day had wished to be unmarried! For my part I know that my affection has done nothing but increase; though, were there but one of you, I should be ashamed of being so strongly attached at my age. Being in love with both, I glory in my passion, and think it a proof of my sense. Why should not two affirmatives make a negative, as well as the reverse? and then a double love will be wisdom—for what is wisdom in reality but a negative? It exists but by correcting folly; and when it has peevishly prevailed on us to abstain from something we have a mind to, it gives itself airs, and inaction pretends to be a personage, a nonentity sets up for a figure of importance. It is the case of most of those phantoms called virtues, which by smothering poor vices, claim a reward as thief-takers do. You know I have a partiality for drunkenness, though I never practised it: it is a reality—but what is sobriety, only the absence of drunkenness!—however, *mes chères femmes*, I make a difference between women and men, and do not extend my doctrine to your sex. Everything is excusable in us, and nothing in you—and pray remember, that I will not lose my flitch of bacon—*though*.

My anxiety increases daily, for still I have no letter. You cannot all three be ill, and if anyone is, I should flatter myself, another would have written, or if any accident has happened. Next to your having met with some ill luck, I should be mortified at being forgotten so suddenly. Of any other vexation I have no fear. So much goodness and good sense as you both possess, would make me perfectly easy, if I were really your husband. I must then suspect some accident, and shall have no tranquillity till a letter puts me out of pain. Jealous I am not, for two young ladies cannot have run away with their father to Gretna Green. Hymen, O, Hymenaee, bring me good news tomorrow . . .

> HORACE WALPOLE, letter to Mary and Agnes Berry, 23/26 June
> 1789

I have been threescore years and ten looking for a society that I perfectly like, and at last there dropped out of the clouds into Lady Herries' room two young gentlewomen, who I so little thought were sent thither on purpose for me, that when I was told they were the charming Miss Berrys I would not even go to the side of the chamber where they sat. But as Fortune never throws anything at one's head without hitting one, I soon found that the charming Berrys were precisely *ce qu'il me fallait*, and that tho' young enough to be my great-granddaughters, lovely enough to turn the heads of all our youths, and sensible enough, if said youths have any brains, to set all their heads to rights again,—yes, sweet damsels, I have found that you can bear to pass half your time with an ante-diluvian without discovering any ennui or disgust, tho' his greatest merit towards you is that he is not one of those old fools who fancy they are in love in their dotage. I have no such vagary, tho' I am not sorry that some folks think I am so absurd, since it frets their selfishness.

> HORACE WALPOLE, letter to Mary and Agnes Berry, 17
> September 1793

I dine on Saturday with the good Widow T——, and blush to say that I have no disposable day before the 26th; by which time you will, I presume, be plucking gooseberries in the suburban regions of Richmond. But think not, O Berries! that that distance, or any other, of latitude or longitude, shall prevent me from following you, plucking you, and eating you. Whatever pleasure men find in the raspberry, in the strawberry, in the coffee-berry, all these pleasures are to my taste concentrated in the May-Fair Berries. Ever theirs,

> SYDNEY SMITH, letter to Mary and Agnes Berry, June 1843

Child of my parents! Sister of my soul!
Thanks in sincerest verse have been elsewhere
Poured out for all the early tenderness
Which I from thee imbibed: and 'tis most true
That later seasons owed to thee no less;
For, spite of thy sweet influence and the touch
Of kindred hands that opened out the springs
Of genial thought in childhood, and in spite
Of all that unassisted I had marked
In life or nature of those charms minute
That win their way into the heart by stealth,
(Still to the very going-out of youth)
I too exclusively esteemed *that* love,
And sought *that* beauty, which, as Milton sings,
Hath terror in it. Thou didst soften down
This over-sternness; but for thee, dear Friend!
My soul, too reckless of mild grace, had stood
In her original self too confident,
Retained too long a countenance severe;
A rock with torrents roaring, with the clouds
Familiar, and a favourite of the stars:
But thou didst plant its crevices with flowers,
Hang it with shrubs that twinkle in the breeze,
And teach the little birds to build their nests
And warble in its chambers. At a time
When Nature, destined to remain so long
Foremost in my affections, had fallen back
Into a second place, pleased to become
A handmaid to a nobler than herself,
When every day brought with it some new sense
Of exquisite regard for common things,
And all the earth was budding with these gifts
Of more refined humanity, thy breath,
Dear Sister! was a kind of gentler spring
That went before my steps.

WILLIAM WORDSWORTH, *The Prelude*, completed 1805

When my father died in 1885 my mother nearly went mad with grief. She
shut herself up, refusing to see her friends in a dumb despair.

One afternoon Oscar [Wilde] called: I told him of her desperate state, and he said he must see her. She stubbornly refused, and I went back to him to say I could not prevail on her. 'But she must see me,' he replied. 'She must. Tell her I shall stay here till she does.' Back I went, and for a few minutes my mother sat, crying and wringing her hands, and saying 'I can't. Send him away.' Then she arose and went into the room where he was waiting, crying as she went. I saw Oscar take both her hands and draw her to a chair, beside which he set his own; then I left them alone. He stayed a long time, and before he went I heard my mother laughing.

When he had gone she was a woman transformed. He had made her talk; had asked questions about my father's last illness and allowed her to unburden her heart of those torturing memories. Gradually he had talked of my father, of his music, of the possibilities of a memorial exhibition of his pictures. Then, she didn't know how, he had begun to tell her all sorts of things which he contrived to make interesting and amusing. 'And then I laughed,' she said. 'I thought I should never laugh again.'

I should not have been surprised if, after my father's death, Oscar had not been near us for a while. But he not only came, he exercised all his gifts, his insight, his patience, his wit, to draw the poison from the wound of a woman not young, not socially important; a woman who had been hospitable to him and for whom he felt a simple affection.

H. M. SWANWICK (Helena Sickert), *I Have Been Young*, 1935

Women always find me antipathetic, before they know me. (Let us not speak about men: they detest me and I detest them; I have no friends. And even my dearest friends are women.)

Women always find me antipathetic; but later they love me. You too will love me . . .

On one occasion, last year, we—Vallini, Bassi, Vugliano, and others —were in the room where the newspapers are, you—alone—in the one with the magazines, standing, upright, with your arm stretched out, leafing through the reviews on the table. And among us this is more or less what was being said:

—She is beautiful.

—Yes, she is beautiful!

—But she writes.

—And not badly . . .

—Who is that D. M. who introduces her work?

—Dino Mantovani.

—He compares her to Gaspara Stampa and to Sappho . . .

—He must know her.

—Evidently: I bet he's paying court to her.

—And she?

—And she, like all women, perhaps permits it just enough so that she can make use of him when necessary.

—But is it certain?

—Not certain. I'm guessing. But it is reasonable to infer it. For us who are not young ladies, there is no critic who would make every effort like that.

—And she is a very respectable lady from a very good family . . .

—They certainly say that she is respectable.

—She is, she is: I guarantee it: I know the family.

—What a pity!

—What is?

—That she is a young lady.

—And that she is respectable.

—What a pity: she is really beautiful!

—If only she were illiterate.

—But she writes!

—Women who write really are detestable!

—If they write badly they annoy us.

—If they write well they humiliate us.

—Shut up! She's coming this way.

And you, my Friend, passed among us, proud dignified tranquil. But certainly as you passed you sensed something which displeased you; like a certain hostility—(no: hostility is too much)—but an indefinable coldness; and in the air you still felt there was something unfavourable, ironically petty and vulgar (as all of us men are petty and vulgar, deep down. All of us: do not deceive yourself). I have put this recollection into dialogue-form for you, my friend, in order to define that indefinable feeling which was separating us and which you sensed and which I sensed: it was the surroundings, the vulgar irony of the surroundings.

On the other hand, now that we are distant from each other—I am seriously ill and exiled from the city for two or three years: perhaps more—we are well able to be friends. You have spoken to me about us corresponding. Most certainly! But I wish to be honest right from the start, as tradesmen do: I am not a spiritual friend: I am at best a mediocre cerebral interlocutor . . . I do not believe in the soul and I have a deep contempt for my spirit and yours, to which I do not attach any more importance than to the energy which moves an earthworm and the chlorophyll which colours a stalk of grass: and that very song of yours, so disdainful even in passion, so high and pure and chaste, is only the cry of your agitated modesty, shrinking under the lash of instinct, of that instinct which provides for the continuation of the species . . . Do you accept as a friend a man who says this to you?

Be warned that my way of thinking will lead me sometimes to write to you things of a coarseness such as to border on impropriety . . . Will you be so highminded as to forgive me?

And start to forgive me for the prolixity of this letter—we are on the third sheet of paper, I think!—Today my friends from Genoa were here, as they often are, journalists and poets, all soulmates and all ill of our same illness, my good Friend.

We went on a boat, as usual, we recited verses, as usual, and we also, an unaccustomed pleasure, had a good blow-out on bananas and medlars. We let ourselves drift all the day, until it was twilight, on a sea the colour of nothing, so that we seemed to be flying.

I recited, and without the book, several of your sonnets: I think I know about fifteen by heart, perfectly and without having studied them. Little by little I shall absorb the whole volume.

> GUIDO GOZZANO, letter to Amalia Guglielminetti, 10 June 1907;
> tr. J. G. Nichols

Yes: I was mean not to give you my book. I wrote to you about it before you wrote to me—blowing me up—which you did with a vengeance. I was mean. I had to buy all the copies I gave, and did not think your beaux—(I cannot remember how to spell the word) worth 24/-. There! I have owned the fact, you may make the most of it. But, dear Kate, I would give you ten times twenty four shillings ten times over in any more pleasant way, fitting for yourself. One gives presentation copies to old fogies & such like. When you write a book, you will of course give one to me. You are a young lady.—A ring, a lock of my hair, or a rose-bud would be the proper present for you: not two huge volumes weighing no end of pounds. Believe me, I would have been very wrong to send it to you . . .

Tell me whom you see, socially, & what you are doing socially and as regards work. I didn't at all understand how you are living, where—with whom—or on what terms. But I don't know that it matters. How little we often know in such respects of those we love dearest. Of what I am at home, you can have no idea;—not that I mean to imply that I am of those you love dearest. And yet I hope I am.

> ANTHONY TROLLOPE, letter to Kate Field, 23 August 1862; in his *Autobiography* Trollope wrote of this American journalist: 'In the last fifteen years she has been, out of my own family, my most chosen friend. She is a ray of light to me, from which I can always strike a spark by thinking of her.'

Your kind reply to my letter gave me a deep pleasure such as I have not felt for a long time, but you know the common characteristic of human nature: the more good you receive, the more you want, and though I promised you I would not resort to self-indulgence, I am beginning to doubt my own strength, for I am permitting myself to turn to you with a big request that may seem oddly disagreeable to you, though surely a person who lives as ascetically as I do will inevitably arrive at the conclusion that everything that people call social relationships, the rules of society, proprieties, and such-like, has become, as far as she is concerned, but a sound without meaning. I do not know fully your view on this matter, Pyotr Ilich, but from some of my observations of you, it seems to me that you least of all will condemn me for this; if I am mistaken, then I sincerely ask you to tell me openly and bluntly, and after that to turn down my request which is this: give me your photograph; I have got two of them, but I want to have one from you. I want to search out in your face those inspirations, those feelings under the influence of which you compose your music which carries a being into a world of sensations, expectations and desires that life can never satisfy. . . . The first of your works that I heard was *The Tempest*. I cannot describe the impression that it made on me; for several days I was as one delirious, and I could do nothing to free myself from this state. I must tell you that I cannot separate the musician from the man, and in him, the servant of such a high art, even more than in other people, I wish and expect to find those human qualities which I worship. My ideal man is certainly a musician, but in him talent must be equally matched by his human qualities; only then will he make a deep and complete impression . . . And so, as soon as I had recovered from the first impression of your work, I straightway wanted to know what sort of man had written such a piece. I began to seek out opportunities to discover as much as I could about you, never missed any occasion when I might hear something, paid attention to the opinion of the public, to individual judgements, to every remark —and on this I will tell you that often what they censured in you sent me into raptures—everyone has his own taste. Only the other day from a casual conversation I learned of one of your opinions which so delighted me, with which I felt such sympathy that, as it were, you immediately became close to me—or, at any rate, dear to me. It seems to me, you see, that it is not only relationships that make people close, but even more a similarity of opinion, equal capacities for feelings, and an identity of sympathies, so that it is possible to be close when one is far distant.

I am so interested to know everything about you that at almost any time I can tell where you are and, to a certain extent, what you are doing. . . . There was a time when I very much wanted to meet you. Now, however, the more I am enchanted by you, the more I fear acquaintance —I feel I would not be in a condition to begin talking with you —although if we should unexpectedly meet face to face anywhere, I could not behave towards you as to a stranger, and I would hold out my hand to you, though only to press yours—but I should not speak a word. Now I prefer to think of you from a distance, to hear you in your music and to feel myself at one with you in it.

NADEZHDA VON MECK, letter to Tchaikovsky, 19 March 1877

You are quite right, Nadezhda Filaretovna, in supposing that I am in a condition to understand fully the peculiarities of your spiritual organism. I dare to think that you are not mistaken in believing me close to you as a person. Just as you have tried to listen to judgements made by the public on me, so I on my part have not missed an opportunity of learning details of you and your mode of living. I have always been interested in you as a person whose moral temper has many features in common with my own nature. There is certainly one trait that draws us together—that we both suffer from one and the same illness. That illness is misanthropy—but a misanthropy of a particular kind, at the root of which there is absolutely no hatred and contempt for people. People who suffer from this illness have no fear of that injury which can come from the machinations of someone who is close; instead they fear that disenchantment, that yearning for the ideal that follows upon every intimacy. There was a time when I was so oppressed by the yoke of this terror of people that I almost went out of my mind. . . . By now I have emerged sufficiently victorious from this struggle for life to have long ago ceased to be unbearable. I have been saved by work—work that is at the same time enjoyment . . .

From what I have said above, you will easily understand that I am in no way surprised that, loving my music, you are not attempting to make the acquaintance of its author. You fear that you will not find in me those qualities with which your imagination, inclined to idealization, has invested me. And you are quite right. I feel that, on closer acquaintance with me, you would not find that correspondence, that complete harmony between the musician and the man, of which you dream.

> Pyotr Ilich Tchaikovsky, letter to Nadezhda von Meck, 28 March 1877; both letters tr. David Brown

Very well, you shan't meet me in the flesh if you'd rather not. There is something deeply touching in that—did you *never* meet a man who would bear meeting and knowing? Perhaps you're right: Oscar Wilde said of me 'An excellent man: he has no enemies; and none of his friends like him.' And that's quite true: they don't like me; but they are my friends, and some of them love me. If you value a man's regard, *strive* with him. As to *liking*, you like your newspaper—and despise it. I had rather you remembered one thing I said for three days than *liked* me (only) for 300,000,000,000,000,000,000 years.

> George Bernard Shaw, letter to Ellen Terry, 25 September 1896

I know the thing that's most uncommon
    (Envy be silent and attend!);
I know a Reasonable Woman,
    Handsome and witty, yet a Friend.

Not warp'd by Passion, aw'd by Rumour,
    Not grave thro' Pride, or gay thro' Folly,
An equal Mixture of good Humour,
    And sensible soft Melancholy.

'Has she no Faults then (Envy says) Sir?'
  Yes, she has one, I must aver:
When all the World conspires to praise her,
  The Woman's deaf, and does not hear.

            POPE, 'On a Certain Lady at Court', *c.* 1725

In this imperfect, gloomy scene
  Of complicated ill,
How rarely is a day serene,
  The throbbing bosom still!
Will not a beauteous landscape bright,
  Or music's soothing sound,
Console the heart, afford delight,
  And throw sweet peace around?
They may, but never comfort lend
Like an accomplish'd female friend!

With such a friend, the social hour
  In sweetest pleasure glides;
There is in female charms a power
  Which lastingly abides—
The fragrance of the blushing rose,
  Its tints and splendid hue,
Will with the season decompose,
  And pass as flitting dew;
On firmer ties his joys depend
Who has a polish'd female friend!

The pleasures which from thence arise
  Surpass the blooming flower,
For though it opens to the skies,
  It closes in an hour!
Its sweetness is of transient date,
  Its varied beauties cease—
They can no lasting joys create,
  Impart no lasting peace;
While both arise, and duly blend
In an accomplish'd female friend!

As orbs revolve and years recede,
   As seasons onward roll,
The fancy may on beauties feed,
   With discontented soul!
A thousand objects bright and fair
   May for a moment shine,
Yet many a sigh and many a tear
   But mark their swift decline;
While lasting joys the man attend
Who has a faithful female friend!

CORNELIUS WHUR, 'The Female Friend', 1837

The Frederica who conducted experiments in sex in Cambridge was looking for an ideal lover. At one level. At another, she was conducting a battle with the whole male sex. She often said 'I like men', as one might say 'I like strong cheese, or, I like bitter chocolate, or, I like red wine.' She came to pronounce that each relationship was what it was—dancing, sex, talk, friendship—as many as there were men. This was true, and she believed it, but it was not the whole truth. Her behaviour was more dictated by generalizations about men, or Men, than she was at first aware.

Men had their group behaviour. Together they talked about girls as they might talk about motor cars or beer, joking about breast measurements and legs, planning campaigns of seduction like army or teenage gang manoeuvres. For these men women were better or worse, easier or more rarefied sex. Simply. Frederica did the same, at first half-consciously, then with deliberation. She judged and categorized men. Quality of skin, size of backside, texture of hair, skill. Men discussed whether girls would or wouldn't. Frederica furiously categorized those men who could and couldn't. If men wanted 'only' one thing, so could, and would, and did, Frederica Potter. She took some pride in the fact that there was no one who could feel able to refer to her as his girl-friend . . .

It should by now be clear that Frederica was more than once both cruel and destructive. In extenuation it can be argued that she had not been led by custom or by cultural mythology to suppose that men had feelings. Men were deceivers ever, the bad ones, and masterful, the good ones. The world was their world and what she wanted was to live in that world, not to be sought out as a refuge from or adjunct to it.

She might have been instructed by literature. She had read endless descriptions of the shyness and desperation of male first love. But whereas she recognized the humiliation of Lucy Snowe, of Rosamond Lehmann's brave, doomed girls, and the death of the heart, from some fund of ancient knowledge, she did not recognize, or believe in, the professional coquettes or pure young girls, or mysterious animal presences of the male novels. None of these were anything to do with Frederica Potter, who was brisk, businesslike, interested in but not obsessed by sex, and wanted to make friends of the creatures if they would have it. Women in male novels were unreal and it was beyond Frederica's comprehension that young men might suppose she was any or all of these characters . . . When one desperate man whom she found unexciting, apart from an encyclopaedic knowledge of Thomas Mann, burst into tears and said she was mocking him she could only stare, become wholly silent, and go home.

A. S. BYATT, *Still Life*, 1985; the time is the mid-1950s

Oliver Cromwell and Beethoven both
Died in the middle of thunderstorms. Ruth
Didn't know this, but knew Kierkegaard's Dad
Cursed God from a hilltop, or so it was said.
Yet none of these things was at all familiar
To Mary, or Nora, or Helen, or Pamela.

But Pamela knew of some laws of Justinian's,
Helen listened to Schutz and had read *The Virginians*,
And Nora and Mary liked Wallace Stevens,
So in general terms it worked out evens
—Except that none of them, only Amanda,
Knew that Oliver Cromwell had died during thunder.

Still, here were these women with items of knowledge
Picked up in one and another college
—And here am I with not quite all their gaps
In my knowledge of all these high-powered chaps,
Doing well with the female population
And their limited but charming conversation.

ALAN BROWNJOHN, 'Peter Daines at a Party', 1969

And now, my dear Boy, do you be very sensible, and tell me one thing—think of it in your bed, and over your cigar, and for a whole week, and then send me word directly—shall I marry?—I vow to the Lord that I am upon the brink of saying 'Miss —— do you think you could marry me?' to a plain, sensible, girl, without a farthing! There now you have it—. . . Now write me word quickly: lest the deed be done! To be sure, there is one thing: I think it is extremely probable that the girl wouldn't have me: for her parents are very strict in religion, and look upon me as something of a Pagan—When I think of it, I know what your decision will be—NO!—How you would hate to stay with me & my spouse, dining off a mutton chop, and a draught of sour, thin, beer, in a clay-cold country—You would despair—you would forsake me—if I know anything of myself, no wife would ever turn me against you: besides, I think no person that I should like would be apt to dislike you: for I must have a woman of some humour lurking about her somewhere: humour half hidden under modesty—But enough of these things—my paper is done, & I must wash myself, & dress for breakfast . . .

FitzGerald, letter to Thackeray, 29 July 1835

It seems my men friends are all alike; they make themselves, on the whole, soft-mannered towards me; they defer to me also. You are right, I value the friendship of men more than that of women. Do not suppose I have no men friends. I could show you two men who claim me as their heart's best brother; there is another, home for the vacation, who has been with me every available moment—till I am tired, I confess. But of David and Jonathan—it is as impossible as magnificent love between a woman and me. It is like this (I am going to hold forth). You measure a friend by the breadth of his understanding; by understanding I mean that delicate response from the chords of feeling which is involuntary. Various folk vibrate to various frequencies, tones, whatever you like. Now a woman's soul of emotion is not so organized, so distinctly divided and active in part as a man's. Set a woman's soul vibrating in response to your own, and it is her whole soul which trembles with a strong, soft note of uncertain quality. But a man will respond, if he be a friend, to the very chord you strike, with clear and satisfying timbre, responding with a part, not the whole, of his soul. It makes a man much more satisfactory. But then the soul of a man is a stubborn and unwieldy instrument. Ever so many chords are slack, and won't sound; most of the subtle semi-notes are missing; you may call from him the notes of the scale of C, but hardly more; the deep bottom tones, and the shrill, sharp notes at the top which verge on madness, they are all missing, and one must turn to a woman. Set up her response, and the whole range of her chords of feeling vibrates with incoherent frenzy. But better a woman vibrating with incoherent hum than a man altogether dumb, eh? So to make a Jonathan for me, it would take the natures of ten men such as I know to complete the keyboard. Any man might say exactly the same. To make a real wife for me would need a woman with a great range of swift and subtle feeling; a woman whose melody of soul is not numbed by the murmur of her whole soul answering at once, when there is no call for such an answer; a vague, wearying sound; like bees in a great lime tree, hidden altogether, so that the tree seems to be speaking and saying nothing. Women can feel, but often, very often, they do not understand, understand in their souls, I mean.

D. H. LAWRENCE, letter to Blanche Jennings, 20 July 1908

January 31 1907. I reflected sadly today how I tended to squabble with my women-friends. Here have I dropped out of all or nearly all my feminine friendships. I never see Lady P., I hear nothing of Countess B. I have lost sight of B. M. I have insulted M. C., alienated Mrs L., shut up Mrs S.—and so on. Yet I do not squabble with my men-friends . . . I think it is a certain bluntness, frankness, coarseness, which does not offend men, but which aggravates women. The thing which has tended to terminate my women-friendships is that at a certain juncture they begin to disapprove and to criticize my course, and to feel a responsibility to say disagreeable things. One ought to take it smilingly and courteously; and one would, if one liked the sex—but I *don't* like the sex. Their mental processes are obscure to me; I don't like their superficial ways, their mixture of emotion with reason. One's men-friends never criticize, they take one for better and worse. One gets plenty of criticism from foes, and one supplies the harshest condemnation oneself. My own feeling is that one's duty to a friend is to encourage and uplift and compliment and believe in him. Women, I think, when they get interested in one, have a deadly desire to improve one. They think that the privilege of friendship is to criticize; they want deference, they don't want frankness.

A. C. BENSON (1862–1925), *Diary*, ed. Percy Lubbock

[After hearing a radio broadcast of John Masefield's play, Melloney Holtspur, *in November 1952, Audrey Napier-Smith wrote a grateful letter to the author, then aged 74. Thus began a correspondence which lasted until Masefield's death fifteen years later. The two met only five times. Masefield gave Miss Napier-Smith, a violinist with the Hallé Orchestra, the name of 'Reyna' ('hidden in your name'), a Spanish word for 'Queen'.]*

Many thanks for your very kind letter about *Melloney* and my other writings.

I am glad to think they had the happy fortune to give you pleasure.

Might I be allowed, do you think, just to keep the link between us still in being? Writers seldom meet with readers and are grateful to them.

Early December 1952

Your very charming kind letter made me very happy. Thank you. I am so glad to know that you will not be vexed by a book now and then: and much honoured by your liking the photograph . . .

About the 20th [January], when you are to play in Oxford. I have been very ill, and cannot go to hear you play, alas; but we wonder whether you would care to come out just to see us after your concert? Would that be too tiring for you, after playing? We could give you tea.

A reliable woman-driver would bring you here, if the roads should be free of fog, ice and snow. There should be a young moon, and after tea the driver would take you back to Oxford, and get you there by 6 p.m. or so. Please, dear Reader, let me arrange all this; if it will not be too cold or too tiring.

You will not find us terrifying: only too glad to see a new friend who is a musician as well as a reader. We do not play, but have had much fondness for your art, and old age is touched to the quick by youth and loves every sight of it.

January 1953

Friendship is very rare, my dear, & very precious, & grows rarer & more precious in old age, so do not ever think that if the head becomes stupider the heart is deader.

1954

Jowett was Master of Balliol where ACS [Swinburne] was a somewhat unusual undergraduate. He asked ACS to read a play that he had written.

This was *Bothwell*, which ACS read through in (about) 5½ hours of rapturous eloquence. At the end ACS asked what he thought of it. J (in the tale) said that it was this, and then that it was that, but that on the whole, perhaps, might it not be considered long? ACS is said to have said, 'Perhaps you're right.'

During what was left of the night J is said to have reflected that he was dealing with a very impulsive young man, & ought to have spoken with a greater tact, & more emphatic generosity. So he bade ACS come to breakfast, and said, 'Thinking over your play—to me it is not a breath too long. I ought not to have made that comment.'

ACS is said to have looked a little blank, & to have said, 'I'm sorry about that. You see . . . I've burned it.'

Then J looked a little blank, but ACS at once said, 'O, it doesn't matter. I can easily write it again.'

1955

What fun for you to meet old friends, 'vingt ans après', & one who had known Brahms.

One sometimes met men who remembered the past great ones.

I met a man, who had met a lady, who had seen Shelley (he being then un-married).

'What would you do, Mr Shelley, if you had all these children?' This is rather a staggerer for a bachelor, but the poet in him rose upon glittering wings:

'Do with them?' he cried. 'I'd shut them into a room, with tubs of water & bowls of oranges.'

Then I met a man who had met 3 men who had known Keats, & had no new thing from any one of them; & I met a man (among several such) who had known Wm Morris and said, 'It was a treat to hear him swear.'

1958

Please will you, some day, if you can, tell me of this Club named after me (or after someone of my name)?

I have heard of a writer who was told that there was a Club named after him. The Club had an address, a note-paper, & published its proceedings in a little printed magazine written by the members (12 members, I think, all gifted writers).

The author received this magazine for some years & enjoyed it very much & felt that he knew all the 12 members as personal friends.

After a while the Club was disbanded, as Clubs will, & that was that.

But after some years the writer heard that the Club was fictitious.

A man in great sorrow had invented the whole thing to keep himself from going mad; he had written all the Club's proceedings & papers, after inventing the different members, & had kept himself sane all the time. He owned up to the writer, & it makes quite a pleasant story.

1962

Please, I want to say this to you.

You have given me lovely, thoughtful & treasured gifts, leather cases, precious books, a dagger that cuts open all my mail: and you are ever generous & a wonder.

But please, I am coming to an end, & I know that within a few years I shall leave all these things, & I cannot bear to think of your dear gifts going to others.

So, please, may I ask you to give me a letter instead of a gift, in any time of gifts?

1965

I often wonder how primitive people who cannot read or write, manage when they are in love [and apart] as no doubt they often are.

Can their minds communicate, and tell each other, by what we call telepathy?

Even with us, now, in a modern land, our minds can communicate: the distant soul can shake the distant friend's soul and make the longing felt, over untold miles. What our modern minds, often so full of rubbish, can do through the rubbish, primitive minds may do like wild fire: and what can quench wild fire? It does not go at death, but it undergoes a change then . . .

My heart's dear pleasure, bless you for your kind long friendship. I hope I haven't been a great pest.

1966

I thank you for your kind and loving note on this so memorable day [the fourteenth anniversary of their first meeting].

I grieve that I cannot write a fitting note now, having a rather grim piece of work to try to finish.

But my blessing & thanks.

I hope that all is well with you.

20 January 1967

JOHN MASEFIELD, *Letters to Reyna*, published 1983

LOVE AND FRIENDSHIP

Love is like the wild rose-briar,
Friendship is like the holly-tree—
The holly is dark when the rose-briar blooms
But which will bloom most constantly?

The wild rose-briar is sweet in spring,
Its summer blossoms scent the air;
Yet wait till winter comes again
And who will call the wild-briar fair?

Then scorn the silly rose-wreath now
And deck thee with the holly's sheen,
That when December blights thy brow
He still may leave thy garland green.

EMILY BRONTË, 'Love and Friendship', written 1839

Friendship is a serious affection; the most sublime of all affections, because it is founded on principle, and cemented by time. The very reverse may be said of love. In a great degree, love and friendship cannot subsist in the same bosom; even when inspired by different objects they weaken or destroy each other, and for the same object can only be felt in succession. The vain fears and fond jealousies, the winds which fan the flame of love, when judiciously or artfully tempered, are both incompatible with the tender confidence and sincere respect of friendship.

MARY WOLLSTONECRAFT, *A Vindication of the Rights of Women*, 1792

Why should my anxious breast repine,
Because my youth is fled?
Days of delight may still be mine;
Affection is not dead.
In tracing back the years of youth,

One firm record, one lasting truth,
  Celestial consolation brings;
Bear it, ye breezes, to the seat,
Where first my heart responsive beat—
  'Friendship is Love without his wings!'

Through few, but deeply chequer'd years,
  What moments have been mine!
Now half obscured by clouds of tears,
  Now bright in rays divine;
Howe'er my future doom be cast,
My soul, enraptured with the past,
  To one idea fondly clings;
Friendship! that thought is all thine own,
Worth worlds of bliss, that thought alone—
  'Friendship is Love without his wings!'

              .   .   .

Oh, Love! before thy glowing shrine
  My early vows were paid;
My hopes, my dreams, my heart was thine,
  But these are now decay'd;
For thine are pinions like the wind,
No trace of thee remains behind,
  Except, alas! thy jealous stings.
Away, away! delusive power,
Thou shalt not haunt my coming hour;
  Unless, indeed, without thy wings.

              .   .   .

Ye few! my soul, my life is yours,
  My memory and my hope;
Your worth a lasting love ensures,
  Unfetter'd in its scope;
From smooth deceit and terror sprung
With aspect fair and honey'd tongue,
  Let Adulation wait on kings;
With joy elate, by snares beset,
We, we, my friends, can ne'er forget
  'Friendship is Love without his wings!'

LORD BYRON, from 'L'Amitié est l'Amour sans Ailes', written
1806

Friendship is a disinterested commerce between equals; love, an abject intercourse between tyrants and slaves.

GOLDSMITH, The Good-Natured Man, 1768

What sex adds to friendship is possessiveness.

ALEXANDER THEROUX, An Adultery, 1988

Nature weaves with a wide loom, and crosses the threads; and erotic passion may be as easily provoked peripherally by deeper impulses as be itself the root of other propensities. Lovers sometimes pretend at first to be only friends, and friends have sometimes fancied, at first blush, that they were lovers; it is as easy for one habit or sentiment as for the other to prove the radical one, and to prevail in the end.

SANTAYANA, Soliloquies in England

True friendship is self-love at second-hand; where, as in a flattering mirror, we may see our virtues magnified and our errors softened, and where we may fancy our opinion of ourselves confirmed by an impartial and faithful witness. He (of all the world) creeps closest to our bosoms, into our favour and esteem, who thinks of us most nearly as we do of ourselves. Such a one is indeed the pattern of a friend, another self—and our gratitude for the blessing is as sincere, as it is hollow in most other cases! This is one reason why entire friendship is scarcely to be found except in love. There is a hardness and severity in our judgements of one another; the spirit of competition also intervenes, unless where there is too great an inequality of pretension or difference of taste to admit of mutual sympathy and respect; but a woman's vanity is interested in making the object of her choice the God of her idolatry; and in the intercourse with that sex, there is the finest balance and reflection of opposite and answering excellences imaginable! . . . This is a dangerous string, which I ought never to touch upon; but the shattered cords vibrate of themselves!

HAZLITT, 'On the Spirit of Obligations'

Time, which strengthens friendships, weakens love.

It is more common to see an extreme love than a perfect friendship.

In friendship we see only the faults which can harm our friends. In love we see in the beloved only those faults from which we ourselves shall suffer.

LA BRUYÈRE, *Les Caractères*

Fidelity between friends is better able than that of lovers to resist the trials of separation, old age and physical and intellectual changes. We may be separated from a friend for long years, in the course of which both of us have changed considerably. Yet when we meet again it generally takes little time and little effort to recreate the feeling of friendship and to take up once again an existential dialogue, as if there had been no interruption. The reason for such fidelity must be sought in the fact that friendship, unlike love, is grounded in the spiritual, in what is permanent in human nature. Our condition of life, our physical appearance, indeed, our ideas and convictions may have changed or developed, but in our deepest selves we are always the same as we were years ago.

LEPP, *The Ways of Friendship*; tr. Bernard Murchland

Lovers are always talking to one another about their love; Friends hardly ever about their Friendship. Lovers are normally face to face, absorbed in each other; Friends, side by side, absorbed in some common interest.

Friendship, unlike Eros, is uninquisitive. You become a man's Friend without knowing or caring whether he is married or single or how he earns his living. What have all these 'unconcerning things, matters of fact' to do with the real question, *Do you see the same truth?*

C. S. LEWIS, *The Four Loves*

That most women are little moved by friendship is because it is vapid after the experience of love.

LA ROCHEFOUCAULD, *Maximes*

People always call friendship peaceful: there is no peaceful friendship any more than peaceful love: it is a passion like love, it too is ardent and often lasts no longer.

EUGÈNE DELACROIX, letter to George Sand, 21 November 1844

'A temple to Friendship,' said Laura, enchanted,
  'I'll build in this garden,—the thought is divine!'
Her temple was built, and she now only wanted
  An image of Friendship to place on the shrine.
She flew to a sculptor, who set down before her
  A Friendship, the fairest his art could invent.
But so cold and so dull, that the youthful adorer
  Saw plainly this was not the idol she meant.
'Oh! never,' she cried, 'could I think of enshrining
  An image, whose looks are so joyless and dim;—
But yon little god upon roses reclining,
  We'll make, if you please, Sir, a Friendship of him.'
So the bargain was struck; with the little god laden
  She joyfully flew to her shrine in the grove:
'Farewell,' said the sculptor, 'you're not the first maiden
  Who came but for Friendship and took away Love.'

THOMAS MOORE, 'A Temple to Friendship', 1815

All love is sacred, and the marriage-tie
Hath much of honour and divinity,
But lust, design, or some unworthy ends
May mingle there, which are despised by friends;
Passion hath violent extremes, and thus
All oppositions are contiguous;
So, when the end is served, their love will bate
If friendship make it not more fortunate:
Friendship, that love's elixir, that pure fire
Which burns the clearer 'cause it burns the higher . . .
Friendship, like heraldry, is hereby known
Richest when plainest, bravest when alone,

Calm as a virgin, and more innocent
Than sleeping doves are, and as much content
As saints in visions.

KATHERINE PHILIPS, from 'Friendship'

Love! in what poyson is thy Dart
Dipt, when it makes a bleeding heart?
None know, but they who feel the smart.

It is not thou, but we are blind,
And our corporeal eyes (we find)
Dazle the Opticks of our Mind . . .

How happy he that loves not, lives!
Him neither Hope nor Fear deceives,
To Fortune who no Hostage gives.

How unconcern'd in things to come!
If here uneasie, finds at *Rome*,
At *Paris*, or *Madrid* his Home.

Secure from low, and private Ends,
His Life, his Zeal, his Wealth attends
His Prince, his Country, and his Friends.

Danger, and Honour are his Joy;
But a fond Wife, or wanton Boy,
May all those Generous Thoughts destroy . . .

Old *Rome* of Children took no care,
They with their Friends their beds did share,
Secure, t'adopt a hopeful Heir.

Love drowsie days, and stormy nights
Makes, and breaks Friendship, whose delights
Feed, but not glut our Appetites.

Well chosen Friendship, the most noble
Of Vertues, all our joys makes double,
And into halves divides our trouble.

But when the unlucky knot we tye,
Care, Avarice, Fear, and Jealousie
Make Friendship languish till it dye.

The Wolf, the Lyon, and the Bear
When they their prey in pieces tear,
To quarrel with themselves forbear.

Yet timerous Deer, and harmless Sheep
When Love into their veins doth creep,
That law of Nature cease to keep.

Who then can blame the Amorous Boy,
Who the Fair *Helen* to enjoy,
To quench his own, set fire on *Troy?*

Such is the world's preposterous fate,
Amongst all Creatures, mortal hate
Love (though immortal) doth Create.

Sir John Denham, from 'Friendship and Single Life against
Love and Marriage', 1668

Beware of a woman with too many girl-friends, for they will always try
to destroy the conjugal we. One girl-friend is worse, unless afterwards
we marry her. In America every woman has her set of girl-friends; some
are cousins, the rest are gained at school. These form a permanent
committee who sit on each other's affairs, who 'come out' together,
marry and divorce together, and who end as those groups of bustling,
heartless well-informed club-women who govern society. Against them
the Couple or Ehepaar is helpless and Man in their eyes but a biological
interlude.

Connolly, *The Unquiet Grave*

Astrov. Why are you so melancholy today? Are you sorry for the Professor, or what?

Voynitsky. Let me alone.

Astrov. Or perhaps you are in love with the Professor's lady?

Voynitsky. She is my friend!

Astrov. Already?

Voynitsky. What do you mean by 'already'?

Astrov. A woman can become a man's friend only in the following sequence: first agreeable acquaintance, then mistress, then friend.

Voynitsky. A vulgar theory.

ANTON CHEKHOV, *Uncle Vanya*, 1897; tr. Constance Garnett

It [jealousy] will make the nearest and dearest friends fall out; they will endure all other things to be common, goods, lands, moneys, participate of each other's pleasures, and take in good part any disgraces, injuries in another kind; but as Propertius well describes it in an elegy of his, in this they will suffer nothing, have no corrivals.

> Stab me with sword, or poison strong
>   Give me to work my bane:
> So thou court not my lass, so thou
>   From mistress mine refrain.
> Command myself, my body, purse,
>   As thine own goods take all,
> And as my ever dearest friend,
>   I ever use thee shall.
> O spare my love, to have alone
>   Her to myself I crave,
> Nay, Jove himself I'll not endure
>   My rival for to have.

BURTON, *The Anatomy of Melancholy*

> This Palamon gan knytte his browes tweye.
> 'It nere,' quod he, 'to thee no greet honour   *would not be*
> For to be fals, ne for to be traitour
> To me, that am thy cosyn and thy brother

Ysworn ful depe, and ech of us til oother,
That nevere, for to dyen in the peyne,   *under torture*
Til that the deeth departe shal us tweyne,   *part*
Neither of us in love to hyndre oother,
Ne in noon oother cas, my leeve brother;
But that thou sholdest trewely forthren me   *help*
In every cas, as I shal forthren thee,—
This was thyn ooth, and myn also, certeyn;
I woot right wel, thou darst it nat withseyn.'   *deny*

This Arcite ful proudly spak ageyn:
'Thow shalt,' quod he, 'be rather fals than I . . .
I pose that thow lovedest hire biforn;   *grant for*
Wostow nat wel the olde clerkes sawe,   *argument's sake*
That "who shal yeve a lovere any lawe?"   *give*
Love is a gretter lawe, by my pan,   *head*
Than may be yeve to any erthely man;
And therfore positif lawe and swich decree   *formal*
Is broken al day for love in ech degree.
A man moot nedes love, maugree his heed.   *despite himself*
He may not fleen it, thogh he sholde be deed,
Al be she mayde, or wydwe, or elles wyf.'   *whether she be*

GEOFFREY CHAUCER, 'The Knight's Tale', *The Canterbury Tales*,
probably begun *c*.1387

Couldest thou *Euphues* for the love of a fruitelesse pleasure, vyolate the
league of faythfull friendeshippe? Diddest thou waye more the entising
lookes of a lewd wenche, then the entyre love of a loyall friende?

JOHN LYLY, *Euphues. The Anatomy of Wit*, 1578

So far as our story approaches the end,
    Which do you pity the most of us three?—
My friend, or the mistress of my friend
    With her wanton eyes, or me?

My friend was already too good to lose,
   And seemed in the way of improvement yet,
When she crossed his path with her hunting-noose
   And over him drew her net.

When I saw him tangled in her toils,
   A shame, said I, if she adds just him
To her nine-and-ninety other spoils,
   The hundredth for a whim!

And before my friend be wholly hers,
   How easy to prove to him, I said,
An eagle's the game her pride prefers,
   Though she snaps at a wren instead!

So, I gave her eyes my own eyes to take,
   My hand sought hers as in earnest need,
And round she turned for my noble sake,
   And gave me herself indeed.

The eagle am I, with my fame in the world,
   The wren is he, with his maiden face.
—You look away and your lip is curled?
   Patience, a moment's space!

For see, my friend goes shaking and white;
   He eyes me as the basilisk:
I have turned, it appears, his day to night,
   Eclipsing his sun's disk.

And I did it, he thinks, as a very thief:
   'Though I love her—that, he comprehends—
One should master one's passions (love, in chief),
   And be loyal to one's friends!'

And she—she lies in my hand as tame
   As a pear late basking over a wall;
Just a touch to try and off it came;
   'Tis mine—can I let it fall?

With no mind to eat it, that's the worst!
　　Were it thrown in the road, would the case assist?
'Twas quenching a dozen blue-flies' thirst
　　When I gave its stalk a twist.

And I—what I seem to my friend, you see:
　　What I soon shall seem to his love, you guess:
What I seem to myself, do you ask of me?
　　No hero, I confess.

'Tis an awkward thing to play with souls,
　　And matter enough to save one's own.
Yet think of my friend, and the burning coals
　　He played with for bits of stone!

One likes to show the truth for the truth;
　　That the woman was light is very true:
But suppose she says—Never mind that youth!
　　What wrong have I done to you?

Well, any how, here the story stays,
　　So far at least as I understand;
And, Robert Browning, you writer of plays,
　　Here's a subject made to your hand!

　　　　　　　ROBERT BROWNING, 'A Light Woman', 1855

Friendship often ends in love; but love in friendship—never.

　　　　　　　COLTON, *Lacon*, Vol. II, 1822

'A married woman must accept her husband's opinion, at all events about men.' He plunged on into the ancient quagmire. 'A man may know with impunity what is injurious if it enters a woman's mind.'

'I don't believe that. I can't and won't believe it.'

He made a gesture of despair.

'We differ hopelessly. It was all very well to discuss these things when you could do so in a friendly spirit. Now you say whatever you know will irritate me, and you say it on purpose to irritate me.'

'No; indeed I do not. But you are quite right that I find it hard to be friendly with you. Most earnestly I wish to be your friend—your true and faithful friend. But you won't let me.'

'Friend!' he cried scornfully. 'The woman who has become my wife ought to be something more than a friend, I should think. You have lost all love for me—there's the misery.'

Monica could not reply. That word 'love' had grown a weariness to her upon his lips. She did not love him; could not pretend to love him. Every day the distance between them widened, and when he took her in his arms she had to struggle with a sense of shrinking, of disgust. The union was unnatural; she felt herself constrained by a hateful force when he called upon her for the show of wifely tenderness. Yet how was she to utter this? The moment such a truth had passed her lips she must leave him. To declare that no trace of love remained in her heart, and still to live with him—that was impossible . . .

'You don't love me,' he continued in harsh, choking tones. 'You wish to be my *friend*. That's how you try to compensate me for the loss of your love.'

GEORGE GISSING, The Odd Women, 1893

I am indeed pleased that you are satisfied with the *Surintendant* [Nicolas Fouquet, Financial Secretary]: it is a sign that he is seeing reason, and that he does not take things so much to heart as he used to. When you do not want what others want, Madame, it is necessary for others to want what you want; we are still only too happy to remain among your friends. There is scarcely anyone else in the kingdom who can reduce those who love her to content themselves with friendship; we see no one who, rejected in love, does not become an enemy; and I am persuaded that it takes a woman of extraordinary merit to behave in such a way that the spite of an ill-treated lover does not lead to a clamorous rupture.

> COMTE DE BUSSY RABUTIN, letter to Madame de Sévigné, 17 August 1654; Bussy Rabutin, who had long been in the same position, wrote in his *Mémoires* that Fouquet 'transformed his love into esteem for a virtue which until then had been unknown to him'

Enter Lord Mountararat and Lord Tolloller

Lord Mount. Phyllis! My darling!

Lord Toll. Phyllis! My own!

Phyl. Don't! How dare you? Oh, but perhaps you're the two noblemen I'm engaged to?

Lord Mount. I am one of them.

Lord Toll. I am the other.

Phyl. Oh, then, my darling! [*to Lord Mountararat*] My own! [*to Lord Tolloller*] Well, have you settled which it's to be?

Lord Toll. Not altogether. It's a difficult position. It would be hardly delicate to toss up. On the whole we would rather leave it to you.

Phyl. How can it possibly concern me? You are both Earls, and you are both rich, and you are both plain.

Lord Mount. So we are. At least I am.

Lord Toll. So am I.

Lord Mount. No, no!

Lord Toll. I am indeed. Very plain.

Lord Mount. Well, well—perhaps you are.

Phyl. There's really nothing to choose between you. If one of you would forgo his title, and distribute his estates among his Irish tenantry, why, then, I should then see a reason for accepting the other.

Lord Mount. Tolloller, are you prepared to make this sacrifice?

Lord Toll. No!

Lord Mount. Not even to oblige a lady?

Lord Toll. No! not even to oblige a lady.

Lord Mount. Then, the only question is, which of us shall give way to the other? Perhaps, on the whole, she would be happier with me. I don't know. I may be wrong.

Lord Toll. No. I don't know that you are. I really believe she would. But the awkward part of the thing is that if you rob me of the girl of my heart, we must fight, and one of us must die. It's a family tradition that I have sworn to respect. It's a painful position, for I have a very strong regard for you, George.

Lord Mount. [*much affected*] My dear Thomas!

Lord Toll. You are very dear to me, George. We were boys together—at least *I* was. If I were to survive you, my existence would be hopelessly embittered.

Lord Mount. Then, my dear Thomas, you must not do it. I say it again and again—if it will have this effect upon you, you must not do it. No, no. If one of us is to destroy the other, let it be me!

Lord Toll. No, no!

Lord Mount. Ah, yes!—by our boyish friendship I implore you!

Lord Toll. [*much moved*] Well, well, be it so. But, no—no!—I cannot consent to an act which would crush you with unavailing remorse.

Lord Mount. But it would not do so. I should be very sad at first—oh, who would not be?—but it would wear off. I like you *very much*—but not, perhaps, as much as you like me.

Lord Toll. George, you're a noble fellow, but that tell-tale tear betrays you. No, George; you are very fond of me, and I cannot consent to give you a week's uneasiness on my account.

Lord Mount. But, dear Thomas, it would not last a week! Remember, you lead the House of Lords! on your demise I shall take your place! Oh, Thomas, it would not last a day!

Phyl. [*coming down*] Now, I do hope you're not going to fight about me, because it's really not worth while.

Lord Toll. [*looking at her*] Well, I don't believe it is!

Lord Mount. Nor I. The sacred ties of Friendship are paramount.

Quartette—Lord Mountararat, Lord Tolloller, Phyllis, and Private Willis

Lord Toll. Though p'r'aps I may incur your blame,
    The things are few
    I would not do
In Friendship's name!

Lord Mount. And I may say I think the same;
    Not even love
    Should rank above
True Friendship's name!

Phyl. Then free me, pray; be mine the blame;
    Forget your craze
    And go your ways
In Friendship's name!

All. Oh, many a man, in Friendship's name,
    Has yielded fortune, rank, and fame!
    But no one yet, in the world so wide,
    Has yielded up a promised bride!

Willis. Accept, O Friendship, all the same,

All. This sacrifice to thy dear name!

    [*Exeunt Lord Mountararat and Lord Tolloller, lovingly, in one direction, and Phyllis in another. Exit Private Willis*]

W. S. Gilbert, *Iolanthe*, 1882

Youth and Age

EASY come, easy go: the young, we gather, make and unmake friendships with bewildering speed. The great exception appears to be school friendships, notably those formed at public schools (in other countries, more logically, 'private'). Cyril Connolly professes himself quite worn out by their intensities, the heights and the depths experienced: the rest of life can only be a long autumnal anticlimax. Disraeli, another Etonian, dwells on the passion, the rapture and the wretchedness, and Leigh Hunt spoke of 'the disembodied transport' arising from his friendships at Christ's Hospital, the Blue-Coat School.

'We twa hae paidl'd in the burn / Frae morning sun till dine . . .' (Burns). Much used to be made of the springlike innocence of such relations, though rather less during recent decades. But schoolgirl friendships, judging by the authors quoted here, seem to have been intellectually livelier and more sophisticated, and without the protagonists turning into world-weary Messalinas *à la* Connolly.

The 'exchange of good offices' which, we have noted, is thought to lower the tone, certainly operates at school: the clever boy does the other's work for him, while the other, more athletic or 'savage' (Byron's term), protects him against bullies. In a variation, Steerforth, the elder by several years, helps David Copperfield with his sums, while in return David serves as a kind of Reader's Digest. Thomas Hughes, a pupil of Dr Arnold at Rugby, is more earnest or muscularly Christian: homesick little Arthur is toughened up physically and emotionally, and reciprocates spiritually, by making the Bible come alive. It is worth mentioning that in answering questions put by a correspondent in 1933, A. E. Housman declared that Oxford had little effect on him except that he met his greatest friend there.

In Aristotle's opinion the elderly, lumped together with the morose, do not make friends easily, since 'there is little in them to give pleasure to a companion'. And Hazlitt, writing in the manner of La Rochefoucauld, held that acquaintances of long standing would have repeated over and over again whatever they had to say, and the soil of friendship was worn out with constant use: 'Old friends might be compared to old married people without the tie of children.' Horace Walpole, on the contrary, believed that old friends were a great blessing in our later years: 'half a word creates one's meaning'. The theme is developed in Julian Barnes's passage on missing 'context', the sorrowful absence of that half a word.

In age, while some people are tenacious of their old friendships and ready to make new ones, others prefer memories of the past to present enactments and thinking of friends to going out and meeting them. There can be that imperceptible casting off of commitments, so well portrayed in Mrs Moore in Forster's *A Passage to India*: 'Why can't I finish my duties and be gone? . . . everything sympathy and confusion and bearing one another's burdens . . .' She is instinctively preparing for the 'rather grim piece of work' that Masefield alluded to.

It has been observed that children often get on more easily with their grandparents than with their parents. Meetings are spaced out and therefore 'special', the gap in age and responsibility reduces stress, and both parties make concessions. To generalize is foolhardy. When one party is interestingly knowledgeable and the other receptive, friendships between the distinctly old and the truly young can be rewarding, even if such equable relationships are relatively infrequent. In a rather stilted postscript to his letter to De Quincey, given in these pages, Wordsworth feared he had expressed himself coldly regarding a visit to Grasmere. 'You speak of yourself as being very young; and therefore may have many engagements of great importance with respect to your worldly concerns and future happiness in life': if, without neglecting these, De Quincey could manage to visit so remote a spot, Wordsworth would be very glad to see him. And in a letter to Swift in 1736 Pope spoke of a few young men, chance acquaintances acquired without his seeking, who recommended themselves by looking rather to the past than the present ('and therefore the future may have some hopes of them'): yet the friends who had been dead for twenty years were more real to him than those he saw daily.

According to a contemporary, Lewis Carroll always used to say that if he found he was taking off his hat when he met one of his child-friends in the street, then he knew it was time for the friendship to end.

———

Pleasure seems to be the motive of young people's friendships. They live by their emotions, and what they most care for is amusement and the interests of the moment. Also their taste in pleasure changes as they grow older; consequently the young make friends quickly and drop them quickly, because their affection alters as their taste in pleasure alters, and pleasure of that sort changes rapidly. The young are given to falling in love, because love is largely guided by emotion and based on pleasure. Consequently they form attachments quickly and break them off quickly, often changing over in the course of twenty-four hours. But young people who are friends, unlike the old, do want to pass their time in one another's company; that is how their friendship is carried on.

ARISTOTLE, *Nicomachean Ethics*; tr. H. Rackham

> for the friendships of youth are more instant
> than Nescafé, needing not even
> hot water . . .

DARYL HINE, *In and Out*, 1989

In general children's friendships are far from placid. Perhaps because of the gregariousness of school life they make and break friends with a rapidity disconcerting to the adult spectator . . .

The finger of friendship is the little finger. They link the little fingers of their right hands and shake them up and down, declaring:

> Make friends, make friends,
> Never, never break friends.

They quarrel, and their friendship is ended with the formula,

> Break friends, break friends,
> Never, never make friends,

repeated in a like manner . . . They make up again, intoning,

> We've broken before,
> We break now—

and they separate their little fingers,

> We'll never break any more,

and they intertwine their little fingers again, squeezing tightly . . . Alternatively, . . . they say,

> Make up, make up, never row again,
> If we do we'll get the cane,

and thereupon they slap hands or smack each other.

> IONA and PETER OPIE, *The Lore and Language of Schoolchildren*,
> 1959

Brian and I don't like each other now as he bosses me about and I boss him, but we will be friends again soon I hope.

Another thing about John is that he is sensible and nise [*sic*]. Whenever we are playing rocket ships he never starts laughing when we get to an awkward point.

I have two friends called Carol and Brenda. I like Brenda because she is very funny and very small. I also like Carol because when she has any sweets she always gives me some, and she has lovely curly hair, and she is very nice.

> 9-year-olds, quoted in above

> Magical feelings
> growing inside you
> warm and good.
> Happy and glad
> you have found a friend.
> Friendship can start
> in little terms—
> 'Hello, hello'—
> but soon you will find
> you have happiness
> for a lifetime.

> EMILY MARSHALL, aged 10, 'Friendship', 1988

Hermione.   Come, I'll question you
   Of my lord's tricks, and yours, when you were boys.
   You were pretty lordings then?
Polixenes.   We were, fair Queen,
   Two lads that thought there was no more behind
   But such a day tomorrow as today,
   And to be boy eternal.
Her.   Was not my lord
   The verier wag o'th'two?
Pol. We were as twinned lambs that did frisk i'th'sun,
   And bleat the one at th'other. What we changed
   Was innocence for innocence: we knew not
   The doctrine of ill-doing, nor dreamed
   That any did. Had we pursued that life,
   And our weak spirits ne'er been higher reared
   With stronger blood, we should have answered heaven
   Boldly 'Not guilty', the imposition cleared
   Hereditary ours.
Her.   By this we gather
   You have tripped since.
Pol.   O my most sacred lady,
   Temptations have since then been born to's: for
   In those unfledged days was my wife a girl;
   Your precious self had then not crossed the eyes
   Of my young playfellow.
Her.   Grace to boot!
   Of this make no conclusion, lest you say
   Your queen and I are devils. Yet go on:
   Th'offences we have made you do we'll answer,
   If you first sinned with us, and that with us
   You did continue fault, and that you slipped not
   With any but with us.

SHAKESPEARE, *The Winter's Tale*, 1610–11

   Harken that happy shout—the schoolhouse door
   Is open thrown and out the younkers teem
   Some run to leap-frog on the rushy moor
   And others dabble in the shallow stream

Catching young fish and turning pebbles oer
For mussel clams—Look in that mellow gleam
Where the retiring sun that rests the while
Streams through the broken hedge—How happy seem
Those schoolboy friendships leaning oer the stile
Both reading in one book—anon a dream
Rich with new joys doth their young hearts beguile
And the books pocketed most hastily
Ah happy boys well may ye turn and smile
When joys are yours that never cost a sigh.

JOHN CLARE, 'Evening schoolboys', 1835

We two boys together clinging,
One the other never leaving,
Up and down the roads going, North and South excursions making,
Power enjoying, elbows stretching, fingers clutching,
Arm'd and fearless, eating, drinking, sleeping, loving,
No law less than ourselves owning, sailing, soldiering, thieving,
    threatening,
Misers, menials, priests alarming, air breathing, water drinking, on
    the turf or the sea-beach dancing,
Cities wrenching, ease scorning, statutes mocking, feebleness
    chasing,
Fulfilling our foray.

WALT WHITMAN, 'We two boys together clinging', 1860

Our mutual loss, my dear Temple, will be great. I shall never cease to
regret you, nor will you find it easy to replace the friend of your youth.
You may find friends of equal merit; you may esteem them equally; but
few connections form'd after five and twenty strike root like that early
sympathy, which united us almost from infancy, and has increas'd to the
very hour of our separation.

What pleasure is there in the friendships of the spring of life, before the
world, the mean unfeeling selfish world, breaks in on the gay mistakes of
the just-expanding heart, which sees nothing but truth, and has nothing
but happiness in prospect!

I am not surpris'd the heathens rais'd altars to friendship: 'twas natural for untaught superstition to deify the source of every good; they worship'd friendship, which animates the moral world, on the same principle as they paid adoration to the sun, which gives life to the world of nature.

FRANCES BROOKE, *The History of Emily Montague*, 1769; letter from Edward Rivers to John Temple

The prodigy of our School days was George Sinclair (son of Sir John): he made exercises for half the School (*literally*), verses at will, and themes without it . . . He was a friend of mine, and in the same remove, and used at times to beg me to let him do my exercise—a request always most readily accorded, upon a pinch, or when I wanted to do something else, which was usually once an hour. On the other hand, he was pacific, and I savage; so I fought for him, or thrashed others for him, or thrashed himself to make him thrash others, whom it was necessary, as a point of honour and stature, that he should so chastise. Or, we talked politics, for he was a great politician, and were very good friends.

My School friendships were with *me passions* (for I was always violent), but I do not know that there is one which has endured (to be sure, some have been cut short by death) till now. That with Lord Clare began one of the earliest and lasted longest, being only interrupted by distance, that I know of. I never hear the word '*Clare*' without a beating of the heart even *now*, and I write it with the feelings of 1803–4–5 ad infinitum.

BYRON, 'Detached Thoughts', 1821

'What a queer chum for Tom Brown' was the comment at the fire; and it must be confessed so thought Tom himself, as he lighted his candle, and surveyed the new green-baize curtains and the carpet and sofa with much satisfaction.

'I say, Arthur, what a brick your mother is to make us so cosy. But look here now, you must answer straight up when the fellows speak to you, and don't be afraid. If you're afraid, you'll get bullied. And don't you say you can sing; and don't you ever talk about home, or your mother and sisters.'

Poor little Arthur looked ready to cry.

'But please,' said he, 'mayn't I talk about—about home to you?'

'O yes, I like it. But don't talk to boys you don't know, or they'll call you homesick, or mamma's darling, or some such stuff. What a jolly desk! Is that yours? And what stunning binding! why, your school-books look like novels.'

And Tom was soon deep in Arthur's goods and chattels, all new, and good enough for a fifth-form boy, and hardly thought of his friends outside till the prayer-bell rang.

'Tell you what, Tommy,' East would say, 'you'll spoil young Hopeful with too much coddling. Why can't you let him go about by himself and find his own level? He'll never be worth a button, if you go on keeping him under your skirts.'

'Well, but he ain't fit to fight his own way yet; I'm trying to get him to it every day—but he's very odd. Poor little beggar! I can't make him out a bit. He ain't a bit like anything I've ever seen or heard of—he seems all over nerves; anything you say seems to hurt him like a cut or blow.'

'That sort of boy's no use here,' said East, 'he'll only spoil. Now I'll tell you what to do, Tommy. Go and get a nice large bandbox made, and put him in with plenty of cotton wool, and a pap-bottle, labelled "With care—this side up", and send him back to mamma.'

'I think I shall make a hand of him, though,' said Tom, smiling, 'say what you will. There's something about him, every now and then, which shows me he's got pluck somewhere in him. That's the only thing after all that'll wash, ain't it, old Scud? But how to get at it and bring it out?'

After supper that night, and almost nightly for years afterwards, Tom and Arthur, and by degrees East occasionally, and sometimes one, sometimes another, of their friends, read a chapter of the Bible together, and talked it over afterwards. Tom was at first utterly astonished, and almost shocked, at the sort of way in which Arthur read the book and talked about the men and women whose lives are there told. The first night they happened to fall on the chapters about the famine in Egypt, and Arthur began talking about Joseph as if he were a living statesman; just as he might have talked about Lord Grey and the Reform Bill; only that they were much more living realities to him. The book was to him, Tom saw, the most vivid and delightful history of real people, who might do right or wrong, just like anyone who was walking about in Rugby—the Doctor, or the masters, or the sixth-form boys. But the astonishment soon passed off, the scales seemed to drop from his eyes, and the book became at once and for ever to him the great human and divine book, and the men and women, whom he had looked upon as something quite different from himself, became his friends and counsellors.

What a bother all this explaining is! I wish we could get on without it. But we can't. However, you'll all find, if you haven't found it out already, that a time comes in every human friendship when you must go down into the depths of yourself, and lay bare what is there to your friend, and wait in fear for his answer. A few moments may do it; and it may be (most likely will be, as you are English boys) that you never do it but once. But done it must be, if the friendship is to be worth the name. You must find what is there, at the very root and bottom of one another's hearts; and if you are at one there, nothing on earth can or at least ought to sunder you.

THOMAS HUGHES, *Tom Brown's Schooldays*, 1857

At school, friendship is a passion. It entrances the being; it tears the soul. All loves of after-life can never bring its rapture, or its wretchedness; no bliss so absorbing, no pangs of jealousy or despair so crushing and so keen! What tenderness and what devotion; what illimitable confidence; infinite revelations of inmost thoughts; what ecstatic present and romantic future; what bitter estrangements and what melting reconciliations; what scenes of wild recrimination, agitating explanations, passionate correspondence; what insane sensitiveness, and what frantic sensibility; what earthquakes of the heart and whirlwinds of the soul are confined in that simple phrase, a schoolboy's friendship! 'Tis some indefinite recollection of these mystic passages of their young emotion that makes grey-haired men mourn over the memory of their schoolboy days. It is a spell that can soften the acerbity of political warfare, and with its witchery can call forth a sigh even amid the callous bustle of fashionable saloons.

BENJAMIN DISRAELI, *Coningsby*, 1844; of Eton

Were I to deduce any system from my feelings on leaving Eton, it might be called *The Theory of Permanent Adolescence*. It is the theory that the experiences undergone by boys at the great public schools, their glories and disappointments, are so intense as to dominate their lives and to arrest their development . . .

Although to the world I appeared a young man going up to Oxford 'with the ball at his feet', I was, in fact, as promising as the Emperor Tiberius retiring to Capri. I knew all about power and popularity, success and failure, beauty and time, I was familiar with the sadness of the lover and the bleak ultimatums of the beloved. I had formed my ideas and made my friends and it was to be years before I could change them. I lived entirely in the past, exhausted by the emotions of adolescence, of understanding, loving and learning.

CYRIL CONNOLLY, *Enemies of Promise*, 1938

An accidental circumstance cemented the intimacy between Steerforth and me, in a manner that inspired me with great pride and satisfaction, though it sometimes led to inconvenience. It happened on one occasion, when he was doing me the honour of talking to me in the playground, that I hazarded the observation that something or somebody—I forget what now—was like something or somebody in Peregrine Pickle. He said nothing at the time; but when I was going to bed at night, asked me if I had got that book.

I told him no, and explained how it was that I had read it, and all those other books of which I have made mention.

'And do you recollect them?' Steerforth said.

Oh yes, I replied; I had a good memory, and I believed I recollected them very well.

'Then I tell you what, young Copperfield,' said Steerforth, 'you shall tell 'em to me. I can't get to sleep very early at night, and I generally wake rather early in the morning. We'll go over 'em one after another. We'll make some regular Arabian Nights of it.'

I felt extremely flattered by this arrangement, and we commenced carrying it into execution that very evening. What ravages I committed on my favourite authors in the course of my interpretation of them, I am not in a condition to say, and should be very unwilling to know; but I had a profound faith in them, and I had, to the best of my belief, a simple, earnest manner of narrating what I did narrate; and these qualities went a long way.

The drawback was, that I was often sleepy at night, or out of spirits and indisposed to resume the story; and then it was rather hard work, and it must be done; for to disappoint or displease Steerforth was of course out of the question. In the mornings, too, when I felt weary and should have enjoyed another hour's repose very much, it was a tiresome thing to be roused, like the Sultana Scheherazade, and forced into a long story before the getting-up bell rang; but Steerforth was resolute; and as he explained to me, in return, my sums and exercises, and anything in my tasks that was too hard for me, I was no loser by the transaction. Let me do myself justice, however. I was moved by no interested or selfish motive, nor was I moved by fear of him. I admired and loved him, and his approval was return enough. It was so precious to me that I look back on these trifles, now, with an aching heart.

Steerforth was considerate, too; and showed his consideration, in one particular instance, in an unflinching manner that was a little tantalizing, I suspect, to poor Traddles and the rest. Peggotty's promised letter—what a comfortable letter it was!—arrived before 'the half' was many weeks old; and with it a cake in a perfect nest of oranges, and two bottles of cowslip wine. This treasure, as in duty bound, I laid at the feet of Steerforth, and begged him to dispense.

'Now, I'll tell you what, young Copperfield,' said he: 'the wine shall be kept to wet your whistle when you are story-telling.'

I blushed at the idea, and begged him, in my modesty, not to think of it. But he said he had observed I was sometimes hoarse—a little roopy was his exact expression—and it should be, every drop, devoted to the purpose he had mentioned. Accordingly, it was locked up in his box, and drawn off by himself in a phial, and administered to me through a piece of quill in the cork, when I was supposed to be in want of a restorative. Sometimes, to make it a more sovereign specific, he was so kind as to squeeze orange juice into it, or to stir it up with ginger, or dissolve a peppermint drop in it; and although I cannot assert that the flavour was improved by these experiments, or that it was exactly the compound one would have chosen for a stomachic, the last thing at night and the first thing in the morning, I drank it gratefully and was very sensible of his attention.

DICKENS, *David Copperfield*, 1849–50

Injurious Hermia, most ungrateful maid,
Have you conspired, have you with these contrived

To bait me with this foul derision?
Is all the counsel that we two have shared—
The sisters' vows, the hours that we have spent
When we have chid the hasty-footed time
For parting us—O, is all forgot?
All schooldays' friendship, childhood innocence?
We, Hermia, like two artificial gods
Have with our needles created both one flower,
Both on one sampler, sitting on one cushion,
Both warbling of one song, both in one key,
As if our hands, our sides, voices, and minds
Had been incorporate. So we grew together
Like to a double cherry, seeming parted
But yet an union in partition,
Two lovely berries moulded on one stem,
So with two seeming bodies but one heart,
Two of the first, like coats in heraldry,
Due but to one, and crownèd with one crest.
And will you rent our ancient love asunder,
To join with men in scorning your poor friend?
It is not friendly, 'tis not maidenly.

SHAKESPEARE, *A Midsummer Night's Dream*, c.1595–6; Helena speaking

'You will never come back again, Lucilla,' said one of her companions; 'you will marry some enchanting Italian with a beautiful black beard, and a voice like an angel; and he'll sing serenades to you, and do all sorts of things: oh, how I wish I was you!'

'That may be,' said Miss Marjoribanks, 'but I shall never marry an Italian, my dear. I don't think I shall marry anybody for a long time. I want to amuse myself. I wonder, by the way, if it would improve my voice to take lessons in Italy. Did I ever tell you of the Italian nobleman that was so very attentive to me that Christmas I spent at Sissy Vernon's? He was very handsome. I suppose they really are all very handsome . . . but I did not pay any attention to him. My object, dear, and you know it, is to return home as well educated as possible, to be a comfort to dear papa.'

'Yes, dear Lucilla,' said the sympathetic girl, 'and it is so good of you; but do tell me about the Italian nobleman—what did he look like—and what did he say?'

'Oh, as for what he said, that is quite a different matter,' said Lucilla; 'but it is not what they say, but the way they say it, that is the fun. I did not give him the least encouragement. As for that, I think, a girl can always stop a man when she does not care for him. It depends on whether you intend him to commit himself or not,' Miss Marjoribanks continued, and fixed her eyes meditatively, but intently, upon her friend's face.

'Whether I intend?—oh goodness, Lucilla! how can you speak so? as if I ever intended anything,' said her companion, confused, yet flattered, by the possibility; to which the elder sage answered calmly, with all the composure in the world—

'No, I never supposed you did; I was thinking of myself,' said Lucilla, as if, indeed, that was the only reasonable subject of thought. 'You know I have seen a good deal of the world, one way and another, with going to spend the holidays, and I could tell you quantities of things. It is quite astonishing how much experience one gets. When I was at Midhurst, at Easter, there was my cousin Tom, who was quite ridiculous; I declare, he nearly brought things to an explanation, Fanny—which, of course, of all things in the world I most wanted to avoid.'

'Oh, but why, Lucilla?' asked Fanny, full of delight and wonder; 'I do so want to know what they say when they make—explanations, as you call them. Oh, do tell me, Lucilla, why?'

'My dear,' said Miss Marjoribanks, 'a cousin of my own! and only twenty-one, and reading for the bar! In the first place, my aunt would never have forgiven me, and I am very fond of my aunt . . . Fortunately he did not just say the words, so I escaped that time; but, of course, I could understand perfectly what he meant.'

'But, oh, Lucilla, tell me the words,' cried the persistent questioner; 'do, there's a darling! I am quite sure you have heard them—and I should so like to know exactly what they say;—do they go down on their knees?—or do they try to take your hand as they always do in novels?—or what do they do?—Oh, Lucilla, tell me, there's a dear!'

'Nonsense,' said Lucilla; 'I only want you to understand that I am not likely to fall into any danger of that sort. My only ambition, Fanny, as I have told you often, is to go home to Carlingford and be a comfort to dear papa.'

'Yes,' said Fanny, kissing her devoted companion, 'and it is so good of you, dear; but then you cannot go on all your life being a comfort to dear papa,' said the intelligent girl, bethinking herself, and looking again with some curiosity in Lucilla's face.

'We must leave that to Providence,' said Miss Marjoribanks, with a sense of paying a compliment to Providence in entrusting it with such a responsibility.

MARGARET OLIPHANT, Miss Marjoribanks, 1866

'Do you think Miss Brodie ever had sexual intercourse with Hugh?' said Jenny.

'She would have had a baby, wouldn't she?'

'I don't know.'

'I don't think they did anything like that,' said Sandy. 'Their love was above all that.'

'Miss Brodie said they clung to each other with passionate abandon on his last leave.'

'I don't think they took their clothes off, though,' Sandy said, 'do you?'

'No. I can't see it,' said Jenny.

'I wouldn't like to have sexual intercourse,' Sandy said.

'Neither would I. I'm going to marry a pure person.'

'Have a toffee.'

They ate their sweets, sitting on the carpet. Sandy put some coal on the fire and the light spurted up, reflecting on Jenny's ringlets. 'Let's be witches by the fire, like we were at Hallowe'en.'

They sat in the twilight eating toffees and incanting witches' spells. Jenny said, 'There's a Greek god at the museum standing up with nothing on. I saw it last Sunday afternoon but I was with Auntie Kate and I didn't have a chance to *look* properly.'

'Let's go to the museum next Sunday,' Sandy said. 'It's research.'

MURIEL SPARK, The Prime of Miss Jean Brodie, 1961

Although now in the fifth form, Laura had remained childish for her age: whereas Evelyn was over eighteen, and only needed to turn up her hair to be quite grown-up. She had matriculated the previous Christmas, and was at present putting away a rather desultory half-year, before leaving school for good. In addition, she was rich, pampered and very pretty —the last comrade in the world for drab little Laura . . .

In all the three years Laura had been at school, she had not got beyond a surface friendliness with any of her fellows. Even those who had been her 'chums' had wandered like shades through the groves of her affection: . . . to none of them had she been drawn by any deeper sense of affinity. And though she had come to believe, in the course of the last, more peaceful year, that she had grown used to being what you would call an unpopular girl—one, that is, with whom no one ever shared a confidence—yet seldom was there a child who longed more ardently to be liked, or suffered more acutely under dislike. Apart however from the brusque manner she had contracted, in her search after truth, it must be admitted that Laura had but a small talent for friendship; she did not grasp the constant give-and-take intimacy implies; the liking of others had to be brought to her, unsought, she, on the other hand, being free to stand back and consider whether or no the feeling was worth returning. And friends are not made in this fashion.

But Evelyn had stoutly, and without waiting for permission, crossed the barrier; and each new incident in her approach was pleasanter than the last. Laura was pleased, and flattered, and round the place where her heart was, she felt a warm and comfortable glow.

She began to return the liking, with interest, after the manner of a lonely, bottled-up child. And everything about Evelyn made it easy to grow fond of her. To begin with, Laura loved pretty things and pretty people; and her new friend was out and away the prettiest girl in the school. Then, too, she was clever, and that counted; you did not make a friend of a fool. But her chief characteristics were a certain sound common sense, and an inexhaustible fund of good-nature—a careless, happy, laughing sunniness, that was as grateful to those who came into touch with it as a rare ointment is grateful to the skin. This kindliness arose, it might be, in the first place from indolence: it was less trouble to be merry and amiable than to put oneself out to be selfish, which also meant standing a fire of disagreeable words and looks; and then, too, it was really hard for one who had never had a whim crossed to be out of humour. But, whatever its origin, the good-nature was there, everlastingly; and Laura soon learnt that she could cuddle in under it, and be screened by it, as a lamb is screened by its mother's woolly coat.

On the night Laura learned that her friend had again met the loathly 'Jim', there was a great to-do. In vain Evelyn laughed, reasoned, expostulated. Laura was inconsolable.

'Look here, Poppet,' said Evelyn at last, and was so much in earnest that she laid her hairbrush down, and took Laura by both her bony little shoulders. 'Look here, you surely don't expect me to be an old maid, do you?—*me?*' The pronoun signified all she might not say: it meant wealth, youth, beauty, and an unbounded capacity for pleasure.

'Evvy, you're not going to *marry* that horrid man?'

'Of course not, goosey. But that doesn't mean that I'm never going to marry at all, does it?'

Laura supposed not—with a tremendous sniff.

'Well, then, what *is* all the fuss about?'

It was not so easy to say. She was of course reconciled, she sobbed, to Evelyn marrying some day: only plain and stupid girls were left to be old maids: but it must not happen for years and years and years to come, and when it did, it must be to someone much older than herself, someone she did not greatly care for: in short, Evelyn was to marry only to escape the odium of the single life.

Having drawn this sketch of her future word by word from the weeping Laura, Evelyn fell into a fit of laughter which she could not stifle. 'Well, Poppet,' she said when she could speak, 'if that's your idea of happiness for me, we'll postpone it just as long as ever we can. I'm all there. For I mean to have a good time first—a jolly good time—before I tie myself up for ever, world without end, amen.'

'That's just what I hate so—your good time, as you call it,' retorted Laura, smarting under the laughter.

'Everyone does, child. You'll be after it yourself when you're a little older.'

'Me?—never!'

'Oh, yes, indeed you will.'

'I won't. I hate men and I always shall. And oh, I thought'—with an upward, sobbing breath—'I thought you liked me best.'

'Of course I like you, you silly child! But that's altogether different. And I don't like you any less because I enjoy having some fun with them, too.'

'I don't want your old leavings!' said Laura savagely. It hurt, almost as much as having a tooth pulled out, did this knowledge that your friend's affection was wholly yours only as long as no man was in question.

HENRY HANDEL RICHARDSON, *The Getting of Wisdom*, 1910

You distress me, dear and sweet friend (there ought to be another word, since for me you are not what is generally meant by 'friend', even at its best), you distress me when you talk of your death. Imagine what would happen to me. A wandering soul, like a bird above the flooded earth, I wouldn't find the smallest rock, not a patch of ground, where I could relieve my weariness . . .

I long to see what you have done since we parted. In four or five weeks we shall read it together, alone, just ourselves, *chez nous*, far from the world and the bourgeois, holed up like bears, growling under our threefold fur.

We shall be neighbours this winter, old fellow. We shall be able to see each other every day, we'll make plans. We'll talk together round my fireside, while the rain falls or the snow covers the roofs. No, I can't find it in me to complain when I think that I have your friendship, that we have hours free to spend entirely together. No matter how bare a rock may be, it isn't miserable when seaweed has clung to it, refreshing the granite with pearls of water from its locks. If I were to lose you, what would be left to me? What should I have in my inner life, that's to say my true one? . . .

Adieu, dear Alfred. Try, if it's *possible*, and for love of me, to go easy with the bottle.

> Gustave Flaubert, letters to Alfred Le Poittevin, 13 May 1845, July 1845

While affectionate and rather gentle with each other, we wore a swash-buckling manner to the outer world. It was our business to be regardless of consequences, to be always looking for preposterous adventures and planning crazy feats, and to be most ready for a brush with constituted authority. 'Booms' were a great fashion. Their inventors were, I think, Hubert Howard and the generation preceding ours, but we developed them into a science. It was a 'boom' to canoe an incredible distance between a winter's dawn and dusk; to set out to walk to London at a moment's notice; to get horses, choose a meeting-place, mark down compass-courses and ride them out, though the way lay through back gardens and flooded rivers; to sleep out of doors in any weather; to scramble at midnight over Oxford roofs; and to devise all manner of fantastic practical jokes. To stop to think of consequences was the mark of a 'heygate' [careerist]. All this, of course, was the ordinary high spirits of young men delighting in health and strength, which happily belong to

the Oxford of every generation. The peculiar features of our circle were
that this physical exuberance was found among men of remarkable
intellectual power, and that it implied no corresponding *abandon* in their
intellectual life. In the world of action we were ripe for any adventure; in
the things of the mind we were critical, decorous, chary of enthusiasm
—*revenants* from the Augustan age . . .

He [Raymond Asquith] spoke best when he was merely fooling—after
dinner, or at the meetings of a social club, or in the midst of a 'boom',
when the call came for oratory. During my 'Greats' schools I had a free
afternoon, and Raymond and I resolved to be American tourists. We
bought wideawake hats, hired an open carriage, and with Baedekers in
our hands and our feet on the cushions drove into the country. In some
village the name of which I have forgotten we drew up at an inn, and
Raymond addressed the assembled rustics on the virtues of total abstin-
ence. It was the most perfect parody conceivable of a temperance speech,
and it completely solemnized his hearers. Then he ordered beer all round.

> JOHN BUCHAN, *These For Remembrance: Memoirs of 6 Friends Killed in
> the Great War*, privately printed 1919

I had some friends—but I dreamed that they were dead—
Who used to dance with lanterns round a little boy in bed;
Green and white lanterns that waved to and fro:
But I haven't seen a Firefly since ever so long ago!

I had some friends—their crowns were in the sky—
Who used to nod and whisper when a little boy went by,
As the nuts began to tumble and the breeze began to blow:
And I haven't seen a Cocoa-palm since ever so long ago!

I had a friend—he came up from Cape Horn,
With a Coal-sack on his shoulder when a little boy was born.
He heard me learn to talk, and he helped me thrive and grow:
But I haven't seen the Southern Cross since ever so long ago!

I had a boat—I out and let her drive,
Till I found my dream was foolish, for my friends were all alive.
The Cocoa-palms were real, and the Southern Cross was true:
And the Fireflies were dancing—so I danced too!

> RUDYARD KIPLING, 'The Friends', 1927

With optimism at the thrill of it—
The rarity of a taxi, suitcases stowed
On the floorboards and the furniture sold—
They drove through green shadows at the ends of lanes
To where-you-will in every New-Found-Land,
Ontario, North Island, New South Wales.
And always our mothers would say, 'Give them
Something of yours, the thing you love best'—
An envied marble, the left-handed boxing glove—
Knowing that their mothers would say the same—
A triangular stamp, a lightweight Egyptian piastre;
And anyone with cash or curiosity
Attended the auctions of gardening tools,
Bicycles, wireless sets and the forlorn shoes.
Boys would fight for the last time and shake hands,
Our clumsily affectionate farewells!
'Goodbye,' girls said to each other, 'Goodbye.'
At the exchange of gifts, at tea-parties
Invented out of rationed tea and sugar,
There seemed the promise of love to others
Waiting for them in the lands of the atlas.
In a place they wouldn't recognize, the wind
In the remaining tree cries in its wisdom,
Its leaves repeating the summer noise for For Ever
To names I can't remember as I listen to
Emigrant songs, the sundered families.
One butterfly where once there were so many.

DOUGLAS DUNN, 'The Departures of Friends in Childhood', 1988

My dearest Margery,—
   I have received a very pretty portrait of a very pretty girl, but although
the pretty girl is prettier than the pretty portrait, I am very glad to have
the pretty portrait as a pretty souvenir of the very pretty original.
   Thank you, my dear and pretty Margery, for your very pretty present.
                              Always affectionately yours,
                                             W. S. Gilbert

W. S. GILBERT, letter to Margery Maude, 30 December 1910

Among my early recollections are those of receiving always at Christmas-time the most sumptuous and enormous box of chocolates from the then Mr Gilbert. For which I used to write laboured little epistles of thanks in return on much decorated notepaper. I always signed it 'Your affectionate little friend, Margery Maude.' After one of these letters I received a lovely copy of the *Bab Ballads* inscribed to 'Miss Margery Maude, from her affectionate little friend, the Author.' . . .

What endless laughter there always was throughout our visit—the scintillating wit to which we listened and the teasing to which we submitted, because it was all such fun. I shall never forget his wonderful sympathy and sweetness and understanding of child-minds. He gained the confidence and love of a child at once and seemed really to enjoy their companionship as much as that of their elders. The last time I was at Grim's Dyke I wanted to get a good snapshot of him, and he at once posed for me in a fantastic attitude rather like a ballet-dancer. I put the photo in my album, and he wrote under it, 'How ill grey hairs become a fool or jester.'

> MARGERY MAUDE (Mrs Joseph Burden); in *W. S. Gilbert: His Life and Letters*, Sidney Dark and Rowland Grey

There is a sort of veteran women of condition, who, having lived always in the *grand monde*, and having possibly had some gallantries, together with the experience of five and twenty or thirty years, form a young fellow better than all the rules that can be given him. These women, being past their bloom, are extremely flattered by the least attention from a young fellow; and they will point out to him those manners and *attentions* that pleased and engaged them, when they were in the pride of their youth and beauty. Wherever you go, make some of those women your friends, which a very little matter will do. Ask their advice, tell them your doubts or difficulties as to your behaviour; but take great care not to drop one word of their experience; for experience implies age, and the suspicion of age, no woman, let her be ever so old, ever forgives.

> LORD CHESTERFIELD, letter to his son, 11 January 1750

It is impossible not to be pleased when one is told that one has given so much pleasure: and it is to me a still higher gratification to find that my poems have impressed a stranger with such favourable ideas of my character as a man. Having said this which is easily said I find some difficulty in replying more particularly to your Letter.

It is needless to say that it would be out of nature were I not to have kind feelings towards one who expresses sentiments of such profound esteem and admiration of my writings as you have done. You can have no doubt but that these sentiments however conveyed to me must have been acceptable; and I assure you that they are still more welcome coming from yourself. You will then perceive that the main end which you proposed to yourself in writing to me is answered, viz. that I am already kindly disposed towards you. My friendship it is not in my power to give: this is a gift which no man can make, it is not in our own power: a sound and healthy friendship is the growth of time and circumstance, it will spring up and thrive like a wildflower when these favour, and when they do not, it is in vain to look for it.

I do not suppose that I am saying any thing which you do not know as well as myself. I am simply reminding you of a common place truth which your high admiration of me may have robbed perhaps of that weight which it ought to have with you. And this leads me to what gave me great concern, I mean the very unreasonable value which you set upon my writings, compared with those of others. You are young and ingenuous and I wrote with a hope of pleasing the young the ingenuous and the unworldly above all others, but sorry indeed should I be to stand in the way of the proper influence of other writers. You will know that I allude to the great names of past times, and above all to those of our own Country. I have taken the liberty of saying this much to hasten on the time, when you will value my poems not less, but those of others, more. That time I know would come of itself; and may come sooner for what I have said, which at all events I am sure you cannot take ill.

> WILLIAM WORDSWORTH, letter to Thomas De Quincey, 29 July 1803; De Quincey was 18 at the time.

I was keenly aware of a Mr Hardy who was a kind, small man, with a thin beard, in the background of London tea parties . . . and in the background of my mind . . . I remember very distinctly the tea party at which I was introduced to him by Mrs Lynn Lynton with her paralysing, pebble-blue eyes, behind gleaming spectacles. Mrs Lynn Lynton, also a novelist, was a Bad Woman, my dear. One of the Shrieking Sisterhood! . . .

So, out of a sort of cloud of almost infantile paralysis—I must have been eighteen to the day—I found myself telling a very very kind, small, ageless, soft-voiced gentleman with a beard, the name of my first book, which had been published a week before. And he put his head on one side and uttered, as if he were listening to himself, the syllables: 'Ow ... Ow ...'

I was petrified with horror ... not because I thought he had gone mad or was being rude to me, but because he seemed to doom my book to irremediable failure ...

I do not see how I can here avoid mentioning that my first book was called *The Brown Owl* and that it was only a fairy tale ... I will add that the publisher—for whom Mr Edward Garnett was literary adviser—paid me ten pounds for it and that it sold many thousands more copies than any other book I ever wrote ... and keeps on selling to this day ...

My ambition in those days was to be an Army Officer!

And then suddenly, in Mrs Lynn Lynton's dim, wicked drawing-room, in face of this kind, bearded gentleman, I was filled with consternation and grief. Because it was plain that he considered that the vowel sounds of the title of my book were ugly and that, I supposed, would mean that the book could not succeed. So I made the discovery that I—but tremendously!—wished that the book should succeed ... even though I knew that if the book should succeed it would for ever damn my chances as one of Her Majesty's officers ...

And I could feel Mr Hardy feeling the consternation and grief that had come up in me, because he suddenly said in a voice that was certainly meant to be consolatory:

'But of course you meant to be onomatopoeic. Ow—ow—representing the lamenting voices of owls ... Like the repeated double O's of the opening of the Second Book of *The Aeneid* ...'

And he repeated:

> 'C*O*nticuer' *O*mnes intentiqu' *O*ra tenebant
> Inde t*O*r*O* pater Aeneas sic *O*rsus ab alt*O*'—

making me really hear the Oh ... Oh's of those lamenting lines ...

I was struck as dumb as a stuck pig. I could not get out a word whilst he went on talking cheerfully. He told me some anecdotes of the brown owl and then remarked that it might perhaps have been better if, supposing I had wanted to represent in my title the cry of the brown owl, instead of two 'ow' sounds I could have found two 'oo's' ... And he reflected and tried over the sound of 'the brooding coots' and 'the muted lutes' ...

And then he said, as if miraculously to my easement:

'But of course you're quite right . . . One shouldn't talk of one's books at tea parties . . . Drop in at Max Gate when you are passing and we'll talk about it all in peace . . .'

Marvellously kind . . . and leaving me still with a new emotional qualm of horror . . . Yes, I was horrified . . . because I had let that kind gentleman go away thinking that my book was about birds . . . whereas it was about Princesses and Princes and magicians and such twaddle . . . I had written it to amuse my sister Juliet . . . So I ran home and wrote him a long letter telling him that the book was not about birds and begging his pardon in several distinct ways.

FORD MADOX FORD, 'Thomas Hardy', *Mightier than the Sword*, 1938

It was never more than a couple of miles a day now, and Kim's shoulders bore all the weight of it—the burden of an old man, the burden of the heavy food-bag with the locked books, the load of the writings on his heart, and the details of the daily routine. He begged in the dawn, set blankets for the lama's meditation, held the weary head on his lap through the noonday heats, fanning away the flies till his wrists ached, begged again in the evenings, and rubbed the lama's feet, who rewarded him with promise of Freedom—today, tomorrow, or, at furthest, the next day.

'Never was such a *chela*. I doubt at times whether Ananda more faithfully nursed Our Lord. And thou art a Sahib? When I was a man—a long time ago—I forgot that. Now I look upon thee often, and every time I remember that thou art a Sahib. It is strange.'

'Thou hast said there is neither black nor white. Why plague me with this talk, Holy One? Let me rub the other foot. It vexes me. I am *not* a Sahib. I am thy *chela*, and my head is heavy on my shoulders.'

'Patience a little! We reach Freedom together. Then thou and I, upon the far bank of the River, will look back upon our lives as in the Hills we saw our days' marches laid out behind us. Perhaps I was once a Sahib.'

' 'Was never a Sahib like thee, I swear it.'

'I am certain the Keeper of the Images in the Wonder House was in past life a very wise Abbot. But even his spectacles do not make my eyes see. There fall shadows when I would look steadily. No matter—we know the tricks of the poor stupid carcass—shadow changing to another shadow. I am bound by the illusion of Time and Space. How far came we today in the flesh?'

'Perhaps half a *koss*.' (Three quarters of a mile, and it was a weary march.)

'Half a *koss*. Ha! I went ten thousand thousand in the spirit. How we are all lapped and swathed and swaddled in these senseless things.' He looked at his thin blue-veined hand that found the beads so heavy. '*Chela*, hast thou never a wish to leave me?'

Kim thought of the oilskin packet and the books in the food-bag. If some one duly authorized would only take delivery of them the Great Game might play itself for aught he then cared. He was tired and hot in his head, and a cough that came from the stomach worried him.

'No,' he said almost sternly. 'I am not a dog or a snake to bite when I have learned to love.'

'Thou art too tender towards me.'

'Not that either. I have moved in one matter without consulting thee. I have sent a message to the Kulu woman by that woman who gave us the goat's milk this morn, saying that thou wast a little feeble and wouldst need a litter. I beat myself in my mind that I did not do it when we entered the Doon. We stay in this place till the litter returns.'

'I am content. She is a woman with a heart of gold, as thou sayest, but a talker—something of a talker.'

'She will not weary thee. I have looked to that also. Holy One, my heart is very heavy for my many carelessnesses towards thee.' An hysterical catch rose in his throat. 'I have walked thee too far: I have not picked good food always for thee; I have not considered the heat; I have talked to people on the road and left thee alone.... I have—I have ... *Hai mai!* But I love thee ... and it is all too late.... I was a child.... Oh, why was I not a man? ...' Overborne by strain, fatigue, and the weight beyond his years, Kim broke down and sobbed at the lama's feet.

'What a to-do is here!' said the old man gently. 'Thou hast never stepped a hair's breadth from the Way of Obedience. Neglect *me*? Child, I have lived on thy strength as an old tree lives on the lime of a new wall. Day by day, since Shamlegh down, I have stolen strength from thee. *Therefore*, not through any sin of thine, art thou weakened. It is the Body—the silly, stupid Body—that speaks now. Not the assured Soul. Be comforted! Know at least the devils that thou fightest. They are earth-born—children of illusion. We will go to the woman from Kulu. She shall acquire merit in housing us, and specially in tending me. Thou shalt run free till strength returns. I had forgotten the stupid Body. If there be any blame, I bear it. But we are too close to the Gates of

Deliverance to weigh blame. I could praise thee, but what need? In a
little—in a very little—we shall sit beyond all needs.'

And so he petted and comforted Kim with wise saws and grave texts on
that little-understood beast, our Body, who, being but a delusion, insists
on posing as the Soul, to the darkening of the Way, and the immense
multiplication of unnecessary devils.

KIPLING, Kim, 1901

'By rights,' remarked the turnkey, when she was first shown to him, 'I
ought to be her godfather.'

The debtor irresolutely thought of it for a minute, and said, 'Perhaps
you wouldn't object to really being her godfather?'

'Oh! *I* don't object,' replied the turnkey, 'if you don't.'

Thus it came to pass that she was christened one Sunday afternoon,
when the turnkey, being relieved, was off the lock; and that the turnkey
went up to the font of Saint George's church, and promised and vowed
and renounced on her behalf, as he himself related when he came back,
'like a good 'un'.

This invested the turnkey with a new proprietary share in the child,
over and above his former official one. When she began to walk and talk,
he became fond of her; bought a little armchair and stood it by the high
fender of the lodge fireplace; liked to have her company when he was on
the lock; and used to bribe her with cheap toys to come and talk to him.
The child, for her part, soon grew so fond of the turnkey, that she would
come climbing up the lodge-steps of her own accord at all hours of the
day. When she fell asleep in the little armchair by the high fender, the
turnkey would cover her with his pocket handkerchief; and when she sat
in it dressing and undressing a doll . . . he would contemplate her from
the top of his stool, with exceeding gentleness . . .

At what period of her early life, the little creature began to perceive
that it was not the habit of all the world to live locked up in narrow yards
surrounded by high walls with spikes at the top, would be a difficult
question to settle. But she was a very, very, little creature indeed, when
she had somehow gained the knowledge, that her clasp of her father's
hand was to be always loosened at the door which the great key opened;
and that while her own light steps were free to pass beyond it, his feet
must never cross that line. A pitiful and plaintive look, with which she

had begun to regard him when she was still extremely young, was perhaps a part of this discovery.

With a pitiful and plaintive look for everything indeed, but with something in it for only him that was like protection, this Child of the Marshalsea and child of the Father of the Marshalsea, sat by her friend the turnkey in the Lodge, kept the family room, or wandered about the prison-yard, for the first eight years of her life . . .

Wistful and wondering, she would sit in summer weather by the high fender in the Lodge, looking up at the sky through the barred window, until bars of light would arise, when she turned her eyes away, between her and her friend, and she would see him through a grating, too.

'Thinking of the fields,' the turnkey said once, after watching her, 'ain't you?'

'Where are they?' she enquired.

'Why, they're—over there, my dear,' said the turnkey, with a vague flourish of his key. 'Just about there.'

'Does anybody open them, and shut them? Are they locked?'

The turnkey was discomfited. 'Well!' he said. 'Not in general.'

'Are they very pretty, Bob?' She called him Bob, by his own particular request and instruction.

'Lovely. Full of flowers. There's buttercups, and there's daisies, and there's'—the turnkey hesitated, being short of floral nomenclature—'there's dandelions, and all manner of games.'

'Is it very pleasant to be there, Bob?'

'Prime,' said the turnkey.

'Was father ever there?'

'Hem!' coughed the turnkey. 'Oh yes, he was there, sometimes.'

'Is he sorry not to be there now?'

'N—not particular,' said the turnkey.

'Nor any of the people?' she asked, glancing at the listless crowd within. 'O are you quite sure and certain, Bob?'

At this difficult point of the conversation Bob gave in, and changed the subject to hard-bake: always his last resource when he found his little friend getting him into a political, social, or theological corner. But this was the origin of a series of Sunday excursions that these two curious companions made together. They used to issue from the Lodge on alternate Sunday afternoons with great gravity, bound for some meadows or green lanes that had been elaborately appointed by the turnkey in the course of the week; and there she picked grass and flowers to bring home, while he smoked his pipe. Afterwards, there were tea-gardens, shrimps, ale, and other delicacies; and then they would come back hand in hand, unless she was more than usually tired, and had fallen asleep on his shoulder.

DICKENS, Little Dorrit, 1855-7

For Yurii Andreievich the encounter was a tremendous, unforgettable event. He was seeing the idol of his childhood, the teacher who had dominated his mind as a boy.

His gray hair was becoming to him, and his loose foreign suit fitted him well. He was very young and handsome for his years.

Admittedly, he was overshadowed by the grandeur of the events; seen beside them, he lost in stature. But it never occurred to Yurii Andreievich to measure him by such a yardstick.

He was surprised at Nikolai Nikolaievich's calm, at his light and detached tone in speaking of politics. He was more self-possessed than most Russians could be at that time. It marked him as a new arrival, and it seemed old-fashioned and a little embarrassing.

But it was something very different from politics that filled those first few hours of their reunion, that made them laugh and cry and throw their arms around each other's necks, and punctuated their first feverish conversation with frequent moments of silence.

Theirs was a meeting of two artists, and although they were close relatives, and the past arose and lived again between them and memories surged up and they informed each other of all that had happened during their separation, the moment they began to speak of the things that really matter to creative minds, all other ties between them vanished, their kinship and difference of age were forgotten, all that was left was the confrontation of elemental forces, of energies and principles.

For the last ten years Nikolai Nikolaievich had had no opportunity to speak about the problems of creative writing as freely and intimately as now. Nor had Yurii Andreievich ever heard views as penetrating, apt, and inspiring as on that occasion.

Their talk was full of exclamations, they paced excitedly up and down the room, marvelling at each other's perspicacity, or stood in silence by the window drumming on the glass, deeply moved by the exalting discovery of how completely they understood each other.

Such was their first meeting, but later the doctor had seen his uncle a

few times in company, and then Nikolai Nikolaievich was completely
different, unrecognizable.

BORIS PASTERNAK, *Doctor Zhivago*, completed in 1955; tr. Max
Hayward and Manya Harari

My Lord,—I did not leave your Lordship without a painful desire of
returning to wait on you again; I say a painful one, because I knew the
condition of my sick family would not allow me, so soon as I
apprehended you would be going out of town. Accordingly, my poor old
Nurse, who has lived in constant attendance & care of me, ever since I
was an Infant at her breast, dyed the other day. I think it a fine verse, that
of your friend Mr Prior.

—and by his side,
A Good man's greatest loss, a faithful Servant, dy'd!

and I dont think one of my own an ill one, speaking of a Nurse,

The tender Second to a Mother's cares.

Hom. Odyss. 7.

Surely this Sort of Friend is not the least, and this sort of Relation, when
continued thro life, Superior to most that we call so. She having been
tryd, & found, kind & officious so long, thro so many accidents and needs
of life, is surely Equal to a meer Natural Tye. Indeed tis Nature that
makes us Love, but tis Experience that makes us Grateful.

POPE, letter to the Earl of Oxford, 7 November 1725

My dear Mamma,

I have felt very uncomfortable since I got here about Everest. I fear that
at the time you told me—I was so occupied with Jack & Harrow that I did
not think about it seriously. Now however—I have a very uneasy
conscience on the subject. It is quite easy, dear Mamma, for you to say
that it is not my business or for you to refuse to read what I have got to
say—but nevertheless I feel I ought in common decency to write to you
at length on the subject.

In the first place if I allowed Everest to be cut adrift without protest in
the manner which is proposed I should be extremely ungrateful—
besides I should be very sorry not to have her at Grosvenor Square

—because she is in my mind associated—more than anything else with *home*.

She is an old woman—who has been your devoted servant for nearly 20 years—she is more fond of Jack and I than of any other people in the world & to be packed off in the way the Duchess suggests would possibly, if not probably break her down altogether.

Look too at the manner in which it would be done. She is sent away—nominally for a holiday as there is no room at Grosvenor Square for her. Then her board wages are refused her—quite an unusual thing. Finally she is to be given her congé by letter—without having properly made up her mind where to go or what to do.

At her age she is invited to find a new place & practically begin over again. Of course I am extremely fond of Everest & it [is] perhaps from this reason that I think such proceedings cruel & rather mean.

I know you have no choice in the matter & that the Duchess has every right to discharge a servant for whom she has 'no further use'. But I do think that you ought *to arrange that she remains at Grosvenor Square—until I go* back to Sandhurst & Jack to school.

In the meantime she will have ample time to make up her mind where to go—to find a place & resign herself to a change.

Then when a *good* place *has been* secured for her she could leave and be given a pension—which would be sufficient to keep her from want—& which should continue during her life.

This is what I should call a fair and generous method of treating her. It is in your power to explain to the Duchess that she *cannot* be sent away until she has got a good place.

She has for 3 months been boarding herself out of her own money and I have no doubt is not at all well off. Dearest Mamma—I know you are angry with me for writing—I am very sorry but I cannot bear to think of Everest not coming back much less being got rid of in such a manner.

> WINSTON CHURCHILL, letter to Lady Randolph, 29 October 1893; Mrs Everest, his old nurse, died in July 1895, and he wrote to his mother: 'I shall never know such a friend again.'

Mr Pickwick himself continued to reside in his new house, employing his leisure hours in arranging the memoranda which he afterwards presented to the secretary of the once famous club, or in hearing Sam Weller read aloud, with such remarks as suggested themselves to his mind, which never failed to afford Mr Pickwick great amusement. Mr Pickwick is somewhat infirm now; but he retains all his former juvenility of spirit, and may still be frequently seen, contemplating the pictures in the Dulwich Gallery, or enjoying a walk about the pleasant neighbourhood on a fine day. He is known by all the poor people about, who never fail to take their hats off, as he passes, with great respect. The children idolize him, and so indeed does the whole neighbourhood. Every year, he repairs to a large family merry-making at Mr Wardle's; on this, as on all other occasions, he is invariably attended by the faithful Sam, between whom and his master there exists a steady and reciprocal attachment which nothing but death will terminate.

DICKENS, *The Pickwick Papers*, 1837

Gregory wondered if this was what being old meant: everything you wanted to say required a context. If you gave the full context, people thought you a rambling old fool. If you didn't give the context, people thought you a laconic old fool. The very old needed interpreters just as the very young did. When the old lost their companions, their friends, they also lost their interpreters: they lost love, but they also lost the full power of speech.

JULIAN BARNES, *Staring at the Sun*, 1986

Strangers, Enemies, Friends

CRUSOE'S reflections on Friday will strike certain (none too careful) readers as patronizing, since in recent times old heroes have mutated into new villains and old villains into new heroes, so that Caliban is seen as a noble or at any rate exploited indigene, Prospero as an arrogant colonist, and Ariel as a servile civil servant or quisling. As that 'secret spark' cuts across the accidents of birth and upbringing, both Crusoe and Melville's Ishmael declare their new friends more Christian in behaviour than many professed Christians: which was intended in tribute, though it may not carry much force these days.

We include the extract from *The Revolt of Islam* chiefly because it anticipated Wilfred Owen, giving him the title for the poem that follows it here, and also some turns of thought and phrase: the strange land, the strange friend, the spear modernized into a bayonet, the vain weeping and useless glee, ill flowing still from ill. Owen's poem, because the poet knew more intimately what he was talking about, is the less rhetorical, the more palpable and impelling. The difference between the two men in 'Strange Meeting', their nominal antagonism, is obvious; what is to be revealed is the affinity between them.

Angel Clare realizes how misleading received ideas can be, for people individualize themselves in your perception as you come to know them; and George Borrow begins to wonder whether, far from being 'broken Gorgios', the Romanies may not even have built Rome. Miss Mitford's apothecary, his professional interest aroused, overcomes his fierce prejudice against the Abbé's nationality, while the relationship between Fielding and Aziz, still savouring of inequality, remains troubled, partial or potential: 'No, not yet . . . No, not there.'

We shall probably never know what fearful misapprehension Beethoven fell into concerning Herr Hummel; but if the dating of the letters is correct the squabble was peculiarly brief. Nor do we know the nature of the strangers who asked protection of Emily Dickinson; no matter, her moral is an old and sound one: do as you would be done by.

These Strangers, in a foreign World,
Protection asked of me—
Befriend them, lest Yourself in Heaven
Be found a Refugee—

EMILY DICKINSON, 'These Strangers, in a foreign World'

Another foreign neighbour, described by Miss Mitford, was an old French *émigré* who came to reside in 'the small town of Hazelby'; a pretty little place where everything seemed at a standstill. . . . 'It has not even a cheap shop,' she remarks, 'for female gear. . . . The very literature of Hazelby is doled out at the pastry-cook's, in a little one-windowed shop, kept by Matthew Wise. Tarts occupy one end of the counter and reviews the other; whilst the shelves are parcelled out between books, and dolls, and gingerbread. It is a question by which of his trades poor Matthew gains least.'

Here it was that the old *émigré* lodged 'in a low three-cornered room, over the little shop, which Matthew Wise designated his "first floor".' Little was known of him, but that he was a thin, pale, foreign-looking gentleman, who shrugged his shoulders in speaking, took a great deal of snuff, and made a remarkably low bow. But it soon appeared from a written paper placed in a conspicuous part of Matthew's shop, that he was an Abbé, and that he would do himself the honour of teaching French to any of the nobility and gentry of Hazelby who might think fit to employ him. Pupils dropped in rather slowly. The curate's daughters, and the attorney's son, and Miss Deane the milliner—but she found the language difficult, and left off, asserting that M. l'Abbé's snuff made her nervous. At last poor M. l'Abbé fell ill, really ill, dangerously ill, and Matthew Wise went in all haste to summon Mr Hallett (the apothecary) . . .

'Now Mr Hallett was what is usually called a rough diamond. He piqued himself on being a plain downright Englishman [and] he had such an aversion to a Frenchman, in general, as a cat has to a dog: and was wont to erect himself into an attitude of defiance and wrath at the mere sight of the object of his antipathy. He hated and despised the whole nation, abhorred the language, and "would as lief," he assured Matthew, "have been called in to a toad." He went, however, grew interested in the case, which was difficult and complicated; exerted all his skill, and in about a month accomplished a cure.

By this time he had also become interested in his patient, whose piety, meekness, and resignation had won upon him in an extraordinary degree. The disease was gone, but a languor and lowness remained, which Mr Hallett soon traced to a less curable disorder, poverty. The thought of the debt to himself evidently weighed on the poor Abbé's spirits, and our good apothecary at last determined to learn French purely to liquidate his own long bill.

It was the drollest thing in the world to see this pupil of fifty, whose habits were so entirely unfitted for a learner, conning his task . . . He was a most unpromising scholar, shuffled the syllables together in a manner that would seem incredible, and stumbled at every step of the pronunciation, against which his English tongue rebelled amain. Every now and then he solaced himself with a fluent volley of execrations in his own language, which the Abbé understood well enough to return, after rather a polite fashion, in French. It was a most amusing scene. But the motive! the generous noble motive!

M. l'Abbé after a few lessons detected this delicate artifice, and, touched almost to tears, insisted on dismissing his pupil, who, on his side, declared that nothing should induce him to abandon his studies. At last they came to a compromise. The cherry-cheeked Margaret . . . [who kept the doctor's house] took her uncle's post as a learner, which she filled in a manner much more satisfactory; and the good old Frenchman not only allowed Mr Hallett to administer gratis to his ailments, but partook of his Sunday dinner as long as he lived.'

CONSTANCE HILL, *Mary Russell Mitford and her Surroundings*, 1920

But I needed none of all this precaution; for never man had a more faithful, loving, sincere servant, than Friday was to me; without passions, sullenness, or designs, perfectly oblig'd and engag'd; his very affections were ty'd to me, like those of a child to a father; and I dare say he would have sacrific'd his life for the saving mine upon any occasion whatsoever; the many testimonies he gave me of this, put it out of all doubt, and soon convinc'd me that I needed to use no precautions as to my safety on his account.

This frequently gave me occasion to observe, and that with wonder, that, however it had pleas'd God in His providence, and in the government of the works of His hands, to take from so great a part of His creatures, the best uses to which their faculties and the powers of their souls are adapted; yet that He has bestow'd upon them the same powers, the same reason, the same affections, the same sentiments of kindness and obligation, the same passions and resentments of wrongs, the same sense of gratitude, sincerity, fidelity, and all the capacities of doing good and receiving good, that He has given to us; and that when He pleases to offer to them occasions of exerting these, they are as ready, nay, more ready to apply them to the right uses for which they were bestowed, than we are: and this made me very melancholly sometimes, in reflecting as the several occasions presented, how mean a use we make of all these, even though we have these powers enlighten'd by the great lamp of instruction, the spirit of God, and by the knowledge of His word, added to our understanding . . .

But to return to my new companion: I was greatly delighted with him, and made it my business to teach him every thing that was proper to make him useful, handy, and helpful; but especially to make him speak, and understand me when I spake, and he was the aptest scholler that ever was, and particularly was so merry, so constantly diligent, and so pleas'd, when he could but understand me, or make me understand him, that it was very pleasant to me to talk to him; and now my life began to be so easy, that I began to say to my self, that could I but have been safe from more savages, I cared not if I was never to remove from the place while I lived.

DANIEL DEFOE, *Robinson Crusoe*, 1719

The Friendship which Wawatam testified for Henry the fur-trader, as described in the latter's 'Adventures', so almost bare and leafless, yet not blossomless nor fruitless, is remembered with satisfaction and security. The stern imperturbable warrior, after fasting, solitude, and mortification of body, comes to the white man's lodge, and affirms that he is the white brother whom he saw in his dream, and adopts him henceforth. He buries the hatchet as it regards his friend, and they hunt and feast and make maple-sugar together. 'Metals unite from fluxility; birds and beasts from motives of convenience; fools from fear and stupidity; and just men at sight.' If Wawatam would taste the 'white man's milk' with his tribe, or take his bowl of human broth made of the trader's fellow-countrymen, he first finds a place of safety for his Friend, whom he has rescued from a similar fate. At length, after a long winter of undisturbed and happy intercourse in the family of the chieftain in the wilderness, hunting and fishing, they return in the spring to Michilimackinac to dispose of their furs; and it becomes necessary for Wawatam to take leave of his Friend at the Isle aux Outardes, when the latter, to avoid his enemies, proceeded to the Sault de Sainte Marie, supposing that they were to be separated for a short time only. 'We now exchanged farewells,' says Henry, 'with an emotion entirely reciprocal. I did not quit the lodge without the most grateful sense of the many acts of goodness which I had experienced in it, nor without the sincerest respect for the virtues which I had witnessed among its members. All the family accompanied me to the beach; and the canoe had no sooner put off than Wawatam commenced an address to the Kichi Manito, beseeching him to take care of me, his brother, till we should next meet.—We had proceeded to too great a distance to allow of our hearing his voice, before Wawatam had ceased to offer up his prayers.' We never hear of him again.

> THOREAU, *A Week on the Concord and Merrimack Rivers*; the reference is to Alexander Henry's *Travels and Adventures in Canada and the Indian Territories*, published in 1809

With much interest I sat watching him. Savage though he was, and hideously marred about the face—at least to my taste—his countenance yet had a something in it which was by no means disagreeable. You cannot hide the soul. Through all his unearthly tattooings, I thought I saw the traces of a simple honest heart; and in his large, deep eyes, fiery black and bold, there seemed tokens of a spirit that would dare a thousand devils. And besides all this, there was a certain lofty bearing about the Pagan, which even his uncouthness could not altogether maim. He looked like a man who had never cringed and never had had a creditor. Whether it was, too, that his head being shaved, his forehead was drawn out in freer and brighter relief, and looked more expansive than it otherwise would, this I will not venture to decide; but certain it was his head was phrenologically an excellent one. It may seem ridiculous, but it reminded me of General Washington's head, as seen in the popular busts of him. It had the same long regularly graded retreating slope from above the brows, which were likewise very projecting, like two long promontories thickly wooded on top. Queequeg was George Washington cannibalistically developed . . .

As I sat there in that now lonely room; the fire burning low, in that mild stage when, after its first intensity has warmed the air, it then only glows to be looked at; the evening shades and phantoms gathering round the casements, and peering in upon us silent, solitary twain; the storm booming without in solemn swells; I began to be sensible of strange feelings. I felt a melting in me. No more my splintered heart and maddened hand were turned against the wolfish world. This soothing savage had redeemed it. There he sat, his very indifference speaking a nature in which there lurked no civilized hypocrisies and bland deceits. Wild he was; a very sight of sights to see; yet I began to feel myself mysteriously drawn towards him. And those same things that would have repelled most others, they were the very magnets that thus drew me. I'll try a pagan friend, thought I, since Christian kindness has proved but hollow courtesy. I drew my bench near him, and made some friendly signs and hints, doing my best to talk with him meanwhile. At first he little noticed these advances; but presently, upon my referring to his last night's hospitalities, he made out to ask me whether we were again to be bedfellows. I told him yes; whereat I thought he looked pleased, perhaps a little complimented.

We then turned over the book together, and I endeavoured to explain to him the purpose of the printing, and the meaning of the few pictures that were in it. Thus I soon engaged his interest; and from that we went to jabbering the best we could about the various outer sights to be seen in this famous town. Soon I proposed a social smoke; and, producing his pouch and tomahawk, he quietly offered me a puff. And there we sat exchanging puffs from that wild pipe of his, and keeping it regularly passing between us.

If there yet lurked any ice of indifference towards me in the Pagan's breast, this pleasant, genial smoke we had, soon thawed it out, and left us cronies. He seemed to take to me quite as naturally and unbiddenly as I to him; and when our smoke was over, he pressed his forehead against mine, clasped me round the waist, and said that henceforth we were married; meaning, in his country's phrase, that we were bosom friends; he would gladly die for me if need should be. In a countryman, this sudden flame of friendship would have seemed far too premature, a thing to be much distrusted; but in this simple savage those old rules would not apply.

After supper, and another social chat and smoke, we went to our room together. He made me a present of his embalmed head; took out his enormous tobacco wallet, and groping under the tobacco, drew out some thirty dollars in silver; then spreading them on the table, and mechanically dividing them into two equal portions, pushed one of them towards

me, and said it was mine. I was going to remonstrate; but he silenced me
by pouring them into my trousers' pockets. I let them stay. He then went
about his evening prayers, took out his idol, and removed the paper
fireboard. By certain signs and symptoms, I thought he seemed anxious
for me to join him; but well knowing what was to follow, I deliberated a
moment whether, in case he invited me, I would comply or otherwise.

I was a good Christian; born and bred in the bosom of the infallible
Presbyterian Church. How then could I unite with this wild idolater in
worshipping his piece of wood? But what is worship? thought I. But what
is worship?—to do the will of God—*that* is worship. And what is the will
of God?—to do to my fellowman what I would have my fellowman to do
to me—*that* is the will of God. Now, Queequeg is my fellowman. And
what do I wish that this Queequeg would do to me? Why, unite with me
in my particular Presbyterian form of worship. Consequently, I must
then unite with him in his; ergo, I must turn idolater. So I kindled the
shavings; helped prop up the innocent little idol; offered him burnt biscuit
with Queequeg; salaamed before him twice or thrice; kissed his nose; and
that done, we undressed and went to bed, at peace with our own
consciences and all the world. But we did not go to sleep without some
little chat.

How it is I know not; but there is no place like a bed for confidential
disclosures between friends. Man and wife, they say, there open the very
bottom of their souls to each other; and some old couples often lie and
chat over old times till nearly morning. Thus, then, lay I and Queequeg
—a cosy, loving pair.

HERMAN MELVILLE, *Moby Dick*, 1851

The Fathers frequently and freely admonished the King [Akbar the
Great]; but their conscientious readiness in doing this never lessened, still
less put an end to, the kindly friendship of the King towards them. Nay
more, when the King perceived that it was the sincerity of their hearts
that led them to feel themselves free to correct him, he took it in such
good part that he always seemed not only to favour them, but to heap
honours upon them in his desire to show his affection towards them. For
when they saluted him, which they did with uncovered heads, he
answered with a nod and a bright smile. He did not allow them to keep
their heads uncovered when they were in his presence. When a council
was being held, or when he summoned them to his private audience-

chamber for familiar conversation, he used to make them sit beside him. He shook hands with them cordially and familiarly. He frequently left the public audience-chamber to converse with them in private. Several times he paced up and down with his arm round Rudolf's shoulders. Once, when he was in camp, he desired another of the priests, in the middle of a crowd of his nobles, to help him fasten on his sword, which service the Father performed, amidst the envy and wonder of all the courtiers. He wished the priests to be sharers of his inmost thoughts, both in good and ill fortune—no common mark of love and kindness. He ordered his door-keepers to grant them entrance, whenever they wished, even into the inner courtyard of the palace, where only the most distinguished nobles had the right of entrance. He sent them food from his own table—a mark of distinction which he is said never to have conferred upon anybody before. He visited one of the Fathers when he was ill, and greeted him in Portuguese as a sign of respect. There would have been no end to his gifts, had the Fathers not frequently told him that all they needed was food and clothing, and these of the most simple description. This reply pleased him so much that he repeated it publicly: and each month sent them as much money, under the guise of alms, as he thought would be sufficient for their daily expenses.

The Commentary of Father Monserrate, SJ, 1582; tr. J. S. Hoyland and S. N. Banerjee

By and by, sure enough, I catched a glimpse of fire, away through the trees. I went for it, cautious and slow. By and by I was close enough to have a look, and there laid a man on the ground. It most give me the fan-tods. He had a blanket around his head, and his head was nearly in the fire. I set there behind a clump of bushes, in about six foot of him, and kept my eyes on him steady. It was getting grey daylight, now. Pretty soon he gapped, and stretched himself, and hove off the blanket, and it was Miss Watson's Jim! I bet I was glad to see him. I says:

'Hallo, Jim!' and skipped out.

He bounced up and stared at me wild. Then he drops down on his knees, and puts his hands together and says:

'Doan' hurt me—don't! I hain't ever done no harm to a ghos'. I awluz liked dead people, en done all I could for 'em. You go en git in de river agin, whah you b'longs, en doan' do nuffn to Ole Jim, 'at 'uz awluz yo' fren'.'

Well, I warn't long making him understand I warn't dead. I was ever so glad to see Jim. I warn't lonesome, now. I told him I warn't afraid of *him* telling the people where I was.

When breakfast was ready, we lolled on the grass and eat it smoking hot; Jim laid it in with all his might, for he was most about starved. Then when we had got pretty well stuffed, we laid off and lazied.

By and by Jim says:

'But looky here, Huck, who wuz it dat 'uz killed in dat shanty, ef it warn't you?'

Then I told him the whole thing, and he said it was smart. He said Tom Sawyer couldn't get up no better plan than what I had. Then I says:

'How do you come to be here, Jim, and how'd you get here?'

He looked pretty uneasy, and didn't say nothing for a minute. Then he says:

'Maybe I better not tell.'

'Why, Jim?'

'Well, dey's reasons. But yo wouldn' tell on me ef I 'uz to tell you, would you, Huck?'

'Blamed if I would, Jim.'

'Well, I b'lieve you, Huck, I—I *run off*.'

'Jim!'

'But mind, you said you wouldn't tell—you know you said you wouldn't tell, Huck.'

'Well, I did. I said I wouldn't, and I'll stick to it. Honest injun I will. People would call me a low down Ablitionist and despise me for keeping mum—but that don't make no difference. I ain't a-going to tell, and I ain't a-going back there anyways. So now, le's know all about it.'

'Well, you see, it 'uz dis way. Ole Missus—dat's Miss Watson—she pecks on me all de time, en treats me pooty rough, but she awluz said she wouldn' sell me down to Orleans. But I noticed dey wuz a nigger trader roun' de place considable, lately, en I begin to git oneasy. Well, one night I creeps to de do', pooty late, en de do' warn't quite shet, en I hear ole missus tell the widder she gwyne to sell me down to Orleans, but she didn' want to, but she could git eight hund'd dollars for me, en it 'uz sich a big stack o' money she couldn' resis'. De widder she try to git her to say she wouldn' do it, but I never waited to hear de res'. I lit out mighty quick, I tell you.'

Some young birds come along, flying a yard or two at a time and lighting. Jim said it was a sign it was going to rain. He said it was a sign when young chickens flew that way, and so he reckoned it was the same way when young birds done it. I was going to catch some of them, but Jim wouldn't let me. He said it was death. He said his father lay mighty sick once, and some of them catched a bird, and his old granny said his father would die, and he did.

And Jim said you mustn't count the things you are going to cook for dinner, because that would bring bad luck. The same if you shook the table-cloth after sundown. And he said if a man owned a beehive, and that man died, the bees must be told about it before sun-up next morning, or else the bees would all weaken down and quit work and die. Jim said bees wouldn't sting idiots; but I didn't believe that, because I had tried them lots of times myself, and they wouldn't sting me.

I had heard about some of these things before, but not all of them. Jim knowed all kinds of signs. He said he knowed most everything. I said it looked to me like all the signs was about bad luck, and so I asked him if there warn't any good-luck signs. He says:

'Mighty few—an' *dey* ain' no use to a body. What you want to know when good luck's a-comin' for? want to keep it off?' And he said, 'Ef you's got hairy arms en a hairy breas', it's a sign dat you's a-gwyne to be rich. Well, dey's some use in a sign like dat, 'kase it's so fur ahead. You see, maybe you's got to be po' a long time fust, en so you might git discourage' en kill yo'self 'f you didn' know by de sign dat you gwyne to be rich bymeby.'

'Have you got hairy arms and a hairy breast, Jim?'

'What's de use to axe dat question? don' you see I has?'

'Well, are you rich?'

'No, but I been rich wunst, and gwyne to be rich agin. Wunst I had foteen dollars, but I tuck to speculat'n', en got busted out.'

'What did you speculate in, Jim?'

'Well, fust I tackled stock.'

'What kind of stock?'

'Why, live stock. Cattle, you know. I put ten dollars in a cow. But I ain' gwyne to resk no mo' money in stock. De cow up 'n' died on my han's.'

'So you lost the ten dollars.'

'No, I didn' lose it all. I on'y los' 'bout nine of it. I sole de hide en taller for a dollar en ten cents.' . . .

'Well, it's all right, anyway, Jim, long as you're going to be rich again some time or other.'

'Yes—en I's rich now, come to look at it. I owns mysef, en I's wuth eight hund'd dollars. I wisht I had de money, I wouldn' want no mo'.'

MARK TWAIN, *The Adventures of Huckleberry Finn*, 1884

To cement a new friendship, especially between foreigners or persons of a different social world, a spark with which both were secretly charged must fly from person to person, and cut across the accidents of place and time.

SANTAYANA, *Persons and Places: The Middle Span*, 1945

So we find Angel Clare at six-and-twenty here at Talbothays as a student of kine, and, as there were no houses near at hand in which he could get a comfortable lodging, a boarder at the dairyman's . . .

At first he lived up above entirely, reading a good deal, and strumming upon an old harp which he had bought at a sale, saying when in a bitter humour that he might have to get his living by it in the streets some day. But he soon preferred to read human nature by taking his meals downstairs in the general dining-kitchen, with the dairyman and his wife, and the maids and men, who all together formed a lively assembly . . . The longer Clare resided here the less objection had he to his company, and the more did he like to share quarters with them in common.

Much to his surprise he took, indeed, a real delight in their companionship. The conventional farm-folk of his imagination—personified in the newspaper-press by the pitiable dummy known as Hodge—were obliterated after a few days' residence. At close quarters no Hodge was to be seen. At first, it is true, when Clare's intelligence was fresh from a contrasting society, these friends with whom he now hobnobbed seemed a little strange. Sitting down as a level member of the dairyman's household seemed at the outset an undignified proceeding. The ideas, the modes, the surroundings, appeared retrogressive and unmeaning. But with living on there, day after day, the acute sojourner became conscious of a new aspect in the spectacle. Without any objective change whatever, variety had taken the place of monotonousness. His host and his host's household, his men and his maids, as they became intimately known to Clare, began to differentiate themselves as in a chemical process. The thought of Pascal's was brought home to him: 'A mesure qu'on a plus d'esprit, on trouve qu'il y a plus d'hommes originaux. Les gens du commun ne trouvent pas de différence entre les hommes.' The typical and unvarying Hodge ceased to exist. He had been disintegrated into a number of varied fellow-creatures—beings of many minds, beings infinite in difference; some happy, many serene, a few depressed, one here and there bright even to genius, some stupid, others wanton, others austere; some mutely Miltonic, some potentially Cromwellian; into men who had private views of each other, as he had of his friends; who could applaud or condemn each other, amuse or sadden themselves by the contemplation of each other's foibles or vices; men every one of whom walked in his own individual way the road to dusty death.

THOMAS HARDY, *Tess of the D'Urbervilles*, 1891

From this time I had frequent interviews with Jasper, sometimes in his tent, sometimes on the heath, about which we would roam for hours, discoursing on various matters ... I soon found that I had become acquainted with a most singular people, whose habits and pursuits awakened within me the highest interest. Of all connected with them, however, their language was doubtless that which exercised the greatest influence over my imagination. I had at first some suspicion that it would prove a mere made-up gibberish. But I was soon undeceived. Broken, corrupted, and half in ruins as it was, it was not long before I found that it was an original speech, far more so, indeed, than one or two others of high name and celebrity ... But where did this speech come from, and who were they who spoke it? These were questions which I could not solve, and which Jasper himself, when pressed, confessed his inability to answer. 'But, whoever we be, brother,' said he, 'we are an old people, and not what folks in general imagine, broken gorgios; and if we are not Egyptians, we are at any rate Rommany Chals!'

'Rommany Chals! I should not wonder after all,' said I, 'that these people had something to do with the foundation of Rome. Rome, it is said, was built by vagabonds, who knows but that some tribe of the kind settled down thereabouts, and called the town which they built after their name; but whence did they come originally? ah! there is the difficulty.'

But abandoning these questions, which at that time were far too profound for me, I went on studying the language, and at the same time the characters and manners of these strange people. My rapid progress in the former astonished, while it delighted, Jasper. 'We'll no longer call you Sap-engro [hunter of snakes], brother,' said he; 'but rather Lav-engro, which in the language of the gorgios meaneth Word Master.' 'Nay, brother,' said Tawno Chikno, with whom I had become very intimate, 'you had better call him Cooro-mengro, I have put on *the gloves* with him, and find him a pure fist master; I like him for that, for I am a Cooro-mengro myself, and was born at Brummagem.'

'I likes him for his modesty,' said Mrs Chikno; 'I never hears any ill words come from his mouth, but, on the contrary, much sweet language. His talk is golden, and he has taught my eldest to say his prayers in Rommany, which my rover had never the grace to do.' 'He is the pal of my rom,' said Mrs Petulengro, who was a very handsome woman, 'and therefore I likes him, and not less for his being a rye; folks calls me high-minded, and perhaps I have reason to be so; before I married Pharaoh I had an offer from a lord—I likes the young rye, and, if he chooses to follow us, he shall have my sister.'

'Sit down, brother,' said Mr Petulengro, 'and take a cup of good ale.'

I sat down. 'Your health, gentlemen,' said I, as I took the cup which Mr Petulengro handed to me.

'Aukko tu pios adrey Rommanis. Here is your health in Rommany, brother,' said Mr Petulengro; who, having refilled the cup, now emptied it at a draught . . .

'And now, brother,' said Mr Petulengro, 'seeing that you have drunk and been drunken, you will perhaps tell us where you have been, and what about?'

'I have been in the Big City,' said I, 'writing lils.'

'How much money have you got in your pocket, brother?' said Mr Petulengro.

'Eighteen pence,' said I; 'all I have in the world.'

'I have been in the Big City, too,' said Mr Petulengro; 'But I have not written lils—I have fought in the ring—I have fifty pounds in my pocket—I have much more in the world. Brother, there is considerable difference between us.'

'I would rather be the lil-writer, after all,' said the tall, handsome black man; 'indeed, I would wish for nothing better.'

'Why so?' said Mr Petulengro.

'Because they have so much to say for themselves,' said the black man, 'even when dead and gone. When they are laid in the churchyard, it is their own fault if people a'n't talking of them. Who will know, after I am dead, or bitchadey pawdel, that I was once the beauty of the world, or that you, Jasper, were—'

'The best man in England of my inches. That's true, Tawno—however, here's our brother will perhaps let the world know something about us.'

'Not he,' said the other, with a sigh; 'he'll have quite enough to do in writing his own lils, and telling the world how handsome and clever he was; and who can blame him? Not I. If I could write lils, every word should be about myself and my own tacho Rommanis—my own lawful wedded wife, which is the same thing. I tell you what, brother, I once heard a wise man say in Brummagem, that "there is nothing like blowing one's own horn", which I conceive to be much the same thing as writing one's own lil.'

After a little more conversation, Mr Petulengro arose, and motioned me to follow him. 'Only eighteen pence in the world, brother!' said he, as we walked together.

'Nothing more, I assure you. How came you to ask me how much money I had?'

'Because there was something in your look, brother, something very much resembling that which a person showeth who does not carry much money in his pocket. I was looking at my own face this morning in my wife's looking-glass—I did not look as you do, brother.'

'I believe your sole motive for inquiring,' said I, 'was to have an opportunity of venting a foolish boast, and to let me know that you were in possession of fifty pounds.'

'What is the use of having money unless you let people know you have it?' said Mr Petulengro. 'It is not everyone can read faces, brother; and, unless you knew I had money, how could you ask me to lend you any?'

'I am not going to ask you to lend me any.'

'Then you may have it without asking; as I said before, I have fifty pounds, all lawfully-earned money, got by fighting in the ring—I will lend you that, brother.'

'You are very kind,' said I; 'but I will not take it.'

'Then the half of it?'

'Nor the half of it; but it is getting towards evening, I must go back to the Great City.'

'And what will you do in the Boro Foros?'

'I know not,' said I.

'Earn money?'

'If I can.'

'And if you can't?'

'Starve!'

'You look ill, brother,' said Mr Petulengro.

'I do not feel well; the Great City does not agree with me. Should I be so fortunate as to earn some money, I would leave the Big City, and take to the woods and fields.'

'You may do that, brother,' said Mr Petulengro, 'whether you have money or not. Our tents and horses are on the other side of yonder wooded hill, come and stay with us; we shall all be glad of your company.'

GEORGE BORROW, *Lavengro*, 1851

But the friendships had to be made first. I think they grew out of some material basis, a feeling of common interest that showed itself by accident. I remember that on the second or third day—we were out of Belfast and steaming past the shores of Northern Ireland—having realized that crowded though we were everyone else was ignoring the lack of privacy and making himself at home, I plucked up courage to take out my fiddle and play softly to myself. I was in fact murdering Beethoven's first violin sonata as usual. I was sitting on my bunk, which was in the bottom tier, as I played, and I was suddenly aware of a man standing above me gesticulating furiously. I had already marked him down as a fellow to be avoided, for his aspect seemed to me villainous. He was a huge man, whose face, except for his tiny eyes and red bulbous nose that looked as though it had been shoved on as an afterthought, was almost wholly obscured by a shaggy beard. He was dressed in the most outlandish garments, in a Russian peasant blouse, his feet and legs bound up in rags. He was a man I shrank from, and there he was, seemingly about to snatch my fiddle from me by its neck and then standing back and playing an imaginary violin in pantomime and, that done, jerking his thumb furiously at his chest. It took me a little time to gather what he meant, and then, so enormously did he loom above me and so ferocious did he appear, there seemed nothing for it but to hand him the instrument. He stared at it with delight. In those great hairy hands it looked like a toy fiddle. I was in agony lest he should break it, for to tell the truth, I no more regarded the fellow as human than if he had been a gorilla. But his face was lit up with joy, and with two strides he was in the middle of the steerage, the fiddle tucked beneath his worn doormat of a beard, and the bow on the strings was making music of a kind I had never heard before. It was wild, passionate and melancholy; I found it almost physically frightening for it seemed to pluck at a nerve in my stomach. It was most decidedly not Beethoven's first sonata; it was not to my mind civilized at all but an expression of primitive and intense melancholy. As he played, quietness fell on the steerage. Everyone was listening, and after a time some of the passengers began to dance, and again it was a dance the like of which I have not seen before or since. For years I was haunted by this music my friend, for the loan of the instrument made him my friend, conjured from my fiddle . . . It was not until quite recent years, with the coming of wireless, that I heard anything like it again, and then I realized it was Tzigane music, the music of the Hungarian gipsies, but played by my friend with a barbaric pathos and splendour beyond anything I ever heard on the BBC.

He was my first friend. When he returned the fiddle to me I gave him to understand that he could use it whenever he liked. To my embarrassment, he embraced me. But thereafter we spent much of the day together. We could converse only by smile and gesture, for his language was beyond me entirely, and though he told me what I assumed was his name I could not pronounce it. He on his side managed 'Billy' very satisfactorily, and no sooner was I under his protection than I was 'Billy' to all the members of his national group, whatever it was, and they made me richly welcome. For my part, I felt both proud and safe with this uncouth giant, who was the slave of gratitude, at my side.

> WALTER ALLEN, *All in a Lifetime*, 1959; sailing steerage to New York, *c.* 1896

Therefore the Oxford party went off to adorn for the dinner.
  Be it recorded in song who was first, who last, in dressing.
Hope was first, black-tied, white-waistcoated, simple, His Honour;
For the postman made out he was heir to the Earldom of Ilay
(Being the younger son of the younger brother, the Colonel) . . .
  Hope was first, His Honour, and next to His Honour the Tutor.
Still more plain the Tutor, the grave man, nicknamed Adam,
White-tied, clerical, silent, with antique square-cut waistcoat
Formal, unchanged, of black cloth, but with sense and feeling
    beneath it;

Skilful in Ethics and Logic, in Pindar and Poets unrivalled;
Shady in Latin, said Lindsay, but *topping* in Plays and Aldrich.
  Somewhat more splendid in dress, in a waistcoat work of a lady,
Lindsay, succeeded; the lively, the cheery, cigar-loving Lindsay,
Lindsay the ready of speech, the Piper, the Dialectician,
This was his title from Adam because of the words he invented,
Who in three weeks had created a dialect new for the party;
This was his title from Adam, but mostly they called him the Piper.
Lindsay succeeded, the lively, the cheery, cigar-loving Lindsay.
  Hewson and Hobbes were down at the *matutine* bathing; of course
    too
Arthur, the bather of bathers, *par excellence*, Audley by surname,
Arthur they called him for love and for euphony; they had been
    bathing,
Where in the morning was custom, where over a ledge of granite
Into a granite basin the amber torrent descended,
Only a step from the cottage, the road and larches between them.
Hewson and Hobbes followed quick upon Adam; on them followed
    Arthur.
  Airlie descended the last, effulgent as god of Olympus;
Blue, perceptibly blue, was the coat that had white silk facings,
Waistcoat blue, coral-buttoned, the white tie finely adjusted,
Coral moreover the studs on a shirt as of crochet of women:
When the fourwheel for ten minutes already had stood at the
    gateway,
He, like a god, came leaving his ample Olympian chamber.
  And in the fourwheel they drove to the place of the clansmen's
    meeting.

  Then was the dinner served, and the Minister prayed for a
    blessing,
And to the viands before them with knife and with fork they beset
    them;
Venison, the red and the roe, with mutton; and grouse succeeding;
Such was the feast, with whisky of course, and at top and bottom
Small decanters of sherry, not overchoice, for the gentry.
So to the viands before them with laughter and chat they beset them.
And, when on flesh and on fowl had appetite duly been sated,
Up rose the Catholic Priest and returned God thanks for the dinner.

Then on all tables were set black bottles of well-mixed toddy,
And, with the bottles and glasses before them, they sat, digesting,
Talking, enjoying, but chiefly awaiting the toasts and speeches.

    Two orations alone the memorial song will render;
For at the banquet's close spake thus the lively Sir Hector,
Somewhat husky with praises exuberant, often repeated,
Pleasant to him and to them, of the gallant Highland soldiers
Whom he erst led in the fight;—something husky, but ready, though
      weary,
Up to them rose and spoke the grey but gladsome chieftain:—
    Fill up your glasses, my friends, once more,—With all the
      honours!
There was a toast I forgot, which our gallant Highland homes have
Always welcomed the stranger, delighted, I may say, to see such
Fine young men at my table—My friends! are you ready? the
      Strangers.
Gentlemen, here are your healths,—and I wish you—With all the
      honours!
    So he said, and the cheers ensued, and all the honours.

Up to them rose and spoke the poet and radical Hewson.
    I am, I think, perhaps the most perfect stranger present.
I have not, as have some of my friends, in my veins some tincture,
Some few ounces of Scottish blood; no, nothing like it.
I am therefore perhaps the fittest to answer and thank you.
So I thank you, sir, for myself and for my companions,
Heartily thank you all for this unexpected greeting,
All the more welcome, as showing you do not account us intruders,
Are not unwilling to see the north and the south forgather.
And, surely, seldom have Scotch and English more thoroughly
      mingled;
Scarcely with warmer hearts, and clearer feeling of manhood,
Even in tourney, and foray, and fray, and regular battle,
Where the life and the strength came out in the tug and tussle,
Scarcely, where man met man, and soul encountered with soul, as
Close as do the bodies and twining limbs of the wrestlers,
When for a final bout are a day's two champions mated,—
In the grand old times of bows, and bills, and claymores,
At the old Flodden-field—or Bannockburn—or Culloden.

—(And he paused a moment, for breath, and because of some
      cheering)
We are the better friends, I fancy, for that old fighting,
Better friends, inasmuch as we know each other the better,
We can now shake hands without pretending or shuffling.
    On this passage followed a great tornado of cheering,
Tables were rapped, feet stamped, a glass or two got broken.

> ARTHUR HUGH CLOUGH, *The Bothie of Tober-na-Vuolich: A Long-
> Vacation Pastoral,* 1848; an undergraduate reading-party in the
> Highlands

It was most touching news to be told, as we were lately, that Christians
on the Continent were praying together for the spiritual well-being of
England. May they gain light, while they aim at unity, and grow in faith
while they manifest their love! We too have our duties to them; not of
reviling, not of slandering, not of hating, though political interests
require it; but the duty of loving brethren still more abundantly in spirit,
whose faces, for our sins and their sins, we are not allowed to see in the
flesh.

> JOHN HENRY NEWMAN, *The British Critic,* 1840

BOSWELL: '*You* should like his book, Mrs Knowles, as it maintains, as you
friends do, that courage is not a Christian virtue.' MRS KNOWLES: 'Yes,
indeed, I like him there; but I cannot agree with him, that friendship is not
a Christian virtue.' JOHNSON: 'Why, Madam, strictly speaking, he is right.
All friendship is preferring the interest of a friend, to the neglect, or,
perhaps, against the interest of others; so that an old Greek said, "He that
has *friends* has *no friend.*" Now Christianity recommends universal benevolence, to consider all men as our brethren, which is contrary to the
virtue of friendship, as described by the ancient philosophers. Surely,
Madam, your sect must approve of this; for, you call all men *friends.*' MRS
KNOWLES: 'We are commanded to do good to all men, "but especially to
them who are of the household of Faith".' JOHNSON: 'Well, Madam. The
household of Faith is wide enough.' MRS KNOWLES: 'But, Doctor, our
Saviour had twelve Apostles, yet there was *one* whom he *loved.* John was
called "the disciple whom JESUS loved".' JOHNSON (with eyes sparkling

benignantly): 'Very well, indeed, Madam. You have said very well.'
BOSWELL: 'A fine application. Pray, Sir, had you ever thought of it?'
JOHNSON: 'I had not, Sir.'

From this pleasing subject, he, I know not how or why, made a sudden transition to one upon which he was a violent aggressor; for he said, 'I am willing to love all mankind, *except an American*': and his inflammable corruption bursting into horrid fire, he 'breathed out threatenings and slaughter'; calling them, 'Rascals—Robbers—Pirates'; and exclaiming, he'd 'burn and destroy them'. Miss Seward, looking to him with mild but steady astonishment, said, 'Sir, this is an instance that we are always most violent against those whom we have injured.'—He was irritated still more by this delicate and keen reproach; and roared out another tremendous volley, which one might fancy could be heard across the Atlantick. During this tempest I sat in great uneasiness, lamenting his heat of temper; till, by degrees, I diverted his attention to other topicks.

> BOSWELL, *Life of Johnson*, 15 April 1778. Among those discussing Soame Jenyns's *View of the Internal Evidence of the Christian Religion* were Mrs Mary Knowles, 'the ingenious Quaker lady', and Miss Anna Seward, 'the poetess of Lichfield'. The 'old Greek' is Diogenes Laertius

North. How do you account, my dearest Shepherd, for the steadiness and perseverance of my affection for thee, seeing that I am naturally and artificially the most wayward, fickle, and capricious of all God's creatures? Not a friend but yourself, James, with whom I have not frequently and bitterly quarrelled, often to the utter extinction of mutual regard—but towards my incomprehensible Brownie my heart ever yearns—

Shepherd. Haud your leein tongue, ye tyke, you've quarrelled wi' me mony thousan' times, and I've borne at your hands mair ill-usage than I wad hae taen frae ony ither mortal man in his Majesty's dominions. Yet I weel believe that only the shears o' Fate will ever cut the cords o' our friendship. I fancy it's just the same wi' you as wi' me, we maun like ane anither whether we wull or no—and that's the sort o' freendship for me—for it flourishes, like a mountain flower, in all weathers—braid and bricht in the sunshine, and just faulded up a wee in the sleet, sae that it micht maist be thocht dead, but fu' o' life in its cozy bield   *shelter*

ahint the mossy stane, and peering out again in a' its beauty, at
the sang o' the rising laverock.

    North. This world's friendships, James—

    Shepherd. Are as cheap as crockery, and as easily broken by a
fa'. They seldom can bide a clash, without fleein intil flinders.   *fragments*

> Christopher North (John Wilson), *Noctes Ambrosianae*, March
> 1827; dialogue with James Hogg, 'The Ettrick Shepherd'

Don't come to me any more! You are a false dog, and may the hangman
do away with all false dogs.

You are an honest fellow and I now realize that you were right. So come
to me this afternoon. You will find Schuppanzigh [violinist] here too and
we shall both blow you up, cudgel you and shake you so that you will
have a thoroughly good time.

    Kisses from your Beethoven, also called dumpling.

> Ludwig van Beethoven, letters thought to be addressed to
> Johann Nepomuk Hummel, pianist and composer, on successive
> days *c.*1779; tr. Emily Anderson

As the Knight of the Couchant Leopard continued to fix his eyes
attentively on the yet distant cluster of palm-trees, it seemed to him as if
some object was moving among them. The distant form separated itself
from the trees, which partly hid its motions, and advanced towards the
knight with a speed which soon showed a mounted horseman, whom his
turban, long spear, and green caftan floating in the wind, on his nearer
approach, showed to be a Saracen cavalier. 'In the desert,' saith an
Eastern proverb, 'no man meets a friend.'

. . . in the last encounter the Saracen had lost his sword and his quiver of
arrows, both of which were attached to the girdle, which he was obliged
to abandon. He had also lost his turban in the struggle. These disadvant-
ages seemed to incline the Moslem to a truce: he approached the
Christian with his right hand extended, but no longer in a menacing
attitude.

    'There is truce betwixt our nations,' he said, in the lingua franca commonly used for the purpose of communication with the Crusaders; 'wherefore should there be war betwixt thee and me?—Let there be peace betwixt us.'

'I am well contented,' answered he of the Couchant Leopard; 'but what security dost thou offer that thou wilt observe the truce?'

'The word of a follower of the Prophet was never broken,' answered the Emir. 'It is thou, brave Nazarene, from whom I should demand security, did I not know that treason seldom dwells with courage.'

The Crusader felt that the confidence of the Moslem made him ashamed of his own doubts.

'By the cross of my sword,' he said, laying his hand on the weapon as he spoke, 'I will be true companion to thee, Saracen, while our fortune wills that we remain in company together.'

'By Mahommed, Prophet of God, and by Allah, God of the Prophet,' replied his late foeman, 'there is not treachery in my heart towards thee. And now wend we to yonder fountain, for the hour of rest is at hand, and the stream had hardly touched my lip when I was called to battle by thy approach.'

The Knight of the Couchant Leopard yielded a ready and courteous assent; and the late foes, without an angry look, or gesture of doubt, rode side by side to the little cluster of palm-trees.

SIR WALTER SCOTT, *The Talisman*, 1825

'Soldiers, our brethren and our friends are slain.
    Ye murdered them, I think, as they did sleep!
Alas, what have ye done? the slightest pain
    Which ye might suffer, there were eyes to weep,
    But ye have quenched them—there were smiles to steep
Your hearts in balm, but they are lost in woe;
    And those whom love did set his watch to keep
Around your tents, truth's freedom to bestow,
Ye stabbed as they did sleep—but they forgive ye now.

'Oh wherefore should ill ever flow from ill,
    And pain still keener pain for ever breed?
We all are brethren—even the slaves who kill
    For hire, are men; and to avenge misdeed
    On the misdoer, doth but Misery feed

With her own broken heart! O Earth, O Heaven!
   And thou, dread Nature, which to every deed
And all that lives or is, to be hath given,
Even as to thee have these done ill, and are forgiven!

'Join then your hands and hearts, and let the past
   Be as a grave which gives not up its dead
To evil thoughts.'—A film then overcast
   My sense with dimness, for the wound, which bled
   Freshly, swift shadows o'er mine eyes had shed.
When I awoke, I lay mid friends and foes,
   And earnest countenances on me shed
The light of questioning looks, whilst one did close
My wound with balmiest herbs, and soothed me to repose;

And one whose spear had pierced me, leaned beside,
   With quivering lips and humid eyes;—and all
Seemed like some brothers on a journey wide
   Gone forth, whom now strange meeting did befall
   In a strange land, round one whom they might call
Their friend, their chief, their father, for assay
   Of peril, which had saved them from the thrall
Of death, now suffering. Thus the vast array
Of those fraternal bands were reconciled that day.

     Pᴇʀᴄʏ Bʏssʜᴇ Sʜᴇʟʟᴇʏ, *The Revolt of Islam*, 1818; an allegorized
     version of the French Revolution

It seemed that out of battle I escaped
Down some profound dull tunnel, long since scooped
Through granites which titanic wars had groined.
Yet also there encumbered sleepers groaned,
Too fast in thought or death to be bestirred.
Then, as I probed them, one sprang up, and stared
With piteous recognition in fixed eyes,
Lifting distressful hands as if to bless.
And by his smile I knew that sullen hall,
By his dead smile I knew we stood in Hell.
With a thousand pains that vision's face was grained;

Yet no blood reached there from the upper ground,
And no guns thumped, or down the flues made moan.
'Strange friend,' I said, 'here is no cause to mourn.'
'None,' said the other, 'save the undone years,
The hopelessness. Whatever hope is yours,
Was my life also; I went hunting wild
After the wildest beauty in the world,
Which lies not calm in eyes, or braided hair,
But mocks the steady running of the hour,
And if it grieves, grieves richlier than here.
For by my glee might many men have laughed,
And of my weeping something had been left,
Which must die now. I mean the truth untold,
The pity of war, the pity war distilled.
Now men will go content with what we spoiled,
Or, discontent, boil bloody, and be spilled.
They will be swift with swiftness of the tigress,
None will break ranks, though nations trek from progress.
Courage was mine, and I had mystery,
Wisdom was mine, and I had mastery:
To miss the march of this retreating world
Into vain citadels that are not walled.
Then, when much blood had clogged their chariot-wheels,
I would go up and wash them from sweet wells,
Even with truths that lie too deep for taint.
I would have poured my spirit without stint
But not through wounds; not on the cess of war.
Foreheads of men have bled where no wounds were.
I am the enemy you killed, my friend.
I knew you in this dark: for so you frowned
Yesterday through me as you jabbed and killed.
I parried; but my hands were loath and cold.
Let us sleep now . . .'

WILFRED OWEN (1893–1918), 'Strange Meeting'

Caesar.   Go charge Agrippa
    Plant those that have revolted in the vant,
    That Antony may seem to spend his fury
    Upon himself.   [*Exeunt*]

Enobarbus. Alexas did revolt and went to Jewry on
    Affairs of Antony; there did persuade
    Great Herod to incline himself to Caesar
    And leave his master Antony. For this pains
    Caesar hath hanged him. Canidius and the rest
    That fell away have entertainment, but
    No honourable trust. I have done ill,
    Of which I do accuse myself so sorely
    That I will joy no more.
        [Enter a Soldier of Caesar's]
Soldier.   Enobarbus, Antony
    Hath after thee sent all thy treasure, with
    His bounty overplus. The messenger
    Came on my guard, and at thy tent is now
    Unloading of his mules.
Eno.   I give it you.
Sold. Mock not, Enobarbus.
    I tell you true. Best you safed the bringer
    Out of the host. I must attend mine office
    Or would have done't myself. Your emperor
    Continues still a Jove.   *[Exit]*
Eno. I am alone the villain of the earth,
    And feel I am so most. O Antony,
    Thou mine of bounty, how wouldst thou have paid
    My better service, when my turpitude
    Thou dost so crown with gold! This blows my heart.
    If swift thought break it not, a swifter mean
    Shall outstrike thought; but thought will do't, I feel.
    I fight against thee? No, I will go seek
    Some ditch wherein to die; the foul'st best fits
    My latter part of life.

SHAKESPEARE, *Antony and Cleopatra*, 1606–7

Eighteen years ago my husband and I moved into our first house. Two weeks later our neighbours arrived next door. We thought they were rather standoffish, and they, in return, were not too keen on us.

But over the years we have blessed the day they came to live next door. We have shared happy times. They were godparents to our daughter.

And when trouble was at its worst they were always at hand with help.

Now they have paid us the biggest compliment ever. My husband recently changed his job and we had to move 200 miles. The parting was just too much. Rather than say goodbye, my neighbour's husband has changed his job, and they have moved with us.

Although we are not neighbours, we are only five minutes away from each other. This is a friendship that really has stood the test of time.

Correspondence, *The People*, 12 October 1969

I'm going out to dine at Gray's
    With Bertie Morden, Charles and Kit,
And Manderly who never pays
    And Jane who wins in spite of it,
    And Algernon who won't admit
The truth about his curious hair
    And teeth that very nearly fit:—
And Mrs Roebeck will be there.

And then tomorrow someone says
    That someone else has made a hit
In one of Mister Twister's plays,
    And off we go to yawn at it;
    And when it's petered out we quit
For number 20, Taunton Square,
    And smoke, and drink, and dance a bit:—
And Mrs Roebeck will be there.

And so through each declining phase
    Of emptied effort, jaded wit,
And day by day of London days
    Obscurely, more obscurely, lit;
    Until the uncertain shadows flit
Announcing to the shuddering air
    A Darkening, and the end of it:—
And Mrs Roebeck will be there.

Envoi

Prince, on their iron thrones they sit,
    Impassable to our despair,
The dreadful Guardians of the Pit:—
    And Mrs Roebeck will be there.

HILAIRE BELLOC, 'Ballade of Hell and of Mrs Roebeck', 1923

My wife and I have asked a crowd of craps
To come and waste their time and ours: perhaps
You'd care to join us? In a pig's arse, friend.
Day comes to an end.
The gas fire breathes, the trees are darkly swayed.
And so *Dear Warlock-Williams: I'm afraid—*

Funny how hard it is to be alone.
I could spend half my evenings, if I wanted,
Holding a glass of washing sherry, canted
Over to catch the drivel of some bitch
Who's read nothing but *Which*;
Just think of all the spare time that has flown

Straight into nothingness by being filled
With forks and faces, rather than repaid
Under a lamp, hearing the noise of wind,
And looking out to see the moon thinned
To an air-sharpened blade.
A life, and yet how sternly it's instilled

All solitude is selfish. No one now
Believes the hermit with his gown and dish
Talking to God (who's gone too); the big wish
Is to have people nice to you, which means
Doing it back somehow.
Virtue is social. Are, then, these routines

Playing at goodness, like going to church?
Something that bores us, something we don't do well
(Asking that ass about his fool research)

But try to feel, because, however crudely,
It shows us what should be?
Too subtle, that. Too decent, too. Oh hell,

Only the young can be alone freely.
The time is shorter now for company,
And sitting by a lamp more often brings
Not peace, but other things.
Beyond the light stand failure and remorse
Whispering *Dear Warlock-Williams: Why, of course—*

PHILIP LARKIN, 'Vers de Société', 1974

Two of us were transferred together from the Bareilly District Gaol to
the Dehra Dun Gaol—Govind Ballabh Pant and I. To avoid the
possibility of a demonstration, we were not put on the train at Bareilly,
but at a wayside station fifty miles out. We were taken secretly by
motor-car at night, and, after many months of seclusion, that drive
through the cool night air was a rare delight.

Before we left Bareilly Gaol, a little incident took place which moved
me then and is yet fresh in my memory. The Superintendent of Police of
Bareilly, an Englishman, was present there, and, as I got into the car, he
handed to me rather shyly a packet which he told me contained old
German illustrated magazines. He said that he had heard that I was
learning German and so he had brought these magazines for me. I had
never met him before, nor have I seen him since. I do not even know his
name. This spontaneous act of courtesy and the kindly thought that
prompted it touched me and I felt very grateful to him . . .

How different was the behaviour of a person acting as an individual
and obeying his own impulses from his behaviour as an official or a unit
in an army. The soldier, stiffening to attention, drops his humanity, and,
acting as an automaton, shoots and kills inoffensive and harmless
persons who have done him no ill. So also, I thought, the police officer
who would hesitate to do an unkindness to an individual would, the day
after, direct a *lathi* charge on innocent people. He would not think of
himself as an individual then, nor will he consider as individuals those
crowds whom he beats down or shoots.

JAWAHARLAL NEHRU, *An Autobiography*, 1936

'Before you go, for you are evidently in a great hurry, will you please unlock that drawer? Do you see a piece of brown paper at the top?'

'Yes.'

'Open it.'

'Who is this?'

'She was my wife. You are the first Englishman she has ever come before. Now put her photograph away.'

He was astonished, as a traveller who suddenly sees, between the stones of the desert, flowers. The flowers have been there all the time, but suddenly he sees them. He tried to look at the photograph, but in itself it was just a woman in a sari, facing the world. He muttered, 'Really, I don't know why you pay me this great compliment, Aziz, but I do appreciate it.'

'Oh, it's nothing; she was not a highly educated woman or even beautiful; but put it away. You would have seen her, so why should you not see her photograph?'

'You would have allowed me to see her?'

'Why not? I believe in the purdah, but I should have told her you were my brother, and she would have seen you. Hamidullah saw her, and several others.'

'Did she think they were your brothers?'

'Of course not, but the word exists and is convenient. All men are my brothers, and as soon as one behaves as such he may see my wife.'

'And when the whole world behaves as such, there will be no more purdah?'

'It is because you can say and feel such a remark as that, that I show you the photograph,' said Aziz gravely . . .

The eye-flies became worse than ever and danced close up to their pupils, or crawled into their ears. Fielding hit about wildly. The exercise made him hot, and he got up to go.

'You might tell your servant to bring my horse. He doesn't seem to appreciate my Urdu.'

'I know. I gave him orders not to. Such are the tricks we play on unfortunate Englishmen. Poor Mr Fielding! But I will release you now. O dear! With the exception of yourself and Hamidullah, I have no one to talk to in this place. You like Hamidullah, don't you?'

'Very much.'

'Do you promise to come at once to us when you are in trouble?'

'I never can be in trouble.'

'There goes a queer chap, I trust he won't come to grief,' thought Aziz, left alone. His period of admiration was over, and he reacted towards patronage. It was difficult for him to remain in awe of anyone who played with all his cards on the table. Fielding, he discovered on closer acquaintance, was truly warm-hearted and unconventional, but not what can be called wise . . .

But they were friends, brothers. That part was settled, their compact had been subscribed by the photograph, they trusted one another, affection had triumphed for once in a way.

India a nation! What an apotheosis! Last comer to the drab nineteenth-century sisterhood! Waddling in at this hour of the world to take her seat! She, whose only peer was the Holy Roman Empire, she shall rank with Guatemala and Belgium perhaps! Fielding mocked again. And Aziz in an awful rage danced this way and that, not knowing what to do, and cried: 'Down with the English, anyhow. That's certain. Clear out, you fellows, double quick, I say. We may hate one another, but we hate you most. If I don't make you go, Ahmed will, Karim will, if it's fifty five-hundred years we shall get rid of you; yes, we shall drive every blasted Englishman into the sea, and then'—he rode against him furiously—'and then,' he concluded, half kissing him, 'you and I shall be friends.'

'Why can't we be friends now?' said the other, holding him affectionately. 'It's what I want. It's what you want.'

But the horses didn't want it—they swerved apart; the earth didn't want it, sending up rocks through which riders must pass single file; the temples, the tank, the jail, the palace, the birds, the carrion, the Guest House, that came into view as they issued from the gap and saw Mau beneath: they didn't want it, they said in their hundred voices: 'No, not yet', and the sky said: 'No, not there.'

E. M. FORSTER, *A Passage to India*, 1924

Gentile or Hebrew or simply one
Whose face has been lost to us in time;
We shall not rescue from oblivion
Now the silent letters of his name.

He knew of mercy what a bandit may
Whom Judea has nailed to a cross.
And we today are at a loss
About the time preceding. That day

At his task of dying crucified,
He heard, amid the crowd's mockery,
That he who was dying at his side
Was a god, and said to him blindly,

Remember me when you inherit
Your kingdom, and the inconceivable voice
That shall judge one day each man's merit
Promised him from the terrible cross

Paradise. Nothing more was said
Until the end came, but history
Shall preserve from death the memory
Of the afternoon on which they died.

Oh friends, the innocence of this friend
Of Jesus, the candour that moved him
From the ignominy of his end
To ask for Heaven and receive it,

Was the very same that so many times
Had hurled him into sin and bloody crimes.

JORGE LUIS BORGES, 'Luke 23', 1960; tr. Irving Feldman

Assorted Affinities

Souls of Poets dead and gone
What Elysium have ye known,
Happy field or mossy cavern,
Choicer than the Mermaid Tavern? (Keats)

VARIETIES of conviviality, odd though harmless capers, joking, smoking, eating, drinking, playing cards (a respectable pursuit as long as one wins), 'excellent discourse of all sorts', photography as an *aide-mémoire*, friendship with a tree, with a desk, with a Tintoretto, an increasingly cordial relationship between an American customer and the staff of a London bookshop, a poet's 'fancy' or fantasy friends, imaginary or dead companions and comforters, the (sometimes equivocal) entreaties of lonely hearts . . .

Sydney Smith was no lonely heart. His discovery of a soul mate through mutual dislike of gravy chimes with a remark of C. S. Lewis's, that a friendship typically opens with some such expression as 'What? You too? I thought I was the only one.'

Friendship under stress and worse is illustrated by Seneca and Captain Scott facing death, by wartime comradeship, persecution and oppression, and the embarrassments of fraternizing under military occupation. Margarete Buber-Neumann said that while the SS could treat prisoners in the concentration camp as slaves, as 'disembodied numbers', threaten them with death, and prohibit everything else, in the feeling she and Milena Jesenská had for each other 'we remained free and unassailable'. As a schoolgirl of 13, in June 1942, shortly before she went into hiding from the Nazis in Amsterdam, Anne Frank wrote that though she had lots of friends, not one of them was close, it was 'just fun and games', and so she would make her diary the friend she had been waiting for, and call it Kitty: 'There is a saying that "paper is more patient than man" . . .'

Most London dinners evaporate in whispers to one's next-door neighbour. I make it a rule never to speak a word to mine, but fire across the table; though I broke it once when I heard a lady who sat next to me, in a low, sweet voice, say, 'No gravy, Sir.' I had never seen her before, but I turned suddenly round and said, 'Madam, I have been looking for a person who disliked gravy all my life; let us swear eternal friendship.' She looked astonished, but took the oath, and, what is better, kept it. You laugh, Miss—; but what more usual foundation for friendship, let me ask, than similarity of tastes?

SYDNEY SMITH; in Lady Holland's *Memoir*

I accompanied Franz Kafka home from his office.

At the entrance to his parents' house we unexpectedly met Felix Weltsch, Max Brod and his wife. They exchanged a few words and arranged to meet in the evening at Oskar Baum's.

When Kafka's friends had left us, he remembered suddenly that I had never met Brod's wife before.

'And I didn't introduce you properly,' he said. 'I am really very sorry.'

'It doesn't matter,' I said. 'I could at least look at her all the better.'

'Did you like her?'

'She has wonderful blue eyes,' I said.

Kafka was astonished.

'You noticed that at once?'

'I make a study of eyes. They tell me more than words,' I said pompously.

But Franz Kafka did not hear. He gazed gravely into the distance.

'All my friends have wonderful eyes,' he said. 'The light of their eyes is the only illumination of the dark dungeon in which I live. And even that is only artificial light.'

He laughed, gave me his hand, and went into the house.

GUSTAV JANOUCH, *Conversations with Kafka*, 1951; tr. Goronwy Rees

one of my friends has green fingers,
she grows grasshoppers quicker than flowers.

another, always wanting to get me a better job,
peruses the classified ads avidly for his own next stop.

another, once a staunch undergrad socialist,
now scoffs at all stupid, rash idealists.

another, pitying the starving millions of the third world,
merely prattles & even this world becomes a blur.

another, a devout practising vegetarian,
eats eggs with a heap of chopped onion.

another, who celebrates each & every religious festivity,
has given all gods a rest & taken up other civilities.

i have yet to meet them all at once
for fear of the confusion that will arise:
civil eggs with chopped idealists,
grasshopper jobs with fringe-benefit onions,
ex-green-fingered socialists, floral vegetarians.
(o gawd, another friend's injunction)

ARTHUR YAP, 'some friends', 1977

I planted a young tree when I was young:
But now the tree is grown and I am old:
There wintry robin shelters from the cold
        And tunes his silver tongue.

A green and living tree I planted it,
A glossy-foliaged tree of evergreen:
All through the noontide heat it spread a screen
        Whereunder I might sit.

But now I only watch it where it towers:
I, sitting at my window, watch it tost
By rattling gale or silvered by the frost;
        Or, when sweet summer flowers,

Wagging its round green head with stately grace
In tender winds that kiss it and go by.
It shows a green full age: and what show I?
    A faded wrinkled face.

So often have I watched it, till mine eyes
Have filled with tears and I have ceased to see,
That now it seems a very friend to me,
    In all my secrets wise.

A faithful pleasant friend, who year by year
Grew with my growth and strengthened with my strength,
But whose green lifetime shows a longer length;
    When I shall not sit here

It still will bud in spring, and shed rare leaves
In autumn, and in summer-heat give shade,
And warmth in winter: when my bed is made
    In shade the cypress weaves.

                        CHRISTINA ROSSETTI, 'A Dumb Friend', written 1863

I hear it was charged against me that I sought to destroy institutions,
But really I am neither for nor against institutions,
(What indeed have I in common with them? or what with the
    destruction of them?)
Only I will establish in the Mannahatta and in every city of these
    States inland and seaboard,
And in the fields and woods, and above every keel little or large that
    dents the water,
Without edifices or rules or trustees or any argument,
The institution of the dear love of comrades.

                        WHITMAN, 'I hear it was charged against me', 1860

... and then to Knipp again and there stayed, reading of Waller's verses
while she finished her dressing—her husband being by, I had no other
pleasure ... Then carried her home, and myself to the Pope's Head,

where all the Houblons were, and Dr Croone; and by and by to an exceeding pretty supper—excellent discourse of all sorts; and indeed, are a set of the finest gentlemen that ever I met withal in my life. Here Dr Croone told me that at the meeting at Gresham College tonight (which it seems they now have every Wednesday again) there was a pretty experiment, of the blood of one dog let out (till he died) into the body of another on one side, while all his own run out on the other side. The first died upon the place, and the other very well, and likely to do well. This did give occasion to many pretty wishes, as of the blood of a Quaker to be let into an Archbishop, and such like. But, as Dr Croone says, may if it takes be of mighty use to man's health, for the amending of bad blood by borrowing from a better body. After supper James Houblon and another brother took me aside, and to talk of some businesses of their own, where I am to serve them, and will . . . Here we sat talking till past one in the morning, and then home—where my people sat up for me, my wife and all; and so to bed.

SAMUEL PEPYS, *Diary*, 14 November 1666

27 December, 1756. Just almost as we were going to bed, in came Tho. Fuller, Mr Will. Piper and John Cayley, and as Mr Will. Piper and T. Fuller are such (what shall I say?) spongers—no, only old Piper—that they must stay and smoke one pipe, they stayed smoking and drinking until they two was very drunk; and at last, poor fools, they must quarrel, and for no other reason that I can judge but because Tho. Fuller told that which in my opinion was really true, *viz.*, Master Piper, being lavish of his professions of kindness, and how much he loved his dear neighbour, which at last occasioned Tho. Fuller to tell him that he could never recollect any favour or kindness he ever showed him. But he did remember that once, on some emergent occasion, he wanted to borrow about £4 of him for a few days, but the poor old man would not let him have it, though he was well assured he had the money by him and could have spared it; and told him of many such-like mean actions, which made the poor old man at last so angry that he cried and bellowed about like a great calf. But, however, they all went away about 2 o'clock. Now let me shift the scene and meditate on the vice of drinking to see how despicable it makes a person look in the eyes of one that is sober. How often does it set the best friends at variance, and even incapacitates a man from acting in any respect like an human being because it totally deprives him of reason, and he is not capable of acting with reason, it is much to be doubted he will be guilty of that which is most vile and sinful.

16 January 1759. About 6.50 Joseph Durrant and I walk down to Whyly where I supped on some boiled chicken, cold turkey minced, a shoulder of mutton roasted, a cold chine, a cold ham, tarts etc., in company with Mr Porter and his wife, Jos. Durrant and his wife, Mrs Coates and Mrs Atkins, Mrs Virgoe and Mrs Vine, Tho. Fuller and his wife, Mr Will. Piper and his brother and Mrs Gibbs. We played at brag in the even. My wife and I lost 3s. 7d. and gave the maid 6d. each. We came home about 1.40 in good order, though I am quite sick of this trade, for it must certainly be useless or hurtful to a tradesman. Neither do I think it consistent with religion, and I should much rather be left out of the number and should think it a greater honour to be absent than present at any of their entertainments.

23 January. About 8.10 I went down to Mrs Atkins's where I supped on a piece of cold roast beef, a loin of veal roasted, tarts etc. in company with Mr Porter and his wife, Mr French and his wife, Mr Calverley, Tho. Fuller and his wife, Joseph Fuller, and Mrs Virgoe. We played at brag in the even. My wife and I won 3s. 2d. We gave the maid only 6d. We came home about 1.10 in very good order.

The Diary of Thomas Turner

December 4, 1779. This evening by Mr Cary came Bill's [nephew] present to me, viz: a large Moorish sword and a curious Moor's purse made of Morocco leather with some coins in it. He also sent me two curious shells and a quill that came from Falklands Island. It is some gratitude in him I must confess—but he expects something in return as he complains in his letter to me of being very low in pocket.

December 31, 1780. This being the last day of the year we sat up till after 12 o'clock, then drank a Happy New Year to all our Friends and went to bed. We were very merry indeed after Supper till 12. Nancy [niece] and Betsie Davie locked me into the great Parlour, and both fell on me and pulled my Wigg almost to Pieces.—I paid them for it however.

February 3, 1781. Had but an indifferent night of Sleep, Mrs Davie and Nancy made me up an Apple Pye Bed last night.

February 12. We did not go to bed till after 12 this night, the Wind being still very high. We were as merry as we could be, I took of Mrs Davie's Garter tonight and kept it. I gave her my Pair of Garters and I am to have her other tomorrow.

JAMES WOODFORDE, *The Diary of a Country Parson 1758–1802*

You dear nice woman! there you are! a bright cheering apparition to surprise one on a foggy October morning, over one's breakfast—that most trying institution for people who are 'nervous' and 'don't sleep'!

It (the photograph) made our breakfast this morning 'pass off', like the better sort of breakfasts in Deerbrook [Harriet Martineau's novel], in which people seemed to have come into the world chiefly to eat breakfast in every possible variety of temper!

Blessed be the inventor of photography! I set him above even the inventor of chloroform! It has given more positive pleasure to poor suffering humanity than anything that has 'cast up' in my time or is like to—this art by which even the 'poor' can possess themselves of tolerable likenesses of their absent dear ones. And mustn't it be acting favourably on the morality of the country? I assure you I have often gone into my own room, in the devil's own humour—ready to swear at 'things in general', and some things in particular—and, my eyes resting by chance on one of my photographs of long-ago places or people, a crowd of sad, gentle thoughts has rushed into my heart, and driven the devil out, as clean as ever so much holy water and priestly exorcisms could have done! I have a photograph of Haddington church tower, and my father's tombstone in it—of every place I ever lived at as a home—photographs of old lovers! old friends, old servants, old dogs! In a day or two, you, dear, will be framed and hung up among the 'friends'. And that bright, kind, indomitable face of yours will not be the least efficacious face there for exorcizing my devil, when I have him! Thank you a thousand times for keeping your word! Of course you would—that is just the beauty of you, that you would never deceive nor disappoint.

JANE WELSH CARLYLE, letter to Mrs Stirling, 21 October 1859

He [Henry James] lived in terror of being thought rich, worldly or luxurious, and was forever contrasting his visitors' supposed opulence and self-indulgence with his own hermit-like asceticism, and apologizing for his poor food while he trembled lest it should be thought too good. I have often since wondered if he did not find our visits more of a burden than a pleasure, and if the hospitality he so conscientiously offered and we so carelessly enjoyed did not give him more sleepless nights than happy days.

I hope not; for some of my richest hours were spent under his roof. From the moment when I turned the corner of the grass-grown street mounting steeply between squat brick houses, and caught sight, at its upper end, of the wide Palladian window of the garden-room, a sense of joyous liberation bore me on. There *he* stood on the doorstep, the white-panelled hall with its old prints and crowded book-cases forming a background to his heavy loosely-clothed figure. Arms outstretched, lips and eyes twinkling, he came down to the car, uttering cries of mock amazement and mock humility at the undeserved honour of my visit. The arrival at Lamb House was an almost ritual performance, from those first ejaculations to the large hug and the two solemn kisses executed in the middle of the hall rug. Then, arm in arm, through the oak-panelled morning-room we wandered out onto the thin worn turf of the garden, with its ancient mulberry tree, its unkempt flower-borders, the gables of Watchbell Street peeping like village gossips over the creeper-clad walls, and the scent of roses spiced with a strong smell of the sea. Up and down the lawn we strolled with many pauses, exchanging news, answering each other's questions, delivering messages from the other members of the group, inspecting the strawberries and lettuces in the tiny kitchen-garden, and the chrysanthemums 'coming along' in pots in the green-house; till at length the parlour-maid appeared with a tea-tray, and I was led up the rickety outside steps to the garden-room, that stately and unexpected appendage to the unadorned cube of the house.

Sometimes, too, our little knot of friends would contrive to be in London at the same time, and I recall one happy evening when Howard Sturgis, Walter Berry, Percy Lubbock and Gaillard Lapsley were dining with me at my hotel. We had hoped that James would join us; but he was already booked for a fashionable dinner from which it was useless to try to detach him. Hardly had we sat down when, to our astonishment, in he walked, resplendent in white waistcoat and white tie, and rubbing his hands as though he nursed between his palms the smile striking up into his face. He had made a mistake in his date; had presented himself at the great house, and been told the dinner was not till the next evening; so here he was, and did we still want him, and was there room for him at the table—oh, he could squeeze into the least little corner, if we'd only let him! And let him we did; and how he enjoyed his dinner, and his glass of champagne (he who, at Rye, thought he could digest nothing heavier than a squeeze of orange juice!), and what a good evening of talk and laughter we had! As I write I yearn back to those lost hours, all the while aware that those who read of them must take their gaiety, their jokes and laughter, on faith, yet unable to detach my memory from them, and loath not to give others a glimpse of that jolliest of comrades, the laughing, chaffing, jubilant yet malicious James, who was so different from the grave personage known to less intimate eyes.

EDITH WHARTON, *A Backward Glance*, 1934

Miss Helene Hanff   9 April 1951
14 East 95th Street
New York City

Dear Miss Hanff,

I expect you are getting a bit worried that we have not written to thank you for your parcels and are probably thinking we are an ungrateful lot. The truth is that I have been chasing round the country in and out of various stately homes of England trying to buy a few books to fill up our sadly depleted stock. My wife was starting to call me the lodger who just went home for bed and breakfast, but of course when I arrived home with a nice piece of MEAT, to say nothing of dried eggs and ham, then she thought I was a fine fellow and all was forgiven. It is a long time since we saw so much meat all in one piece.

We should like to express our appreciation in some way or other, so we are sending by Book Post today a little book which I hope you will like. I remember you asked me for a volume of Elizabethan love poems some time ago—well, this is the nearest I can get to it.

Yours faithfully,
Frank Doel
For MARKS & Co.
Booksellers
84, Charing Cross Road
London, WC 2

New York City
16 April 1951

To All at 84, Charing Cross Road:

Thank you for the beautiful book. I've never owned a book before with pages edged all round in gold. Would you believe it arrived on my birthday?

I wish you hadn't been so over-courteous about putting the inscription on a card instead of on the flyleaf. It's the bookseller coming out in you all, you were afraid you'd decrease its value. You would have increased it for the present owner. (And possibly for the future owner. I love inscriptions on flyleaves and notes in margins, I like the comradely sense of turning pages someone else turned, and reading passages some one long gone has called my attention to.) . . .

I send you greetings from America—faithless friend that she is, pouring millions into rebuilding Japan and Germany while letting England starve. Some day, God willing, I'll get over there and apologize personally for my country's sins (and by the time I come home my country will certainly have to apologize for mine) . . .

Yours,
Helene Hanff

New York City
15 October 1951

WHAT KIND OF A PEPYS' DIARY DO YOU CALL THIS?

this is not pepys' diary, this is some busybody editor's miserable collection of EXCERPTS from pepys' diary may he rot.

i could just spit.

where is jan. 12, 1668, where his wife chased him out of bed and round the bedroom with a red-hot poker?

where is sir w. pen's son that was giving everybody so much trouble with his Quaker notions? ONE mention does he get in this whole pseudo-book. and me from philadelphia . . .

HH

P.S. Fresh eggs or powdered for Xmas? I know the powdered last longer but 'fresh farm eggs flown from Denmark' have got to taste better. you want to take a vote on it?

London
20 October 1951

Dear Miss Hanff,

First of all, let me apologize for the Pepys. I was honestly under the impression that it was the complete Braybrooke edition and I can understand how you must have felt when you found your favourite passages missing . . .

About the eggs—I have talked to the rest of the inmates here and we all seem to think that the fresh ones would be nicer . . .

With best wishes,
Yours sincerely,
Frank Doel

London
14 February 1952

Dear Helene,

I quite agree it is time we dropped the 'Miss' when writing to you. I am not really so stand-offish as you may have been led to believe, but as copies of letters I have written to you go into the office files the formal address seemed more appropriate. But as this letter has nothing to do with books, there will be no copy.

We are quite at a loss to know how you managed the nylons which appeared this noon as if by magic. All I can tell you is that when I came back from lunch they were on my desk with a note reading: 'From Helene Hanff' . . . The girls are very thrilled . . .

With best wishes from us all,
Frank Doel

New York City
15 August 1959

sir:

i write to say i have got work.

i won it. i won a $5,000 Grant-in-Aid off CBS, it's supposed to support me for a year while I write American History dramatizations. I am starting with a script about New York under seven years of British Occupation and i MARVEL at how i rise above it to address you in friendly and forgiving fashion, your behavior over here from 1776 to 1783 was simply FILTHY.

Is there such a thing as a modern-English version of the Canterbury Tales? I have these guilts about never having read Chaucer but I was

talked out of learning Early Anglo-Saxon/-Middle English by a friend
who had to take it for her Ph.D. They told her to write an essay in Early
Anglo-Saxon on any-subject-of-her-own-choosing. 'Which is all very
well,' she said bitterly, 'but the only essay subject you can find enough
Early Anglo-Saxon words for is "How to Slaughter a Thousand Men in a
Mead Hall".' . . .

hh

London
2 September 1959

Dear Helene,

We were all delighted to hear that you've won a Grant-in-Aid and are
working again. We are prepared to be broad-minded about your choice
of subject matter, but I must tell you that one of the young inmates here
confessed that until he read your letter he never knew that England had
ever owned 'the States'.

With regard to Chaucer, the best scholars seem to have fought shy of
putting him into modern English, but there was an edition put out by
Longmans in 1934, the Canterbury Tales only, a modernized version by
Hill, which I believe is quite good. It is (of course!) out of print and I am
trying to find a nice clean second-hand copy.

Sincerely,
Frank

HELENE HANFF, *84, Charing Cross Road*, 1971

Men are more evanescent than pictures, yet one sorrows for lost friends,
and pictures *are* my friends. I have none others. I am never long enough
with men to attach myself to them; and whatever feelings of attachment I
have are to material things. If the great Tintoret here were to be
destroyed, it would be precisely to me what the death of Hallam was to
Tennyson—as far as *this* world is concerned—with an addition of
bitterness and indignation, for my friend would perish murdered, *his* by a
natural death. Hearing of plans for its restoration is just the same to me as
to another man hearing talk behind an Irish hedge of shooting his
brother.

RUSKIN, letter to his father, 28 January 1852

Pratt elegantly referred all diseases to debility, and with a proper contempt for symptomatic treatment, went to the root of the matter with port wine and bark; Pilgrim was persuaded that the evil principle in the human system was plethora, and he made war against it with cupping, blistering, and cathartics. They had both been long established in Milby, and as each had a sufficient practice, there was no very malignant rivalry between them; on the contrary, they had that sort of friendly contempt for each other which is always conducive to a good understanding between professional men; and when any new surgeon attempted, in an ill-advised hour, to settle himself in the town, it was strikingly demonstrated how slight and trivial are theoretic differences compared with the broad basis of common human feeling. There was the most perfect unanimity between Pratt and Pilgrim in the determination to drive away the obnoxious and too probably unqualified intruder as soon as possible. Whether the first wonderful cure he effected was on a patient of Pratt's or of Pilgrim's, one was as ready as the other to pull the interloper by the nose, and both alike directed their remarkable powers of conversation towards making the town too hot for him.

GEORGE ELIOT, 'Janet's Repentance', *Scenes of Clerical Life*, 1857

Truth of a modest sort I can promise you, and also sincerity. That complete, praiseworthy sincerity which, while it delivers one into the hands of one's enemies, is as likely as not to embroil one with one's friends.

'Embroil' is perhaps too strong an expression. I can't imagine among either my enemies or my friends a being so hard up for something to do as to quarrel with me. 'To disappoint one's friends' would be nearer the mark. Most, almost all, friendships of the writing period of my life have come to me through my books; and I know that a novelist lives in his work.

JOSEPH CONRAD, 'A Familiar Preface', *A Personal Record*, 1912

If it be true that poets, as you say,
Envisage in their verse and populate,
By dreams that shall come true, the future state,
I must be careful whom I shall portray

Lest I sit down, forever and for aye,
With the strange characters I celebrate.
O awful thought: our Fancy is our Fate!
(Let me erase some writings while I may!)
But one thing I am sure of, dear A. E.:
I will confront the malcreated crew,
Victims or merely subjects of my song,
If I can reach the bourne where you shall be
Creating kindness as you always do,
And I may bring my fancy friends along.

OLIVER ST JOHN GOGARTY, 'To a Friend', 1938

The war separated
Me, the writer of plays, from my friend the stage designer.
The cities where we worked are no longer there.
When I walk through the cities that still are
At times I say: that blue piece of washing
My friend would have placed it better.

BERTOLT BRECHT, 'The Friends', *c.*1948; tr. Michael Hamburger

'O, ah, yes, of course, the Mole and the Badger,' said Toad lightly. 'What's become of them, the dear fellows? I had forgotten all about them.'

'Well may you ask!' said the Rat reproachfully. 'While you were riding about the country in expensive motor-cars, and galloping proudly on blood-horses, and breakfasting on the fat of the land, those two poor devoted animals have been camping out in the open, in every sort of weather, living very rough by day and lying very hard by night; watching over your house, patrolling your boundaries, keeping a constant eye on the stoats and the weasels, scheming and planning and contriving how to get your property back for you. You don't deserve to have such true and loyal friends, Toad, you don't, really. Some day, when it's too late, you'll be sorry you didn't value them more while you had them!'

Toad was inclined to be sulky at first; but he brightened up immediately, like the good fellow he was.

'Well, well,' he said; 'perhaps I am a bit of a talker. A popular fellow such as I am—my friends get round me—we chaff, we sparkle, we tell witty stories—and somehow my tongue gets wagging. I have the gift of conversation. I've been told I ought to have a *salon*, whatever that may be.'

'Mayn't I sing them just one *little* song?' he pleaded piteously.

'No, not *one* little song,' replied the Rat firmly ... 'It's no good, Toady; you know well that your songs are all conceit and boasting and vanity; and your speeches are all self-praise and—and—well, and gross exaggeration and—and—'

'And gas,' put in the Badger, in his common way.

'It's for your own good, Toady,' went on the Rat. 'You know you *must* turn over a new leaf sooner or later, and now seems a splendid time to begin; a sort of turning-point in your career. Please don't think that saying all this doesn't hurt me more than it hurts you.'

Toad remained a long while plunged in thought. At last he raised his head, and the traces of strong emotion were visible on his features. 'You have conquered, my friends,' he said in broken accents. 'It was, to be sure, but a small thing that I asked—merely leave to blossom and expand for yet one more evening, to let myself go and hear the tumultuous applause that always seems to me—somehow—to bring out my best qualities. However, you are right, I know, and I am wrong. Henceforth I will be a very different Toad. My friends, you shall never have occasion to blush for me again. But, O dear, O dear, this is a hard world!'

KENNETH GRAHAME, *The Wind in the Willows*, 1908

Hermes goes through the world. He meets a dog.

—I am a god, Hermes introduces himself politely.

The dog sniffs his feet.

—I feel lonely. Humans betray gods: but unknowing, mortal animals, we crave them. In the evening, after a whole day wandering, we will sit down under an oak. I will tell you then that I feel old and want to die. It will be a necessary lie, so you will lick my hands.

—All right, the dog carelessly replies, I will lick your hands. They are cool, and have a strange smell.

They walk, they walk. They meet a star.

—I am Hermes, the god says, and produces one of his very best faces. Would you like to go with us to the end of the world? I will make it frightening there, so you will have to lean your head on my shoulder.

—Good, the star replies with a glassy voice. It's all the same to me where I go; but the end of the world, that is naïve. Unfortunately there is no end of the world.

They go. They go. The dog, Hermes, and the star. They hold hands. Hermes thinks that if he sets out to find friends another time, he won't be so frank.

ZBIGNIEW HERBERT, 'Hermes, Dog, and Star', 1957; tr. John Carpenter and Bogdana Carpenter

Can someone make my simple wish come true?
Male biker seeks female for touring fun.
Do you live in North London? Is it you?

Gay vegetarian whose friends are few,
I'm into music, Shakespeare and the sun.
Can someone make my simple wish come true?

Executive in search of something new—
Perhaps bisexual woman, arty, young.
Do you live in North London? Is it you?

Successful, straight and solvent? I am too—
Attractive Jewish lady with a son.
Can someone make my simple wish come true?

I'm Libran, inexperienced and blue—.
Need slim non-smoker under twenty-one.
Do you live in North London? Is it you?

Please write (with photo) to Box 152.
Who knows where it may lead once we've begun?
Can someone make my simple wish come true?
Do you live in North London? Is it you?

WENDY COPE, 'Lonely Hearts', 1982

BASSOONIST, GARDENER, Kapellmeister, linguist, 52; fine teenage son; degrees: geology, philosophy; lived Europe; seeks friendship unattached intelligent woman under 50.

VEGETARIAN SINGLE STILL SEEKING that special friend? Meet compatible veggies nationwide. All interests, ages, outlooks. Discretion assured. Full details only $1.00.

HANDSOME NYC POET EMERITUS, 59, seeks beautiful, bright, non-smoking woman. Dutch treat, naturally.

MANHATTAN WOMAN SEEKS bright, non-smoking SM 40s+ for exchange of ideas. Non-professional interests include: psychology, brain research, origin of consciousness, creativity, serious paranormal research, robotics and AI. Intellectual eccentrics welcome.

NIGERIAN Ph.D. STUDENT, 27, 5′4″, non-smoker, non-drinker, seeks sincere single lady for eternal companionship.

QUIET, SENSITIVE, VERY GENTLE AND SHY, old-fashioned lady, mid-fifties, overeducated and unencumbered, interested in esoterical, spiritual and mystical matters, is looking for kindred soul, music lover or musician. New York area.

POOR AND UGLY SWM—29 enjoys company of Faulkner, Calvino, Woolf, but they're all dead. Seeking slim, intelligent SWF for espresso, conversation, museums and the City.

WOMAN POET, 43, wants platonic correspondence with biblio-biophiles any age, gender, culture: modern literature, art; chu-song, pottery, Soseki; natural history, science.

BROKEN-WINGED, CAGED, SHY, 37, MARRIED—longs for wounded male, British? Black? Asian?, suspected of nearly knowing everything. To write to and maybe learn to sing with.

WOMAN Ph.D, ON TROPICAL ISLAND seeks intellectual correspondences to combat mental entropy.

NON-ROMANTIC FRIENDSHIP sought by Jewish, single, 44 years old, well read but not intellectual, pleasant, if a little girlish-looking; for walks in park, possibly theatre, outings with children welcome.

RIGHT-WING CONSERVATIVE REPUBLICAN Born-again Fundamental Baptist lady, 60 years old, would like to meet humorous gentleman with similar values. Or have all the real men of this persuasion gone the way of the dinosaurs—extinct?

GAY FATHER OF 2 SONS, 7 & 9, sometime mime, singer, feminist, gardener, explorer of cities and mountains, seeks new options for friendship, collaboration, partnership.

> Personal column, *New York Review of Books*, between 1986 and 1989

Dear Dr Duck,
I'm in need of help and would like to know if you can help me. I'm 25-years-old and totally unable to make friends with other people. I find it difficult to talk and what to talk about. I become very nervous and self-conscious. All my communications are short, straightforward. What I think is known as small talk. Up to now, I haven't mixed with people because of being unable to talk. I don't have any friends. Besides being born a quiet, shy chap, I had a very religious, sheltered life. Because of this I become very selfconceited and pompous. Please can you help me. Thanks.
Yours sincerely,
Alfred

> STEVE DUCK: *Friends, for Life: The Psychology of Close Relationships*, 1983

> It is the awaited hour
> over the table falls
> interminably
> the lamp's spread hair
> Night turns the window to immensity
> There is no one here
> presence without name surrounds me
>
> OCTAVIO PAZ, 'Friendship', 1961; tr. Charles Tomlinson

IMAGINARY FRIENDS

When children are playing alone on the green,
In comes the playmate that never was seen.
When children are happy and lonely and good,
The Friend of the Children comes out of the wood.

Nobody heard him and nobody saw,
His is a picture you never could draw,
But he's sure to be present, abroad or at home,
When children are happy and playing alone.

He lies in the laurels, he runs on the grass,
He sings when you tinkle the musical glass;
Whene'er you are happy and cannot tell why,
The Friend of the Children is sure to be by!

He loves to be little, he hates to be big,
'Tis he that inhabits the caves that you dig;
'Tis he when you play with your soldiers of tin
That sides with the Frenchmen and never can win.

'Tis he, when at night you go off to your bed,
Bids you go to your sleep and not trouble your head;
For wherever they're lying, in cupboard or shelf,
'Tis he will take care of your playthings himself!

ROBERT LOUIS STEVENSON, 'The Unseen Playmate', 1885

My grandmother did one thing for me which made me feel very fond of her. For several years I had been deeply attached to a toy cow. Originally a solid cow on a wooden stand, she had gradually become a limp and flattened piece of leather. This had been caused by my keeping her under my pillow after her early detachment from the wooden stand. With sympathetic awareness of Moocow's importance, Grandmama stitched up her burst sides and inserted wash-leather patches, to my complete satisfaction. Moocow had, I suppose, become a sort of fetish. I used to converse with her when I was alone, and around her I created a dream existence. She ceased to be a toy cow, and became a companionable character with whom I shared interesting adventures, in regions of escape from my surroundings. (I called her 'she', but I thought of her as neither one thing nor the other—my idea about men and women being that they dressed differently so as to show the difference; I hadn't as yet consciously considered the question of how bulls differed from cows.)

Moocow's friends and relations lived in a country inhabited by people called 'Mezenthrums'; I used to talk to them down a small hole in the cement between the blue and white Dutch tiles on the bathroom wall. I gave them messages from Moocow, visualizing them in a vague way as a crowd of people among whom there were some whom I gradually got to know quite well. (This device was probably suggested by the speaking-tube which went from outside the dining-room to the lower regions.) I also used to unscrew one of the brass knobs on my bedstead and by doing this 'get into another world' where anything I wished for could happen in my mind . . . The people in my other world were human but quite unlike anything I had seen or heard about; they were neither dream nor reality; I just invented them. My attachment to Moocow lasted until I was nearly nine; by then I had gradually discarded her as something a bit babyish for a boy of my age.

SIEGRIED SASSOON, *The Old Century*, 1938

There is a dotty woman
Who when she does her shopping
And sees a hopscotch in the street
Goes hophop hophop hopping.

A game she often wins
Though no one else is there;
She plays a childhood friend, who'd now
Be quite as old as her.

And sometimes she denounces
That friend of long ago,
And says to all the empty air:
You KNOW you cheated, Flo!

GERDA MAYER, 'Her Friend Flo', 1978

'The Watcher in Spanish' was the latest of our conceits. The phrase came,
I believe, from a line in a poem, about: 'The Watcher in Spanish cape . . .'
We imagined him as a macabre but semi-comic figure, not unlike Guy
Fawkes, or a human personification of Poe's watching raven. He
appeared to us, we said, at moments when our behaviour was particularly
insincere; one might, for example, be telling a boastful story, or pretending an interest in heraldry, or flattering the wife of a don—and there,
suddenly, he would be standing, visible only to ourselves. He made no
gesture, never spoke. His mere presence was a sufficient reminder and
warning. Mutely, he reminded us that the 'two sides' continued to exist,
that our enemies remained implacable, beneath all their charming,
expensive, scholarly disguises; he warned us never to betray ourselves by
word or deed. He was our familiar, our imaginary mascot, our guardian
spirit. We appealed to him, made fun of him, tried to deceive him. Often,
when we were alone together, we spoke to him aloud. 'Come out of that
corner!' Chalmers would shout. 'You needn't think we can't see you!
Now, leave us alone—do you hear? We're busy.'

    It was the Watcher, we said, who disapproved of my presence at
Black's poker parties and vetoed all Ashmeade's invitations to bring
Chalmers with me to coffee after Hall; in other words, we were jealous of
each other's friends. On the rare occasions when we attempted jointly to
entertain, the Watcher immediately put in his appearance; our whole
behaviour, when a third party was in the room, became so strained and
falsified that we seemed to each other to be acting in a disgraceful kind of
charade. Every word, every laugh, rang sham as a bad penny, every smile
or gesture was an act of treason to our dearest beliefs. As soon as the
visitors had gone, our mutual accusations would begin, half in joke,
half in earnest. Very soon, we both agreed to keep our respective
acquaintances to ourselves.

Christopher Isherwood, Lions and Shadows, 1938

> Old Eben Flood, climbing alone one night
> Over the hill between the town below
> And the forsaken upland hermitage
> That held as much as he should ever know
> On earth again of home, paused warily.
> The road was his with not a native near;
> And Eben, having leisure, said aloud,
> For no man else in Tilbury Town to hear:

'Well, Mr Flood, we have the harvest moon
Again, and we may not have many more;
The bird is on the wing, the poet says,
And you and I have said it here before.
Drink to the bird.' He raised up to the light
The jug that he had gone so far to fill,
And answered huskily: 'Well, Mr Flood,
Since you propose it, I believe I will.'

Alone, as if enduring to the end
A valiant armour of scarred hopes outworn,
He stood there in the middle of the road
Like Roland's ghost winding a silent horn.
Below him, in the town among the trees,
Where friends of other days had honoured him,
A phantom salutation of the dead
Rang thinly till old Eben's eyes were dim.

Then, as a mother lays her sleeping child
Down tenderly, fearing it may awake,
He set the jug down slowly at his feet
With trembling care, knowing that most things break;
And only when assured that on firm earth
It stood, as the uncertain lives of men
Assuredly did not, he paced away,
And with his hand extended paused again:

'Well, Mr Flood, we have not met like this
In a long time; and many a change has come
To both of us, I fear, since last it was
We had a drop together. Welcome home!'
Convivially returning with himself,
Again he raised the jug up to the light;
And with an acquiescent quaver said:
'Well, Mr Flood, if you insist, I might.

'Only a very little, Mr Flood—
For auld lang syne. No more, sir; that will do.'
So, for the time, apparently it did,
And Eben evidently thought so too;

For soon amid the silver loneliness
Of night he lifted up his voice and sang,
Secure, with only two moons listening,
Until the whole harmonious landscape rang—

'For auld lang syne.' The weary throat gave out,
The last word wavered, and the song was done.
He raised again the jug regretfully
And shook his head, and was again alone.
There was not much that was ahead of him,
And there was nothing in the town below—
Where strangers would have shut the many doors
That many friends had opened long ago.

EDWIN ARLINGTON ROBINSON, 'Mr Flood's Party', 1921

All the time that I was climbing alone I had a strong feeling that I was
accompanied by a second person. This feeling was so strong that it
completely eliminated all loneliness I might otherwise have felt. It even
seemed that I was tied to my 'companion' by a rope, and that if I slipped
'he' would hold me. I remember constantly glancing back over my
shoulder, and once, when after reaching my highest point, I stopped to
try and eat some mint cake, I carefully divided it and turned round with
one half in my hand. It was almost a shock to find no one to whom to give
it. It seemed to me that this 'presence' was a strong, helpful and friendly
one, and it was not until Camp VI was sighted that the link connecting
me, as it seemed at the time, to the beyond, was snapped, and, although
Shipton and the camp were but a few yards away, I suddenly felt alone.

F. S. SMYTHE, 'The Second Assault', in *Everest 1933*, Hugh
Ruttledge, 1934

I lay me down and slumber
    And every morn revive.
Whose is the night-long breathing
    That keeps a man alive?

When I was off to dreamland
   And left my limbs forgot,
Who stayed at home to mind them,
   And breathed when I did not?

*   *   *

—I waste my time in talking,
   No heed at all takes he,
My kind and foolish comrade
   That breathes all night for me.

A. E. Housman, *More Poems* XIII, 1936

UNDER STRESS

My dear Barrie

We are pegging out in a very comfortless spot—Hoping this letter may be found & sent to you I write a word of farewell—It hurt me grievously when you partially withdrew your friendship or seemed so to do—I want to tell you that I never gave you cause—If you thought or heard ill of me it was unjust—Calumny is ever to the fore. My attitude towards you and everyone connected with you was always one of respect and admiration—Under these circumstances I want you to think well of me and my end and more practically I want you to help my widow and my boy your godson—We are showing that Englishmen can still die with a bold spirit fighting it out to the end. It will be known that we have accomplished our object in reaching the Pole and that we have done everything possible even to sacrificing ourselves in order to save sick companions. I think this makes an example for Englishmen of the future and that the country ought to help those who are left behind to mourn us—I leave my poor girl and your godson, Wilson leaves a widow, and Edgar Evans also a widow in humble circumstances. Do what you can to get their claims recognized.

Goodbye. I am not at all afraid of the end but sad to miss many a simple pleasure which I had planned for the future on our long marches—I may not have proved a great explorer, but we have done the greatest march ever made and come very near to great success. Goodbye my dear friend.

Yours ever,

R. Scott

We are in a desperate state feet frozen &c, no fuel and a long way from food, but it would do your heart good to be in our tent, to hear our songs and the cheery conversation as to what we will do when we get to Hut Point.

Later.—We are very near the end but have not and will not lose our good cheer—we have four days of storm in our tent and now have no food or fuel—We did intend to finish ourselves when things proved like this but we have decided to die naturally in the track.

As a dying man my dear friend be good to my wife & child—Give the boy a chance in life if the State won't do it—He ought to have good stuff in him—and give my memory back the friendship which you inspired. I never met a man in my life whom I admired and loved more than you but I never could show you how much your friendship meant to me—for you had much to give and I nothing.

> Captain Robert Falcon Scott, letter to J. M. Barrie, March 1912

Livingstone's Journal, 14 March 1872—'Mr. Stanley leaves. I commit to his care my Journal, sealed with five seals; the impressions are those of an American gold coin, anna, and half-anna, and cake of paint with royal arms, positively not to be opened.'

Stanley.—'At dawn we were up. The bales and baggage were taken outside, and the men prepared themselves for their first march homewards. We had a sad breakfast together. I couldn't eat, my heart was too full; nor did my companion seem to have any appetite. We found something to do which kept us together. At eight I was not gone, and I had thought to have been off at five a.m. "Doctor, I'll leave two of my men. May be you've forgotten something in the hurry. I'll halt a day at Tara for your last word and your last wish. Now, we must part. There's no help for it. Good-bye."

"Oh, I'm coming with you a little way. I must see you on the road."

"Thank you. Now, my men, home! Kirangoze, lift the flag. March!"

On the walk Livingstone once more told his plans, and it was settled that his men should be hired for two years from arrival at Unyanyembe, to give ample margin for the completion of his work.

"Now, my dear Doctor, the best friends must part. You have come far enough."

"Well, I will say this to you. You have done what few men could do; far better than some great travellers I know. And I am grateful to you for what you have done for me. God guide you safe home, and bless you, my friend."

"And may God bring you safe back to us all, my dear friend. Farewell."

"Farewell."

We wrung each other's hands, and I had to tear myself away before I was unmanned. But Susi, and Chumah, and Hamaydah, the Doctor's faithful fellows, they must all shake and kiss my hands; before I could quite turn away I betrayed myself.'

Stanley resolutely turned his face eastward, but now and then would take a look round at the deserted figure of an old man in gray clothes, who with bended head and slow steps was returning to his solitude. A drop in the path came which would hide him from view. 'I took one more look at him. He was standing near the gate of Kwihaha with his servants near him. I waved a handkerchief to him, and he responded by lifting his cap.'

This was Livingstone's last sight of a white man.

THOMAS HUGHES, *David Livingstone*, 1889

Nero, his fair disciple, having sent his satellites or officers toward him to denounce the decree of his death to him , . . . Seneca, with a reposed and undaunted countenance, listened attentively to their charge, and presently demanded for paper and ink to make his last will and testament, which the captain refusing him, he turned towards his friends and thus bespake them: 'Sith, my loving friends, I cannot bequeath you any other thing in remembrance or acknowledgement of what I owe you, I leave you at least the richest and best portion I have, that is, the image of my manners and my life, which I beseech you to keep in memory; which doing you may acquire the glory and purchase the name of truly sincere and absolutely true friends.' And therewithal, sometimes appeasing the sharpness of the sorrow he saw them endure for his sake, with mild and gentle speeches, sometimes raising his voice to chide them: 'Where are,' said he, 'those memorable precepts of Philosophy? What is become of those provisions which for so many years together we have laid up against the brunts and accidents of Fortune? Was Nero's innated cruelty unknown unto us? What might we expect or hope for at his hands, who had murdered his mother and massacred his brother, but that he would also do his tutor and governor to death that hath fostered and brought him up?'

Having uttered these words to all the bystanders, he turned him to his wife, as she was ready to sink down, and with the burthen of her grief to faint in heart and strength; he called and embraced her about the neck, and heartily entreated her, for the love of him, somewhat more patiently to bear this accident; and that his hour was come, wherein he must shew no longer by discourse and disputation, but in earnest effect, declare the fruit he had reaped by his study; and that undoubtedly he embraced death, not only without grief but with exceeding joy. 'Wherefore, my dear dear heart, do not dishonour it by thy tears, lest thou seem to love thyself more than my reputation . . .' To whom Paulina, having somewhat roused her drooping spirits, and by a thrice noble affection awakened the magnanimity of her high-settled courage, answered thus: 'No, Seneca, think not that in this necessity I will leave you without my company. I would not have you imagine that the virtuous examples of your life have not also taught me to die; and when shall I be able to do it or better, or more honestly, or more to mine own liking, than with yourself? And be resolved I will go with you and be partaker of your fortune.'

MONTAIGNE, 'Of Three Good Women'

Taking my meditative way along to the other extremity of our trench, I was genially desired by Corporal Worley to take cocoa with him; he was just bringing it to the boil over some shreds of sandbag and tallow candle. Scarcely had I grasped the friendly mug when a rifle-grenade burst with red-hot fizzing on the parapet behind me and another on the parados behind him; and we were unhit. Worley's courtesy and warm feeling went on, undiverted as though a butterfly or two had settled on a flower. A kinder heart there never was; a gentler spirit never. With his blue eyes a little doubtfully fixed on me, his red cheeks a little redder than usual, he would speak in terms of regret for what he thought his roughness, saying dolefully that he had been in the butchering trade all his time. Where now, Frank Worley? I should like an answer. He was for ever comforting those youngsters who were so numerous among us; even as the shrapnel burst low over the fire-bay he would be saying without altered tone, 'don't fret, lay still', and such things.

In M Camp I acquired an extraordinary facility in issuing the nightly rum ration. There were so many (I forget the exact tally) to be served from each jar; each man brought his own favourite vessel at the welcome call 'Roll up for your Rum', and the dispenser was confronted with the need for all sorts of mental mensurations. The indefatigable dear Worley held up his candle, or turned on his pocket torch, as I stood at the door of each billet, and it was rare that anyone went short. The precious drops were fairly distributed, and when all was done Worley would prolong my visitation, in defiance of military principles, by luring me into his tent to join a party of old stagers whose bread and cheese was the emblem of an unforgettable kindness. And there was an occasion or two in which Cassells and myself were the guests of those good souls at a veritable banquet. An estaminet by St Jans ter Biezen was then the scene of much music, much champagne and a dinner of the best: there's no higher honour to come. Daniels, Davey, Ashford, Roberts, Worley, Clifford, Seall, Unsted, do you remember me yet? I should know you among ten thousand. Your voices are heard, and each man longed for, beyond the maze of mutability.

EDMUND BLUNDEN, *Undertones of War*, 1928

He talked of Africa,
    That fat and easy man.
I'd but to say a word,
    And straight the tales began.

And when I'd wish to read,
    That man would not disclose
A thought of harm, but sleep;
    Hard-breathing through his nose.

Then when I'd wish to hear
    More tales of Africa,
'Twas but to wake him up,
    And but a word to say

To press the button, and
    Keep quiet; nothing more;
For tales of stretching veldt,
    Kaffir and sullen Boer.

O what a lovely friend!
    O quiet easy life!
I wonder if his sister
    Would care to be my wife . . .

     IVOR GURNEY, 'Companion–North-East Dug-out', 1919

My desk, most loyal friend
    thank you. You've been with me on
every road I've taken.
    My scar and my protection.

My loaded writing mule.
    Your tough legs have endured
the weight of all my dreams, and
    burdens of piled-up thoughts.

Thank you   for toughening me.
    No worldly joy could pass
your severe looking-glass
    you blocked the first temptation,

and every base desire
    your heavy oak outweighed
lions of hate, elephants
    of spite   you intercepted.

Thank you for growing with me
    as my need grew in size
I've been laid out across you
    so many years   alive . . .

I celebrate thirty years
    of union   truer than love
I know every notch in your wood.
    You know the lines in my face.

Haven't you written them there?
    devouring reams of paper
denying me any tomorrow
    teaching me only today.

You've thrown my important letters
    and money   in floods together,
repeating: for every single verse
    today has to be the deadline.

You've warned me of retribution
    not to be measured in spoonfulls.
And when   my body will be laid out,
    Great fool! Let it be on you then.

Marina Tsvetayeva, from 'Desk', 1933–5; tr. Elaine Feinstein

The moon, weary in the pall of cloud,
cast a murky glance at the hill.
The table was laid for six,
and only one place was empty.

My husband, myself and my friends
are seeing the new year in.
Why are my fingers covered as with blood?
Why does the wine burn like poison?

The host with full glass raised
was impressive—immobile.
'I drink to the earth of our own forest glades,
in which we all lie.'

A friend looked at my face,
suddenly remembered God knows what,
and exclaimed: 'I drink to her songs
in which we all live!'

But a third, not understanding,
as he went out into the dark,
answering my thoughts
said: 'We ought to drink to him
who is not with us yet.'

ANNA AKHMATOVA, 'New Year Ballad', 1932;
tr. Richard McKane

There were girls among them who lived through a typhus attack
without staying in bed. Two of their friends would take the sick comrade
between them, when she had a temperature of 103°F. and saw everything
as a blur, and drag her along with their labour gang; out in the fields they
would lay her down under a shrub, and in the evening they would march
her back to camp—all to avoid her being sent to the hospital hut and so
being exposed to the danger of a selection.

Under the pressure of a concentration camp you grew more closely
attached to people than you would have done otherwise in such a short
time.

ELLA LINGENS-REINER, *Prisoners of Fear*, 1948;
of Auschwitz

On August 10, 1943, Milena's Czech friends showed their affection for
her. Suspecting that this would be her last birthday, they decided to give
her a real party. In the orderly room of a barracks with a Czech
Blockälteste, the table was covered with presents. All those who loved
Milena were present . . . Someone went to get the birthday child and she

was led to the table. The gifts consisted of handkerchiefs embroidered with a prisoner's number, tiny cloth hearts marked with the name 'Milena', figurines carved from toothbrush handles, flowers that had been smuggled into camp.

Milena, who was very ill by then and too weak to keep up all her friendships, was moved to tears: 'What a surprise!' she said. 'And I thought you'd all forgotten me and weren't friends with me any more. Forgive me for not coming to see you more often. But from now on I'll be better.' Surrounded by her Czech friends, Milena was all joy and gratitude. I, the 'little Prussian', stood a little to one side, watching the others laugh, enjoying the unusual atmosphere. I felt transported to Prague, to Milena's natural surroundings. What Milena wanted most in the world was to have friends. She once wrote: 'If you have two or three people, but what am I saying, if you have just one person with whom you can be weak, miserable, and contrite, and who won't hurt you for it, then you are rich. You can expect indulgence only of one who loves you, never from others and, above all, never from yourself.'

MARGARETE BUBER-NEUMANN, *Milena*, 1977,
tr. Ralph Manheim; Ravensbrück camp

[*In May–June 1944 large convoys of Hungarian prisoners arrived at Auschwitz, 'filling the void which the Germans had not neglected to create with a series of diligent selections'.*]

I tried, in a fragmentary fashion, to explain to him that the place he had landed in was not for polite or quiet people. I tried to convince him of a few recent discoveries of mine (in truth, not yet well digested): that down there, in order to get by, it was necessary to get busy, organize illegal food, dodge work, find influential friends, hide one's thoughts, steal, and lie; that whoever did not do so was soon dead, and that his saintliness seemed dangerous to me and out of place. And since, as I have said, twenty bricks are heavy, on our fourth trip, instead of taking twenty of them off the wagon, I took seventeen and showed him that if you placed them on the litter in a certain way, with an empty space in the lower layer, no one would ever suspect that there weren't twenty. This was a ruse I thought I had invented (I found out later that it was, however, in the public domain), and that I had used several times with success . . .

Bandi was very sensitive about his condition of '*Zugang*', that is, new arrival, and to the condition of social subjection that derived from it. Therefore he did not object, but neither did he show any enthusiasm for my invention. 'If there are seventeen, why should we make them believe that there are twenty?'

'But twenty bricks weigh more than seventeen,' I answered impatiently, 'and if they're well arranged, no one will notice. Besides, they're not going to be used to build your house or mine.'

'Yes,' he said, 'but they're still seventeen bricks and not twenty.' He was not a good disciple.

We worked together for a few more weeks in the same squad. He told me that he was a Communist sympathizer, not a Party member, but his language was that of a proto-Christian. At work he was dexterous and strong, the best worker in the squad, but he did not try to profit from this superiority of his, or show off to the German foremen, or lord it over us. I told him that in my opinion working like this was a waste of energy, and that it was also politically wrong, but Bandi gave no sign of understanding me; he did not want to lie. In that place we were supposed to work; so he worked as best he could. In no time, with his radiant and childlike face, his energetic voice and awkward gait, Bandi became very popular, everybody's friend.

August came, with an extraordinary gift for me: a letter from home —an unprecedented event. In June, with frightful irresponsibility, and through the mediation of a 'free' Italian labourer who was a bricklayer, I had written a message for my mother, who was hidden in Italy, and addressed it to a woman friend of mine named Bianca Guidetti Serra. I had done all this as one observes a ritual, without really hoping for success. Instead, my letter had arrived without difficulty, and my mother had answered via the same route. The letter from the sweet world burned in my pocket; I knew that it was elementary prudence to keep silent, and yet I had to talk about it.

At that time we were cleaning cisterns. I went down into my cistern and Bandi was with me. By the weak gleam of the light bulb, I read the miraculous letter, hastily translating it into German. Bandi listened attentively. Certainly he could not understand much because German was neither my language nor his, and also because the message was scant and reticent. But he understood what was essential for him to understand: that that piece of paper in my hands, which had reached me in such a precarious way and which I would destroy before nightfall, represented a breach, a small gap in the black universe that closed tightly around us, and through that breach hope could pass. At least I believe that Bandi, even though he was a *Zugang*, understood or sensed all this, because when I was through reading he came close to me, rummaged at length in his pocket, and finally, with loving care, pulled out a radish. He gave it to me, blushing deeply, and said with shy pride: 'I've learned. This is for you. It's the first thing I've stolen.'

PRIMO LEVI, 'A Disciple', 1981; tr. Ruth Feldman

It is good to have friends even in hell.

Spanish proverb

He had met and shuddered at the kind of German who assured him that they had known nothing about Belsen. Such an assurance, so far from being a sign of conscience or grace, seemed as repulsive as the touch of a leper. That in itself might be salutary—guilt should be contagious perhaps—and to harp on one's innocence was a sure sign of guilt. But the Linkmann family were as frankly untouched by what had gone on as a happy English household would have been untouched by the existence of slums and squalor in the same town. The concept of national guilt meant no more to them than the concept of social guilt means to the average man anywhere.

Oliver was thankful for this. Guilt feelings on a grand scale were surely for the saints: they were unnatural for most people and could only do harm. However precarious and ill-founded it might be, the appearance of innocence was something to be grateful for. It should not be questioned. Oliver could talk seriously about sex with Liese and Herman—no conversational holds of that kind were barred—and yet it would, he knew, be indefensibly gross even to hint at the existence of concentration camps or the slaughter of the Jews. It would be a rape of hospitality, an outrage which he felt his hosts could never forget or forgive. None of them were delicate people, but friendship and shared pleasure create their own delicacy, even in the shadow of war. By his silence, and his acceptance of what he was offered, Oliver condoned and shared the guilt of his friends. They had agreed together to put it from them. Did the Victorians put things from them in the same spirit, he wondered, and if so, would these horrors come home to roost one day, instead of dissolving in the sweetness and light their present friendship seemed superficially to let in?

> JOHN BAYLEY, *In Another Country*, 1955; Oliver is a young
> lieutenant in British Intelligence, in occupied Germany

A customer entered the store. It was Margerine, an old, greying African man wearing broken eyeglasses mended with bits of Scotch tape; he had been given his name by an English memsahib who was unable to pronounce his clan name M'gheren'he, and said she thought it sounded terribly like Margerine. He often ran errands for Fong in return for jelly beans or small cubes of greasy homemade soap . . .

'What is there to see? Just more trouble,' said Margarine. 'Remember in nineteen fifty-six when the Queen came? A nice lady, the Queen. We were all happy. Then in sixty Philip [he pronounced this Philipy] took the flag down; bye-bye, I said. I felt like crying. All my friends were happy. We're free, they said. I said to them, you *buggers* wait one year and you will be crying too.' . . .

The Chinamen had watched it all with respectful awe. 'You speak that black language?' asked the taller one.

'Oh, yes,' said Fong. 'I can even sing hymns in Swahili.'

'That man is your friend?' asked the other.

'They're all my friends,' said Fong. 'When you're a grocer even one enemy is too many.' Well put, he thought.

> PAUL THEROUX, *Fong and the Indians*, 1968

> Crouch'd on the pavement close by Belgrave Square,
> A tramp I saw, ill, moody, and tongue-tied;
> A babe was in her arms, and at her side
> A girl; their clothes were rags, their feet were bare.
>
> Some labouring men, whose work lay somewhere there,
> Pass'd opposite; she touch'd her girl, who hied
> Across, and begg'd, and came back satisfied.
> The rich she had let pass with frozen stare.

Thought I: Above her state this spirit towers;
She will not ask of aliens, but of friends,
Of sharers in a common human fate.

She turns from that cold succour, which attends
The unknown little from the unknowing great,
And points us to a better time than ours.

MATTHEW ARNOLD, 'West London', 1867

Animals

GILBERT WHITE's testimony to the spirit of community among animals is the more persuasive since his *Natural History* makes plain that he was no sentimentalist on the subject.

'So close a friend, and yet so remote,' Thomas Mann says of his dog, invoking an extreme instance of the mixture of likeness and unlikeness held to characterize the most rewarding relationships. Scott and Wordsworth both celebrated in verse the faithful dog who guarded the body of his dead master, on Helvellyn, for three months: how the animal kept alive, only 'He knows, who gave that love sublime; / And gave that strength of feeling . . .' According to T. H. White in *The Sword in the Stone*, the second-century historian and soldier Flavius Arrianus recommended that dogs should sleep with people 'because it makes them more human and because they rejoice in the company of human beings'; White added, 'Imagine a modern MFH going to bed with his hounds.' It is not beyond our imagining.

'It often happens that a man is more humanely related to a cat or dog than to any human being' (Thoreau). Of late those caring bodies whose attentions can barely cope with the proliferating cares that beset us have advised the elderly and lonely to keep pets; the very act of stroking them, cats in particular, the physical contact with a living creature, can have therapeutic value. The theory receives support from Cowper and the leverets who helped him at a time when human companionship was beyond his strength. And Wyatt's falcons must have provided a semblance of affection and loyalty when his friends at court abandoned him.

In a poem Melville represented the little pilot-fish as friends of the Maldive shark: 'friendly they guide him to prey', and in return, somewhat like public schoolboys, though they 'never partake of the treat', they find a haven in the shark's jaws 'when peril's abroad'. An engaging Icelandic folk-tale tells of a man stranded on an ice floe when crossing from the island of Grims Ey to the mainland. An amicable she-bear kept him warm through the night, and suckled him together with her cubs. Over succeeding days the bear induced the man to climb on her back, whereupon she shook him off. By the fourth day the bewildered man was able to stay in place, no matter how violently she shook herself. She then swam to the island with him mounted safely on her. In reciprocation the man gave her fresh milk from his cows and slaughtered two of his rams, binding them across her back, before she returned to her cubs.

Coriolanus sounds a manifestly unsentimental note on which to close. 'Nature teaches beasts to know their friends,' says Sicinius, the sancti-monious demagogue. 'Pray you,' asks Menenius, the cynical patrician, 'who does the wolf love?' 'The lamb.' 'Ay, to devour him . . .'

———

Selborne, 15 August 1775

There is a wonderful spirit of sociality in the brute creation, independent of sexual attachment: the congregation of gregarious birds in the winter is a remarkable instance.

Many horses, though quiet with company, will not stay one minute in a field by themselves: the strongest fences cannot restrain them. My neighbour's horse will not only not stay by himself abroad, but he will not bear to be left alone in a strange stable, without discovering the utmost impatience, and endeavouring to break the rack and manger with his fore-feet. He has been known to leap out at a stable-window, through which dung was thrown, after company; and yet in other respects is remarkably quiet. Oxen and cows will not fatten by themselves; but will neglect the finest pasture that is not recommended by society. It would be needless to instance in sheep, which constantly flock together.

But this propensity seems not to be confined to animals of the same species; for we know a doe, still alive, that was brought up from a little fawn with a dairy of cows; with them it goes afield, and with them it returns to the yard. The dogs of the house take no notice of this deer, being used to her; but if strange dogs come by, a chase ensues; while the master smiles to see his favourite securely leading her pursuers over hedge, or gate, or stile, till she returns to the cows, who, with fierce lowings and menacing horns, drive the assailants quite out of the pasture.

Even great disparity of kind and size does not always prevent social advances and mutual fellowship. For a very intelligent and observant person has assured me, that in the former part of his life, keeping but one horse, he happened also on a time to have but one solitary hen. These two incongruous animals spent much of their time together, in a lonely orchard, where they saw no creature but each other. By degrees an apparent regard began to take place between these two sequestered individuals. The fowl would approach the quadruped with notes of complacency, rubbing herself gently against his legs; while the horse would look down with satisfaction, and move with the greatest caution and circumspection, lest he should trample on his diminutive companion. Thus, by mutual good offices, each seemed to console the vacant hours of the other; so that Milton, when he puts the following sentiment in the mouth of Adam, seems to be somewhat mistaken:—

> Much less can bird with beast, or fish with fowl
> So well converse, nor with the ox the ape.

GILBERT WHITE, *The Natural History of Selborne*

The greenhouse is my summer seat;
My shrubs displac'd from that retreat
   Enjoy'd the open air;
Two goldfinches, whose sprightly song
Had been their mutual solace long,
   Liv'd happy prisoners there.

They sang, as blithe as finches sing
That flutter loose on golden wing,
   And frolic where they list;
Strangers to liberty, 'tis true,
But that delight they never knew,
   And, therefore, never miss'd.

But nature works in ev'ry breast;
Instinct is never quite suppress'd;
   And Dick felt some desires,
Which, after many an effort vain,
Instructed him at length to gain
   A pass between his wires.

The open windows seem'd to invite
The freeman to a farewell flight;
   But Tom was still confin'd;

And Dick, although his way was clear,
Was much too gen'rous and sincere
  To leave his friend behind.

For, settling on his grated roof,
He chirp'd and kiss'd him, giving proof
  That he desir'd no more;
Nor would forsake his cage at last,
Till gently seized I shut him fast,
  A pris'ner as before.

Oh ye, who never knew the joys
Of Friendship, satisfied with noise,
  Fandango, ball and rout!
Blush, when I tell you how a bird,
A prison, with a friend, preferr'd
  To liberty without.

COWPER, 'The Faithful Friend', 1795

William . . . asks me to set down the story of Barbara Wilkinson's Turtle
Dove. Barbara is an old maid. She had 2 turtle Doves. One of them died
the first year I think. The other bird continued to live alone in its cage for
9 years, but for one whole year it had a companion and daily visitor, a
little mouse that used to come and feed with it, and the Dove would
caress it, and cower over it with its wings, and make a loving noise to it.
The mouse though it did not testify equal delight in the Dove's company
yet it was at perfect ease. The poor mouse disappeared and the Dove was
left solitary till its death. It died of a short sickness and was buried under a
tree with funeral ceremony by Barbara and her maiden, and one or two
others.

DOROTHY WORDSWORTH, *Grasmere Journals*, 30 January 1802

'Twas in that place o' Scotland's isle,
That bears the name o' Auld King Coil,   *Kyle*
Upon a bonie day in June,
When wearing thro' the afternoon,

Twa dogs, that were na thrang at hame,   *busy*
Forgather'd ance upon a time.

  The first I'll name, they ca'd him Cæsar,
Was keepit for his Honor's pleasure;
His hair, his size, his mouth, his lugs,   *ears*
Shew'd he was nane o' Scotland's dogs,
But whalpit some place far abroad,
Whare sailors gang to fish for Cod.

  His lockèd, letter'd, braw brass collar
Shew'd him the gentleman and scholar;
But tho' he was o' high degree,
The fient a pride, na pride had he,   *devil*
But wad hae spent an hour caressin,
Ev'n wi' a tinkler-gypsey's messin: *mongrel*
At kirk or market, mill or smiddie,
Nae tawted tyke, tho' e'er sae duddie,   *matted cur, ragged*
But he wad stan't, as glad to see him,   *stand*
And stroan't on stanes an' hillocks wi' him.   *watered*

  The tither was a ploughman's collie,
A rhyming, ranting, raving billie,
Wha for his friend and comrade had him,
And in his freaks had Luath ca'd him,
After some dog in Highland sang,
Was made lang syne, Lord knows how lang.

  He was a gash an' faithful tyke,   *wise*
As ever lap a sheugh or dyke.   *leapt a ditch*
His honest, sonsie, baws'nt face   *white-striped*
Ay gat him friends in ilka place;
His breast was white, his touzie back   *shaggy*
Weel clad wi' coat o' glossy black;
His gawcie tail, wi' upward curl,   *ample*
Hung owre his hurdies wi' a swirl.   *buttocks*

  Nae doubt but they were fain o' ither,
An' unco pack an' thick thegither;   *intimate*
Wi' social nose whyles snuff'd an' snowkit,   *scented*

Whyles mice an' moudieworts they howkit;　　*moles, dug up*
Whyles scour'd awa in lang excursion,
An' worry'd ither in diversion;
Till tir'd at last wi' mony a farce,
They sat them down upon their arse,
And there began a lang digression
About the *lords o' the creation.*

ROBERT BURNS, from 'The Twa Dogs', 1786

You are to know then, that as 'tis Likeness that begets Affection, so my Favorite Dog is a Little one, a lean one, and none of the finest Shap'd . . . If it be the chief point of Friendship to comply with a Friend's Motions & Inclinations, he possesses this in an eminent degree; he lyes down when I sitt, & walks where I walk, which Is more than many very good Friends can pretend to, Witness Our Walk a year ago in St James's Park —Histories are more full of Examples of the Fidelity of Dogs than of Friends, but I will not insist upon many of 'em, because It is possible some may be almost as fabulous as those of Pylades & Orestes, &c. I will only say for the honour of Dogs that the Two most ancient and esteemable Books, Sacred and prophane, extant, (viz: the Scripture and Homer) have shown a particular Regard to these Animals. That of Toby [Book of Tobit] is the more remarkable, because there was no manner of reason to take notice of the Dog besides the great humanity of the Author. And Homer's Account of Ulysses's Dog Argus, is the most pathetic imaginable, all the Circumstances consider'd, and an excellent Proof of the Old Bard's Goodnature. Ulysses had left him at Ithaca when he embarkd for Troy, & found him on his return after 20 years, (which by the way is not unnatural, as some Criticks have said, since I remember the Dam of my Dog who was 22 years old when she dy'd: May the Omen of Longevity prove fortunate to her Successour!) You shall have it in Verse.

ARGUS

When wise Ulysses from his native Coast
Long kept by Wars, and long by Tempests tost,
Arrivd at last, poor, old, disguis'd, alone,
To all his Friends & ev'n his Queen unknown,
Chang'd as he was, with Age, & Toils, & Cares,

Furrowd his rev'rend Face, & white his hairs,
In his own Palace forc'd to ask his Bread,
Scornd by those Slaves his former Bounty fed,
Forgot of all his own Domestic Crew;
His faithful Dog his rightful Master knew!
Unfed, unhousd, neglected, on the Clay,
Like an old Servant, now cashier'd, he lay,
And tho' ev'n then expiring on the Plain,
Touch'd with Resentment of ungrateful Man,
And longing to behold his Ancient Lord again.
Him when he Saw—he rose, & crawld to meet,
(Twas all he cou'd) and fawn'd, and kist his feet,
Seiz'd with dumb Joy—then falling by his Side,
Own'd his returning Lord, Look'd up, & Dy'd.

POPE, letter to Henry Cromwell, 19 October 1709

Ah Bounce! ah gentle Beast! why wouldst thou dye,
When thou hadst Meat enough and Orrery?

POPE to Bounce, 1744. Pope's dog Bounce died while in the care
of Lord Orrery, to whom Pope explained that in writing this
couplet (probably his last) he was thinking of some lines of
Chaucer, rendered as 'Ah Arcite! gentle Knight! why wouldst
thou die,/When thou hadst Gold enough, and Emilye?'

Master, by Styx!—which is the poets' oath,
And the dread bourne of dogs and poets both—
Dear Master, destined soon my fate to share,
'Twas not for want of meat or love, I swear,
Bounce left thee early for the Stygian shore:
I went ('twas all I could) to be before;
To wait, as oft in life, when thou wouldst roam,
I watched to have thy greeting coming home.
So here I prick my ears and strain to mark
Thy slight form coming after through the dark,
And leap to meet thee; with my deep bark drown
Thy: 'Bounce! why Bounce, old friend! nay, down, Bounce, down!'
Then, master, shall I turn and, at thy side,

Pace till we reach the river's foetid tide.
The monstrous shapes and terrors of the way
Shall flee, themselves in terror, at my bay;
Gorgons, chimaeras, hydras at my growl
Scatter, and harpies prove pacific fowl;
Charon shall give prompt passage; what is more,
Seem civil till we reach the farther shore;
And last—for this is dog's work—at the Gate
Where the three-headed Cerberus lies in wait,
Thou shalt not need or lyre or hydromel
To mollify the gruesome Hound of Hell
But may'st pass through unscath'd: he will not mind
Seeing with thee, a female of his kind.

There must I leave thee; there to feel thy hand
Bestow a final pat, great Bounce shall stand,
Knowing, alas, that I may do no more
Than gaze and grieve and, while I can, adore.
Watching thy cheerful, firm, unhurried tread
Down that long road declining to the dead,
And think, to see that dwindling shade depart:
'So small a master, but how great a heart!'

A. D. HOPE, 'Bounce to Pope', 1978

So he stands and looks and listens, gathering from what I say and the tone of it that I distinctly approve of his existence—the very thing which I am at pains to imply. And suddenly he thrusts out his head, opening and shutting his lips very fast, and makes a snap at my face as though he meant to bite off my nose. It is a gesture of response to my remarks, and it always makes me recoil with a laugh, as Bashan knows beforehand that it will. It is a kiss in the air, half caress, half teasing, a trick he has had since puppyhood, which I have never seen in any of his predecessors. And he immediately begs pardon for the liberty, crouching, wagging his tail, and behaving funnily embarrassed.

Extraordinary creature! So close a friend, and yet so remote; so different from us, in certain ways, that our language has not power to do justice to his canine logic. For instance, what is the meaning of that frightful circumstantiality—unnerving alike to the spectator and to the parties themselves—attendant on the meeting of dog and dog; or on their first acquaintance or even on their first sight of each other? My excursions with Bashan have made me witness to hundreds of such encounters, or, I might better say, forced me to be an embarrassed spectator at them. And every time, for the duration of the episode, my old familiar Bashan was a stranger to me, I found it impossible to enter into his feelings or behaviour or understand the tribal laws which governed them. Certainly the meeting in the open of two dogs, strangers to each other, is one of the most painful, thrilling, and pregnant of all conceivable encounters; it is surrounded by an atmosphere of the last uncanniness, presided over by a constraint for which I have no preciser name; they simply cannot pass each other, their mutual embarrassment is frightful to behold . . .

I speak of these things only to show how under stress of circumstance the character of a near friend may reveal itself as strange and foreign. It is dark to me, it is mysterious; I observe it with head-shakings and can only dimly guess what it may mean. And in all other respects I understand Bashan so well, I feel such lively sympathy for all his manifestations! For example, how well I know that whining yawn of his when our walk has been disappointing, too short, or devoid of sporting interest; when I have begun the day late and only gone out for a quarter of an hour before dinner. At such times he walks beside me and yawns—an open, impudent yawn to the whole extent of his jaws, an animal, audible yawn insultingly expressive of his utter boredom. 'A fine master I have!' it seems to say.

When I sit reading in a corner of the garden wall, or on the lawn with my back to a favourite tree, I enjoy interrupting my intellectual preoccupations to talk and play with Bashan. And what do I say to him? Mostly his own name, the two syllables which are of the utmost personal interest because they refer to himself and have an electric effect upon his whole being. I rouse and stimulate his sense of his own ego by impressing upon him—varying my tone and emphasis—that he *is* Bashan and that Bashan is his name. By continuing this for a while I can actually produce in him a state of ecstasy, a sort of intoxication with his own identity, so that he begins to whirl round on himself and send up loud exultant barks to heaven out of the weight of dignity that lies on his chest. Or we amuse ourselves, I by tapping him on the nose, he by snapping at my hand as though it were a fly. It makes us both laugh, yes, Bashan has to laugh too;

and as I laugh I marvel at the sight, to me the oddest and most touching thing in the world. It is moving to see how under my teasing his thin animal cheeks and the corners of his mouth will twitch, and over his dark animal mask will pass an expression like a human smile, or at least some ungainly, pathetic semblance of one. It gives way to a look of startled embarrassment, then transforms the face by appearing again.

THOMAS MANN, from 'A Man and His Dog', 1919; tr. H. T. Lowe-Porter

Be kind to dogs, dear reader; they deserve your sympathy and even gratitude. For they are the universal consoler. The love which was once lavished upon you or which you once so ardently sought and then found insufferable and escaped from, it is all now lavished on them. They have taken your place, and enable you to live in carefree independence and freedom elsewhere. But for them there is no escape. To extricate yourself from the possessive, jealous and interfering clutches of wife, mummy, sister or mistress, a number of courses were open to you—the army, the colonies, murder, the divorce court, or simply the train and desertion. But poor doggie, the universal consoler *malgré lui*, has no such means. He mops up for you, in the slobber on his coat, the eternal tears of the world, tears of frustrated love, of grief, of rage, which you have caused to flow. That love from which you fled with a shudder, he is the substitute victim of it now. Anything you revolted against—loss of freedom, nagging, jealousy, emotional scenes and so on—the whole bag of tricks is your legacy to him. Do not hate or despise him: he is your saviour; he earns your pity and gratitude.

So when you see a lady dragging a little dog along on a string, think to yourself, 'There, but for the grace of God, go I.'

J. R. ACKERLEY, *My Sister and Myself: Diaries*, 11 October 1950

His friends he loved. His direst earthly foes—
    Cats—I believe he did but feign to hate.
My hand will miss the insinuated nose,
    Mine eyes the tail that wagg'd contempt at Fate.

WILLIAM WATSON, 'An Epitaph', 1884

The day before yesterday, I appeased a life-long ambition: I held a young fox in my arms. He was an orphan—in other words, the vixen had been killed—a small rickety orphan, when he was given to Mrs Cox six months ago. Now he is the elegant young friend of the family; gentler than a dog, more demonstrative than a cat. I held him in my arms, & snuffed his wild geranium smell, and suddenly he thrust his long nose under my chin, and burrowed against my shoulder, and subsided into bliss. His paws are very soft, soft as raspberries. Everything about him is elegant—an Adonis of an animal. His profile is intensely sophisticated, his full face is the image of artless candour. His fur is like rather coarse, very thick, swansdown, & he wears a grey stomacher.

> Sylvia Townsend Warner, letter to George Plank, 4
> September 1958

In the year 1774, being much indisposed both in mind and body, incapable of diverting myself either with company or books, and yet in a condition that made some diversion necessary, I was glad of any thing that would engage my attention without fatiguing it. The children of a neighbour of mine had a leveret given them for a plaything; it was at that time about three months old. Understanding better how to tease the poor creature than to feed it, and soon becoming weary of their charge, they readily consented that their father, who saw it pining and growing leaner every day, should offer it to my acceptance. I was willing enough to take the prisoner under my protection, perceiving that in the management of such an animal, and in the attempt to tame it, I should find just that sort of employment which my case required. It was soon known among the neighbours that I was pleased with the present, and the consequence was, that in a short time I had as many leverets offered to me as would have stocked a paddock. I undertook the care of three . . .

Puss grew presently familiar, would leap into my lap, raise himself upon his hinder feet, and bite the hair from my temples. He would suffer me to take him up and to carry him about in my arms, and has more than once fallen asleep upon my knee. He was ill three days, during which time I nursed him, kept him apart from his fellows that they might not molest him (for, like many other wild animals, they persecute one of their own species that is sick), and by constant care and trying him with a variety of herbs, restored him to perfect health. No creature could be more grateful than my patient after his recovery; a sentiment which he most significantly expressed, by licking my hand, first the back of it, then the palm, then every finger separately, then between all the fingers, as if anxious to leave no part of it unsaluted; a ceremony which he never performed but once again upon a similar occasion. Finding him extremely tractable, I made it my custom to carry him always after breakfast into the garden, where he hid himself generally under the leaves of a cucumber vine, sleeping or chewing the cud till evening; in the leaves also of that vine he found a favourite repast. I had not long habituated him to this taste of liberty, before he began to be impatient for the return of the time when he might enjoy it. He would invite me to the garden by drumming upon my knee, and by a look of such expression as it was not possible to misinterpret. If this rhetoric did not immediately succeed, he would take the skirt of my coat between his teeth, and pull at it with all his force. Thus Puss might be said to be perfectly tamed, the shyness of his nature was done away, and on the whole it was visible, by many symptoms which I have not room to enumerate, that he was happier in human society than when shut up with his natural companions . . .

Puss is still living, and has just completed his tenth year, discovering no signs of decay, nor even of age, except that he is grown more discreet and less frolicksome than he was. I cannot conclude, without observing that I have lately introduced a dog to his acquaintance, a spaniel that had never seen a hare to a hare that had never seen a spaniel. I did it with great caution, but there was no real need of it. Puss discovered no token of fear, nor Marquis the least symptom of hostility. There is therefore, it should seem, no natural antipathy between dog and hare, but the pursuit of the one occasions the flight of the other, and the dog pursues because he is trained to it; they eat bread at the same time out of the same hand, and are in all respects sociable and friendly.

COWPER, 'Puss, Tiney, and Bess', *The Gentleman's Magazine*, June 1784

The wanton Troopers riding by
Have shot my Fawn and it will die.
Ungentle men! They cannot thrive
To kill thee. Thou ne'er didst alive
Them any harm: alas, nor could
Thy death yet do them any good . . .

Thenceforth I set my self to play
My solitary time away,
With this: and very well content,
Could so mine idle Life have spent.
For it was full of sport; and light
Of foot, and heart; and did invite
Me to its game: it seem'd to bless
Its self in me. How could I less
Than love it? O I cannot be
Unkind t'a Beast that loveth me . . .

With sweetest milk, and sugar, first
I it at mine own fingers nurs'd.
And as it grew, so every day
It wax'd more white and sweet than they.
It had so sweet a Breath! And oft
I blush'd to see its foot more soft,
And white—shall I say than my hand?
Nay, any Lady's of the Land.

It is a wond'rous thing, how fleet
'Twas on those little silver feet.
With what a pretty skipping grace,
It oft would challenge me the Race:
And when't had left me far away,
'Twould stay, and run again, and stay.
For it was nimbler much than Hinds;
And trod as on the foür Winds.

I have a Garden of my own,
But so with Roses overgrown,
And Lilies, that you would it guess
To be a little Wilderness.
And all the Springtime of the year
It only lovèd to be there.
Among the beds of Lilies, I
Have sought it oft, where it should lie;
Yet could not, till it self would rise,
Find it, although before mine Eyes.
For, in the flaxen Lilies' shade,
It like a bank of Lilies laid.

Upon the Roses it would feed,
Until its Lips ev'n seem'd to bleed:

And then to me 'twould boldly trip,
And print those Roses on my Lip.
But all its chief delight was still
On Roses thus its self to fill:
And its pure virgin Limbs to fold
In whitest sheets of Lilies cold.
Had it liv'd long, it would have been
Lilies without, Roses within.

O help! O help! I see it faint:
And die as calmly as a Saint.
See how it weeps. The Tears do come
Sad, slowly dropping like a Gum.
So weeps the wounded Balsam: so
The holy Frankincense doth flow.
The brotherless Heliades
Melt in such Amber Tears as these.

I in a golden Vial will
Keep these two crystal Tears; and fill
It till it do o'erflow with mine;
Then place it in Diana's Shrine.

Now my Sweet Fawn is vanish'd to
Whither the Swans and Turtles go:
In fair Elysium to endure,
With milk-white Lambs, and Ermines pure.
O do not run too fast: for I
Will but bespeak thy Grave, and die.

ANDREW MARVELL (1621–78), from 'The Nymph complaining
for the death of her Fawn'

One day at Kasur a squirrel's nest fell on the dining-room table from the roof. In it were two pink bits of jelly. It was really difficult to tell which was head, which was tail; but they were young squirrels. I know no animal born so helpless, except possibly marsupials; but as a girl I had reared most young things. I essayed to rear these, and with the help of a sparrow's feather nipple to an essence bottle, and a bit of hot brick always kept warm in their basket, I succeeded. No more dainty pets could be imagined than the lovely little creatures who were so absolutely fearless. Tweedledum and Tweedledee I called them, for they were absolutely alike. Handsome little souls no bigger than small rats, with their barred bushy tails and dark markings down their backs. And they were useful to me also. They travelled everywhere with me, and I wonder how many friends I made through their dainty ways! They were an unfailing source of amusement, and in some cases they served as introduction, as when an old Brahman said to me, 'The *mem* must be a servant of Ram's since she is so good to Ram's creatures.' Then he told me the following legend:

'When the great God Ram lost his peerless wife, Sita, through the wickedness of the evil demon Ravana, He called on all His creatures to aid Him in His search for her. Now the first of all His creatures to respond was the squirrel; bright, and cheerful, and golden; for in those days it had no marks upon its back. And it leapt to Ram's arms and sate awaiting orders. But the great God's heart was gentle. He saw the beauty of the little creature. So He said, "Not so! Thou art too pretty for strife. Live to show mankind the beauty of a life untouched by care." So He laid His hand on the squirrel's back in blessing; and lo! the imprint of His fingers remained dark on the golden body to show that even the touch of care can cloud a life.

'For Ram was sorrowful.'

Anyhow the little creatures have brought much pleasure into my life . . . They were, however, extraordinarily wilful. They could not bear my writing. They would try to stop it by laying hold of the pen and jerking it, and if that did not succeed would absolutely pass along the line with their dainty feet, and lick off the ink as I wrote. This was done with a determination to have their own way which was unmistakable; and success brought about an instant change of attitude which was almost touching. Dumtoo would snuggle down into the palm of my hand, and with her bushy tail almost covering her eyes look at me, as who would say, 'You're a dear! I thought you would give in.' This may seem to some an exaggerated picture, but the more one lives with animals, the more things do we see that are inexplicable except by postulating much more power of ratiocination than the majority of mankind are inclined to grant to animals.

Flora Annie Steel, *The Garden of Fidelity: The Autobiography of
Flora Annie Steel, 1847–1929*, 1930

> It had a velvet cap,
> And would sit upon my lap,
> And seek after small wormès,
> And sometime white bread-crumbès;

And many times and oft
Between my breastès soft
It wouldè lie and rest;
It was proper and prest.

    Sometime he would gasp
When he saw a wasp;
A fly or a gnat,
He would fly at that;
And prettily he would pant
When he saw an ant,
Lord, how he would pry
After the butterfly!
Lord, how he would hop
After the gressop!
And when I said, 'Phip, Phip!'
Then he would leap and skip,
And take me by the lip.
Alas, it will me slo   *slay*
That Philip is gone me fro! . . .

    For it would come and go,
And fly so to and fro;
And on me it wouldè leap
When I was asleep,
And his feathers shake,
Wherewith he wouldè make
Me often for to wake,
And for to take him in
Upon my naked skin.
God wot, we thought no sin;
What though he crept so low?
It was no hurt, I trow
He did nothing, perdè,
But sit upon my knee.
Philip, though he were nice,
In him it was no vice.
Philip had leave to go
To peck my little toe;
Philip might be bold

And do what he wold:
Philip would seek and take
All the fleas black
That he could there espy
With his wanton eye.

JOHN SKELTON (*c.*1460–1529), from *Philip Sparrow*, a girl's lament
for her pet, killed by the family cat

Lux, my fair falcon, and your fellows all,
　How well pleasaunt it were your liberty!
Ye not forsake me that fair might ye befall.
　But they that sometime lik'd my company,
Like lice away from dead bodies they crawl:
　Lo, what a proof in light adversity!
But ye, my birds, I swear by all your bells,
Ye be my friends, and so be but few else.

SIR THOMAS WYATT (1503–42), 'Lux, my fair falcon'

The children had pets of their own, too, of course. Among them
guinea-pigs were the stand-bys—their highly unemotional nature fits
them for companionship with adoring but overenthusiastic young masters and mistresses. Then there were flying squirrels, and kangaroo-rats,
gentle and trustful, and a badger whose temper was short but whose
nature was fundamentally friendly. The badger's name was Josiah; the
particular little boy whose property he was used to carry him about,
clasped firmly around what would have been his waist if he had had any.
Inasmuch as when on the ground the badger would play energetic games
of tag with the little boy and nip his bare legs, I suggested that it would be
uncommonly disagreeable if he took advantage of being held in the little
boy's arms to bite his face; but this suggestion was repelled with scorn as
an unworthy assault on the character of Josiah. 'He bites legs sometimes,
but he never bites faces,' said the little boy. We also had a young black
bear whom the children christened Jonathan Edwards, partly out of
compliment to their mother, who was descended from that great Puritan
divine, and partly because the bear possessed a temper in which gloom
and strength were combined in what the children regarded as Calvinistic

proportions. As for the dogs, of course there were many, and during their lives they were intimate and valued family friends, and their deaths were household tragedies. One of them, a large yellow animal of several good breeds and valuable rather because of psychical than physical traits, was named 'Susan' by his small owners, in commemoration of another retainer, a white cow; the fact that the cow and the dog were not of the same sex being treated with indifference.

THEODORE ROOSEVELT, *An Autobiography*, 1913

Goblins came, on mischief bent,
To Saint Anthony in Lent.

'Come, ye goblins, small and big,
We will kill the hermit's pig.

'While the good monk minds his book,
We, the hams will cure and cook.

'While he goes down on his knees,
We will fry the sausages.

'While he on his breast doth beat,
We will grill the tender feet.

'While he David's Psalms doth sing,
We will all to table bring.'

On his knees went Anthony
To those imps of Barbary.

'Good, kind goblins, spare his life,
He to me is child and wife.

'He indeed is good and mild
As 'twere any chrisom child.

'He is my felicity,
Spare, oh spare my pig to me!'

But the pig they did not spare,
Did not heed the hermit's prayer.

They the hams did cure and cook,
Still the good Saint read his book.

When they fried the sausages,
Still he rose not from his knees.

When they grilled the tender feet
He ceasèd not his breast to beat.

They did all to table bring,
He for grace the Psalms did sing.

All at once the morning broke,
From his dream the monk awoke.

There in the kind light of day
Was the little pig at play.

'The Temptation of St Anthony', adapted from an old French
song by R. L. Gales (1862–1927)

Let sordid mortals toil all day,
    For gold and silver search and dig;
A greater treasure I enjoy
    In this, my charming talking pig.

Though mighty monarchs on their thrones
    In pride and state look fierce and big,
They are not so content and blessed
    As is old Tony with his pig.

I neither care who's in or out,
    Whether Tory, whether Whig,
I love my country, King and Queen,
    But best of all I love my pig.

FREDERICK FORREST, from 'St Anthony and his Pig. A Cantata',
1766

Each of us pursues his trade,
I and Pangur my comrade,
His whole fancy on the hunt,
And mine for learning ardent.

More than fame I love to be
Among my books and study,
Pangur does not grudge me it,
Content with his own merit.

When—a heavenly time!—we are
In our small room together
Each of us has his own sport
And asks no greater comfort.

While he sets his round sharp eye
On the wall of my study
I turn mine, though lost its edge
On the great wall of knowledge.

Now a mouse drops in his net
After some mighty onset
While into my bag I cram
Some difficult darksome problem.

When a mouse comes to the kill
Pangur exults, a marvel!
I have when some secret's won
My hour of exultation.

Though we work for days and years
Neither the other hinders;
Each is competent and hence
Enjoys his skill in silence.

Master of the death of mice,
He keeps in daily practice,
I, too, making dark things clear,
Am of my trade a master.

FRANK O'CONNOR, 'The Scholar and the Cat', from the Irish,
early middle ages

For I will consider my Cat Jeoffry.

For he is the servant of the Living God, duly and daily serving
him . . .

For his tongue is exceeding pure so that it has in purity what it wants
in music.

For he is docile and can learn certain things.

For he can sit up with gravity, which is patience upon approbation.

For he can fetch and carry, which is patience in employment.

For he can jump over a stick, which is patience upon proof positive.

For he can spraggle upon waggle at the word of command.

For he can jump from an eminence into his master's bosom.

For he can catch the cork and toss it again.

For he is hated by the hypocrite and miser.

For the former is afraid of detection.

For the latter refuses the charge.

For he camels his back to bear the first notion of business.

For he is good to think on, if a man would express himself neatly.

For he made a great figure in Egypt for his signal services.

For he killed the Icneumon rat, very pernicious by land.

For his ears are so acute that they sting again.

For from this proceeds the passing quickness of his attention.

For by stroking of him I have found out electricity.

For I perceived God's light about him both wax and fire.

For the electrical fire is the spiritual substance which God sends from
heaven to sustain the bodies both of man and beast.

For God has blessed him in the variety of his movements.

For, though he cannot fly, he is an excellent clamberer.

For his motions upon the face of the earth are more than any other
quadruped.

For he can tread to all the measures upon the music.

For he can swim for life.

For he can creep.

> CHRISTOPHER SMART, from *Jubilate Agno*, written between 1758
> and 1763

Tiber makes love to you for the good reason that he loves you, and loves
making love. Cats are passionate and voluptuous, they get satisfaction
from mating but no pleasure (the females dislike it and this is wounding
to the male), no voluptuousness; *and no appreciation* . . .

We had a dark grey cat (Norfolk bred, very Norfolk in character) called Tom. He was reserved, domineering, voluptuous—much as I imagine Tiber to be. When he was middle-aged he gave up nocturnal prowlings and slept on my bed, against my feet. One evening I was reading in bed when I became aware that Tom was staring at me. I put down my book, said nothing, watched. Slowly, with a look of intense concentration, he got up and advanced on me, like Tarquin with ravishing strides, poised himself, put out a front paw, and stroked my cheek as I used to stroke his chops. A human caress from a cat. I felt very meagre and ill-educated that I could not purr. It had never occurred to me that their furry love develops from what was shown them as kittens.

SYLVIA TOWNSEND WARNER, letter to David Garnett, 18 June
1973

Pet was never mourned as you,
Purrer of the spotless hue,
Plumy tail, and wistful gaze
While you humoured our queer ways,
Or outshrilled your morning call
Up the stairs and through the hall—
Foot suspended in its fall—
While, expectant, you would stand
Arched, to meet the stroking hand;
Till your way you chose to wend
Yonder, to your tragic end.

Never another pet for me!
Let your place all vacant be;
Better blankness day by day
Than companion torn away.
Better bid his memory fade,
Better blot each mark he made,
Selfishly escape distress
By contrived forgetfulness,
Than preserve his prints to make
Every morn and eve an ache.

From the chair whereon he sat
Sweep his fur, nor wince thereat;
Rake his little pathways out
Mid the bushes roundabout;
Smooth away his talons' mark
From the claw-worn pine-tree bark,
Where he climbed as dusk embrowned,
Waiting us who loitered round.

Strange it is this speechless thing,
Subject to our mastering,
Subject for his life and food
To our gift, and time, and mood;
Timid pensioner of us Powers,
His existence ruled by ours,
Should—by crossing at a breath
Into safe and shielded death,
By the merely taking hence
Of his insignificance—
Loom as largened to the sense,
Shape as part, above man's will,
Of the Imperturbable.

As a prisoner, flight debarred,
Exercising in a yard,
Still retain I, troubled, shaken,
Mean estate, by him forsaken;
And this home, which scarcely took
Impress from his little look,
By his faring to the Dim
Grows all eloquent of him.

Housemate, I can think you still
Bounding to the window-sill,
Over which I vaguely see
Your small mound beneath the tree,
Showing in the autumn shade
That you moulder where you played.

HARDY, 'Last Words to a Dumb Friend', dated 2 October 1904

Fears, Failures, and False Friends

'FRIENDSHIP is the marriage of the soul, and this marriage is liable to divorce' (Voltaire). The following pages look at the darker side of our subject: reservations, inadequacies, misunderstandings, excessive candour, negligence, ingratitude, envy, deceit, the 'petty provocations and incivilities peevishly returned' which Johnson registered in describing the rupture between Addison and Pope, and friendships foundering (often for 'a slip of the tongue', for 'some trick not worth an egg', like too much baking soda in the bread), or exploited, or betrayed. La Fontaine's fable suggests an alternative interpretation of the reputedly Chinese proverb quoted on p. 29: that's to say, exercise discretion when doing a friend a good turn. Kierkegaard commented (1849) that Job could endure everything, until his friends came to comfort him, whereupon he grew impatient.

> Alas! they had been friends in youth;
> But whispering tongues can poison truth,

Coleridge wrote of Lord Roland and Sir Leoline in *Christabel*,

> And constancy lives in realms above;
> And life is thorny; and youth is vain;
> And to be wroth with one we love,
> Doth work like madness in the brain.

'Sweetest things turn sourest by their deeds', and friendships that fester may grow into rank enmity: 'a grief unto death', in the words of Ecclesiasticus.

The case of the narrator in the passage taken from Proust, seemingly perverse, has its special interest. Friends are most welcome *in absentia*, in theory; he fears that active friendship will detract or distract from his individuality by bringing out what is shared and similar. He is (in Bacon's phrase) a cannibal of his own heart, dedicated to singularity, haecceity, the mapping of selfhood. This is not to be wondered at, he being a writer, and the author of *A la recherche du temps perdu*.

'My birthplace hate I, and my love's upon / This enemy town': in his dealings with the Volscians and their general Aufidius, Coriolanus

proves the speciousness of the saying, 'My enemy's enemy is my friend.'
And in the matter of false friends, one of the harshest ironies occurs when
Othello assures himself,

> O brave Iago, honest and just!
> That hast such noble sense of thy friend's wrong;
> Thou teachest me.

━━━━━

And in the midst of the Great Assembly Palamabron pray'd:
'O God, protect me from my friends, that they have not power over
  me.
Thou hast giv'n me power to protect myself from my bitterest
  enemies.'

BLAKE, *Milton*, 1804–8

Thus human life is nothing but a perpetual illusion; we only deceive and
flatter one another. No one speaks of us in our presence as he does in our
absence. Union between men is founded only on this mutual deceit; and
few friendships would survive if each man knew what his friend says
about him when he is not there, even though it is said sincerely and
dispassionately.

BLAISE PASCAL (1623–62), *Pensées*

The most fatal disease of friendship is gradual decay, or dislike hourly
encreased by causes too slender for complaint, and too numerous for
removal. Those who are angry may be reconciled; those who have been
injured may receive a recompence; but when the desire of pleasing and
willingness to be pleased is silently diminished, the renovation of
friendship is hopeless; as, when the vital powers sink into languor, there
is no longer any use of the physician.

JOHNSON, *The Idler*, 23 September 1758

How is it that we are impelled to treat our old friends so ill when we obtain new ones? The housekeeper says, I never had any new crockery but I began to break the old.

THOREAU, *A Week on the Concord and Merrimack Rivers*

When I wer still a bwoy, an' mother's pride,
A bigger bwoy spoke up to me so kind-like,
'If you do like, I'll treat ye wi' a ride
In theäse wheel-barrow here.' Zoo I wer blind-like
To what he had a-worken in his mind-like,
An' mounted vor a passenger inside;
An' comen to a puddle, perty wide,
He tipp'd me in, a-grinnen back behind-like.
Zoo when a man do come to me so thick-like,
An' sheäke my hand, where woonce he pass'd me by,
An' tell me he would do me this or that,
I can't help thinken o' the big bwoy's trick-like.
An' then, vor all I can but wag my hat
An' thank en, I do veel a little shy.

WILLIAM BARNES, 'False Friends-Like', 1857

Give me the avowed, erect and manly foe;
Firm I can meet, perhaps return the blow;
But of all plagues, good Heaven, thy wrath can send,
Save me, oh, save me, from the candid friend.

GEORGE CANNING, *New Morality*, 1798

To forgive enemies H. does pretend,
Who never in his life forgave a friend.

When H——y finds out what you cannot do,
That is the very thing he'll set you to.
If you break not your neck, 'tis not his fault,

But pecks of poison are not pecks of salt.
And when he could not act upon my life
Hired a villain to bereave my life.

Thy friendship oft has made my heart to ache:
Do be my enemy for friendship's sake.

BLAKE, *MS Notebook*, c.1808; on William Hayley

It was promptly settled between us that he and I were to be great friends for ever, and he would say 'our friendship' as though he were speaking of some important and delightful thing which had an existence independent of ourselves, and which he soon called—not counting his love for his mistress—the great joy of his life. These words made me rather uncomfortable and I was at a loss for an answer, for I did not feel when I was with him and talked to him—and no doubt it would have been the same with everyone else—any of that happiness which it was, on the other hand, possible for me to experience when I was by myself. For alone, at times, I felt surging from the depths of my being one or other of those impressions which gave me a delicious sense of comfort. But as soon as I was with someone else, when I began to talk to a friend, my mind at once 'turned about', it was towards the listener and not myself that it directed its thoughts, and when they followed this outward course they brought me no pleasure. Once I had left Saint-Loup, I managed, with the help of words, to put more or less in order the confused minutes that I had spent with him; I told myself that I had a good friend, that a good friend was a rare thing, and I tasted, when I felt myself surrounded by 'goods' that were difficult to acquire, what was precisely the opposite of the pleasure that was natural to me, the opposite of the pleasure of having extracted from myself and brought to light something that was hidden in my inner darkness. If I had spent two or three hours in conversation with Saint-Loup, and he had expressed his admiration of what I had said to him, I felt a sort of remorse, or regret, or weariness at not having been left alone and ready, at last, to begin my work. But I told myself that one is not given intelligence for one's own benefit only, that the greatest of men have longed for appreciation, that I could not regard as wasted, hours in which I had built up an exalted idea of myself in the mind of my friend; I had no difficulty in persuading myself that I ought to be happy in consequence, and I hoped all the more anxiously that this happiness might never be taken from me simply because I had not yet been conscious of it ... I felt that I was capable of exemplifying the virtues of friendship better than most people (because I should always place the good of my friends before those personal interests to which other people were devoted but which did not count for me), but not of finding happiness in a feeling which, instead of multiplying the differences that there were between my nature and those of other people—as there are among all of us—would cancel them.

PROUST, Within a Budding Grove, 1918; tr. Scott Moncrieff

There are few things in which we deceive ourselves more than in the esteem we profess to entertain for our friends. It is little better than a piece of quackery. The truth is, we think of them as we please—that is, as *they* please or displease us. As long as we are in good humour with them, we see nothing but their good qualities; but no sooner do they offend us than we rip up all their bad ones (which we before made a secret of, even to ourselves) with double malice. He who but now was little less than an angel of light shall be painted in the blackest colours for a slip of the tongue, 'some trick not worth an egg', for the slightest suspicion of offence given or received. We often bestow the most opprobrious epithets on our best friends, and retract them twenty times in the course of a day, while the man himself remains the same. In love, which is all rhapsody and passion, this is excusable; but in the ordinary intercourse of life, it is preposterous.

HAZLITT, Characteristics

O world, thy slippery turns! Friends now fast sworn,
Whose double bosoms seem to wear one heart,
Whose hours, whose bed, whose meal and exercise
Are still together, who twin, as 'twere, in love
Unseparable, shall within this hour,
On a dissension of a doit, break out
To bitterest enmity. So fellest foes,
Whose passions and whose plots have broke their sleep
To take the one the other, by some chance,

> Some trick not worth an egg, shall grow dear friends
> And interjoin their issues.

SHAKESPEARE, *Coriolanus*, c. 1608; Coriolanus to himself

> It often falls (as here it erst befell)
>   That mortall foes doe turne to faithfull friends,
>   And friends profest are chaunged to foemen fell:
>   The cause of both, of both their minds depends,
>   And th'end of both likewise of both their ends.
>   For enmitie, that of no ill proceeds,
>   But of occasion, with th'occasion ends;
>   And friendship, which a faint affection breeds
> Without regard of good, dyes like ill grounded seeds.

EDMUND SPENSER, *The Faerie Queene*, 1596

Before nine o'clock it was pretty well known all along the river that the two partners of the 'Amity Claim' had quarrelled and separated at daybreak. At that time the attention of their nearest neighbour had been attracted by the sounds of altercation and two consecutive pistol-shots. Running out, he had seen, dimly, in the grey mist that rose from the river, the tall form of Scott, one of the partners, descending the hill toward the *cañon*; a moment later, York, the other partner, had appeared from the cabin, and walked in an opposite direction toward the river . . .

The quarrel remained inexplicable. That two men, whose amiability and grave tact had earned for them the title of 'The Peace-makers', in a community not greatly given to the passive virtues—that these men, singularly devoted to each other, should suddenly and violently quarrel, might well excite the curiosity of the camp. A few of the more inquisitive visited the late scene of conflict, now deserted by its former occupants. There was no trace of disorder or confusion in the neat cabin. The rude table was arranged as if for breakfast; the pan of yellow biscuit still sat upon that hearth whose dead embers might have typified the evil passions that had raged there but an hour before. But Colonel Starbottle's eye—albeit somewhat bloodshot and rheumy—was more intent on practical details. On examination, a bullet-hole was found in the door-post, and another, nearly opposite, in the casing of the window. The

Colonel called attention to the fact that the one 'agreed with' the bore of Scott's revolver, and the other with that of York's derringer. 'They must hev stood about yer,' said the Colonel, taking position; 'not mor'n three feet apart, and missed!' There was a fine touch of pathos in the falling inflection of the Colonel's voice, which was not without effect. A delicate perception of wasted opportunity thrilled his auditors . . .

Sandy Bar began to accept the enmity of the former partners as a lifelong feud, and the fact that they had ever been friends was forgotten. The few who expected to learn from the trial [concerning the ownership of the Amity Claim] the origin of the quarrel were disappointed . . .

[After many years of bitterness, York returns to the cabin] A figure started up angrily and came toward him—a figure whose bloodshot eyes suddenly fixed into a vacant state; whose arms were at first outstretched, and then thrown up in warning gesticulation; a figure that suddenly gasped, choked, and then fell forward in a fit.

But before he touched the ground, York had him out into the open air and sunshine. In the struggle both fell and rolled over on the ground. But the next moment York was sitting up, holding the convulsed frame of his former partner on his knee, and wiping the foam from his inarticulate lips. Gradually the tremor became less frequent, and then ceased; and the strong man lay unconscious in his arms.

For some moments York held him quietly thus, looking in his face . . . And then came voices, and two men joined them. 'A fight?' No, a fit; and would they help him bring the sick man to the hotel?

And there, for a week, the stricken partner lay, unconscious of aught but the visions wrought by disease and fear. On the eighth day, at sunrise, he rallied, and opening his eyes, looked upon York, and pressed his hand; then he spoke—

'And it's you. I thought it was only whisky.'

York replied by taking both of his hands, boyishly working them backward and forward, as his elbow rested on the bed, with a pleasant smile.

'And so you've been abroad. How did you like Paris?'

'So, so. How did you like Sacramento?'

'Bully.'

And that was all they could think to say. Presently, Scott opened his eyes again.

'I'm mighty weak.'

'You'll get better soon.'

'Not much.'

A long silence followed ... Then Scott slowly and with difficulty turned his face to York, and said—

'I might hev killed you once.'

'I wish you had.'

They pressed each other's hands again, but Scott's grasp was evidently failing. He seemed to summon his energies for a special effort.

'Old man!'

'Old chap.'

'Closer!'

York bent his head toward the slowly fading face.

'Do ye mind that morning?'

'Yes.'

A gleam of fun slid into the corner of Scott's blue eye, as he whispered—

'Old man, thar *was* too much saleratus [baking soda] in that bread.'

It is said that these were his last words. For when the sun, which had so often gone down upon the idle wrath of these foolish men, looked again upon them reunited, it saw the hand of Scott fall cold and irresponsive from the yearning clasp of his former partner, and it knew that the feud of Sandy Bar was at an end.

BRET HARTE, from 'The Iliad of Sandy Bar', 1873

For it is an old-saide saw, 'there is harde batayle where kinne and frendys doth batayle eyther agenst others', for there may be no mercy, but mortall warre.

SIR THOMAS MALORY, *Le Morte D'Arthur*, finished 1470

A Man often contracts a Friendship with one whom perhaps he does not find out till after a Year's Conversation; when on a sudden some latent ill Humour breaks out upon him, which he never discovered or suspected at his first entering into an Intimacy with him. There are several Persons who in some certain Periods of their Lives are inexpressibly agreeable, and in others as odious and detestable. *Martial* has given us a very pretty Picture of one of this Species in the following Epigram:

In all thy Humours, whether grave or mellow,
Thou 'rt such a touchy, testy, pleasant Fellow;
Hast so much Wit, and Mirth, and Spleen about thee,
There is no living with thee, nor without thee.

JOSEPH ADDISON, *The Spectator*, 18 May 1771

> The nearest friends can go
> With anyone to death, comes so far short
> They might as well not try to go at all.
> No, from the time when one is sick to death,
> One is alone, and he dies more alone.
> Friends make pretence of following to the grave,
> But before one is in it, their minds are turned
> And making the best of their way back to life
> And living people, and things they understand.

ROBERT FROST, from 'Home Burial', 1914

In the misfortunes of our best friends we always find something that isn't displeasing to us.

LA ROCHEFOUCAULD, *Maximes*, 1665

As *Rochefoucauld* his Maxims drew
From Nature, I believe 'em true:
They argue no corrupted Mind
In him; the Fault is in Mankind.

This Maxim more than all the rest
Is thought too base for human Breast;
'In all Distresses of our Friends
We first consult our private Ends,
While Nature kindly bent to ease us,
Points out some Circumstance to please us.'

If this perhaps your Patience move
Let Reason and Experience prove.

We all behold with envious Eyes,
Our *Equal* rais'd above our *Size*;
Who would not at a crowded Show,
Stand high himself, keep others low?
I love my Friend as well as you,
But would not have him stop my View;
Then let me have the higher Post;
I ask but for an Inch at most . . .

What Poet would not grieve to see,
His Brethren write as well as he?
But rather than they should excel,
He'd wish his Rivals all in Hell.

Her End when Emulation misses,
She turns to Envy, Stings and Hisses:
The strongest Friendship yields to Pride,
Unless the Odds be on our Side . . .

I have no Title to aspire;
Yet, when you sink, I seem the higher.
In POPE, I cannot read a Line,
But with a Sigh, I wish it mine:
When he can in one Couplet fix
More Sense than I can do in Six:
It gives me such a jealous Fit,
I cry, Pox take him, and his Wit.

Why must I be outdone by GAY,
In my own hum'rous biting Way?

ARBUTHNOT is no more my Friend,
Who dares to Irony pretend;
Which I was born to introduce,
Refin'd it first, and shew'd its Use.

St. John, as well as Pultney knows,
That I had some Repute for Prose;
And till they drove me out of Date,
Could maul a Minister of State:
If they have mortified my Pride,
And made me throw my Pen aside;
If with such Talents Heav'n hath blest 'em
Have I not Reason to detest 'em?

To all my Foes, dear Fortune, send
Thy Gifts, but never to my Friend:
I tamely can endure the first,
But, this with Envy makes me burst.

Jonathan Swift, from 'Verses on the Death of Dr Swift', 1739

There are persons who cannot make friends. Who are they? Those who cannot be friends. It is not the want of understanding or good nature, of entertaining or useful qualities, that you complain of: on the contrary, they have probably many points of attraction; but they have one that neutralizes all these—they care nothing about you, and are neither the better nor worse for what you think of them. They manifest no joy at your approach; and when you leave them, it is with a feeling that they can do just as well without you. This is not sullenness, nor indifference, nor absence of mind; but they are intent solely on their own thoughts, and you are merely one of the subjects they exercise them upon. They live in society as in a solitude ... There is, therefore, something cold and repulsive in the air that is about them—like that of marble. In a word, they are *modern philosophers*; and the modern philosopher is what the pedant was of old—a being who lives in a world of his own, and has no correspondence with this. It is not that such persons have not done you services—you acknowledge it; it is not that they have said severe things of you—you submit to it as a necessary evil: but it is the cool manner in which the whole is done that annoys you—the speculating upon you, as if you were nobody—the regarding you, with a view to an experiment *in corpore vili*—the principle of dissection—the determination to spare no blemishes—to cut you down to your real standard;—in short, the utter absence of the partiality of friendship, the blind enthusiasm of affection, or the delicacy of common decency, that whether they 'hew you as a carcass fit for hounds, or carve you as a dish fit for the gods', the operation on your feelings and your sense of obligation is just the same; and, whether they are demons or angels in themselves, you wish them equally *at the devil*!

HAZLITT, 'On Disagreeable People', 1827

There is a certain sort of people who easily make friends with everyone, hate him just as quickly, and then love him again. If one looks at the human race as a whole, where every part fits in its place, then such people are fillers, so to speak, that can be dropped in anywhere. One seldom finds great geniuses among this sort, although they are readily taken for such.

GEORG CHRISTOPH LICHTENBERG, *Sudelbuch*, 1765–70

A certain Bear, whose dam had licked him ill,
Dwelt in a lonely forest on a hill.
A new Bellerophon, he shunned his kind,
Till the seclusion, telling on his mind,
Went near to drive him melancholy-mad.
Though speech be good, and silence better still,
Too much of either turns to bad,
And sense consorts not long with solitude.
The other animals tabooed
His unattractive domicile;
And he, for all his bearishness,
Relished his isolation less and less.
   Meanwhile, in the same neighbourhood
There lived a Greybeard, who was likewise bored.
He had a taste for gardening, and adored
Both Flora and Pomona, whose employ,
Though always pleasant, yields a fuller joy
If shared with some congenial friend;
For gardens rarely talk (except in Fable).
   At length, dissatisfied to spend
His life in circles purely vegetable,
One day he gave his silent loves the slip
In search of livelier companionship.
The Bear, impelled by a like yearning,

Had left his cheerless eminence,
And by an odd coincidence
They met each other at a turning.
The Man took fright, but what was to be done?
'Twas not the faintest use to run;
And feeling that on such a case
'Tis well to put one's boldest face,
He managed to dissemble his alarm.
The Bear, whose manner failed in courtly charm,
Muttered a grumpy invitation.
    'Nay,' said the other, 'won't Your Lordship grace
My humble cot, which you can see from here,
And condescend to rustic cheer
Of milk and fruit? No doubt a strange collation
For one of your distinguished race,
But 'tis the best I have.' The bear agreed.
They were good friends before they reached the door;
And though 'tis better, by the wise man's creed,
To live alone than with a bore,
Once there, they got on very well indeed.
The Man could garden undisturbed all day,
For Bruin barely had two words to say.
He went a-hunting to supply their need;
But his great line was shooing flies away
From his friend's forehead as a-drowse he lay.
Once while the Oldster snored in deep repose,
A bluebottle assailed his nose
With such persistence that the Bear
At last was driven to despair.
'I'll swat you, ma'am, for this,' he growled—'here goes!'
Therewith he hurled a brickbat through the air,
Which squashed the fly—but broke the sleeper's head.
His aim was better than his reasoning,
And the result of all his pains
Was that his chum lay doornail-dead.

An idiotic friend's a dangerous thing:
I'ld sooner have a foe with brains.

> JEAN DE LA FONTAINE, 'The Bear and the Garden Lover', *Fables*,
> 1678; tr. Edward Marsh

Voltaire's reception in Prussia was such as might well have elated a less vain and excitable mind. He wrote to his friends at Paris, that the kindness and the attention with which he had been welcomed surpassed description, that the King was the most amiable of men, that Potsdam was the paradise of philosophers. He was created chamberlain, and received, together with his gold key, the cross of an order, and a patent ensuring to him a pension of eight hundred pounds sterling a year for life. A hundred and sixty pounds a year were promised to his niece if she survived him. The royal cooks and coachmen were put at his disposal ... But even amidst the delights of the honeymoon, Voltaire's sensitive vanity began to take alarm. A few days after his arrival, he could not help telling his niece that the amiable King had a trick of giving a sly scratch with one hand while patting and stroking with the other ...

This eccentric friendship was fast cooling. Never had there met two persons so exquisitely fitted to plague each other. Each of them had exactly the fault of which the other was most impatient; and they were, in different ways, the most impatient of mankind. Frederic was frugal, almost niggardly. When he had secured his plaything he began to think that he had bought it too dear. Voltaire, on the other hand, was greedy, even to the extent of imprudence and knavery; and conceived that the favourite of a monarch who had barrels full of gold and silver laid up in cellars ought to make a fortune which a receiver-general might envy. They soon discovered each other's feelings. Both were angry; and a war began, in which Frederic stooped to the part of Harpagon, and Voltaire to that of Scapin. It is humiliating to relate, that the great warrior and statesman gave orders that his guest's allowance of sugar and chocolate should be curtailed. It is, if possible, a still more humiliating fact, that Voltaire indemnified himself by pocketing the wax candles in the royal antechamber ...

Causes of quarrel multiplied fast ... Voltaire was soon at war with the other men of letters who surrounded the King; and this irritated Frederic, who, however, had himself chiefly to blame: for, from that love of tormenting which was in him a ruling passion, he perpetually lavished extravagant praises on small men and bad books, merely in order that he might enjoy the mortification and rage which on such occasions Voltaire took no pains to conceal. His Majesty, however, soon had reason to regret the pains which he had taken to kindle jealousy among the members of his household. The whole palace was in a ferment with literary intrigues and cabals. It was to no purpose that the imperial voice, which kept a hundred and sixty thousand soldiers in order, was raised to quiet the contention of the exasperated wits. It was far easier to stir up such a storm than to lull it. Nor was Frederic, in his capacity of wit, by any means without his own share of vexations. He had sent a large quantity of verses to Voltaire, and requested that they might be returned, with remarks and corrections. 'See,' exclaimed Voltaire, 'what a quantity of his dirty linen the King has sent me to wash!' Talebearers were not wanting to carry the sarcasm to the royal ear; and Frederic was as much incensed as a Grub Street writer who had found his name in the *Dunciad*.

This could not last . . . They parted with cold civility; but their hearts were big with resentment. Voltaire had in his keeping a volume of the King's poetry, and forgot to return it. This was, we believe, merely one of the oversights which men setting out upon a journey often commit. That Voltaire could have meditated plagiarism is quite incredible. He would not, we are confident, for the half of Frederic's kingdom, have consented to father Frederic's verses. The King, however, who rated his own writings much above their value, and who was inclined to see all Voltaire's actions in the worst light, was enraged to think that his favourite compositions were in the hands of an enemy, as thievish as a daw and as mischievous as a monkey. In the anger excited by this thought, he lost sight of reason and decency, and determined on committing an outrage at once odious and ridiculous.

Voltaire had reached Frankfort. His niece, Madame Denis, came thither to meet him. He conceived himself secure from the power of his late master, when he was arrested by order of the Prussian resident. The precious volume was delivered up. But the Prussian agents had, no doubt, been instructed not to let Voltaire escape without some gross indignity. He was confined twelve days in a wretched hovel. Sentinels with fixed bayonets kept guard over him. His niece was dragged through the mire by the soldiers. Sixteen hundred dollars were extorted from him by his insolent gaolers.

THOMAS BABINGTON MACAULAY, 'Frederic the Great', 1842

What can I say to you? How can I now retract
    All that that fool, my voice, has spoken—
Now that the facts are plain, the placid surface cracked,
    The protocols of friendship broken?

> I cannot walk by day as now I walk at dawn
>   Past the still house where you lie sleeping.
> May the sun burn away these footprints on the lawn
>   And hold you in its warmth and keeping.

VIKRAM SETH, 'Protocols', 1989

... As soon as I was informed, that you had denied having used certain expressions, I did not hesitate a moment (nor was it in my power to do so) to give you my fullest faith, and approve to my own consciousness the truth of my declaration, that I should have felt it as a blessing, tho' my Life had the same instant been hazarded as the pledge, could I with firm conviction have given Montagu the Lie at the conclusion of his Story, even as at the very first sentence I exclaimed—'Impossible! It is impossible!'—The expressions denied were indeed only the most offensive part to the feelings—but at the same time I learnt that you did not hesitate instantly to express your conviction, that Montagu never said those words & that I had invented them—or (to use your own words) 'had forgotten myself'. Grievously indeed, if I know aught of my nature, must I have forgotten both myself & common Honesty, could I have been villain enough to have invented & persevered in such atrocious falsehoods.—Your message was that 'if I declined an explanation, you begged I would no longer continue to talk about the affair'.—When, Wordsworth, did I ever decline an explanation?

Even to her [Mary Lamb] I did not intend to mention it; but alarmed by the wildness & paleness of my Countenance & agitation I had no power to conceal, she entreated me to tell her what was the matter. In the first attempt to speak, my feelings overpowered me, an agony of weeping followed, & then alarmed at my own imprudence and conscious of the possible effect on her health & mind if I left her in that state of suspense, I brought out convulsively some such words as—Wordsworth—Wordsworth has given me up. *He* has no hope of me—I have been an absolute Nuisance in his family—And when long Weeping had relieved me, & I was able to relate the occurrence connectedly, she can bear witness for me, that disgraceful, as it was, that I should be made the Topic of vulgar Gossip, yet that 'had the whole & ten times worse, been proclaimed by a Speaking Trumpet from the Chimneys, I should have smiled at it—or indulged indignation only as far as it excited me to pleasurable activity—;—but that *you* had said it, this & this only, was the Sting! the Scorpion-tooth!'

But one thing more—the last Complaint that you will hear from me, perhaps. When without my knowledge dear Mary Lamb, just then on the very verge of a Relapse, wrote to Grasmere, was it kind or even humane to have returned such an answer, as Lamb deemed it unadvisable to shew me; but which I learnt from the only other person, who saw the answer, amounted in Substance to a Sneer on my reported high Spirits & my wearing Powder?—When & to whom did I ever make a merit of my Sufferings?—Is it consistent *now* to charge me with going about complaining to everybody, & *now* with my high Spirits?—Was I to carry a gloomy face into every society? or ought I not rather to be grateful, that in the natural activity of my Intellect God had given me a counteracting principle to the intensity of my feelings, & a means of escaping from a part of the Pressure?—But for this I had been driven mad—& yet for how many months was there a continual Brooding & going on of the one gnawing Recollection behind the curtain of my outward Being even when I was most exerting myself—and exerting myself more in order the more to benumb it! I might have truly said, with Desdemona,

> I am not merry, but I do beguile
> The Thing I am, by seeming otherwise.

And as to the Powder, it was first put in to prevent my taking Cold after my Hair had been thinned, & I was advised to continue it till I became wholly grey—as in its then state it looked as if I had dirty powder in my hair, & even when known to be only the everywhere intermixed grey, yet contrasting with a face even younger than my real age gave a queer & contradictory character to my whole appearance.—Whatever be the result of this long delayed explanation, I have loved you & yours too long & too deeply to have it in my own power to cease to do so.

SAMUEL TAYLOR COLERIDGE, letter to Wordsworth, 4 May 1812. Basil Montagu had told Coleridge that Wordsworth had 'commissioned' him to say that he held no hopes of him, that Coleridge had been 'an absolute nuisance' in the household and was a 'rotten drunkard'. Wordsworth maintained that he had been misunderstood, and that what he *had* told Montagu solely concerned that gentleman's plan to take Coleridge into his home, which Wordsworth believed would prove injurious to both parties.

You have I suppose heard from Mrs Clarkson that Wordsw. is in town. His being here has contributed too much to distract my mind from what ought to be its sole object of pursuit; but to shun such a man as W. or neglect to seize every occasion of being in his company is beyond my power. I have likewise had an occasion to see him in an interesting situation. I found that he and C. [Coleridge] had no common friend to interfere & by merely being the bearer of civil messages & explanatory letters heal the breach wh. has subsisted between them. And I therefore undertook the task & I rejoice to say with success. But do not speak of it. I wrote an account of the negociation to Mrs Clarkson, because she was privy to the rupture, & was entitled to know the event, but I do not for obvious reasons mention my concern in the reconciliation. That two *such men* as W. and C. (one I believe the greatest man now living in this country & the other a man of astonishing genius & talents tho' not harmoniously blended as in his happier friend to form a great & good man) shd. have their relation towards each other affected by anythg. such a being as I cd. do seems strange & I do not wish to have the thought excited, certainly not by my own uncalled for mention of the transaction. There is no affected humility in this remark . . .

W. without saying a complimentary thing to me has done what really flattered me, has offered to go & visit any one of my friends to whom I wish to introduce him . . .

Coleridge began his course of lectures at Willis's Rooms on Tuesday. He very obligingly gave me a ticket for myself *& friends* . . .

Henry Crabb Robinson, letter to his brother Thomas, 20 May 1812

Miss F. Burney to Mrs Piozzi

10 August 1784

When my wondering eyes first looked over the letter I received last night, my mind instantly dictated a high-spirited vindication of the consistency, integrity, and faithfulness of the friendship thus abruptly reproached and cast away. But a sleepless night gave me leisure to recollect that you were ever as generous as precipitate, and that your own heart would do justice to mine, in the cooler judgement of future reflection. Committing myself, therefore, to that period, I determined simply to assure you, that if my last letter hurt either you or Mr Piozzi, I am no less sorry than surprised; and that if it offended you, I sincerely beg your pardon.

Not to that time, however, can I wait to acknowledge the pain an accusation so unexpected has caused me, nor the heartfelt satisfaction with which I shall receive, when you are able to write it, a softer renewal of regard.

May Heaven direct and bless you!

F. B.

N.B. This is the sketch of the answer which F. B. most painfully wrote to the unmerited reproach of not sending *cordial congratulations* upon a marriage which she had uniformly, openly, and with deep and avowed affliction, thought wrong.

Mrs Piozzi to Miss Burney

13 August 1784

Give yourself no serious concern, sweetest Burney. All is well, and I am too happy myself to make a friend otherwise; quiet your kind heart immediately, and love my husband if you love his and your

H. L. Piozzi

N. B. To this kind note, F. B. wrote the warmest and most affectionate and heartfelt reply; but never received another word! And here and thus stopped a correspondence of six years of almost unequalled partiality, and fondness on her side; and affection, gratitude, admiration, and sincerity on that of F. B., who could only conjecture the cessation to be caused by the resentment of Piozzi, when informed of her constant opposition to the union.

> *Diary and Letters of Madame d'Arblay* (Fanny Burney), edited by her niece

There had been some alarm of housebreakers in Chelsea, which sacrilegious housebreakers, not content with robbing ordinary people, broke into Mr Carlyle's house and ran away again, without carrying off anything more valuable than the dining-room clock. It was the remembrance of this little incident of the seal [sent to Goethe by Carlyle, inscribed 'To the German Master: From friends in England', on the poet's eighty-second birthday] which suggested to some one the idea of replacing the stolen clock, and about fifteen of Carlyle's friends and admirers subscribed to purchase one, a small sign of their respect and goodwill ... It was Carlyle's birthday, and a dismal winter's day, the streets were shrouded in greenish vapours, and the houses looked no less dreary within, than the streets through which we had come. Somewhat chilled and depressed, we all assembled in Lady Stanley's great drawing-room in Dover Street, where the fog had also penetrated, and presently from the further end of the room, advancing through shifting darkness, came Carlyle. There was a moment's pause. No one moved; he stood in the middle of the room without speaking. No doubt the philosopher, as well as his disciples, felt the influence of the atmosphere. Lady Stanley went to meet him. 'Here is a little birthday present we want you to accept from us all, Mr Carlyle,' said she, quickly pushing up before him a small table, upon which stood the clock ticking all ready for his acceptance. Then came another silence, broken by a knell sadly sounding in our ears. 'Eh, what have I got to do with Time any more?' he said. It was a melancholy moment. Nobody could speak. The unfortunate promoter of the scheme felt her heart sinking into her shoes. Had she but the wit to answer him cheerfully, to assure him that anyhow time had a great deal to do with him, the little ceremony might have been less of a fiasco than it assuredly was; and yet I think afterwards the old man must have been pleased, and liked to think that he was remembered.

ANNE THACKERAY RITCHIE, *Chapters from Some Memoirs*, 1894

Lockit. Peachum then intends to outwit me in this affair; but I'll be even with him. The dog is leaky in his liquor, so I'll ply him that way, get the secret from him, and turn this affair to my own advantage. Lions, wolves, and vultures don't live together in herds, droves or flocks. Of all animals of prey, man is the only sociable one. Every one of us preys upon his neighbour, and yet we herd together. Peachum is my companion, my friend—according to the custom of the world, indeed, he may quote thousands of precedents for cheating me. And shall not I make use of the privilege of friendship to make him a return?

AIR: Packington's pound

> *Thus gamesters united in friendship are found,*
> *Though they know that their industry all is a cheat;*
> *They flock to their prey at the dice-box's sound,*
> *And join to promote one another's deceit.*
> *But if by mishap*
> *They fail of a chap,*   customer
> *To keep in their hands, they each other entrap.*

> *Like pikes, lank with hunger, who miss of their ends,*
> *They bite their companions, and prey on their friends.*

Now, Peachum, you and I, like honest tradesmen, are to have a fair trial which of us two can over-reach the other.

JOHN GAY, *The Beggar's Opera*, 1728

Witwoud. Petulant's my friend, and a very honest fellow, and a very pretty fellow, and has a smattering—faith and troth, a pretty deal of an odd sort of a small wit; nay, I'll do him justice. I'm his friend, I won't wrong him neither. And if he had any judgement in the world, he would not be altogether contemptible. Come, come, don't detract from the merits of my friend.

Fainall. You don't take your friend to be over-nicely bred?

Witwoud. No, no, hang him, the rogue has no manners at all, that I must own: no more breeding than a bum-bailiff, that I grant you: 'tis pity, faith; the fellow has fire and life.

Mirabell. What, courage?

Witwoud. Hum, faith, I don't know as to that, I can't say as to that. Yes, faith, in a controversy, he'll contradict anybody.

Mirabell. Though 'twere a man whom he feared, or a woman whom he loved.

Witwoud. Well, well, he does not always think before he speaks; we have all our failings: you are too hard upon him, you are, faith. Let me excuse him—I can defend most of his faults, except one or two; one he has, that's the truth on't; if he were my brother, I could not acquit him: that, indeed, I could wish were otherwise.

Mirabell. Ay, marry, what's that, Witwoud?

Witwoud. O pardon me!—expose the infirmities of my friend! No, my dear, excuse me there.

Fainall. What, I warrant he's unsincere, or 'tis some such trifle.

Witwoud. No, no; what if he be? 'Tis no matter for that, his wit will excuse that: a wit should no more be sincere, than a woman constant; one argues a decay of parts, as t'other of beauty.

Mirabell. Maybe you think him too positive?

Witwoud. No, no, his being positive is an incentive to argument, and keeps up conversation.

Fainall. Too illiterate?

Witwoud. That! that's his happiness: his want of learning gives him the
more opportunities to show his natural parts.

Mirabell. He wants words?

Witwoud. Ay: but I like him for that now; for his want of words gives me
the pleasure very often to explain his meaning.

Fainall. He's impudent?

Witwoud. No, that's not it.

Mirabell. Vain?

Witwoud. No.

Mirabell. What! he speaks unseasonable truths sometimes, because he has
not wit enough to invent an evasion?

Witwoud. Truths! ha! ha! ha! no, no; since you will have it, I mean, he
never speaks truth at all, that's all. He will lie like a chambermaid, or a
woman of quality's porter. Now that is a fault.

WILLIAM CONGREVE, *The Way of the World*, 1700

Freeze, freeze, thou bitter sky,
That dost not bite so nigh
   As benefits forgot:
Though thou the waters warp,
Thy sting is not so sharp
   As friend remember'd not.
Heigh-ho! sing, heigh-ho! unto the green holly:
Most friendship is feigning, most loving mere folly.

SHAKESPEARE, *As You Like It*

'Ah! I know nothing about the feelings of parents,' said the Water-rat:
'I am not a family man. In fact, I have never been married, and I never
intend to be. Love is all very well in its way, but friendship is much
higher. Indeed, I know of nothing in the world that is either nobler or
rarer than a devoted friendship.'

'And what, pray, is your idea of the duties of a devoted friend?' asked a
green Linnet, who was sitting on a willow-tree hard by, and had
overheard the conversation ...

'What a silly question!' cried the Water-rat. 'I should expect my
devoted friend to be devoted to me, of course.'

'And what would you do in return?' said the little bird, swinging upon a silver spray, and flapping his tiny wings.

'I don't understand you,' answered the Water-rat.

'Let me tell you a story on the subject,' said the Linnet.

'Is the story about me?' asked the Water-rat. 'If so, I will listen to it, for I am extremely fond of fiction.'

'It is applicable to you,' answered the Linnet; and he flew down, and alighting upon the bank, he told the story of The Devoted Friend.

'Once upon a time,' said the Linnet, 'there was an honest little fellow named Hans.'

'Was he very distinguished?' asked the Water-rat.

'No,' answered the Linnet, 'I don't think he was distinguished at all, except for his kind heart, and his funny, round, good-humoured face. He lived in a tiny cottage all by himself, and every day he worked in his garden. In all the countryside there was no garden so lovely as his. Sweet-williams grew there, and Gillyflowers, and Shepherd's-purses, and Fair-maids of France. There were damask Roses, and yellow Roses, lilac Crocuses and gold, purple Violets and white. Columbine and Lady's-smock, Marjoram and Wild Basil, the Cowslip and the Flower-de-luce, the Daffodil and the Clove-Pink bloomed or blossomed in their proper order as the months went by, one flower taking another flower's place, so that there were always beautiful things to look at, and pleasant odours to smell.

'Little Hans had a great many friends, but the most devoted friend of all was big Hugh the Miller. Indeed, so devoted was the rich Miller to little Hans, that he would never go by his garden without leaning over the wall and plucking a large nosegay, or a handful of sweet herbs, or filling his pockets with plums and cherries if it was the fruit season.

'"Real friends should have everything in common," the Miller used to say, and little Hans nodded and smiled, and felt very proud of having a friend with such noble ideas.

'Sometimes, indeed, the neighbours thought it strange that the rich Miller never gave little Hans anything in return, though he had a hundred sacks of flour stored away in his mill, and six milch cows, and a large flock of woolly sheep; but Hans never troubled his head about these things, and nothing gave him greater pleasure than to listen to all the wonderful things the Miller used to say about the unselfishness of true friendship.

'So little Hans worked away in his garden. During the spring, the summer, and the autumn he was very happy, but when the winter came, and he had no fruit or flowers to bring to the market, he suffered a good deal from cold and hunger, and often had to go to bed without any supper but a few dried pears or some hard nuts. In the winter, also, he was extremely lonely, as the Miller never came to see him then.

'"There is no good in my going to see little Hans as long as the snow lasts," the Miller used to say to his wife, "for when people are in trouble they should be left alone and not be bothered by visitors. That at least is my idea about friendship, and I am sure I am right. So I shall wait till the spring comes, and then I shall pay him a visit, and he will be able to give me a large basket of primroses, and that will make him so happy."

'"You are certainly very thoughtful about others," answered the Wife, as she sat in her comfortable armchair by the big pinewood fire; "very thoughtful indeed. It is quite a treat to hear you talk about friendship. I am sure the clergyman himself could not say such beautiful things as you do, though he does live in a three-storied house, and wear a gold ring on his little finger."

'"But could we not ask little Hans up here?" said the Miller's youngest son. "If poor Hans is in trouble I will give him half my porridge, and show him my white rabbits."

'"What a silly boy you are!" cried the Miller; "I really don't know what is the use of sending you to school. You seem not to learn anything. Why, if little Hans came up here, and saw our warm fire, and our good supper, and our great cask of red wine, he might get envious, and envy is a most terrible thing, and would spoil anybody's nature. I certainly will not allow Hans' nature to be spoiled. I am his best friend, and I will always watch over him, and see that he is not led into any temptations. Besides, if Hans came here, he might ask me to let him have some flour on credit, and that I could not do. Flour is one thing, and friendship is another, and they should not be confused. Why, the words are spelt differently, and mean quite different things. Everybody can see that."

'"How well you talk!" said the Miller's Wife, pouring herself out a large glass of warm ale; "really I feel quite drowsy. It is just like being in church."

'"Lots of people act well," answered the Miller; "but very few people talk well, which shows that talking is much the more difficult thing of the two, and much the finer thing also."'

OSCAR WILDE, from 'The Devoted Friend', 1888

Timon. O you gods, think I, what need we have any friends, if we should
ne'er have need of 'em? They were the most needless creatures living
should we ne'er have use for 'em, and would most resemble sweet
instruments hung up in cases, that keeps their sounds to themselves.
Why, I have often wish'd myself poorer that I might come nearer to
you. We are born to do benefits; and what better or properer can we
call our own than the riches of our friends? O what a precious comfort
'tis to have so many like brothers commanding one another's fortunes.
O joy's e'en made away ere't can be born! Mine eyes cannot hold out
water, methinks. To forget their faults, I drink to you.

Steward.   Who is not Timon's?
  What heart, head, sword, force, means, but is Lord Timon's,
  Great Timon, noble, worthy, royal Timon?
  Ah, when the means are gone that buy this praise,
  The breath is gone whereof this praise is made.
  Feast-won, fast-lost; one cloud of winter show'rs,
  These flies are couch'd.
Tim.   Come, sermon me no further.
  No villainous bounty yet hath pass'd my heart;
  Unwisely, not ignobly, have I given.
  Why dost thou weep? Canst thou the conscience lack,
  To think I shall lack friends? Secure thy heart.
  If I would broach the vessels of my love,
  And try the arguments of hearts by borrowing,
  Men and men's fortunes could I frankly use
  As I can bid thee speak.
Stew.   Assurance bless your thoughts.
Tim. And in some sort these wants of mine are crown'd,
  That I account them blessings; for by these
  Shall I try friends. You shall perceive how you
  Mistake my fortunes; I am wealthy in my friends.

Lucullus. And what hast thou there under thy cloak, pretty Flaminius?
Flaminius. Faith, nothing but an empty box, sir, which, in my lord's behalf,
  I come to entreat your honour to supply; who, having great and instant

occasion to use fifty talents, hath sent to your lordship to furnish him, nothing doubting your present assistance therein.

Lucul. La, la, la, la: 'nothing doubting,' says he? Alas, good lord; a noble gentleman 'tis, if he would not keep so good a house . . . Draw nearer, honest Flaminius. Thy lord's a bountiful gentleman: but thou art wise, and thou know'st well enough, although thou com'st to me, that this is no time to lend money, especially upon bare friendship, without security. Here's three solidares for thee; good boy, wink at me, and say thou saw'st me not. Fare thee well.

Tim. My worthy friends, will you draw near? . . . Each man to his stool, with that spur as he would to the lip of his mistress. Your diet shall be in all places alike. Make not a City feast of it, to let the meat cool ere we can agree upon the first place. Sit, sit. The gods require our thanks.

You great benefactors, sprinkle our society with thankfulness. For your own gifts, make yourselves prais'd; but reserve still to give, lest your deities be despis'd. Lend to each man enough, that one need not lend to another; for were your godheads to borrow of men, men would forsake the gods. Make the meat be belov'd, more than the man that gives it. Let no assembly of twenty be without a score of villains. If there sit twelve women at the table, let a dozen of them be as they are. The rest of your fees, O gods, the Senators of Athens, together with the common leg of people—what is amiss in them, you gods, make suitable for destruction. For these my present friends, as they are to me nothing, so in nothing bless them, and to nothing are they welcome.

Uncover, dogs, and lap.

               [The dishes are uncovered and seen to be full of warm water.

Some. What does his lordship mean?

Others.   I know not.

Tim. May you a better feast never behold,
   You knot of mouth-friends! Smoke and lukewarm water
   Is your perfection. This is Timon's last;
   Who, stuck and spangled with your flatteries,
   Washes it off, and sprinkles in your faces
   Your reeking villainy.   *[Throwing the water in their faces.*
                Live loath'd, and long,
   Most smiling, smooth, detested parasites,
   Courteous destroyers, affable wolves, meek bears,
   You fools of fortune, trencher-friends, time's flies,
   Cap-and-knee slaves, vapours, and minute-jacks!

Of man and beast the infinite malady
Crust you quite o'er! What, dost thou go?
Soft, take thy physic first—thou too—and thou!

SHAKESPEARE, *Timon of Athens*, ?1607–8

Who, gratis, shared my social glass,
But when misfortune came to pass,
Referr'd me to the pump? Alas!
My Friend.

THOMAS HOOD, from 'A Lay of Real Life', 1835

The first day in your house,
You more than welcome your guest.
You roast him some fish, you brew him some beer,
You offer him all that is best.

The second day still
You are willing to give
Some milk and some bread,
And so let him live.

On the third day, the food
Becomes somewhat rare—
He may have some rice,
If with you he will share.

On the fourth day, you send him
Out into the fields;
Then after a little bite,
You make him shine up your shields.

The fifth day, your guest
Is as thin as a cricket.
You whisper to your wife,
You've never acted so wicked.

On the sixth day, you hide
So he can't see you;
If you want to eat,
In secret, you so do . . .

On the seventh day, really,
You have had enough!
You throw him out with your fists:
You had to get tough!

You are really not
An unkindly man—
But sometimes one has to
Defend his own stand!

ANON., 'The Guest in Your House', Tanganyika; tr. Charlotte and
Wolf Leslau, 1970

Fish and guests smell at three days old.

Danish proverb

You see, my Lord, I do not wait upon ceremony:
Here I have come, forgetting all acrimony,
Hoping that your present gravity
Will find excuse for my humble levity
Remembering all the good time past.
Your Lordship won't despise an old friend out of favour?
Old Tom, gay Tom, Becket of London,
Your Lordship won't forget that evening on the river
When the King and you and I were all friends together?
Friendship should be more than biting Time can sever.
What, my Lord, now that you recover
Favour with the King, shall we say that summer's over
Or that the good time cannot last?
Fluting in the meadows, viols in the hall,
Laughter and apple-blossom floating on the water,
Singing at nightfall, whispering in chambers,
Fires devouring the winter season,

Eating up the darkness, with wit and wine and wisdom!
Now that the King and you are in amity,
Clergy and laity may return to gaiety,
Mirth and sportfulness need not walk warily.

> T. S. ELIOT, *Murder in the Cathedral*, 1935; the First Tempter
> addressing Archbishop Thomas Becket

I had many friends to help me to fall; but as to rising again, I was so much left to myself, that I wonder now I was not always on the ground. I praise God for His mercy; for it was He only who stretched out His hand to me.

> *The Life of Saint Teresa of Jesus*, written by herself, *c.*1562–8; tr.
> David Lewis

As the Father hath loved me, so have I loved you: continue ye in my love.

If ye keep my commandments, ye shall abide in my love; even as I have kept my Father's commandments, and abide in his love.

These things have I spoken unto you, that my joy might remain in you, and that your joy might be full.

This is my commandment, That ye love one another, as I have loved you.

Greater love hath no man than this, that a man lay down his life for his friends.

Ye are my friends, if ye do whatsoever I command you.

Henceforth I call you not servants; for the servant knoweth not what his lord doeth: but I have called you friends; for all things that I have heard of my Father I have made known unto you.

> St John 15

Then one of the twelve, called Judas Iscariot, went unto the chief priests,

And said unto them, What will ye give me, and I will deliver him unto you? And they covenanted with him for thirty pieces of silver.

And from that time he sought opportunity to betray him.

And the disciples did as Jesus had appointed them; and they made ready the passover.

Now when the even was come, he sat down with the twelve.

And as they did eat, he said, Verily I say unto you, that one of you shall betray me.

And they were exceeding sorrowful, and began every one of them to say unto him, Lord, is it I?

And he answered and said, He that dippeth his hand with me in the dish, the same shall betray me.

The Son of man goeth as it is written of him: but woe unto that man by whom the Son of man is betrayed! it had been good for that man if he had not been born.

Then Judas, which betrayed him, answered and said, Master, is it I? He said unto him, Thou hast said.

And while he yet spake, lo, Judas, one of the twelve, came, and with him a great multitude with swords and staves, from the chief priests and elders of the people.

Now he that betrayed him gave them a sign, saying, Whomsoever I shall kiss, that same is he: hold him fast.

And forthwith he came to Jesus, and said, Hail, master; and kissed him.

And Jesus said unto him, Friend, wherefore art thou come? Then came they, and laid hands on Jesus, and took him.

When the morning was come, all the chief priests and elders of the people took counsel against Jesus to put him to death:

And when they had bound him, they led him away, and delivered him to Pontius Pilate the governor.

Then Judas, which had betrayed him, when he saw that he was condemned, repented himself, and brought again the thirty pieces of silver to the chief priests and elders,

Saying, I have sinned in that I have betrayed the innocent blood. And they said, What is that to us? see thou to that.

And he cast down the pieces of silver in the temple, and departed, and went and hanged himself.

And the chief priests took the silver pieces, and said, It is not lawful for to put them into the treasury, because it is the price of blood.

And they took counsel, and bought with them the potter's field, to bury strangers in.

St Matthew 26, 27

And Jesus saith unto them, All ye shall be offended because of me this night: for it is written, I will smite the shepherd, and the sheep shall be scattered.

But after that I am risen, I will go before you into Galilee.

But Peter said unto him, Although all shall be offended, yet will not I.

And Jesus saith unto him, Verily I say unto thee, That this day, even in this night, before the cock crow twice, thou shalt deny me thrice.

But he spake the more vehemently, If I should die with thee, I will not deny thee in any wise. Likewise also said they all.

And they led Jesus away to the high priest: and with him were assembled all the chief priests and the elders and the scribes.

And Peter followed him afar off, even into the palace of the high priest: and he sat with the servants, and warmed himself at the fire.

And as Peter was beneath in the palace, there cometh one of the maids of the high priest:

And when she saw Peter warming himself, she looked upon him, and said, And thou also wast with Jesus of Nazareth.

But he denied, saying, I know not, neither understand I what thou sayest. And he went out into the porch; and the cock crew.

And a maid saw him again, and began to say to them that stood by, This is one of them.

And he denied it again. And a little after, they that stood by said again to Peter, Surely thou art one of them: for thou art a Galilæan, and thy speech agreeth thereto.

But he began to curse and to swear, saying, I know not this man of whom ye speak.

And the second time the cock crew. And Peter called to mind the word that Jesus said unto him, Before the cock crow twice, thou shalt deny me thrice. And when he thought thereon, he wept.

St Mark 14

Absence and Loss

Does absence really make the heart grow fonder? Not in the opinion of Elizabeth Bowen, for whom the deprived senses override the sentimental heart. Pope, on the other hand, suggests that absence can make the heart see truer. And Francis Beaumont, lying in the country sunshine far from the Mermaid Tavern and the theatres, began his 'Letter to Ben Jonson' by invoking

> The Sun which doth the greatest comfort bring
> To absent friends, because the self-same thing
> They know they see however absent . . .

As if seconding Voltaire, but in a very different tone of voice, Lamb speaks of death as 'the old divorcer'. It is touching to compare Johnson, cagey and stoical, instructing Boswell as to whether or not we shall meet our friends in the afterlife (we shall be satisfied either way), with his early 'Ode on Friendship', said to have been written at the age of 16, which conveys a simpler, wholehearted, more confident view:

> O! shall thy flames then cease to glow
>   When souls to happier climes remove?
> What rais'd our virtue here below
>   Shall aid our happiness above.

Santayana reasoned that if we were to enjoy them in a future life, we should need to find our friends in their bodies and with their familiar ways intact, for it would be 'an insult to affection' to suppose we could be content with some 'eternal formula expressing their idiosyncrasy'.

'After such flickering talk I have to try / To find the idiom of eternity,' Robert Conquest reflects in 'After Writing an Obituary'. As we have seen, it is little things that we commonly look for from our friends, 'recreation and pastime' (Montaigne), 'yarns for the fireside' (Henry Lawson), 'fellowship in joy' rather than 'sympathy in sorrow' (Nietzsche); and it is logical that what we miss should be small, trivial-seeming things. Playing darts or chess, 'killing time', going to a football match or a film, walking together, remembering together, 'a gesture, a trick of expression', 'their costume . . . some manner of the hair' . . . Or arguing together: in a letter recounting T. F. Powys's funeral in 1953, Sylvia

Townsend Warner told how the parson, an old man and an old friend of Powys, stood for some time at the foot of the grave after the blessing, 'in an oddly conversational attitude, as though, for this once, he had got the better of an argument'.

Friendships end in other, less drastic ways, of course: through apathy or preoccupation, 'through sheer inability to cross the street' (Virginia Woolf), through consorting with inferior persons (Beatrice Webb), through 'a woman's bright eyes' or 'a few light words' (Stevenson), through success in life, or failure, or the acquisition of power (Connolly remarked that people with a will to power can have no friends because they will always be *wanting* something).

Emily Dickinson could have had any number of divine deterrents or reprisals in mind—and quite possibly death—when she wrote,

> God is indeed a jealous God—
> He cannot bear to see
> That we had rather not with Him
> But with each other play.

———

> Are Friends Delight or Pain?
> Could Bounty but remain
> Riches were good—
>
> But if they only stay
> Ampler to fly away
> Riches are sad.

> EMILY DICKINSON, 'Are Friends Delight or Pain?'

> Of that short Roll of friends writ in my heart
>   Which with thy name begins, since their depart,
> Whether in the English Provinces they be,
>   Or drink of Po, Sequan, or Danubie,
> There's none that sometimes greets us not, and yet
>   Your Trent is Lethe; that past, you us forget.
> You do not duties of Societies,
>   If from th'embrace of a lov'd wife you rise,

View your fat Beasts, stretch'd Barns, and labour'd fields,
 Eat, play, ride, take all joys which all day yields,
And then again to your embracements go:
 Some hours on us your friends, and some bestow
Upon your Muse, else both we shall repent,
 I that my love, she that her gifts on you are spent.

        JOHN DONNE (1572–1631), 'To Mr I. L.'

Mr Chute tells me that you have taken a new house in Squireland, and have given yourself up for two years more to port and parsons. I am very angry, and resign you to the works of the devil or the church, I don't care which. You will get the gout, turn Methodist, and expect to ride to heaven upon your own great toe. I was happy with your telling me how well you love me, and though I don't love loving, I could have poured out all the fullness of my heart to such an old and true friend—but what am I the better for it, if I am to see you but two or three days in the year? I thought you would at last come and while away the remainder of life on the banks of the Thames in gaiety and old tales. I have quitted the stage, and the Clive [Catherine Raftor Clive, an actress] is preparing to leave it. We shall neither of us ever be grave: dowagers roost all around us, and you could never want cards or mirth. Will you end like a fat farmer, repeating annually the price of oats, and discussing stale newspapers? . . . Your wit and humour will be as much lost upon them as if you talked the dialect of Chaucer: for with all the divinity of wit, it grows out of fashion like a fardingale. I am convinced that the young men at White's already laugh at George Selwyn's bon mots only by tradition. I avoid talking before the youth of the age as I would dancing before them: for if one's tongue don't move in the steps of the day, and thinks to please by its old graces, it is only an object of ridicule, like Mrs Hobart in her cotillion. I tell you we should get together, and comfort ourselves with reflecting on the brave days that we have known—not that I think people were a jot more clever or wise in our youth, than they are now; but as my system is always to live in a vision as much as I can, and as visions don't increase with years, there is nothing so natural as to think one remembers what one does not remember . . .

 Adieu! Though I am very angry with you, I deserve all your friendship, by that I have for you, witness my anger and disappointment.

      HORACE WALPOLE, letter to George Montagu, 15 April 1768

We hear the most improbable tales at this distance. Pray is it true that the young Spartans among you are born with six fingers, which spoils their scanning?—It must look very odd; but use reconciles ... I have many questions to put, but ten Delphic voyages can be made in a shorter time than it will take to satisfy my scruples. Do you grow your own hemp?—What is your staple trade,—exclusive of the national profession, I mean? Your locksmiths, I take it, are some of your great capitalists.

I am insensibly chatting to you as familiarly as when we used to exchange good-morrows out of our old contiguous windows, in pump-famed Hare Court in the Temple. Why did you ever leave that quiet corner?—Why did I?—with its complement of four poor elms, from whose smoke-dyed barks, the theme of jesting ruralists, I picked my first ladybirds! My heart is as dry as that spring sometimes proves in a thirsty August, when I revert to the space that is between us; a length of passage enough to render obsolete the phrases of our English letters before they can reach you. But while I talk I think you hear me,—thoughts dallying with vain surmise—

> Aye me! while thee the seas and sounding shores
> Hold far away.

Come back, before I am grown into a very old man, so as you shall hardly know me. Come, before Bridget walks on crutches. Girls whom you left children have become sage matrons while you are tarrying there. The blooming Miss W——r (you remember Sally W——r) called upon us yesterday, an aged crone. Folks whom you knew die off every year. Formerly, I thought that death was wearing out,—I stood ramparted about with so many healthy friends. The departure of J. W., two springs back, corrected my delusion. Since then the old divorcer has been busy. If you do not make haste to return, there will be little left to greet you, of me, or mine.

> CHARLES LAMB, 'Distant Correspondents', a letter to Barron Field, at Sydney, New South Wales, 1817

The heart may think it knows better: the senses know that absence blots people out. We have really no absent friends. The friend becomes a traitor by breaking, however unwillingly or sadly, out of our own zone: a hard judgement is passed on him, for all the pleas of the heart.

> ELIZABETH BOWEN, *The Death of the Heart*, 1938

Let me tell you I am the better acquainted with you for a long Absence, as
men are with themselves for a long affliction: Absence does but hold off a
Friend, to make one see him the truer.

Pope, letter to Swift, 14 December 1725

Each week or so, by the post,
By phone or over the back fence,
Comes notice of yet another hostile action.
Off to Boston goes Berg; to Dallas Dawes.
And Martin, immovable Martin, suddenly writes
From the farthest reaches of Wichita, 'Keep in touch.'

The enemy
Carries them all away and their houses are sold
And their names are removed from the telephone books and their mail
Is forwarded for a very short time and stops.

Like soldiers
We number them to ourselves and look at each other
And say very little about them because we have neither
A talent for major emotions nor major emotions, being
Pretty much cold fish.

And like soldiers
We accept their replacements with scorn for a suitable period,
Keep to ourselves for as long as conditions permit,
And suddenly, being healthy and normal and soldierly,
Adjust the past to the present by filing the past
Quietly in a most inaccessible drawer.

This is soldierly.

Thus are the trenches,
Hilltops, ridges, beaches,
Rights and freedoms defended. And thus is defended
The soldierly life, our life, which a Dawes, Berg or Martin
Will understand and condone, so we hope, in those enemy
Places, wherever they are, where we hear they are.

Reed Whittemore, 'The Losses', 1956

Antonapoulos! Within Singer there was always the memory of his friend. At night when he closed his eyes the Greek's face was there in the darkness—round and oily, with a wise and gentle smile. In his dreams they were always together . . .

Then years later there was the time Antonapoulos took the rent money from the vase on the mantelpiece and spent it all on the slot machines. And the summer afternoon Antonapoulos went downstairs naked to get the paper. He suffered so from the summer heat. They bought an electric refrigerator on the instalment plan, and Antonapoulos would suck the cubes of ice constantly and even let a few of them melt in the bed with him as he slept. And the time Antonapoulos got drunk and threw a bowl of macaroni in his face.

Those ugly memories wove through his thoughts during the first months like bad threads through a carpet. And then they were gone. All the times that they had been unhappy were forgotten. For as the year went on his thoughts of his friend spiralled deeper until he dwelt only with the Antonapoulos whom he alone could know.

This was the friend to whom he told all that was in his heart. This was the Antonapoulos who no one knew was wise but him. As the year passed his friend seemed to grow larger in his mind, and his face looked out in a very grave and subtle way from the darkness at night. The memories of his friend changed in his mind so that he remembered nothing that was wrong or foolish—only the wise and good.

He saw Antonapoulos sitting in a large chair before him. He sat tranquil and unmoving. His round face was inscrutable. His mouth was wise and smiling. And his eyes were profound. He watched the things that were said to him. And in his wisdom he understood.

This was the Antonapoulos who now was always in his thoughts. This was the friend to whom he wanted to tell things that had come about.

CARSON McCULLERS, *The Heart is a Lonely Hunter*, 1940

A man who has a few friends, or one who has a dozen (if there be any one so wealthy on this earth), cannot forget on how precarious a base his happiness reposes; and how by a stroke or two of fate—a death, a few light words, a piece of stamped paper, a woman's bright eyes—he may be left, in a month, destitute of all.

STEVENSON, *Virginibus Puerisque*, 1881

I have had playmates, I have had companions,
In my days of childhood, in my joyful school-days,
All, all are gone, the old familiar faces.

I have been laughing, I have been carousing,
Drinking late, sitting late, with my bosom cronies,
All, all are gone, the old familiar faces.

I loved a love once, fairest among women:
Closed are her doors on me, I must not see her—
All, all are gone, the old familiar faces.

I have a friend, a kinder friend has no man;
Like an ingrate, I left my friend abruptly;
Left him, to muse on the old familiar faces.

Ghost-like I paced round the haunts of my childhood,
Earth seemed a desert I was bound to traverse,
Seeking to find the old familiar faces.

Friend of my bosom, thou more than a brother,
Why wert not thou born in my father's dwelling?
So might we talk of the old familiar faces—

How some they have died, and some they have left me,
And some are taken from me; all are departed;
All, all are gone, the old familiar faces.

LAMB, 'The Old Familiar Faces', 1798

. . . the shock opened a chasm in life that never closed, and as long as life
lasted, he found himself invariably taking for granted, as a political
instinct, without awaiting further experiment—as he took for granted
that arsenic poisoned—the rule that a friend in power is a friend lost . . .
This, then, was the result of the new attempt at education, down to March
4, 1861; this was all; and frankly, it seemed to him hardly what he wanted.

HENRY ADAMS, *The Education of Henry Adams*, 1907

Meanwhile I have caught up the threads of another friendship. Carrie Darling, when I was a young girl living in my own home, was my first intellectual friendship. She was the first 'professional' woman I had come across. Fresh from Newnham and full of the fervour and enthusiasm of those early pioneers, saved from priggishness and pedantry by having earned her livelihood from fifteen years of age, by being at least three times engaged to be married before she went to college at twenty-eight —with, in fact, all the charms of a bohemian and a highly trained professional—she captivated my imagination. Her friendship was of the utmost value to me: she stimulated all that was good in me—my love of learning and intellectual ambition, all my moral enthusiasm, and to some extent checked the vulgar materialism brought about by life in second-rate fashionable sets. Her personality had a certain distinction and charm ... All this charm is gone ... For these thirteen years she has lived exclusively with inferiors. Eight years in a small Australian town with all its vulgarity and petty intrigues, five years in an Indian military station consorting with clergy and Eurasians, and, above all, five years' servitude to a husband who is her inferior in every respect—a mere elementary schoolteacher in training and a narrow evangelical prig by constitution ... She has practically fled from him. Poor clever Carrie! The whole week we spent in one long tale of married misery. To me the friendship is no longer invigorating. I have lived in some ways a more strenuously 'professional' life than she has, I am satisfied by love, and overburdened with friendships. But there is the supreme value of faithfulness ... to drop a friend or be dropped degrades life—makes life seem a horrid morass where anyone may be left to die uncared for. All ties should be made in their degree secure—to be broken only by mutual consent and for very sufficient reasons. The change from youth to age, from success to failure, is no reason. How I hate anarchism in all its forms!

BEATRICE WEBB, *Diary*, ?19 January 1896

It is the fate of most men who mingle with the world, and attain even the prime of life, to make many real friends, and lose them in the course of nature. It is the fate of all authors or chroniclers to create imaginary friends, and lose them in the course of art. Nor is this the full extent of their misfortunes; for they are required to furnish an account of them besides.

DICKENS, *The Pickwick Papers*

It was on the day, or rather night, of the 27th of June, 1787, between the hours of eleven and twelve, that I wrote the last lines of the last page [of *The Decline and Fall of the Roman Empire*], in a summer-house in my garden. After laying down my pen, I took several turns in a *berceau*, or covered walk of acacias, which commands a prospect of the country, the lake, and the mountains. The air was temperate, the sky was serene, the silver orb of the moon was reflected from the waters, and all nature was silent. I will not dissemble the first emotions of joy on the recovery of my freedom, and, perhaps, the establishment of my fame. But my pride was soon humbled, and a sober melancholy was spread over my mind, by the idea that I had taken an everlasting leave of an old and agreeable companion, and that whatsoever might be the future date of my History, the life of the historian must be short and precarious.

EDWARD GIBBON (1737–94), *Memoirs of my Life and Writings*

By what do we remember our friends? Often by a gesture, a trick of expression, some quaint phrase, or a favourite pose, or some nicety of manner. These were but trivial things in our friendship, perhaps, but they spring first to the mind in the act of recollection.

BUCHAN, *These For Remembrance*

If anybody's friend be dead
It's sharpest of the theme
The thinking how they walked alive—
At such and such a time—

Their costume, of a Sunday,
Some manner of the Hair—
A prank nobody knew but them
Lost, in the Sepulchre—

How warm, they were, on such a day,
You almost feel the date—
So short way off it seems—
And now—they're Centuries from that—

How pleased they were, at what you said—
You try to touch the smile
And dip your fingers in the frost—
When was it—Can you tell—

You asked the Company to tea—
Acquaintance—just a few—
And chatted close with this Grand Thing
That don't remember you—

Past Bows, and Invitations—
Past Interview, and Vow—
Past what Ourself can estimate—
That—makes the Quick of Woe!

EMILY DICKINSON, 'If anybody's friend be dead'

When somebody as dear as he is dead,
Grief must be huge and uninhibited.
Melpomene, to whom, God-given, belong
Lyre and clear voice, teach me a funeral song.

HORACE, from *Odes: Book One*, XXIV, 23 BC, '. . . tam cari capitis';
tr. James Michie

That the world will never be quite—what a cliché—the same
    again
Is what we only learn by the event
When a friend dies out on us and is not there
To share the periphery of a remembered scent

Or leave his thumb-print on a shared ideal;
Yet it is not at floodlit moments we miss him most,
Not intervolution of wind-rinsed plumage of oatfield
Nor curragh dancing off a primeval coast

Nor the full strings of passion; it is in killing
Time where he could have livened it, such as the drop-by-drop
Of games like darts or chess, turning the faucet
On full at a threat to the queen or double top.

LOUIS MACNEICE, 'Tam Cari Capitis', 1948

Life admits not of delays; when pleasure can be had, it is fit to catch it.
Every hour takes away part of the things that please us, and perhaps part
of our disposition to be pleased. When I came to Lichfield, I found my old
friend Harry Jackson dead. It was a loss, and a loss not to be repaired, as
he was one of the companions of my childhood. I hope we may long
continue to gain friends, but the friends which merit or usefulness can
procure us, are not able to supply the place of old acquaintances, with
whom the days of youth may be retraced, and those images revived
which gave the earliest delight. If you and I live to be much older, we shall
take great delight in talking over the Hebridean Journey.

JOHNSON, letter to Boswell, 1 September 1777

Good God! how often are we to die before we go quite off this stage? in
every friend we lose a part of ourselves, and the best part. God keep those
we have left! few are worth praying for, and one's self the least of all.

POPE, letter to Swift, 5 December 1732, the day after John Gay's
death

The deep grief we feel at the loss of a friend arises from the feeling that in
every individual there is something which no words can express, something which is peculiarly his own and therefore irreparable. *Omne
individuum ineffabile*.

We may come to look upon the death of our enemies and adversaries,
even long after it has occurred, with just as much regret as we feel for that
of our friends, viz., when we miss them as witnesses of our brilliant
success.

SCHOPENHAUER, *Parerga and Paralipomena*; tr. T. Bailey Saunders

He was my *Friend*, the truest *Friend* on earth;
A strong and mighty *Influence* joyn'd our *Birth*.
Nor did we envy the most sounding *Name*
   By *Friendship* giv'n of old to *Fame*.
None but his *Brethren* he, and *Sisters* knew,
   Whom the kind youth preferr'd to Me:
   And ev'n in that we did agree,
For much above my self I lov'd them too.

Say, for you saw us, ye immortal *Lights*,
How oft unweari'd have we spent the Nights?
Till the *Ledaean Stars*, so fam'd for *Love*,
   Wondred at us from above.
We spent them not in toys, in lusts, or wine;
   But search of deep *Philosophy*,
   Wit, *Eloquence*, and *Poetry*,
Arts which I lov'd, for they, my *Friend*, were *Thine*.

Ye fields of *Cambridge*, our dear *Cambridge*, say,
Have ye not seen us walking every day?
Was there a *Tree* about which did not know
   The *Love* betwixt us two?
Henceforth, ye gentle *Trees*, for ever fade;
   Or your sad branches thicker joyn,
   And into darksome shades combine,
Dark as the *Grave* wherein my *Friend* is laid.

   ABRAHAM COWLEY, from 'On the Death of Mr William Hervey',
1656

Why sleeps the pen of Young! the friend profess'd,
The known abilities, the knowing best
That heart, which few can equal, none excel,
That heart which lov'd thee and thou lov'd'st so well.
His humbler friends expected, wish'd, and waited
To hear from thee his character completed.

   LADY BRADSHAIGH, in a letter to Samuel Richardson's daughter
   Martha, shortly after Richardson's death in July 1761

When Heav'n would kindly set us free,
  And earth's enchantment end,
It takes the most effectual means,
  And robs us of a friend.

EDWARD YOUNG, *Resignation*, 1762; Young included this passage
on learning of the death of Samuel Richardson, who had begun
to print the poem

When I heard of the death of Coleridge, it was without grief. It seemed to
me that he long had been on the confines of the next world,—that he had
a hunger for eternity. I grieved then that I could not grieve. But since, I
feel how great a part he was of me. His great and dear spirit haunts me. I
cannot think a thought, I cannot make a criticism on men or books,
without an ineffectual turning and reference to him. He was the proof and
touchstone of all my cogitations. He was a Grecian (or in the first form) at
Christ's Hospital, where I was deputy Grecian; and the same subordina-
tion and deference to him I have preserved through a life-long acquaintance. Great in his writings, he was greatest in his conversation. In him
was disproved that old maxim, that we should allow every one his share
of talk. He would talk from morn to dewy eve, nor cease till far midnight,
yet who ever would interrupt him,—who would obstruct that con-
tinuous flow of converse, fetched from Helicon or Zion? He had the tact
of making the unintelligible seem plain. Many who read the abstruser
parts of his 'Friend' would complain that his works did not answer to his
spoken wisdom. They were identical. But he had a tone in oral delivery,
which seemed to convey sense to those who were otherwise imperfect
recipients. He was my fifty years old friend without a dissension. Never
saw I his likeness, nor probably the world can see again. I seemed to love
the house he died at more passionately than when he lived.

LAMB, *The New Monthly Magazine*, February 1835

'There is this consolation,' Mr Disraeli said, 'remaining to us when we
remember our unequalled and irreparable losses, that these great men are
not altogether lost to us, that their words will be often quoted in this
House, that their examples will often be referred to and appealed to, and
that even their expressions may form a part of our discussions. There are,

indeed, I may say, some members of Parliament, who though they may not be present, are still members of this House, are independent of dissolutions, of the caprices of constituencies, and even of the course of time. I think that Mr Cobden was one of these men.'

While the House was still under an impression from these words which was almost religious, Mr [John] Bright, yielding to a marked and silent expectation, rose and tried to say how every expression of sympathy that he had heard had been most grateful to his heart. 'But the time,' he went on in broken accents, 'which has elapsed since in my presence the manliest and gentlest spirit that ever quitted or tenanted a human form took its flight is so short, that I dare not even attempt to give utterance to the feelings by which I am oppressed. I shall leave to some calmer moment when I may have an opportunity of speaking before some portion of my countrymen the lesson which I think may be learned from the life and character of my friend. I have only to say that after twenty years of most intimate and almost brotherly friendship, I little knew how much I loved him until I had lost him.'

JOHN MORLEY, *The Life of Richard Cobden*, 1881

One writes, that 'Other friends remain',
    That 'Loss is common to the race'—
    And common is the commonplace,
And vacant chaff well meant for grain.

That loss is common would not make
    My own less bitter, rather more:
    Too common! Never morning wore
To evening, but some heart did break.

. . .

I wage not any feud with Death
    For changes wrought on form and face;
    No lower life that earth's embrace
May breed with him, can fright my faith.

Eternal process moving on,
    From state to state the spirit walks;
    And these are but the shatter'd stalks,
Or ruin'd chrysalis of one.

Nor blame I Death, because he bare
    The use of virtue out of earth:
    I know transplanted human worth
Will bloom to profit, otherwhere.

For this alone on Death I wreak
    The wrath that garners in my heart;
    He put our lives so far apart
We cannot hear each other speak.

                TENNYSON, *In Memoriam A. H. H.*, 1850

It's an owercome sooth for age an' youth
    And it brooks wi' nae denial,
That the dearest friends are the auldest friends
    And the young are just on trial.

There's a rival bauld wi' young an' auld
    And it's him that has bereft me;
For the sürest friends are the auldest friends
    And the maist o' mines hae left me.

There are kind hearts still, for friends to fill
    And fools to take and break them;
But the nearest friends are the auldest friends
    And the grave's the place to seek them.

       STEVENSON, 'It's an owercome sooth for age an' youth', 1887

I went by footpath and by stile
    Beyond where bustle ends,
Strayed here a mile and there a mile
    And called upon some friends.

On certain ones I had not seen
    For years past did I call,
And then on others who had been
    The oldest friends of all.

It was the time of midsummer
    When they had used to roam;
But now, though tempting was the air,
    I found them all at home.

I spoke to one and other of them
    By mound and stone and tree
Of things we had done ere days were dim,
    But they spoke not to me.

HARDY, 'Paying Calls', 1917

The last word this one spoke
was my name. The last word
that one spoke
was my name.

My two friends
had never met. But when they said
that last word
they spoke to each other.

I am proud to have given them a language
of one word, a narrow space
in which, without knowing it,
they met each other at last.

NORMAN MacCAIG, 'Two friends', 1980

After so long an absence
    At last we meet again:
Does the meeting give us pleasure,
    Or does it give us pain?

The tree of life has been shaken,
    And but few of us linger now,
Like the Prophet's two or three berries
    In the top of the uttermost bough.

We cordially greet each other
  In the old, familiar tone;
And we think, though we do not say it,
  How old and grey he is grown!

We speak of a Merry Christmas
  And many a Happy New Year;
But each in his heart is thinking
  Of those that are not here.

We speak of friends and their fortunes,
  And of what they did and said,
Till the dead alone seem living,
  And the living alone seem dead.

And at last we hardly distinguish
  Between the ghosts and the guests;
And a mist and shadow of sadness
  Steals over our merriest jests.

LONGFELLOW, 'The Meeting', 1873

When I heard the terrible news, that Myris was dead,
I went to his house, although I avoid
going to the houses of Christians,
especially during times of mourning or festivity.

I stood in the corridor. I didn't want
to go further inside because I noticed
that the relatives of the deceased looked at me
with obvious surprise and displeasure.

They had him in a large room
and from the corner where I stood
I could catch a glimpse of it: all precious carpets,
and vessels in silver and gold.

I stood and wept in a corner of the corridor.
And I thought how our parties and excursions
wouldn't be worthwhile now without Myris;
and I thought how I'd no longer see him
at our wonderfully indecent night-long sessions
enjoying himself, laughing, and reciting verses
with his perfect feel for Greek rhythm;
and I thought how I'd lost forever
his beauty, lost forever
the young man I'd worshipped so passionately.

Some old women close to me were talking with lowered voices
about the last day he lived:
the name of Christ constantly on his lips,
his hand holding a cross.
Then four Christian priests
came into the room, and said prayers
fervently, and orisons to Jesus,
or to Mary (I'm not very familiar with their religion).

We'd known of course that Myris was a Christian,
known it from the very start,
when he first joined our group the year before last.
But he lived exactly as we did:
more devoted to pleasure than all of us,
he scattered his money lavishly on amusements.
Not caring what anyone thought of him,
he threw himself eagerly into night-time scuffles
when our group happened to clash
with some rival group in the street.
He never spoke about his religion.
And once we even told him
that we'd take him with us to the Serapeion.
But—I remember now—
he didn't seem to like this joke of ours.
And yes, now I recall two other incidents.
When we made libations to Poseidon,
he drew himself back from our circle and looked elsewhere.
And when one of us in his fervour said:

'May all of us be favoured and protected
by the great, the sublime Apollo'—
Myris, unheard by the others, whispered: 'Not counting me.'

The Christian priests were praying loudly
for the young man's soul.
I noticed with how much diligence,
how much intense concern
for the forms of their religion, they were preparing
everything for the Christian funeral.
And suddenly an odd sensation took hold of me:
indefinably I felt
as if Myris were going from me;
I felt that he, a Christian, was united
with his own people and that I was becoming
a stranger, a total stranger. I even felt
a doubt come over me: that I'd been deceived by my passion
and had always been a stranger to him.
I rushed out of their horrible house,
rushed away before my memory of Myris
could be captured, could be perverted by their Christianity.

> C. P. CAVAFY, 'Myris: Alexandria, AD 340', 1929; tr. Edmund
> Keeley and Philip Sherrard

Unto me hearken, O Elders, to me, aye, me shall ye listen,
'Tis that I weep for my comrade Enkidu, bitterly crying
Like to a wailing woman: my grip is slack'd on the curtleaxe
Slung at my thigh, and the brand at my belt from my sight is
    removèd.
Aye, and my festal attire lends nought of its aid for my pleasure,
Me, me hath sorrow assailèd, and cast me down in affliction.
Comrade and henchman, who chased the wild ass, the pard of the
    desert,
Comrade and henchman, who chased the wild ass, the pard of the
    desert,
Enkidu—we who all haps overcame, ascending the mountains,
Captur'd the Heavenly Bull, and destroy'd him: we o'erthrew
    Humbaba,

He who abode in the Forest of Cedars—O, what is this slumber
Now hath o'ercome thee, for now art thou dark, nor art able to hear
   me?

He who endurèd all hardships with me, whom I lovèd dearly,
Enkidu,—he who endurèd all hardships with me is now perish'd,
Gone to the common lot of mankind! And I have bewail'd him
Day and night long: and unto the tomb I have not consign'd him.
O but my friend cometh not to my call—six days, yea, a se'nnight
He like a worm hath lain on his face—and I for this reason
Find no life, but must needs roam the desert like to a hunter.

     The Epic of Gilgamish, ?2000 BC; translated into English hexameters
     by R. Campbell Thompson

As I go down the highway,
   And through the village street,
I hear the pipers playing
   And the tramp of marching feet.
The men I worked and fought with
   Swing by me four on four,
And at the end you follow
   Whom I shall see no more.

Oh, Stalk, where are you lying?
   Somewhere and far away,
Enemy hands have buried
   Your quiet contemptuous clay.
There was no greeting given,
   No tear of friend for friend,
From us when you flew over
   Exultant to the end.

I couldn't see the paper,
   I couldn't think that you
Would never walk the highway
   The way you used to do.
I turn at every footfall,

   Half-hoping, half-afraid
To see you coming, later
   Than usual for parade.

The old Lairg clique is broken,
  I drove there yesterday,
And the car was full of ghosts that sat
  Beside me all the way.
Ghosts of old songs and laughter,
  Ghosts of the jolly three,
That went the road together
  And go no more with me.

Oh, Stalk, but I am lonely,
  For the old days we knew,
And the bed on the floor at Lesdos
  We slept in, I and you.
The joyful nights in billets
  We laughed and drank and swore—
But the candle's burned out now, Stalk,
  In the mess at Henancourt.

The candle's burned out now, old man,
  And the dawn's come grey and cold,
And I sit by the fire here
  Alone and sad and old.
Though all the rest come back again,
  You lie in a foreign land,
And the strongest link of all the chain
  Is broken in my hand.

E. A. MACKINTOSH (1893–1917), 'In Memoriam R. M. Stalker,
Missing, September 1916'

Well O.K., he was wrong
Getting killed in Spain
Like that. Wal Hannington
Sat and tried to argue him out of going.
He was wrong, he was wrong,

The angel has not descended, the state
Hasn't the faintest chance of withering away,
And nobody is sure which way Hegel is up any more.
He was the greatest hero I've met because he was brave,
And would argue with anybody,
And could interest people because he was interested—
If he was so bloody interested he should have gone on talking, gone
    on talking,
Something might have been talked out.
Near to a saint, he should not have got himself killed,
Thereby making himself an ineffectual angel, a moth.
The Professor of economics was right:
He just couldn't keep still at a public meeting,
He would keep turning round and standing up to see what was
    happening and who was talking,
And this was probably how the bullet got him in the trenches at
    Jarama.

                        MARTIN BELL, 'David Guest', 1967

       Now that we're almost settled in our house
       I'll name the friends that cannot sup with us
       Beside a fire of turf in th' ancient tower,
       And having talked to some late hour
       Climb up the narrow winding stair to bed:
       Discoverers of forgotten truth
       Or mere companions of my youth,
       All, all are in my thoughts tonight being dead.

       Always we'd have the new friend meet the old
       And we are hurt if either friend seem cold,
       And there is salt to lengthen out the smart
       In the affections of our heart,
       And quarrels are blown up upon that head;
       But not a friend that I would bring
       This night can set us quarrelling,
       For all that come into my mind are dead.

Lionel Johnson comes the first to mind,
That loved his learning better than mankind,
Though courteous to the worst; much falling he
Brooded upon sanctity
Till all his Greek and Latin learning seemed
A long blast upon the horn that brought
A little nearer to his thought
A measureless consummation that he dreamed.

And that enquiring man John Synge comes next,
That dying chose the living world for text
And never could have rested in the tomb
But that, long travelling, he had come
Towards nightfall upon certain set apart
In a most desolate stony place,
Towards nightfall upon a race
Passionate and simple like his heart.

And then I think of old George Pollexfen,
In muscular youth well known to Mayo men
For horsemanship at meets or at racecourses,
That could have shown how pure-bred horses
And solid men, for all their passion, live
But as the outrageous stars incline
By opposition, square and trine;
Having grown sluggish and contemplative.

They were my close companions many a year,
A portion of my mind and life, as it were,
And now their breathless faces seem to look
Out of some old picture-book;
I am accustomed to their lack of breath,
But not that my dear friend's dear son,
Our Sidney and our perfect man,
Could share in that discourtesy of death.

For all things the delighted eye now sees
Were loved by him: the old storm-broken trees
That cast their shadows upon road and bridge;
The tower set on the stream's edge;

The ford where drinking cattle make a stir
Nightly, and startled by that sound
The water-hen must change her ground;
He might have been your heartiest welcomer.

When with the Galway foxhounds he would ride
From Castle Taylor to the Roxborough side
Or Esserkelly plain, few kept his pace;
At Mooneen he had leaped a place
So perilous that half the astonished meet
Had shut their eyes; and where was it
He rode a race without a bit?
And yet his mind outran the horses' feet.

We dreamed that a great painter had been born
To cold Clare rock and Galway rock and thorn,
To that stern colour and that delicate line
That are our secret discipline
Wherein the gazing heart doubles her might.
Soldier, scholar, horseman, he,
And yet he had the intensity
To have published all to be a world's delight.

What other could so well have counselled us
In all lovely intricacies of a house
As he that practised or that understood
All work in metal or in wood,
In moulded plaster or in carven stone?
Soldier, scholar, horseman, he,
And all he did done perfectly
As though he had but that one trade alone.

Some burn damp faggots, others may consume
The entire combustible world in one small room
As though dried straw, and if we turn about
The bare chimney is gone black out
Because the work had finished in that flare.
Soldier, scholar, horseman, he,
As 'twere all life's epitome.
What made us dream that he could comb grey hair?

I had thought, seeing how bitter is that wind
That shakes the shutter, to have brought to mind
All those that manhood tried, or childhood loved
Or boyish intellect approved,
With some appropriate commentary on each;
Until imagination brought
A fitter welcome; but a thought
Of that late death took all my heart for speech.

YEATS, 'In Memory of Major Robert Gregory', 1919

Finding him in a very good humour, I ventured to lead him to the subject of our situation in a future state, having much curiosity to know his notions on that point. JOHNSON: 'Why, Sir, the happiness of an unembodied spirit will consist in a consciousness of the favour of GOD, in the contemplation of truth, and in the possession of felicitating ideas.' . . . BOSWELL: 'One of the most pleasing thoughts is, that we shall see our friends again.' JOHNSON: 'Yes, Sir; but you must consider, that when we are become purely rational, many of our friendships will be cut off. Many friendships are formed by a community of sensual pleasures: all these will be cut off. We form many friendships with bad men, because they have agreeable qualities, and they can be useful to us; but, after death, they can no longer be of use to us. We form many friendships by mistake, imagining people to be different from what they really are. After death, we shall see every one in a true light. Then, Sir, they talk of our meeting our relations: but then all relationship is dissolved; and we shall have no regard for one person more than another, but for their real value. However, we shall either have the satisfaction of meeting our friends, or be satisfied without meeting them.'

BOSWELL, *Life of Johnson*, 28 March 1772

Do not come back. Be, if you can bear it,
dead with the dead. The dead are busy. Yet,
so far as this does not distract you, help me,
as the most distant often helps me: in me.

RAINER MARIA RILKE, from 'Requiem for a Friend', 1909

On the death of a friend, we should consider that the fates through confidence have devolved on us the task of a double living, that we have henceforth to fulfil the promise of our friend's life also, in our own, to the world.

Thoreau, *Journal*, 28 February 1840

He loseth nothing that keepeth God for his friend.

Thomas Fuller, *Gnomologia: Adagies and Proverbs*, 1732

Death is but *Crossing* the *World*, as Friends do the Seas; they live in one another still.

For they must needs be present, that love and live in that which is *Omnipresent*.

In this Divine Glass, they see Face to Face; and their Converse is *Free*, as well as *Pure*.

This is the Comfort of Friends, that though they may be said to *Die*, yet their Friendship and Society are, in the best Sense, ever present, because *Immortal*.

Penn, *Some Fruits of Solitude*

Friendly Gestures

SOME of us may have found some of the foregoing testimonies rather intimidating. Our friendships are generally more relaxed, freer from sifting and sounding, rarely perceived as solemn endeavours or spiritual ardours. Indeed, we may not actually have written or spoken much on the subject, not even (or least of all) to our best friends. ('Enemies declare war. The friend never declares his love': Thoreau.) In which case we can take comfort from Wilde's tale of the odious Miller, an adept in differentiating between friendship and flour, between benevolence and benefaction, who reckoned that talking well, especially on this theme, was much more difficult and distinguished than acting well. Related is the misgiving felt by a character in Iris Murdoch's *A Fairly Honourable Defeat*: 'You have so much instinctive wisdom and goodness of heart,' she told her husband, 'It sometimes worries me that you're putting it all into a book, if you see what I mean.'

Yet it is a writer's job, we might say his duty as a friend, to make explicit what is implicit, to question what we take for granted and bring into consciousness what for much of the time goes on unconsciously, to describe, explore and (if one may say so) instruct. Despite the measure of unthinkingness natural and necessary to us, and not merely a product of laziness, we are an enormously inquisitive species, not content for long to leave what we call 'instinct' unexamined, and our relations with others form an essential part of our proper study.

Simple friendliness is ubiquitous in the shape of casual gestures, spontaneous and disinterested, which can mean much in the anonymity and abrasive indifference of our everyday transactions. As the present compilation neared its end, one of the editors queried the smudged signature on a cheque with which he was paying a restaurant bill. 'Could be sent to prison for that sort of thing,' he joked to the Moroccan waitress. 'Would you visit me there?' 'Oh yes,' she replied amenably, 'In my country we have a saying: Your truest friends are those who visit you in prison . . .' He wrote this down on the back of the cheque-book, and adjusted the tip. As Emerson observed, the only way to have a friend is to be one.

For thus the royal *Mandate* ran,
When first the human race began,
'The social, friendly, honest man,
   Whate'er he be,
'Tis *he* fulfils *great Nature's plan*,
   And none but *he*.'

BURNS, from 'Second Epistle to John Lapraik', 1786

We cannot tell the precise moment when friendship is formed. As in filling a vessel drop by drop, there is at last a drop which makes it run over; so in a series of kindnesses there is at last one which makes the heart run over.

JOHNSON, in Boswell's *Life*, 19 September 1777

Forsake not an old friend; for the new is not comparable to him: a new friend is as new wine; when it is old, thou shalt drink it with pleasure.

Ecclesiasticus 9

I love everything that's old: old friends, old times, old manners, old books, old wines; and, I believe, Dorothy, you'll own I have been pretty fond of an old wife.

GOLDSMITH, *She Stoops to Conquer*, 1773

Old Friends are best. King James used to call for his old shoes: they were easiest for his feet.

JOHN SELDEN (1584–1654), *Table Talk*

There are three faithful friends—an old wife, an old dog, and ready money.

FRANKLIN, *Poor Richard's Almanack*, 1747

Henry IV of France one day reproached the Count d'Aubigné, that he still retained his friendship for M. de la Trémouille, who was in disgrace, and banished the court. 'Sire,' said d'Aubigné, 'M. de la Trémouille is sufficiently unfortunate; since he has lost the favour of his master, I could not abandon him in the time when he has the most need of my friendship.'

The Percy Anecdotes

Please telegraph the following to Bret Harte immediately at my cost W. A. Kendall the poet writes that he is friendless & moneyless & is dying by inches as you know doctors say he must return to California & by sea wants to sail the fifteenth will you petition the steamship Company for a pass for him & sign my name & Howells & the other boys to it & forward said pass to Kendall at three twenty three Van Buren street Brooklyn I will send him fifty dollars get him some money if you can I do not know him but I know he is a good fellow and has hard luck.

MARK TWAIN, telegram to W. D. Howells, January 1872

I think without my mentioning it for my sake you would be a friend to Miss Brawne when I am dead. You think she has many faults—but, for my sake, think she has not one—if there is any thing you can do for her by word or deed I know you will do it.

JOHN KEATS, letter to Charles Brown, 30 September 1820

As a rule we are unconscious of that which makes us precious to our friends. X, I am sure, has not the least notion why I love him. I doubt if he knows that he possesses what makes me love him.

We are friends, not through anything peculiar to us, but through the universal, the origin and property of us all.

For what do my friends stand? Not for the clever things they say: I do not remember them half an hour after they are spoken. It is always the unspoken, the unconscious, which is their reality to me.

MARK RUTHERFORD, *Last Pages from a Journal*

It is not that a man has occasion often to fall back upon the kindness of his friends; perhaps he may never experience the necessity of doing so; but we are governed by our imaginations, and they stand there as a solid and impregnable bulwark against all the evils of life.

SYDNEY SMITH, in Lady Holland's *Memoir*

> A little health,
> A little wealth,
> A little house and freedom,
> And at the end
> A little friend
> And little cause to need him.

KILVERT, *Diary*, 3 July 1872: sampler seen in a farmhouse

A Little Health, A Little Wealth, A Little
    House, and Freedom—and at The End
I'd Like a Friend, And *Every* Cause to Need Him.

WILFRED OWEN, postcard to Leslie Gunston, his cousin, 12 February 1918

What is the odds so long as the fire of soul is kindled at the taper of conwiviality, and the wing of friendship never moults a feather!

DICKENS, *The Old Curiosity Shop*, 1841

When men are friendly even water is sweet.

Chinese proverb

The proper office of a friend is to side with you when you are in the wrong. Nearly anybody will side with you when you are in the right.

MARK TWAIN, *Notebook*, published 1935

Laughter is not at all a bad beginning for a friendship, and it is far the best ending for one.

WILDE, *The Picture of Dorian Gray*, 1891

When my friends are one-eyed, I look at them in profile.

JOSEPH JOUBERT (1754–1824), *Pensées*

The best mirror is an old friend.

Proverb

Without wearing any mask we are conscious of, we have a special face for each friend.

OLIVER WENDELL HOLMES, *The Professor at the Breakfast Table*, 1860

Friendship has two garments; an outer and an under one.

LAURENCE STERNE, *Tristram Shandy*, 1759–67

Friendship that flames goes out in a flash.

THOMAS FULLER, *Gnomologia*

The friendship that can end never really began.

PUBLILIUS SYRUS (1st century BC), *Sententiae*

A friend to all is a friend to none.

Gnomologia

He makes no friend who never made a foe.

TENNYSON, 'Lancelot and Elaine', 1859

Sir, more than kisses, letters mingle Souls;
For, thus friends absent speak.

DONNE, from 'To Sir Henry Wotton'

'Letters are no matter of indifference; they are generally a very positive curse.'

'You are speaking of letters of business; mine are letters of friendship.'

'I have often thought them the worse of the two,' replied he coolly. 'Business, you know, may bring money, but friendship hardly ever does.'

JANE AUSTEN, *Emma*; John Knightley and Jane Fairfax

As in political so in literary action a man wins friends for himself mostly by the passion of his prejudices and by the consistent narrowness of his outlook.

CONRAD, *A Personal Record*

What men call social virtues, good fellowship, is commonly but the virtue of pigs in a litter, which lie close together to keep each other warm. It brings men together in crowds and mobs in bar-rooms and elsewhere, but it does not deserve the name of virtue.

THOREAU, *Journal*, 22 October 1852

It is fellowship in joy, not sympathy in sorrow, that makes people friends.

The best friend is likely to acquire the best wife, because a good marriage is based on the talent for friendship.

They are few who will not disclose the private affairs of their friends when at a loss for conversational subjects.

NIETZSCHE, *Human, All Too Human*

There is no man so friendless but what he can find a friend sincere enough to tell him disagreeable truths.

EDWARD GEORGE BULWER-LYTTON, *What Will He Do With It?*, 1858

... if there is anything to one's praise, it is a foolish vanity to be gratified at it; and if it is abuse—why, one is always sure to hear of it from one damned good-natured friend or another.

RICHARD BRINSLEY SHERIDAN, *The Critic*, 1779; on not reading the reviewers

Our friends are generally ready to do everything for us, except the very thing we wish them to do.

HAZLITT, *Characteristics*

We need new friends; some of us are cannibals who have eaten their old friends up; others must have ever-renewed audiences before whom to re-enact the ideal version of their lives.

LOGAN PEARSALL SMITH, *Afterthoughts*, 1931

The real marriage of true minds is for any two people to possess a sense of humour or irony pitched in exactly the same key, so that their joint glances at any subject cross like interarching searchlights.

EDITH WHARTON, *A Backward Glance*

About this time I used to see a good deal of Gilberte with whom I had renewed my old intimacy: for our life, in the long run, is not calculated according to the duration of our friendships. Let a certain period of time elapse and you will see reappear (just as former Ministers reappear in politics, as old plays are revived on the stage) friendly relations that have been revived between the same persons as before, after long years of interruption, and revived with pleasure. After ten years, the reasons which made one party love too passionately, the other unable to endure a too exacting despotism, no longer exist.

PROUST, *The Sweet Cheat Gone*, 1925; tr. Scott Moncrieff

My wife once said that she likes me to be at home, in my own study. She doesn't want to talk to me, or to see me, but she likes to think I'm there. That's exactly how I feel about the small number of my oldest friends.

WALTER RALEIGH, letter to Austen Chamberlain, 10 December 1918

The only reward of virtue is virtue; the only way to have a friend is to be one.

I do then with my friends as I do with my books. I would have them where I can find them, but I seldom use them.

EMERSON, 'Friendship'

How sweet, how passing sweet, is solitude!
But grant me still a friend in my retreat,
Whom I may whisper—solitude is sweet.

COWPER, from 'Retirement', 1782

Everyone has had friends it has seemed a happy thought to bring together, and everyone remembers that his happiest thoughts have not been his greatest successes.

HENRY JAMES, 'The Friends of the Friends', 1896

In Mali, best friends throw excrement at each other and comment loudly on the genitals of their respective parents—this to us unnatural and obscene behaviour is a proof of the love of friends.

ROBERT BRAIN, *Friends and Lovers*, 1976

I wish by the behaviour of my friend toward me to be led to have such regard for myself as for a box of precious ointment. I shall not be so cheap to myself if I see that another values me.

THOREAU, *Journal*, 25 March 1842

The brotherhood of man will only become a reality when the consciousness of alien beings corrects man's myopia, and he realizes that he has more in common with Eskimos and Bengali beggars and black faggots than he has with the form of intelligent life on Solar System X.

GERMAINE GREER, *The Female Eunuch*, 1970

In a paperback copy of *Tristram Shandy* bought in the second-hand bookstore in Alice, this was scribbled in the flyleaf: 'One of the few moments of happiness a man knows in Australia is that moment of meeting the eyes of another man over the tops of two beer glasses.'

BRUCE CHATWIN, *The Songlines*, 1987

Now and then a friend and some sauterne,
    Now and then a haunch of Highland venison:
And for Lotos-lands I'll never yearn
    Maugre Alfred Tennyson.

MORTIMER COLLINS, from 'Lotos Eating', 1855

16 December [1838], Amritsar. Runjeet gave us another of his nautches last night, exactly on the pattern of the one I described before, except that he drank harder himself and got very drunk, and tried hard to make George drink. 'When a man drinks hard enough,' he said, 'he opens his heart and talks all kind of nonsense, and that is right among friends.' He asked if it was true that books are written against drinking, shook his head and said what foolish books they must be.

FANNY EDEN, *Indian Journals*

It is so gratifying of you to say in your letter that you like me. Things of that kind, which can be very important, people usually omit to mention. Personally, I have no use for unspoken affections, and so I will most readily reply that I like you a great deal . . .

SYLVIA TOWNSEND WARNER, letter to Paul Nordoff, 24 July 1939

Fluent with a friend
The only word unspoken
Is *sayonara*.

Anonymous haiku

Your truest friends are those who visit you in prison or in hospital.

Moroccan proverb

It is easier to visit friends than to live with them.

Chinese proverb

How few of his friends' houses would a man choose to be at when he is sick.

JOHNSON, 1783; in Boswell's Life

How many men, I wonder, does one meet with, in a lifetime, whom he would choose for his death-bed companions!

NATHANIEL HAWTHORNE, The Blithedale Romance, 1852

It is beginning to be realized that, for some reason, people with fewer friends are more prone to tonsillitis and cancer ... it has been found time and time again that many coronary patients have small friendship networks and, conversely, that 'loners' are more likely to have heart attacks.

STEVE DUCK, Friends, for Life

My name is DEATH: the last best friend am I!

SOUTHEY, Carmen Nuptiale, 1816

Turn my pages,—never mind
If you like not all you find;
Think not all the grains are gold
Sacramento's sand-banks hold ...

Best for worst shall make amends,
Find us, keep us, leave us friends
Till, perchance, we meet again,
Benedicite,—Amen!

OLIVER WENDELL HOLMES, from 'Programme', 1874

ACKNOWLEDGEMENTS

THE editors and publisher are grateful for permission to include the following copyright material:

J. R. Ackerley, from *My Sister and Myself: Diaries* (Hutchinson 1982). Reprinted by permission of David Higham Associates Ltd.

Anna Akhmatova, 'New Year Ballad', trans. Richard McKane, from *Selected Poems* (Penguin/OUP, 1969). English translation © Richard McKane 1969.

Walter Allen, from *All in a Lifetime* (Chatto & Windus, 1986). Reprinted by permission of David Higham Associates Ltd.

Anon., 'The Guest in Your House' from *African Poems and Love Songs*, trans. Charlotte and Wolf Leslau (1970). Reprinted by permission of the translators and Peter Pauper Press, New York.

Aristotle, extracts from *Aristotle's Ethics for English Readers*, trans. H. Rackham (1945). Reprinted by permission of Basil Blackwell.

David Arkell, from *Ententes Cordiales* (1989). Reprinted by permission of Carcanet Press Ltd.

Julian Barnes, from *Staring at the Sun* (Cape, 1986). Reprinted by permission of the Peters Fraser & Dunlop Group Ltd.

John Bayley, from *In Another Country* (Constable, 1955).

Ludwig van Beethoven, from *The Letters of Beethoven*, vol. i, trans. Emily Anderson (1961). Reprinted by permission of Macmillan.

Martin Bell, 'David Guest' from *Complete Poems*, ed. Peter Porter (Bloodaxe Books Ltd., 1988).

Hilaire Belloc, extract from 'Dedicatory Ode', 'Ballade of Hell and Mrs Roebeck' from *Complete Verse* (Gerald Duckworth & Co. Ltd.) Reprinted by permission of the Peters Fraser & Dunlop Group Ltd.

Elizabeth Bishop, from 'Efforts of Affection: A Memoir of Marianne Moore', from *The Collected Prose*, ed. Robert Giroux. © 1984 by Alice Methfessel. Reprinted by permission of Farrar, Straus and Giroux Inc.

Edmund Blunden, from *Undertones of War* (Collins). Reprinted by permission of the Peters Fraser & Dunlop Group Ltd.

Jorge Luis Borges, 'Luke 23', trans. Irving Feldman, from *A Personal Anthology*, ed. Anthony Kerrigan (E. P. Dutton).

Elizabeth Bowen, from *The Death of the Heart*. Reprinted by permission of Jonathan Cape Limited and Alfred A. Knopf Inc.

Robert Brain, from *Friends and Lovers* (Hart-Davis, 1976). Reprinted by permission of Grafton Books, a division of the Collins Publishing Group.

Bertolt Brecht, 'The Friends', trans. Michael Hamburger, reprinted from *Bertolt Brecht: Poems 1913–1956* (Methuen), eds. John Willett and Ralph Manheim. Reprinted by permission of Michael Hamburger.

Vera Brittain, the extracts from *Testament of Friendship :The Story of Winifred Holtby*, are reprinted by permission of her literary executor and Virago Press.

Alan Brownjohn, 'Peter Daines at a Party' from *Collected Poems 1952–83* (Secker & Warburg, 1983: reprinted with additions, Hutchinson, 1988). Reprinted by permission of the author.

Margaret Buber-Neumann, from *Milena*, trans. Ralph Manheim. Reprinted by permission of Collins Publishers. Copyright in the USA by Henry Holt & Co. Inc.

John Buchan, excerpts from *These For Remembrance: Memoirs of 6 Friends Killed in the Great War*, copyright the Rt. Hon. the Lord Tweedsmuir, CBE, reprinted by permission of Buchan & Enright, Publishers.

A. S. Byatt, from *Still Life* (Chatto, 1985). Reprinted by permission of the Peters Fraser & Dunlop Group Ltd. and Chatto & Windus Ltd.

Jane Welsh Carlyle, letter to Mrs. Stirling, 21 Oct. 1859 from *The Collected Letters of Thomas and Jane Welsh Carlyle*, eds. Charles Richard Sanders and Kenneth J. Fielding (1970). Reprinted by permission of Duke University Press.

C. P. Cavafy, 'Myris: Alexandria, AD 340', from *C. P. Cavafy: Collected Poems*, ed. George Savidis, trans. Edmund Keeley and Philip Sherrard. Trans. © 1975 by Edmund Keeley and Philip Sherrard. Reprinted with the permission of Princeton University Press and Chatto & Windus on behalf of the Estate of C. P. Cavafy.

Bruce Chatwin, extract from *The Songlines*, © Bruce Chatwin 1987. Reprinted by permission of Jonathan Cape Ltd., on behalf of the Estate of Bruce Chatwin and Rogers Coleridge & White Ltd.

Winston Churchill, letter to Lady Randolph 29 Oct. 1893, from *Winston S. Churchill*, vol. I, by Randolph S. Churchill (Heinemann, 1966). Reprinted by permission of Curtis Brown on behalf of the Estate of Sir Winston Churchill, © C & T Publications Ltd.

Cicero/Matius, extracts from *Cicero's Letters to His Friends*, vol. 2, trans. D. R. Shackleton Bailey (1978). Reprinted by permission of Cambridge University Press.

Cyril Connolly, from *The Unquiet Grave* (Hamish Hamilton, 1944). Reprinted by permission of Rogers Coleridge & White Ltd. From *Enemies of Promise*, © 1983 by Deirdre Levi. Reprinted by permission of Rogers Coleridge & White Ltd. and International Creative Management Inc.

Robert Conquest, excerpt from 'After Writing an Obituary' from *New and Collected Poems* (Hutchinson, 1988).

Wendy Cope, 'Lonely Hearts' from *Making Cocoa for Kingsley Amis*. Reprinted by permission of Faber & Faber Ltd.

Emily Dickinson, 'Nature Assigns the Sun', 'These Strangers, in a foreign World', and 'God is indeed a jealous God — . . . ', reprinted by permission of the publishers and the Trustees of Amherst College from *The Poems of Emily Dickinson*, ed. Thomas H. Johnson, Cambridge, Mass.: The Belknap Press of Harvard University Press. Copyright 1951, © 1955, 1979, 1983 by the President and Fellows of Harvard College.

Margaret Drabble, from *The Radiant Way* (1987). Reprinted by permission of the Peters Fraser & Dunlop Group Ltd. and Weidenfeld and Nicolson Ltd.

Steve Duck, from *Friends for Life*: *The Psychology of Close Relationships* (1983). Reprinted by permission of Harvester Wheatsheaf and St Martin's Press Inc.

Douglas Dunn, 'The Departures of Friends in Childhood' from *Northlight*. Reprinted by permission of Faber & Faber Ltd.

Fanny Eden, from *Tigers, Durbars and Kings*: *Fanny Eden's Indian Journals*, ed. Janet Dunbar. Reprinted by permission of John Murray (Publishers) Ltd.

T. S. Eliot, extract from *Murder in the Cathedral*, © 1935 by Harcourt Brace Jovanovich, Inc. and renewed 1963 by T. S. Eliot. Reprinted by permission of Faber & Faber Ltd., and Harcourt Brace Jovanovich, Inc.

The Epic of Gilgamish, trans. R. Campbell Thompson (Luzac & Co., 1928).

Euripides, extract from *Iphigenia in Tauris*, trans. Gilbert Murray (Allen & Unwin, 1913). Reprinted by permission of Unwin Hyman Ltd.

Edward FitzGerald, extracts from *The Letters of Edward FitzGerald, Vol. I: 1830–1850*, Alfred McKinley Terhune and Annabelle Burdick Terhune, eds., © 1980 by Princeton University Press. Reprinted with the permission of Princeton University Press.

E. M. Forster, from *A Passage to India*. Reprinted by permission of Edward Arnold.

Anne Frank, from *Anne Frank*: *The Diary of a Young Girl*, trans. B. M. Mooyaart (Vallentine, Mitchell & Co./Doubleday & Co. Inc., 1952).

Robert Frost, extracts from a letter to Edward Thomas, 31 July 1915 and from a letter to Helen Thomas, 27 Apr. 1917 from *Selected Letters of Robert Frost*, ed. Lawrance Thompson (1965); extract from 'Home Burial' from *The Poetry of Robert Frost*, ed. Edward Connery Lathem (1969), copyright 1930, 1939, © 1969 by Holt, Rinehart & Winston, © 1958 by Robert Frost, © 1967 by Lesley

Frost Ballantine. Reprinted by permission of Jonathan Cape Ltd. on behalf of the Estate of Robert Frost.

Oliver St John Gogarty, 'To a Friend' from *The Collected Poems of Oliver St John Gogarty* (1954), © Oliver D. Gogarty. Reprinted by permission of Devin-Adair Publishers.

Guido Gozzano, letter to Amalia Guglielminetti, trans. J. G. Nichols, in *Guido Gozzano: The Colloquies* (1987). Reprinted by permission of Carcanet Press Ltd.

Germaine Greer, from *The Female Eunuch* (MacGibbon & Kee, 1970). Reprinted by permission of Aitken & Stone Ltd. and Grafton Books, a division of the Collins Publishing Group.

Helene Hanff, extracts from *84, Charing Cross Road*, © 1970 by Helene Hanff. Reprinted by permission of André Deutsch Ltd. and Viking Penguin, a division of Penguin Books USA Inc.

Gwen Harwood, 'Wittgenstein and Engelmann' from *The Lion's Bride*. Reprinted by permission of Angus & Robertson (UK).

Ernest Hemingway, from *A Moveable Feast* (1964). Used with permission.

Zbigniew Herbert, 'Hermes, Dog, and Star', from *Selected Poems*, trans. John and Bogdana Carpenter (1977). Reprinted by permission of Oxford University Press.

Daryl Hine, from *In and Out*, © Daryl Hine 1989. Reprinted by permission of Alfred A. Knopf Inc.

A. D. Hope, 'Bounce to Pope' from *A Book of Answers*. Reprinted by permission of Angus & Robertson (UK).

Horace, from 'Odes. Book One XXIV', from *Horace: Odes*, trans. James Michie (Hart-Davis, 1964). Reprinted by permission of James Michie.

Christopher Isherwood, from *Lions and Shadows*. Reprinted by permission of Methuen, London.

Gustav Janouch, from *Conversations with Kafka*, trans. Goronwy Rees (André Deutsch, 1971). Reprinted by permission of the publisher.

Otto Karrer, from *St Francis of Assisi: The Legends and Lauds* trans. N. Wydenbruck (Sheed & Ward, 1947).

Revd Francis Kilvert, from *Kilvert's Diary*. Reprinted by permission of Jonathan Cape Ltd. on behalf of Mrs Sheila Hooper.

Rudyard Kipling, 'The Friends', copyright 1927 by Rudyard Kipling. Reprinted by permission of the National Trust, from *Rudyard Kipling's Verse: Definitive Edition*. Used by permission of Doubleday, a division of Bantam, Doubleday, Dell Publishing Group Inc.

Jean de La Fontaine, 'The Bear and the Garden Lover' from *The Fables of Jean de La Fontaine*, trans. Edward Marsh. Reprinted by permission of William Heinemann Ltd. and Harper & Row Inc.

Philip Larkin, 'Vers de Société' from *High Windows*, © 1974 by Philip Larkin. Reprinted by permission of Faber & Faber Ltd. and Farrar, Straus & Giroux Inc.

Ingnace Lepp, from *The Ways of Friendship*, trans. Bernard Murchland. Translation © 1966 by Macmillan Publishing Company. Reprinted by permission of Georges Borchardt Inc., and Macmillan Publishing Company.

Primo Levi, from 'A Disciple', from *Moments of Reprieve*, trans. Ruth Feldman. Translation © 1987 by Summit Books. Reprinted by permission of Summit Books, a division of Simon & Schuster Inc.

C. S. Lewis, from *The Four Loves*, © 1960 by Helen Joy Lewis and renewed 1988 by Arthur Owen Barfield. Reprinted by permission of Collins Publishers, and Harcourt Brace Jovanovich, Inc.

Ellen Lingens-Reiner, from *Prisoners of Fear* (Gollancz, 1948).

Norman MacCaig, 'Two Friends' from *Collected Poems*. Reprinted by permission of Chatto & Windus on behalf of the author.

Carson McCullers, from *The Heart is a Lonely Hunter* (Barrie & Jenkins Ltd.). Reprinted by permission of Laurence Pollinger

Louis MacNeice, 'Tam Cari Capitis' from *The Collected Poems of Louis MacNeice*. Reprinted by permission of Faber & Faber Ltd.

Thomas Mann, extract from 'A Man and His Dog', trans. H. T. Lowe-Porter, from *Stories of a Lifetime*, vol. 2, published in the US as *Stories of Three Decades*, copyright 1930, 1931, 1934, 1935, 1936 by Alfred A. Knopf Inc. Reprinted by permission of Martin Secker & Warburg Ltd. and Alfred A. Knopf Inc.

Emily Marshall, 'Friendship'. Used with permission.

John Masefield, extracts from *John Masefield: Letters to Reyna*, ed. William Buchan (Buchan & Enright, Publishers, 1983). Reprinted by permission of The Society of Authors as the literary representative of the Estate of John Masefield.

Gerda Mayer, 'Her Friend Flo' from *The Knockabout Show* (Chatto, 1978). Reprinted by permission of the author.

From *The Commentary of Father Monserrate SJ, 1582*, trans. J. S. Hoyland and annotated by S. N. Banerjee (1922). Reprinted by permission of OUP, India.

Iris Murdoch, from *A Fairly Honourable Defeat* (Chatto & Windus, 1970).

Ogden Nash, 'A Friend In Need Will be Around In Five Minutes', from *Good Intentions*, copyright 1939 by Ogden Nash. First appeared in the *New Yorker*. Reprinted by permission of Curtis Brown, London on behalf of the Estate of Ogden Nash and Little, Brown and Co.

Jawaharlal Nehru, from *An Autobiography*. Reprinted by permission of The Bodley Head on behalf of the Estate of Jawaharlal Nehru.

Friedrich Nietzsche, from *Human, All Too Human*, trans. R. J. Hollingdale. Reprinted by permission of Cambridge University Press.

Frank O'Connor, 'The Scholar and the Cat', translation from the Irish, from *Kings, Lords and Commons* (1959). Reprinted by permission of the Peters Fraser & Dunlop Group Ltd.

Ulick O'Connor, from *Oliver St John Gogarty*. Reprinted by permission of the publisher, Methuen London.

Frank O'Hara, excerpt from 'Poem read at Joan Mitchell's', © 1959 by Maureen Granville-Smith, Administratrix of the Estate of Frank O'Hara; 'John Button Birthday', © 1965 by Maureen Granville-Smith, Administratrix of the Estate of Frank O'Hara. Both reprinted from *The Collected Poems of Frank O'Hara* by permission of Alfred A. Knopf Inc.

Ŏm Ŭi-Gil, 'Sitting at Night', from *Slow Chrysanthemums, Classical Korean Poems in Chinese*, translated and introduced by Kim Jong-gil (1987). Reprinted by permission of Anvil Press Poetry.

Iona and Peter Opie, from *The Lore and Language of Schoolchildren* (1959). Reprinted by permission of Oxford University Press.

Wilfred Owen, postcard to Leslie Gunston, from *Wilfred Owen: Collected Letters*, ed. Harold Owen and John Bell (1967). Reprinted by permission of Oxford University Press.

Boris Pasternak, from *Doctor Zhivago*, trans. Max Hayward and Manya Harari. Reprinted by permission of Collins Publishers.

Octavio Paz, 'Friendship', trans. Charles Tomlinson from *Octavio Paz: The Collected Poems 1957–87* (1988). Reprinted by permission of Carcanet Press Ltd.

Plato, from *Lysis*, trans. Benjamin Jowett. Reprinted by permission of The Jowett Copyright Trustees, Balliol College, Oxford.

Cole Porter, 'Friendship'. Reproduced by kind permission of Warner Chappell Music Ltd.

Peter Porter, from 'A Chagall Postcard' from *Possible Worlds* (OUP, 1989). Reprinted by permission of Oxford University Press.

Ezra Pound, excerpts from *The Selected Letters of Ezra Pound*, ed. by D. D. Paige, copyright 1950 by Ezra Pound. Reprinted by permission of Faber & Faber Ltd. and New Directions Publishing Corporation.

V. S. Pritchett, from 'The Skeleton', from *Collected Stories* (Chatto, 1982). Reprinted by permission of the Peters Fraser & Dunlop Group Ltd. and Chatto & Windus.

Henry Handel Richardson, from *The Getting of Wisdom*. Reprinted by permission of William Heinemann Ltd.

George Santayana, from *Soliloquies in England* (Constable, 1922); from *The Life of Reason*; from *Persons and Places: The Middle Span* (Constable 1945). Reprinted by permission of MIT Press, Cambridge, Mass.

Siegfried Sassoon, from *The Old Century*. Reprinted by permission of George T. Sassoon.

Dorothy L. Sayers, from *Unnatural Death* (Gollancz, 1927). Reprinted by permission of David Higham Associates Ltd.

Arthur Schopenhauer, extracts from *Parerga and Paralipomena*, from *Essays from the Parerga and Paralipomena*, trans. T. Bailey Saunders (Allen & Unwin, 1951). Reprinted by permission of Unwin Hyman Ltd.

Vikram Seth, 'Protocols', from *All You Who Sleep Tonight* (Faber, 1990). Reprinted by permission of the author.

Bernard Shaw, from *Bernard Shaw: Collected Letters 1874–1897*, ed. Dan H. Laurence (Max Reinhardt, 1965). Reprinted by permission of The Society of Authors on behalf of the Bernard Shaw Estate.

Edith Simcox, extracts from 'Autobiography of a Shirt Maker' (MS). © Queen's College, Oxford.

Logan Pearsall Smith, from *Afterthoughts* (Constable, 1931).

Sydney Smith, letter to Mary and Agnes Berry, June 1843, from *The Letters of Sydney Smith*, ed. Nowell C. Smith (1953). Reprinted by permission of Oxford University Press.

F. S. Smythe, 'The Second Assault', in *Everest 1933* by Hugh Ruttledge (A. & C. Black, 1934).

Muriel Spark, from *The Prime of Miss Jean Brodie*, © 1961 by Muriel Spark. Reprinted by permission of David Higham Associates Ltd., and of Harper & Row Publishers Inc.

Christina Stead, from *Dark Places of the Heart*, copyright © 1966 Christina Stead, originally published as *Cotters' England*. Reprinted by permission of Joan Daves and Laurence Pollinger Ltd., on behalf of the Estate of Christina Stead.

H. M. Swanwick, from *I Have Been Young* (Gollancz, 1935).

Pyotr Ilich Tchaikovsky, letter to Nadezhda von Meck, 28 Mar. 1877, and Nadezhda von Meck to Tchaikovsky, 19 Mar. 1877, both from *Tchaikovsky: A Biographical and Critical Study*, vol. 2, by David Brown. Reprinted by permission of Victor Gollancz Ltd.

Alexander Theroux, extract from *An Adultery* (1988). Reprinted by permission of Hamish Hamilton Ltd.

Paul Theroux, from *Fong and the Indians* (Hamish Hamilton; Houghton Mifflin, 1968). Reprinted by permission of Aitken & Stone Ltd.

Hester Lynch Thrale, from *Thraliana: The Diary of Mrs Hester Lynch Thrale, 1776–1809*, ed. Katherine C. Balderston (1942). Reprinted by permission of Oxford University Press.

Marina Tsvetayeva, extract from 'Desk', trans. Elaine Feinstein, from *Selected Poems of Marina Tsvetayeva* (OUP, 1981). Reprinted by permission of Olwyn Hughes.

Arthur Waley, 'Oaths of Friendship' from *Chinese Poems* trans. Arthur Waley, published in the United States as *Translations from the Chinese*, copyright 1919 and renewed 1947 by Arthur Waley. Reprinted by permission of Constable Publishers and Alfred A. Knopf Inc.

Sylvia Townsend Warner, extracts from *Sylvia Townsend Warner: Letters*, © 1982 by Susanna Pinney and William Maxwell. Reprinted by permission of Chatto & Windus on behalf of the Executors of the Sylvia Townsend Warner Estate, and Viking Penguin, a division of Penguin Books USA Inc.

Alec Waugh, from *My Brother Evelyn and Other Profiles* (Cassell & Co.). Reprinted by permission of the Peters Fraser & Dunlop Group Ltd.

Beatrice Webb, from *The Diary of Beatrice Webb*, vol. 2, ed. Norman and Jeanne Mackenzie (Virago, 1983), © London School of Economics.

T. H. White, from *The Sword in the Stone* (Collins, 1937).

Virginia Woolf, from *Mrs Dalloway* (1925) copyright 1925 by Harcourt Brace Jovanovich, Inc., and renewed 1953 by Leonard Woolf; from *The Diary of Virginia Woolf*, vol. II, 1920–4, © 1978 by Quentin Bell and Anjelica Garnett, ed. Anne Olivier Bell (1978), entry for 1 Nov. 1924; from *The Waves* (1931), copyright 1931 by Harcourt Brace Jovanovich and renewed 1959 by Leonard Woolf. Reprinted by permission of Chatto & Windus on behalf of the Executors of the Virginia Woolf Estate and the Hogarth Press, and Harcourt Brace Jovanovich, Inc.

Arthur Yap, 'some friends'. Used with permission.

W. B. Yeats, 'The Lover Pleads with His Friend for Old Friends'. This poem is in the public domain and is taken from *The Poems of W. B. Yeats: A New Edition*, edited by Richard J. Finneran (New York: Macmillan, 1983).

INDEX OF AUTHORS

INDEX OF UNASCRIBED PASSAGES

OXFORD

MORE OXFORD PAPERBACKS

Details of a selection of other Oxford Paperbacks follow. A complete list of Oxford Paperbacks, including The World's Classics, Twentieth-Century Classics, OPUS, Past Masters, Oxford Authors, Oxford Shakespeare, and Oxford Paperback Reference, is available in the UK from the General Publicity Department, Oxford University Press (RS), Walton Street, Oxford, OX2 6DP.

In the USA, complete lists are available from the Paperbacks Marketing Manager, Oxford University Press, 200 Madison Avenue, New York, NY 10016.

Oxford Paperbacks are available from all good bookshops. In case of difficulty, customers in the UK can order direct from Oxford University Press Bookshop, 116 High Street, Oxford, Freepost, OX1 4BR, enclosing full payment. Please add 10 per cent of the published price for postage and packing.

LITERARY BIOGRAPHY AND
CRITICISM IN OXFORD PAPERBACKS

Oxford Paperbacks's impressive list of literary biography and criticism includes works ranging from specialist studies of the prominent figures of the world literature to D. J. Enright on television soap opera.

BRITISH WRITERS OF THE THIRTIES
Valentine Cunningham

'He has steeped himself in the period . . . *British Writers of the Thirties* is by far the best history of its kind published in recent years . . . and it will become required reading for those who wish to look back at a society and a culture in which writers, for all their faults, were taken seriously.' Peter Ackroyd, *The Times*

'a serious and often brilliant book, provoking one to argument, forcing one back to known texts and forward to unread ones . . . it is simply so packed with information that it will speak as much to readers with an interest in social history as to the students of literature for whom it was first intended.' Claire Tomalin, *Independent*

'this should henceforth be the standard treatment . . . a minor classic of literary history' Frank Kermode, *Guardian*

'brilliant survey and analysis . . . Mr Cunningham's narrative is cleverly constructed, wonderfully detailed, and he deploys his findings to great effect.' Charles Causley, *Times Educational Supplement*

Also in Oxford Paperbacks:

Fields of Vision   D. J. Enright
Modern English Literature   W. W. Robson
The Oxford Illustrated History of English Literature
edited by Pat Rogers
The Pursuit of Happiness   Peter Quennell

PAST MASTERS

General Editor: Keith Thomas

Past Masters is a series of concise and authoritative introductions to the life and works of men and women whose ideas still influence the way we think today.

'Put end to end, this series will constitute a noble encyclopaedia of the history of ideas.' Mary Warnock

SHAKESPEARE

Germaine Greer

'At the core of a coherent social structure as he viewed it lay marriage, which for Shakespeare is no mere comic convention but a crucial and complex ideal. He rejected the stereotype of the passive, sexless, unresponsive female and its inevitable concommitant, the misogynist conviction that all women were whores at heart. Instead he created a series of female characters who were both passionate and pure, who gave their hearts spontaneously into the keeping of the men they loved and remained true to the bargain in the face of tremendous odds.'

Germaine Greer's short book on Shakespeare brings a completely new eye to a subject about whom more has been written than on any other English figure. She is especially concerned with discovering why Shakespeare 'was and is a popular artist', who remains a central figure in English cultural life four centuries after his death.

'eminently trenchant and sensible . . . a genuine exploration in its own right' John Bayley, *Listener*

'the clearest and simplest explanation of Shakespeare's thought I have yet read' Auberon Waugh, *Daily Mail*

Also available in Past Masters:

Paine   Mark Philp
Dante   George Holmes
The Buddha   Michael Carrithers
Confucius   Raymond Dawson

ILLUSTRATED HISTORIES IN
OXFORD PAPERBACKS

Lavishly illustrated with over 200 full colour and black and white photographs, and written by leading academics, Oxford Paperbacks' illuminating histories provide superb introductions to a wide range of political, cultural, and social topics.

THE OXFORD ILLUSTRATED HISTORY
OF ENGLISH LITERATURE

Edited by Pat Rogers

Britain possesses a literary heritage which is almost unrivalled in the Western world. In this volume, the richness, diversity, and continuity of that tradition are explored by a group of Britain's foremost literary scholars.

Chapter by chapter the authors trace the history of English literature, from its first stirrings in Anglo-Saxon poetry to the present day. At its heart towers the figure of Shakespeare, who is accorded a special chapter to himself. Other major figures such as Chaucer, Milton, Donne, Wordsworth, Dickens, Eliot, and Auden are treated in depth, and the story is brought up to date with discussion of living authors such as Seamus Heaney and Edward Bond.

'[a] lovely volume . . . put in your thumb and pull out plums'
Michael Foot

'scholarly and enthusiastic people have written inspiring essays that induce an eagerness in their readers to return to the writers they admire' *Economist*

Other illustrated histories in Oxford Paperbacks:

The Oxford Illustrated History of Britain
The Oxford Illustrated History of Medieval Europe

THE OXFORD SHAKESPEARE

General Editor: Stanley Wells

The Oxford Shakespeare offers new and authoritative editions of Shakespeare's plays in which the early printings have been scrupulously re-examined and interpreted on freshly considered principles. An introductory essay provides all relevant background information together with an appraisal of critical views and of the play's effects in performance. The detailed commentaries pay particular attention to language and staging. Reprints of sources, music for songs, genealogical tables, maps, etc. are included when necessary; many of the volumes are illustrated and contain an index.

'This is now *the* paperback edition to have.' *Sunday Times*

THE TWO NOBLE KINSMEN

Edited by Eugene M. Waith

The Royal Shakespeare Company's choice of *The Two Noble Kinsmen* to open the Swan Theatre in 1986 demonstrated that this long-neglected play is at last coming into its own as a stageworthy, humorous, and moving dramatization of the conflicting claims of love and friendship. It was first published in 1634 as 'by the memorable worthies of their time, Mr John Fletcher, and Mr William Shakespeare, Gent' and was probably performed soon after the wedding of Princess Elizabeth, daughter of James I, to the Elector Palatine in February 1613.

The exceptionally full Introduction to this new edition explains the relevance to the play of the ideas of chivalry and of the classical idea of friendship. The edition (which is illuminatingly illustrated) also offers a discussion of the centuries-long debate about the play's authorship and a clarification of its stage action.

Also available in the Oxford Shakespeare:

Hamlet
Julius Caesar
Henry V
The Tempest

A SPLENDID QUARTET OF SHORT STORIES

CLASSIC IRISH SHORT STORIES
Selected and Introduced by Frank O'Connor

The Irish short story, Frank O'Connor believes, is 'a distinct art form' and the stories he has chosen for this collection show how the form has remained peculiarly itself while being developed in various ways in response to changing social and political conditions. Authors include James Joyce, Liam O'Flaherty, Seàn O'Faolàin, George Moore, and Elizabeth Bowen.

CLASSIC ENGLISH SHORT STORIES
Selected and Introduced by Derek Hudson

The years 1930 to 1955 marked a high point in the fortunes of the English short story. Inevitably the Second World War left its mark on many of the tales Derek Hudson has collected here, but, he argues, the dominating impression is that very English characteristic, humour. The authors include Somerset Maugham, Virginia Woolf, Evelyn Waugh, Graham Greene, H. E. Bates, and Rosamond Lehmann.

CLASSIC SCOTTISH SHORT STORIES
Selected and Introduced by J. M. Reid

CLASSIC AMERICAN SHORT STORIES
Selected and Introduced by Douglas Grant

Also in Oxford Paperbacks:
CLASSIC ENGLISH SHORT STORIES

The Dragon's Head
The Killing Bottle
Charmed Lives
The Green Man Revisited

THE OXFORD AUTHORS

General Editor: Frank Kermode

The Oxford Authors is a series of authoritative editions of the major English writers for the student and the general reader. Drawing on the best texts available, each volume contains a generous selection from the writings—poetry and prose, including letters—to give the essence of a writer's work and thinking. Where appropriate, texts have been tactfully modernized and all are complemented by essential Notes, an Introduction, Chronology, and suggestions for Further Reading.

'The Oxford Authors series can always be relied upon to be splendid—with good plain texts and helpful notes.' Robert Nye, *Scotsman*

OSCAR WILDE

Edited by Isobel Murray

The drama of Oscar Wilde's life has for years overshadowed his achievement in literature. This is the first large-scale edition of his work to provide unobtrusive guidance to the wealth of knowledge and allusion upon which his writing stands.

Wilde had studied Greek and Latin and was familiar with American literature, while he was as well read in French as he was in English, following Gautier and Flaubert as well as Pater and Ruskin. Through her Notes Isobel Murray enables the modern reader for the first time to read Wilde as such admiring contemporaries as Pater, Yeats, and Symons read him, in a rich, shared culture of literary and visual arts.

This edition underlines the range of his achievement in many genres, including *The Picture of Dorian Gray, Salome, The Importance of Being Earnest, The Decay of Lying,* and *The Ballad of Reading Gaol.* The text is that of the last printed edition overseen by Wilde.

Also in the Oxford Authors:

Sir Philip Sidney
Ben Jonson
Byron
Thomas Hardy

OXFORD BOOKS

Oxford Books began in 1900 with Sir Arthur Quiller-Couch ('Q')'s *Oxford Book of English Verse*. Since then over 60 superb anthologies of poetry, prose, and songs have appeared in a series that has a very special place in British publishing.

THE OXFORD BOOK OF ENGLISH GHOST STORIES

Chosen by Michael Cox and R. A. Gilbert

This anthology includes some of the best and most frightening ghost stories ever written, including M. R. James's 'Oh Whistle, and I'll Come to You, My Lad', 'The Monkey's Paw' by W. W. Jacobs, and H. G. Wells's 'The Red Room'. The important contribution of women writers to the genre is represented by stories such as Amelia Edwards's 'The Phantom Coach', Edith Wharton's 'Mr Jones', and Elizabeth Bowen's 'Hand in Glove'.

As the editors stress in their informative introduction, a good ghost story, though it may raise many profound questions about life and death, entertains as much as it unsettles us, and the best writers are careful to satisfy what Virginia Woolf called 'the strange human craving for the pleasure of feeling afraid'. This anthology, the first to present the full range of classic English ghost fiction, similarly combines a serious literary purpose with the plain intention of arousing pleasing fear at the doings of the dead.

'an excellent cross-section of familiar and unfamiliar stories and guaranteed to delight' *New Statesman*

Also in Oxford Paperbacks:

The Oxford Book of Short Stories edited by V. S. Pritchett
The Oxford Book of Political Anecdotes
edited by Paul Johnson
The Oxford Book of Ages
edited by Anthony and Sally Sampson
The Oxford Book of Dreams edited by Stephen Brock